2,001 Winning Ads For Real Estate

by Steve Kennedy
and Deborah Johnson, Ph.D.

Argyle Press, Inc.
Carson City, Nevada

Dedications

To my lovely and loving wife, Mary-Ellen—S.K.

To my mother for her unfailing love—D.J.

Requests for permission should be addressed to Argyle Press, Inc., 4800 Numaga Pass, Carson City Nevada, 89703.

This publication is designed to provide accurate and authoritative information in regard to the subject matter covered. It is sold with the understanding that the publisher is not engaged in rendering legal, accounting, or other professional services. If legal advice or other expert assistance is required, the services of a competent professional should be sought.

Original Cover Design by Steve Kennedy, Carson City, Nevada
Updated Cover Design and Graphics by Diana Elkins, Carson City, Nevada.
Proofreading by Alice Nolan, Carlsbad, California.
Editing Assistance by Barbara Shields, Carson City, Nevada.

Library of Congress Cataloging in Publication Data

Kennedy, Steve, 1957-
    2,001 winning ads for real estate / by Steve Kennedy and Deborah Johnson.—3rd ed.
       p.   cm.
    Originally published: 1987.
    Includes index.
    ISBN 1-887145-04-4
    1.Advertising—Real estate business. I. Johnson, Deborah, 1952-
    II. Title III. Title: Two thousand winning ads for real estate
HF6161.R3K44 1995
659.1'933333—dc20

95-25929
CIP

Printed in the United States of America. Second printing of 3rd Edition.

Table of Contents

Introduction

This book is for every real estate agent who wants to maximize the effectiveness of his or her classified ads. It's a simple, easy-to-use guide with 2001 ads you can easily adapt for your own use. We've tried to give you an assortment of ads—long and short, funny and serious—so you can pick whatever best fits your needs.

For easy reference, we've divided the properties according to:

1. Price (Low Priced, Mid-Range & Prestige Homes)
2. Farms, Ranch & Horse Properties
3. Condominiums & Townhomes
4. Mobile Homes
5. Vacation Homes
6. Investment Properties

To start, just look up the kind of property you want to advertise. Once you've found the section describing the particular property you're selling, think about the angle you want to play up in your ad. What appeals to buyers is usually one of the following:

1. Location
2. Size
3. Price/Terms
4. Style
5. Special Features
6. Condition
7. Unique Appeals

Therefore, you'll find each property section handily broken down by the above features. Simply turn to the feature you've selected, then help yourself to the scores of suggestions at your fingertips. You might want to sell one feature the first week, then try another the second.

In this 3rd edition, we have tried to incorporate the Fair Housing Administration's Real Estate Advertising Guidelines. Although every effort has been made to delete any word or phrases that are in the grey area of these guidelines, we cannot make a guarantee. Following is an excerpt from the article *What's in an ad? Words you can use* by Walt Albro in the February 13, 1995 issue of the <u>Realtor News®</u>, National Association of Realtors®.

> "The federal Fair Housing Act prohibits adverisements that state a preference or discrimate on the basis of race, color, religion, sex, handicap, familial status or national origin.
>
> Overtly discriminatory ad phrases such as "whites only," "adults preferred" and "singles preferred" were clearly understood to be violations, say NAR analysts.
>
> Realtors® became concerned, however, when phrases commonly used to describe architectural features or amenities were prohibited by certain newspapers as possible fair housing violations.
>
> HUD's clarifications, Caldwell* says, will end a lot of the uncertainty among real estate ad writers. "It's a good step in the right direction," he adds.
>
> *Robert W. Caldwell of Altamonte Springs, Florida*
> *1994 Chairman of the NAR Equal Opportunity Committee*

HUD gave the following guidelines concerning what words and phrases are acceptable in real estate advertisements:

Handicap

Acceptable:
- Great view
- Fourth-floor walk-up
- Walk-in closets
- Jogging trails
- Walk to bus stop
- Wheelchair ramp

Also acceptable are phrases describing conduct: Non-smoking and sober

Religion

Advertisements that use the legal name of an entity that contains a religious reference—Roselawn Catholic Home, for example—or those which contain a religious symbol, such as a cross, standing alone, may indicate a religious preference. However, if such an advertisement includes a disclaimer, such as the statement, "This home does not discriminate on the basis of race, color, religion, national origin, sex, handicap or familial status," it will not be a violation.

Acceptable:

The use of secularized terms or symbols relating to religious holidays such as:
- Santa Claus
- Easter Bunny
- St. Valentine's Day images

Phrases such as:
- Merry Christmas and Happy Easter

Race, color, national origin

Acceptable:
- Master bedroom
- Rare find
- Desirable neighborhood

Sex

Acceptable:
- Mother-in-law suite
- Bachelor apartment

Familial status

Acceptable:

Ads describing the property, services and facilities or neighborhoods.

Examples:
- Two bedroom
- Cozy
- Family room
- No bicycles allowed
- Quiet streets

A copy of the complete guidelines can be found in Appendix B.

Now, back to the contents of the book. You'll see some similarities in the ads. For example, the fact that they all have headlines. It's a well-known advertising fact that headlines draw readers—approximately 50 to 75% more readers than ads without them. But headlines do cost more. If your budget is big enough, use them whenever possible. Otherwise you may be able to incorporate them into an ad's copy. Similarly, it's also a well-known advertising fact that the longer you can make your ads, the better they'll sell. But unfortunately the reality is that we can't always afford long ads. Sometimes, though, we can't afford not to run them.

The best headlines offer readers a promise or a personal benefit they'll receive if they decide to buy. For example, "Live at the Top of the World." Second-best headlines are news-oriented, using phrases like "Just Listed" or "New on Market." Yet all too many agents fall back on cutesy headlines, trying to provoke a reader's curiosity. However, cutesy seldom works. Would you call about a property with a headline that started, "Z-Z-Z-Z-Z"? What sells a reader is substance. So make sure your headline always has something to say.

That holds true, too, for the body of the copy. Don't run on with just a list of features. Every house is meant to be a home; sell it that way. Make it sound like a place where someone would want to live. Not because of all the great features it has, but because of the way someone would feel if they lived there.

Use a lot of adjectives to get your point across. We'll help you out at the end of the book where you'll find a list of "Selling Words" to help you describe different properties. Remember, adjectives warm up your ad, giving it personality and adding excitement.

It's also important that you end your ad with what advertising pros refer to as a "call to action." It isn't enough to give the price and your phone number, you also need to toss in a final twist of enticement. There are lots of ways to do it, as you'll see in the pages that follow.

Some Realtors® debate over how much to include in an ad. Should they put in the address of the home? Should they quote the price? Studies have shown that you may lose up to 50% of your prospective buyers if you don't include the price in the ad. So you'll find prices in all of our ads. However, the prices used in this book reflect the current market values in the Southern California area where a mid-priced home usually carries a stiff price of over $160,000. What buys a three bedroom suburban ranch in Los Angeles may buy a mansion where you live. Remember, don't take the price quotes literally, they're only for reference.

One thing you'll notice that we've elected not to include in our ads are specific interest rates or down payment amounts. This doesn't mean that we're recommending that you not include them in your ads. However, if you do, you should be aware that the law stipulates that if you choose to mention these amounts in your ad, you must also disclose the exact down payment amount necessary, the number and amount of monthly payments and the APR (annual percentage rate).

Because it's important to keep track of the results from your ads, we've opted for putting your office phone number into the ad and not your full address. This makes it easy to keep tabs on how your ads are doing. If they're not working, try changing your approach. But don't give up if the results aren't stupendous immediately. Remember that advertising is the backbone of sales in this country. After relying on a real estate agent, more home buyers turn to classified ads than anything else. When you get a call from a classified ad, you can be pretty sure the prospective buyer is serious. That's the kind of home he or she is looking for. If that particular one doesn't strike his or her fancy, chances are you know of similar homes for sale. Use your classified ads as lead-getters.

Now that you've become familiar with some of the finer points of ad writing, we're ready to get to the main purpose of this book—classified ads that can help to make you money.

CHAPTER ONE

Low-Priced Homes

LOCATION

COUNTRY

We Saved the Trees

surrounding this delightful country home. Set on its own little hill, this 3 bedroom, 2 bath charmer combines modern convenience with old-fashioned style. Curl up before the warm wood stove in the family room, grow a garden right in your own backyard. Where else can you find clean air, birds & privacy for only $117,000? Better move fast. Call Clarke Realty, 555-7120. Ask for Richard.

Your Cozy Hideaway

Get back to nature in this charming cedar cottage. Big screened porch, old oak tree, & huge fenced yard. Enjoy 3 comfortably-sized bedrooms, 2 baths. Great buy at only $115,000. Call Robert at Clarke Realty, 555-7120. This one won't last long!

Country Charmer

If you'd like to get back to a quiet, simpler lifestyle, consider this 2 bedroom, 2 bath home shaded by tall trees. Front porch for rocking, roomy kitchen for eating, bright & cheery living room. Only 20 min. from town. For $112,000, make it yours today. Call Shirley at Clarke Realty, 555-7120.

Relaxing Rural Retreat...

on an acre all your own. Massive stone fireplace, handmade cabinets...small but loaded with charm. Big windows bring the outdoors in. 1 bedroom, den, updated kitchen & bath. Only $98,000 so hurry! Call Fred at Clarke Realty, 555-7120.

Country Home Waiting for Loving Family

Room for horses, dogs, garden. Put on a pot of soup in the comfortable kitchen. Start a fire in the brick hearth. You'll love the 3 sunny bedrooms, 2 full baths, city conveniences, great schools...not to mention the peace & quiet. Just $107,500. Call Dolores at Clarke Realty, 555-7120. Now.

Make Friends With Nature

in this all-brick ranch. Feed the deer off your private patio, count the butterflies in the garden. 8 years young, this city-style, 2 bedroom, 2 bath home makes life easy. Built-in conveniences, fully carpeted, garage/workshop. Less than an hour from downtown, only $125,000. Call Tom at Clarke Realty, 555-7120. Do it today.

AD TIP: Don't advertise all of your listings. Put in one or two in each price range and location to attract prospects.

Mother Nature Is Waiting

Mellowed by time, this wonderful old cottage is in a place set apart. Trees, birds, flowers make up its beauty. Gingerbread trim & funny nooks & crannies create its charm. The 2 bedrooms are just right for sleeping, while the living/dining room is spacious & bright. 2 baths, too. If you want a home that reflects who you are for only $95,000, call Deena at Clarke Realty, 555-7120. Don't let Mother Nature wait any longer.

Escape Before It's Too Late

Count the stars at night. Breathe the clean air. Feel at peace inside. Come to the country & see this big & bright frame home. Walk around the large fenced yard. Check out the chicken coop. Explore all the possibilities. 3 bedrooms, 2 baths with lots of room for only $95,000. Call George at Clarke Realty, 555-7120.

Come Down a Country Lane

Longing to get away from the hustle & bustle? Afraid of losing the convenience? Have the best of both worlds in this 5 room, wooded retreat just 15 min. off Hwy 99. Features airy loft just right for a library or guest room, master bedroom sitting area, kitchen greenhouse window. Won't last long at $89,500. Call Clarke Realty, 555-7120, & ask for Sue.

If You've Ever Wanted 15 Trees to Call Your Own

don't miss this opportunity. Elms, oaks, pines come with this comfortable country home just outside the city. Solid 3 bedroom brick ranch with good-sized living room, separate dining area, eat-in kitchen, 2 full baths. From your patio look out over a wooded ravine. Enjoy the good life for only $120,000. Call Tom today at Clarke Realty, 555-7120.

Your Home in the Woods

Bring chestnuts to roast in the old-fashioned fireplace of this country beauty. Set amid trees & flowering shrubs, it's a nature lover's delight. Enjoy it from a rocking chair on the front porch. Feel a sense of the past with the hardwood floors, wood windows, old pine cabinets. 2 bedrooms, 2 baths make it perfect. Only $79,500. To see it today, call Noreen at Clarke Realty, 555-7120.

Eat the Apples Right Off the Tree—Yours

If you've ever wanted to reach up & pluck an apple, drive out to this country cottage. Only 45 min. from Center City, it feels worlds apart. Upstairs are 2 bedrooms with quaint dormer windows. Downstairs a family-sized living room & big, window-lined kitchen. 2 baths, too. It's a house for people who enjoy living with nature. If you're one of them call Jeannie at Clarke Realty, 555-7120, & grab it for only $65,000. Don't wait.

Cut Your Own Christmas Tree

Imagine how thrilled your children will be when you step out the back door to chop down your very own evergreen. This traditional home offers a gigantic basement playroom, 3 spread-out bedrooms, 2 full baths & yard with room to roam. Garage has space for tools, bikes & cars. Bargain priced at $119,000. Call Joe today at Clarke Realty, 555-7120.

Listen to the Quiet

If you're tired of the traffic or your neighbor's chatter, try something different...the sound of silence in this cozy 2 bedroom, 2 bath cottage set back from the street. A bargain at $88,000. Call Regina at Clarke Realty, 555-7120.

Hansel & Gretel Cottage

This snug little home would fit right into a storybook with its gabled roof, dormer windows & brick sidewalk. Just 5 min. off Route 81. Cozy fireplace, built-in bookcases, even a dishwasher in the step-saving kitchen. With 2 bedrooms & 2 baths, there's plenty of room. Loaded with personality. Just $75,000. Call Jay at Clarke Realty, 555-7120, now.

WATERFRONT

Bring Your Fishing Pole

& fire up the brick BBQ in your backyard. Enjoy life at the beach in this charming cottage. Tile floors, knotty pine walls, modern galley kitchen, 2 bedrooms, 2 baths. Old, but full of character, just $80,000. Call Tony at Clarke Realty, 555-7120, today to take a look.

Your Own Lazy River

Ever wanted a river to call your own? Well here's your chance in this small window-lined waterfront home new on market. Summer porch, large garage, storage area, big brick fireplace, wood-burning stove. Only 25 min. from downtown. If you're looking for a 2 bedroom, 2 bath home in one of the most peaceful settings around, call George at Clarke Realty, 555-7120. At $75,000, this is a great buy.

AD TIP: Using abbreviations in your ad can save you money. But be sure they are common and people will understand them.

Relax on the Beach

near this comfortable & carefree home with a yard full of flowers. Living room, big built-in hutch, separate dining, country kitchen, 3 good-sized bedrooms with ample closets & 2 full baths. Clean, simple, close to swimming, sunning & lots of beach for running. Even the price is easy, just $99,000. Call Virginia today at Clarke Realty, 555-7120.

Shake the Sand Out of Your Shoes

Set in rolling sand dunes, within hearing distance of the waves, this is a golden opportunity to own a beach home at a reasonable price. 2 bedrooms, 2 baths, living room with French windows, step-saving kitchen, modern bath. Yours for just $65,000. Call Clarke Realty, 555-7120, & ask for Richard. Do it today!

Enjoy a Waterfall Right in Your Own Backyard!

Set in a peaceful glen, this 4 bedroom, 2-story is full of character & charm. Lush, tropical garden, big bookcases flanking the fireplace, cheery breakfast nook where you can watch the stream. 3 full baths & 2 car garage with room for RV. If country living is your style, call Jean at Clarke Realty, 555-7120. Only $95,000.

On the Sand

Spectacular bargain. 1 bedroom beach house just right for a weekend getaway. Watch the surf through sliding glass doors opening to a plant-filled patio. Whip up a snack in the step-saving kitchen, separated from the living room by a convenient breakfast bar. Enjoy the spacious bedroom, with its huge closets & room-sized bath. Life at the beach for only $76,000, but you'd better act fast. Call Tony at Clarke Realty, 555-7120, today.

Waterfront Retreat

Watch the sea gulls dive for their supper, walk for hours along the shore. It's a comfortable, serene lifestyle that's yours for only $105,000. Of course, the 3 bedroom, 2 bath, 2-story house needs a little work. If you're willing to invest some time & labor, you can reap rich rewards. Come out today & see the potential. Call Robert at Clarke Realty, 555-7120.

Beach Bungalow

Afternoons fishing, jumping over waves, building sand castles. Bring back those times in this weathered 3 bedroom, 2 bath cottage. From its shingled roof to the wood windows that look out over the sand, it's the kind of place where you can relax, feel free. Cedar lines the closets, warm woodwork fills the living room. Come back to a place that really has been a home. Call Henry at Clarke Realty, 555-7120. Only $86,000. Hurry.

A Peaceful Brook

runs through the backyard of this sturdy brick home. 3 bedroom, 2 bath ranch, with modern conveniences & old-fashioned style. Hardwood floors, roomy pantry, spacious attic. Just 45 min. from downtown. Only $76,000. Call Jean at Clarke Realty, 555-7120, today.

Can You See Yourself Living at the Beach?

If you love sun & surf, consider this 2 bedroom, 2 bath charmer 3 blocks from the boardwalk. There's a 2 car garage where you can store surfboards, fenced yard for pets, patio big enough for a hot tub. Call Ginger at Clarke Realty, 555-7120. For only $90,000, enjoy the surf all year long.

Beach Fixer

Bring your toolbox to this cozy cottage just 4 blocks from the beach. Cedar shingles, rows of windows, super front porch. Has large living room, 3 spacious bedrooms & 2 full baths. Only $110,000. Great place for family who wants to give their home a personal touch. Call Regina today at Clarke Realty, 555-7120.

Like Fish for Supper?

Enjoy free fish dinners when you move into this home within biking distance of the shoreline. Imagine getting tile floors, custom cabinets, wall-to-wall carpeting, 3 bedrooms & 2 baths—all for only $86,500. Plus a lifestyle you thought you never could afford. Call Suzanne at Clarke Realty, 555-7120, today.

On the Beach

is a charming bungalow that started life as a weekend hideaway. But over the years, it's turned into a full-time home. With 2 bedrooms, 2 baths, giant eat-in kitchen, living room with native stone fireplace. Only $75,000. Call Manuel at Clarke Realty, 555-7120, to see this unbelievable bargain.

Watch the Sunsets

over the lake from the balcony of this 2 bedroom, 2 bath rustic set amid the trees. Huge windows, rock walls, kitchen greenhouse window & eating nook. Park your own sailboat on the beach below. At only $88,000, it's a great buy. Call Thomas at Clarke Realty, 555-7120, today.

AD TIP: Write fast and edit later.

Listen to the Waves

roar just outside the door of this beach bungalow. '40s knotty pine walls, lots of windows, ample closet space & 2 cozy bedrooms & 2 full baths are the basics. But there's also a pier you can fish from, pine trees you can admire, & your nearest neighbor is hidden from view. It's an island retreat along the bay that's hard to find. In a neighborhood of high-priced homes, it's just $88,000. Call Paul today at Clarke Realty, 555-7120.

HILL

Your Mountain Cabin

Perched on the side of a mountain, this old-time cabin overlooks the canyon. Gingerbread trim, gigantic rock fireplace, vine-covered brick patio. 2 bedrooms & an extra room for home office or guest. Updated kitchen & bath. Only $99,000—call George at Clarke Realty, 555-7120, today.

Your Hillside Retreat

Charming cottage with cozy rock courtyard dominated by tall old oak tree. You'll love the glass wall kitchen. Big bedroom with extra storage space. Extra building can be converted into artist's studio or rental unit. Just $101,000. Call Susan at Clarke Realty, 555-7120, today.

Mountain High

Look straight up at the mountains from the wonderfully private patio of this cabin just 45 min. from downtown. Features long, lean kitchen with rock-lined eating nook. Cove ceilings mark the bedroom & a jalousy-windowed porch opens to the trees. Marvelous place to feel in tune with nature. Offered at $95,000. Call Richard at Clarke Realty, 555-7120, today.

Hillside Retreat

Get a magnificent skyline view from the living room of this stunning 2 bedroom, 2 bath contemporary. Features a wall of windows & upper & lower decks where you can relax & enjoy the city lights. At only $96,000, it's sure to go fast. Call Thomas at Clarke Realty, 555-7120, today.

A Home With a View for Only $100,000

Tucked in the foothills, this charming A-frame is surrounded by stones & trees. Swedish fireplace, built-in bookshelves, butler's pantry make it special. So do the 2 bedrooms, each with its own full bath. Redwood deck has room for a spa. Enjoy the serenity of the mountains only minutes from the city. Call Gina today at Clarke Realty, 555-7120.

Hilltop Serenity

Like to feel on top of it all? Then you'll love this home high above the city. Watch the city lights from the living room at night. Enjoy the entertainment-sized kitchen & bright & cheery dining room. Downstairs you'll find 3 bedrooms, 2 baths, surrounded by trees. Only $110,000. If serenity is what you're after, call Marcie at Clarke Realty, 555-7120. Don't wait.

A View & a Whole Lot More

Sleekly designed 3 bedroom, 2 bath home features entire walls of windows overlooking a nature preserve. The 3 bedrooms are set apart in their own wing, while the kitchen, living & dining rooms flow together in one smooth, giant area. If you're looking for a home in great shape, with a view that goes on forever, call Virginia at Clarke Realty, 555-7120. Just reduced to $99,000.

Live Among the Treetops

Inside this comfortable rambler the feeling is open & bright, with light-colored hardwood floors throughout. The 2 bedrooms are big & comfortable...the kitchen a cook's dream. Lots of living space & 2 full baths for only $120,000. Call James at Clarke Realty, 555-7120. Do it today.

Incredible View

is yours in this 3 bedroom, 2 bath hillside home that offers mountain serenity & city convenience. Almost every room has a view. Enjoy the wonderfully private patio. Make it yours today—only $99,500. Call Ronald at Clarke Realty, 555-7120.

Hillside Hideaway

Dramatic 2-level contemporary with lots of open space & balconies. Watch the stars come out from the rooftop patio. Fix dinner in a streamlined, up-to-date kitchen. From the living room step onto the private redwood deck & get your fill of the scenery. Lower level features 3 secluded bedrooms & 2 full baths. A contemporary delight for only $102,000. Call Harold at Clarke Realty, 555-7120. Don't miss out.

Hillside Charmer—$88,000

Double French doors open into the spacious, window-lined living room. Off the combination dining room/kitchen, you'll find a charming redwood-paneled room perfect for reading or studying. Downstairs bedroom & bath. Set in a special location in forest of trees with lots of windows so you can enjoy them. It's sure to sell fast. So call Eugene at Clarke Realty, 555-7120, today.

Want a View & Privacy?

Then consider this new-on-the-market contemporary just 30 min. from town. From the moment you walk through the double entry doors, you can tell this is a quality-built home. A Jenn-air range, top-of-the-line fixtures, oak paneling, whisper-soft carpet & stone fireplace prove it. With 2 spacious bedrooms, 2 full baths & a fenced yard. A bargain at $115,000. Call Clarke Realty, 555-7120, today. Ask for Roger.

City Lights at Night

Enjoy a carpet of lights from the living room of this hillside home. Or step out onto the wraparound redwood deck for a closer view. Built right into the rock, this cozy 2 bedroom, 2 bath home has lots of glass, heart pine floors & a kitchen designed for convenience. Enjoy its peace & quiet for only $96,000. Call Marlene at Clarke Realty, 555-7120. Do it today.

Cabin in the Sky

That's how you'll feel about this rustic log home just outside town. Let it bring out the country in you with its wide planked floors, hand-built cabinets, homespun charm. 4 unique & custom-crafted rooms. Quality like this is hard to find, especially for $87,000. Call Tony at Clarke Realty, 555-7120. This is really something special.

Have the World at Your Feet

in this delightful hilltop home only 45 min. from downtown. Enjoy windows open to the sky & a night blanket of city lights. 3 bedrooms, 2-1/2 baths on a full acre. Natural landscaping for easy care. Only $88,000. Call Paul at Clarke Realty, 555-7120, right now.

DESERT

Wide-Open Spaces

can be yours in this desert home just 10 min. from town. Southwestern style features red tile roof, charming paved courtyard, tile fountain & sky that stretches as far as the eye can see. With 3 bedrooms & 2-1/2 baths, spacious yet full of quiet charm. All for only $87,900. Call Robert today at Clarke Realty, 555-7120.

A Desert Paintbrush

painted this cool & calming home with creamy pastel colors. Wide windows carry you out to the emptiness that goes for miles. Modern in style, this 3 bedroom, 2 bath ranch offers a spa & private deck and workshop/garage for $87,500. Call Joel at Clarke Realty, 555-7120.

Your Desert Retreat

Get away from it all in this cozy desert home. Air conditioned for comfort, filled with all the modern conveniences, far away from the city's hustle. Sit on the quiet patio & admire the night stars, watch the sun bring out nature's glorious colors. If you want an immaculate 2 bedroom, 2 bath home landscaped by nature herself, call Tim at Clarke Realty, 555-7120. Only $99,000.

A Place in the Sun—$90,000

Cactus & rocks surround this 1 bedroom charmer...where the air is clean & the sky bright blue. Spacious veranda, stone fireplace, skylights. If you'd like something different, for only $90,000, call Bill at Clarke Realty, 555-7120. Do it now.

There's Nothing Quite Like a Desert Sunset

Enjoy every evening from the cool, brick-lined patio of this stucco home. Small & cozy, its 2 bedrooms have French doors opening to the garden. In the living room, there's an adobe fireplace. Stained glass windows decorate the kitchen. Ready for someone to love for only $86,000. Call Fred today at Clarke Realty, 555-7120.

GOLF

If Golf Is Your Bag

live only 5 min. away from one of the finest courses in the city. For only $99,000, you can own this 3 bedroom, 2 bath ranch in the friendly neighborhood of Indian Hills. Walk to schools. Great shopping nearby. Lush carpeting, generously-sized rooms, giant basement workshop. Why wait any longer? Call Tony at Clarke Realty, 555-7120, today.

Attention: Golfers!

Consider this spacious 3 bedroom, 2 bath home near the George Rogers golf course. Country-style breakfast nook, roomy garage, sprawling backyard. During the evening, relax next to the crackling fireplace. Call Peter at Clarke Realty, 555-7120, today to see this $99,000 gem.

Ready to Tee Off?

Then head for this 2 bedroom, 1 bath cottage just off the green at the city golf course. Surrounded by a white picket fence, it features a generous front porch, bay windows, lots of room for a garden & bright, shiny hardwood floors, well-cared for. Only $78,000. Call Gina today at Clarke Realty, 555-7120.

Live Near the Green

of the fabulous Monterey Village Golf Course. Less than a mile from the club, you can enjoy this 3 bedroom, 2 bath ranch loaded with convenience. 2 car garage, dishwasher, gas fireplace, wall-to-wall carpeting, automatic sprinklers all designed to save you time. Only $100,000. Call Debbie today at Clarke Realty, 555-7120. Get those clubs ready!

Golfer's Delight

You'll love this 3 bedroom, 2 bath home just 5 min. from Paradise Golf Club. Secluded on 1/4 acre lot, almost hidden by tall trees. Antique fireplace, honey birch cabinets, gleaming hardwood floors. It's a mature beauty that can't be beat. Only $99,000. Call Susan at Clarke Realty, 555-7120, today.

RECREATION/LEISURE

Ski Cabin

Get ready for the snow in this log cabin. Just 5 min. from the lifts, full of old-fashioned charm with massive stone fireplace, broad beams & a loft above the living room with plenty of space for guests. Just $45,000 so hurry & call Edward at Clarke Realty, 555-7120. Move in before the snow falls.

Park Your Boat

at your own dock outside this rambling 2 bedroom, 1 bath cabin on the shore of Lake Michigan. Picnic on the summer porch where cool breezes blow. During the evening, warm yourself near the pot-bellied stove. Spend the afternoon picking up pine cones. Life the way it used to be for only $50,000. Call Mimi today at Clarke Realty, 555-7120.

Winter Wonderland

can be yours in this cozy mountain cabin just 1 hour from the city. Stoke up a roaring fire in the gigantic stone fireplace. Cook in the modern, all-electric kitchen. With 3 bedrooms & 2 baths, what ski-loving family could resist this $90,000 jewel? Call Ruth at Clarke Realty, 555-7120, today. Get ready for ski season!

Bring Your Tennis Racket

to this 2 bedroom, 2 bath ranch just steps from the city courts. Sitting back from the street on a winding sidewalk, it offers an old-fashioned porch, cheerful & bright rooms, big attic storage space. If you're a tennis buff, get into the swing of it with this special home. Only $89,000. Call Gina at Clarke Realty, 555-7120, today.

Like to Hunt?

Then check out this log-style cabin in the state's best hunting area. Fix a big breakfast in the country kitchen. Sit around the fireplace & swap stories. With 2 bedrooms, 2 baths & 1,000 sq. ft., have plenty of room for guests. Your home away from home—only $55,000. Call Carl at Clarke Realty, 555-7120, today.

CONVENIENCE

Tired of Commuting?

Consider this charming home in the city's historical district. Built with 1920's quality, it's an old-fashioned jewel just waiting to be polished. In addition to the satisfaction of restoring its original luster, you'll also have the joy of living close to work, shops, schools. This 3 bedroom, 2 bath home is under $100,000. Call Ed at Clarke Realty, 555-7120, today. Explore the possibilities now.

Walk to Work

If you're tired of fighting the freeways, why do it? Enjoy the quiet elegance of a 1930's home, with gleaming hardwood trim, primrose garden & French windows galore. Hard to believe this 3 bedroom, 2-story is right in the city's hub. 2 baths, too. Only 90,000. Call Tim at Clarke Realty, 555-7120, now.

In the Shadow of Skyscrapers

grows a homemade vegetable garden. And a cute cottage with cheerful gingerbread trim, brick sidewalks & a hammock in the backyard. It's a one of a kind home with 2 bedrooms, modernized kitchen & bath. Just steps away from the the bus line & great schools. Would you believe it's only $65,000? See it today. Call Frank at Clarke Realty, 555-7120.

City Convenience
With Country Charm

Right off Main Street you'll find this sparkling 3 bedroom, 2 bath colonial with plantation shutters. Vaulted ceilings, glassed-in hutch, spacious pantry. In perfect shape, with all the latest appliances, this 2-story is priced at only $87,000. Call Gina at Clarke Realty, 555-7120, today.

Super Schools, Super Price

If you want your kids to have the best, come see this 4 bedroom, 2-story Victorian-style home in the Mendocino school district. At $88,000, it's one of the lowest priced homes in the neighborhood. Your kids can even walk to school. With hand-polished bannisters, family room with fireplace, up-to-the-minute kitchen, 3 full baths & a yard big enough for a playground—it's a great buy. Call Tim at Clarke Realty, 555-7120. Now.

Close to Medical Center

If you'd like to live close to the John Hopkins Medical Complex, consider this contemporary special. From the dramatic slate foyer to the floor-to-ceiling brick fireplace, it's designed to catch everyone's eye. 3 bedrooms, labor-saving galley kitchen, 2 baths, full basement, 2 car garage for only $87,000. See it today. Call Helen at Clarke Realty, 555-7120.

Two Blocks From Mall

Right on the bus line, just minutes from the mall, there's a new home on the market. A cozy frame cottage with a big sun porch for plants, warm wood-paneled living room, 2 gigantic bedrooms, 1-1/2 baths & grand yard for gardening. In the evening, sit in a rocker on the wide front veranda. Or walk around the corner for ice cream. Only $88,000. Call Regina at Clarke Realty, 555-7120, to find out more.

Ford Employees:
Forget the Commute

& pick up the key to this sprawling brick ranch, just 5 min. from Ford. Enjoy quiet evenings on the big screened porch. Roast marshmallows in the huge stone fireplace. It comes with 3 bedrooms, 2 baths, ample closets, farm-style kitchen & 2 car garage for just $98,000. Call Tom at Clarke Realty, 555-7120, now.

5 Min. From Town!

But you'd never believe it when you see this 2 bedroom, 2 bath contemporary. The giant, plant-filled atrium is an oasis of serenity. Living room is big enough for entertaining. There's even a walled garden with a porch swing under the trees. Delightfully decorated, landscaped with care. Yours for only $87,000. Call Warren at Clarke Realty, 555-7120, now.

Walk to Work

Shops, offices & schools are only steps away from this chic city home. Contemporary in style, with giant walls of glass, spiral staircase, sleek modern kitchen & high-tech living room, this 2 bedroom, 2 bath showcase is just $99,000. Call George at Clarke Realty, 555-7120, to see it today.

Enjoy Convenience?

Then stop by this 3 bedroom home just min. from downtown. It features wall-to-wall carpeting, formica countertops, 2 ceramic tile baths, easy neutral decor. Private spa off master bedroom. Only $98,000. Call Ruth at Clarke Realty, 555-7120, for more information.

Take the Kids to the Park

next to this 4 bedroom, 3 bath ranch. Let them enjoy the playground, tennis, feeding the ducks. They can romp in the big basement, while you relax in the private sitting area off the master bedroom. Yours for only $96,000. Call Reginald at Clarke Realty, 555-7120, now.

Jogger's Delight

This 2 bedroom, 2 bath traditional borders a scenic & popular jogging trail. Entertain your friends in the spacious, window-filled living room, where you can enjoy a fire's glow or your spacious redwood deck with its sizzling spa. Plenty of closet space. Priced at $87,000. Call Robert at Clarke Realty, 555-7120.

AD TIP: Make sure your headline calls attention to your ad.

Convenient to Everything

Close to shops, doctors, offices, schools—this 2-story brick beauty is loaded with charm. French windows, planter boxes, glowing hardwood floors & 2 tiled baths make it special. Set back from the street, its 2 bedrooms are far removed from the traffic's roar. For $87,000, it's worth a call to Eunice at Clarke Realty, 555-7120. Make it now.

So Near Yet Feels So Far

Convenient to shops, churches, grocery stores & buses...this charming 2 bedroom, 2 bath home feels far from the city's hustle. Shady elms, a giant garage & wonderful garden are just a few of the features that make this a great value at $87,000. Call Tom at Clarke Realty, 555-7120. Do it today.

Great Schools

are just a few blocks from this friendly, 3 bedroom, 2 bath Cape Cod. After class, the kids can study in the honey paneled family room, or in the privacy of their comfortably-sized bedrooms. Offered at only $97,000...it's one of the lowest priced homes in the Walnut School District. Give your kids the best education in the area. Call Harold at Clarke Realty, 555-7120. Do it today.

Sick of Fighting the Freeways?

Start enjoying life in this city-close, 2 bedroom, 2 bath Victorian home. From the etched glass on the front doors to the hand-carved hutch in the living room & the classy '50s tile in the kitchen, you'll experience a quality of life you've never known before. Only $89,000. Call Richard today at Clarke Realty, 555-7120.

Close to Methodist Hospital

If you've always dreamt about walking to work, this is your chance. A classic 3 bedroom, 2 bath Georgian just across from the hospital. Wide white columns & a sweeping balustrade add an air of prestige. Offered at $90,000. Call Jackie at Clarke Realty, 555-7120. Now.

Want to Save Time?

Then move to an elegant, 3 bedroom, 2 bath home right downtown. Walk through its iron gate & step back into a gentler, more lavish era reflected in the gleaming hardwood floors, floor-to-ceiling windows, built-in conveniences. Priced at only $95,000, it's waiting for the right person. Call Betty today at Clarke Realty, 555-7120.

Tired of Driving?

Then move into this spick & span home near the Southgate mall. With 4 large bedrooms, each kid can have his own. The large kitchen is great for family feasts & there's always room to romp in the unusually large living room. Or send them out to the fenced backyard, where there's an old apple tree perfect for climbing. 3 full baths, too. Enjoy a perfect family home for just $88,000. Call Tom at Clarke Realty, 555-7120. Hurry.

Top Location

You couldn't have planned it better. Beaches, shops, stores, bus lines... they're all within walking distance of this snug Cape Cod. Sitting on a quiet tree-lined street, it's shaded by shrubbery. An oversized garage, delightful garden, 2 big bedrooms & 2 baths are only some of the features creating its charm. At only $95,000, you should see it today. Call Shirley at Clarke Realty, 555-7120.

NEIGHBORHOOD

Children Will Love This Neighborhood

because it's full of friendly families. If you'd like a 3 bedroom, 2 bath old-fashioned home, with flower-filled garden, intriguing wraparound veranda & generous sunlit kitchen, as well as all the modern conveniences, for only $89,000. Call Henry at Clarke Realty, 555-7120. Don't miss it!

Gold Coast Living Without Gold Coast Prices

This snug frame home is in a great neighborhood. Built with craftsmanship & care, it has stained glass windows framing the fireplace, window seats in both bedrooms, mosaic tile. Comfortable & cozy, priced at just $88,000. To see it, call Jim at Clarke Realty, 555-7120.

Belong to a Community of People Who Care

That's what you get when you move into this gorgeous 3 bedroom ranch in suburban Roslyn where people are proud of their homes & it shows. See pride of ownership in the professionally landscaped lawn, custom-built cabinets, 2 full ceramic tile baths, finest draperies & carpets throughout. It's perfect & only $82,000. Call Edward at Clarke Realty, 555-7120. Do it now.

Remember the Old Neighborhood?

where neighbors looked out for each other & children played street tag? You can have that again in this 3 bedroom, 2 bath charmer near Main Street. There's plenty of room to spread out in the gigantic living room, cozy den & huge eat-in kitchen. It's only $87,000. Call Gina at Clarke Realty, 555-7120, today.

Live in the Tudor House
at 4896 Lincoln Street

You've driven by it a million times. Now this 3 bedroom, 2 bath manor can be yours for just $87,000. Imagine the pride you'll feel walking down its grand staircase, or dining with a view of your private rose garden, or reading next to the magnificent fireplace with its mahogany mantel. Live the way you deserve, call Richard at Clarke Realty, 555-7120.

Best Area Only $105,000

It's hard to find a home in prestigious San Marino under $150,000...but this is it. A well cared for 3 bedroom, 2 bath Cape Cod surrounded by high-priced estates. Among its desirable features are a spacious, fully landscaped yard, summer porch, Italian tile entry & fully modernized kitchen. At this price, it's sure to go fast. Call Marcie at Clarke Realty, 555-7120, today.

Hollywood Hills Charm

If you like the feeling of the country but thrive on the energy of the city, consider this bungalow high over Hollywood. Sitting on a winding road hidden by the trees, it's a relaxing retreat for the busy professional. 2 bedrooms, 2 baths make it easy to have guests, while the brick patio is perfect for entertaining. Offered at only $108,000. Call Mimi at Clarke Realty, 555-7120, today.

Artist's Haven

With its many skylights, this uniquely designed home makes the perfect studio. Small but creatively built to make the maximum use of its space. Plenty of storage, compact kitchen, full bath. Even a serene, plant-filled patio. Only $98,000. Call Yolanda at Clarke Realty, 555-7120, now.

Friendly Family Neighborhood

If you'd like your kids to have plenty of friends, come see this charming 3 bedroom, 2 bath stucco. The huge fenced yard makes it perfect for playing, while on rainy days the kids can romp around the big basement. All the rooms, including the kitchen, are generously sized. A genuine family home for just $87,000. To find out more, call Tony at Clarke Realty, 555-7120, today.

Old Towne

This is a sadly neglected home but its quality shows in its hand-carved trim, solid oak cabinets, heavy wood doors. In a neighborhood where many buildings are being restored, it's an opportunity to bring back a little history & make some money, too. 6 rooms in all. It can be yours for just $85,000. Don't miss the opportunity. Call Henry at Clarke Realty, 555-7120.

Live Where the Action Is

If you like to party, check out this stylish 2 bedroom, 2 bath home just off Melrose Avenue. Easy to care for with natural landscaping, automatic sprinklers, 2 car garage...all in tip-top shape. You'll love the bold colors & exciting decor. For only $99,000...it's a real deal. Call Jim at Clarke Realty, 555-7120. Make your move today.

Want a Prestigious Address
for Under $100,000?

Then come to this 2 bedroom, 2 bath cutie right in the middle of estate row. Originally a carriage house, it's packed with charm. Brick floors, huge French windows, an open feeling & warmth... it's small but every inch is quality. Great opportunity for the right person. Call Dee at Clarke Realty, 555-7120, today.

Palm Springs Luxury at a Reasonable Price

Can you believe that $89,000 will give you a home in one of this country's most elite areas? A place full of celebrity homes, where kings & presidents come to visit. Picture yourself in this 2 bedroom, 2 bath, pastel-colored bungalow with bougainvillea twining up your back patio or watching the desert sunset through the living room's picture window. Call Antoinette at Clarke Realty, 555-7120, now.

Live at Sea Point

If you'd like to live in one of Orange County's newest, most thoughtfully planned communities, consider this 3 bedroom Ranger special. Packed with upgrades, it features a full-wall stone fireplace, tile countertops, microwave, 2 full baths, an elegant terrazzo foyer floor. For only $110,000 it's hard to beat. Let Jim at Clarke Realty, 555-7120, show it to you today.

Cul-De-Sac Living at the Right Price

Come see this comfortable 3 bedroom, 2 bath ranch on a secluded cul-de-sac. Set apart by its gently weathered shingles, French windows & lush landscaping, it's peaceful & filled with flowers. You'll love all the conveniences inside. To see it today, call Edward at Clarke Realty, 555-7120. At $98,000, it won't last.

The Right Address

Imagine living on Gold Coast row in a chic 2 bedroom, 2 bath home. With clean lines, colored tile, a sense of intimacy & comfort. For only $88,000 you can't afford to pass it up. Call William at Clarke Realty, 555-7120, today.

Imagine Life the Way It Used to Be for Only $95,000

Sunday afternoon strolls, afternoons lying in a hammock, children riding bikes. That simple lifestyle can be yours again in this delightful Victorian home new on the market. Located in an established neighborhood of custom-built, character-filled homes, it offers 3 sprawling bedrooms, 2 full baths, elegant dark wood trim, hardwood floors, etched glass doors & best of all, a big front porch where you can spend the evening. Call Shirley today at Clarke Realty, 555-7120.

Down a Winding Street

you'll find this cozy Cape Cod. 1 or 2 bedrooms with plenty of room to grow. You'll love the antique fireplace, bay window, highly polished hardwood floors, old-fashioned mosaic tile. Custom quality at rock-bottom price of $76,000. See it today. Call Jim at Clarke Realty, 555-7120.

Prestige Living at a Practical Price

You'll be the envy of all your friends when you live in this neighborhood known for its excellent homes, fine schools & superb restaurants. You don't have to tell them the great deal you made because this 2 bedroom, 1-1/2 bath stunner is a bargain. For just $79,000, you get a free-flowing contemporary with high-tech accents, sun-drenched patio & elegant upstairs balcony. Make it yours. Call Jo at Clarke Realty, 555-7120.

AD TIP: Don't write ads to impress your friends. Write ads to attract prospects.

PRIVACY

A Hidden Delight

Hidden behind towering shrubs & huge trees, this cottage is worlds removed from the city's hustle. 2 cheerful bedrooms, 2 full baths, solid plaster walls, quaint casement windows, a summer porch you can fill with wicker & chimes. Experience a lifestyle you never thought you'd find in the city. Only $89,000. Call Hal today at Clarke Realty, 555-7120.

Your Private Sanctuary

A place you can unwind in total seclusion. Your private road leads to this modern 2 bedroom, 2 bath dream with an efficient galley kitchen, tile floors, walls of glass overlooking the garden. Peace & quiet for just $97,000. Call Sam at Clarke Realty, 555-7120, now.

Cul-De-Sac Privacy

If you're looking for a home that's convenient, yet private—this is it. A 2-story, 3 bedroom, 2 bath traditional set back on a huge lawn at the end of a cul-de-sac. Backyard slopes down to a wooded ravine. Inside the space is generous, well-lit, full of amenities you'll love. Only $87,000. Call William today at Clarke Realty, 555-7120.

Romantic Hideaway

Imagine candle-lit dinners on the brick terrace. Evenings in the tree-shaded spa. Curling up in front of the flickering stone fireplace. Old & charming, this 2 bedroom, 2 bath retreat in the hills is just $89,000. A perfect gift for yourself & someone you love. Call Ginger at Clarke Realty, 555-7120, & let the romance begin.

At the End of the Road

there's a tasteful 3 bedroom, 2 bath home...the kind of place where you can watch flowers grow, feed the deer, enjoy the spectacular view through its walls of glass. Only 30 min. from town. Wall-to-wall carpeting, walk-in closets, wonderfully large kitchen are only a few of its many attractive features. At $98,000, it won't last long. Call Ronald at Clarke Realty, 555-7120, right now.

A Place of Peace

If you're looking for a home that's soothing & quiet, stop by this 3 bedroom, 2 bath retreat. Set far back from the street, beneath huge elms & flowering shrubs, it's carefully planned to create a relaxing environment. From the secluded, cactus-studded garden off the master bedroom to the gentle flagstone patio out back...privacy is maximized. Only $87,000. Call Edward at Clarke Realty, 555-7120, now.

Your Private Retreat

On a winding road high in the hills, you'll find this delightful 2 bedroom, 2 bath hideaway. Concealed from the street, it's open to the trees, flowers, sky. Lots of glass, appliance upgrades, wood trim make it special. It can be yours for only $87,000. Call Judy at Clarke Realty, 555-7120, to see it today.

At Last—Sanctuary

If you don't want to fight traffic, check out this 3 bedroom, 2-1/2 bath ranch on a cul-de-sac. In the evenings, you can unwind on its big screened porch. Or relax with the family in the fireplace-dominated "great room." Or munch a midnight snack at the convenient, tile-topped breakfast bar. Just $89,000. Call Roslyn today at Clarke Realty, 555-7120.

The Haven of Home

tailor-made for comfort & relaxation. 2 bedroom, 2 bath stucco cottage with stone courtyard & fountain, lots of Mexican tile, & secluded spa where you can reward yourself. For only $98,000...call Dean at Clarke Realty, 555-7120, today.

Retreat to Comfort

in this 3 bedroom, 2 bath charmer just minutes from the freeway. Beamed ceilings, brick fireplace, copper-kettle kitchen make it cozy & warm. Secluded cul-de-sac, circular driveway & stone gates insure privacy. Offered at just $95,000. Call Rusty at Clarke Realty, 555-7120.

SAFETY & SECURITY

Enjoy Cul-De-Sac Safety

nestled against an open field. Your kids will love this great 3 bedroom home, with lots of room to run & play. Mom & Dad'll enjoy the spacious bedrooms, cheerful family room, sunny eat-in kitchen & 2-1/2 baths. For $87,000, give the kids room to roam. Call Ann at Clarke Realty, 555-7120, today.

Behind a Guarded Gate

you'll find the ultimate in comfort, a 2 bedroom, 2 bath contemporary home with simple, classical lines. Enjoy the drama of floor-to-ceiling windows, tile patio, whisper-soft carpeting. All in a neighborhood where you can take an evening stroll. Only $98,000. Call Mary today at Clarke Realty, 555-7120.

AD TIP: Keep track of how your ads are doing by asking prospects where they saw the ad.

Enjoy Peace of Mind

in this charming 2 bedroom home. Located in a gated community, it's the kind of place where neighbors look out for each other. Enjoy the labor-saving kitchen, tranquil walled patio, lots of extra storage space & 2 tiled baths. Priced at just $87,000. Call Ronald at Clarke Realty, 555-7120, to see it today.

Through the Gate

you'll find a delightful 1 bedroom home with 24 hour security. When you come home, unwind by puttering in the garden, cooking in the big kitchen or entertaining in the open-beamed living room. Hard to believe it's only $95,000. Call Mrs. Williams at Clarke Realty, 555-7120, to see this lovely home today.

Like to Take an Evening Stroll?

Then move into a neighborhood where you can wander whenever you like. Nothing to worry about here but how fast your flowers will grow. You'll love this 3 bedroom, 2 bath rambler, with its Victorian trim, spacious porch, trees galore. For only $97,000, make this your home. Call John at Clarke Realty, 555-7120.

VIEW

Sunset View

Relax on the redwood patio. Watch the sun's rays filter through the trees around this stone & glass 2 bedroom, 2 bath home. Through the big windows they'll touch lightly on the living room limestone wall, shed a pink glow on the kitchen's white ceramic counters, lengthen the shadows in the peaches & cream dining room. Feel at peace in this affordable $86,000 beauty. Call Roger at Clarke Realty, 555-7120, today.

Love a Spectacular View?

Then come home to it every night in this cedar cottage hugging a mountainside. From each of its rooms, enjoy looking out for miles. Its features are a 2 car garage, pleasant patio & pine walls. At only $85,000, it will sell quickly. Call Gina at Clarke Realty, 555-7120, to see it today.

Bring Your Camera

because this home offers a view of towering cactus that will delight any photographer. It's a spectacular sight all year long & it's yours for only $89,000. You'll love the house, too...a 2 bedroom, 2 bath redwood & glass contemporary, with an open & free feeling. Call Helen at Clarke Realty, 555-7120, today.

A View As Big As the Outdoors

That's what you'll get in this 3 bedroom, 2 bath rustic perched in the Glenoak hills. Follow the winding driveway to the big double doors. Relax in the spacious, airy living room. Watch the wind blow the treetops. It's the perfect escape for those who love the outdoors. Only $97,000. Call Tim at Clarke Realty, 555-7120.

Skyline Drama

belongs to you from the dramatic living room of this clean-cut 2 bedroom, 2 bath contemporary. Smooth, sweeping lines make the lower floor a "great room," while a circular stairway takes you upstairs to the loft & sleeping areas. Perfect for professionals. Only $102,000. Call Marietta at Clarke Realty, 555-7120, to see it today.

Watch the City Lights Twinkle

for only $86,000 when you move into this 2 bedroom, 2 bath ranch high above the city. Shingled roof, cedar siding, brick walks add to its charm. Call Sam at Clarke Realty, 555-7120, today.

Enjoy the Sunsets

from the brick-walled patio of this secluded home in the mountains. Live with nature just outside your back door while enjoying the convenience of the city. Plenty of comfort with 3 bedrooms & 2 baths. Priced at just $98,000. Call Henry at Clarke Realty, 555-7120, now.

Creekside View

is yours from the vine-covered patio of this comfortable 3 bedroom, 2 bath rambler. If you like wide open rooms, lots of glowing wood, big windows & lush plants, you'll love this home. It can be yours for only $97,000. Call Richard today at Clarke Realty, 555-7120.

A View for Under $100,000?

That's right in this cozy Victorian home just off Sand Ridge. From the glassed-in porch, you can see forever. 2 bedrooms, 2 baths, a wood-burning stove & a den for just $98,000. Call George today at Clarke Realty, 555-7120.

You Can See Forever

from every room of this 2 bedroom, 2 bath charmer in the exclusive Sierra Canyon. From the colorful rock patio, enjoy nature at its finest. In the cozy, wood-paneled living room, see the city lights below you. Only $87,000. Call Eugene at Clarke Realty, 555-7120, now.

SIZE

STARTER HOMES

Looking for Your First Home?

Then start here in this 2 bedroom, 2 bath ranch in one of the city's best neighborhoods. For only $87,000 you can enjoy a spacious living room with built-in bookcases, fireplace, tons of storage space & the joy of owning a home. Call Peter at Clarke Realty, 555-7120, today.

Start Here

in this immaculate, 2 bedroom California-style ranch in south Diamond Bar. Easy neutral decor. Plant shelves. Lots of light & windows. 2 full baths. Bargain priced at $77,000. Call John at Clarke Realty, 555-7120, to find out how easy it is to make this charming home yours.

ATTENTION:
First Time Buyers

If you've been dreaming about a home of your own, come see this quaint cottage on a quiet tree-lined street. New on the market, it shows lots of tender loving care. You can tell by the glowing hard-wood floors, handmade wood box by the fireplace, corner cupboard in the dining room. Made for comfortable living, this 2 bedroom, 2 bath home is only $87,000. Call Tina at Clarke Realty, 555-7120.

Own With Ease

Generous terms & a rock-bottom price make this 3 bedroom, 2 bath traditional perfect. You'll love the roomy fenced yard, save tons of time with the latest appliances, delight in the convenient workshop/garage. All for only $98,000. Call Henry at Clarke Realty, 555-7120, today.

Beginner's Luck

can be yours in this spick & span 2 bedroom, 2 bath charmer. Snuggled behind a white picket fence, with fruit trees, a sun porch & winding sidewalk, it's a great first home. Convenient to bus lines & downtown, just $87,000. Call Tom today at Clarke Realty, 555-7120.

A Gingerbread Cottage

with wood trim, French doors, & a hot, bubbly spa just off the master bedroom. Wall-to-wall carpets make housework easy, while the kitchen is a gourmet cook's dream. 2 bedrooms, 2 baths for just $87,000. Hurry & call Ted at Clarke Realty, 555-7120, to take a look today.

> AD TIP: *Talk to your readers one-on-one by using words like you and yours.*

Why Rent
When You Can Own?

Come see this smart 2 bedroom, 2 bath contemporary in move-in condition. No maintenance worries with easy-care carpet, top-of-the-line floors, new paint job & natural landscaping. Can you believe it's only $85,000? Call Henry at Clarke Realty, 555-7120, & see it for yourself.

Charming Beginner

From the pitched roof to the intricate porch, this home is made for romantics. Shiny hardwood floors will show off your precious antiques. There's a breakfast nook you can fix up with gingham. Put lace curtains over the big French windows in the 2 bedrooms. 2 baths, too. Finally, a place you can make your own...for just $87,000. Call Virgie at Clarke Realty, 555-7120, today.

Writer's Cottage

The perfect place to write a best-selling novel. A secluded cottage set back from the street. With a step-saving kitchen, warm & cozy fireplace, screened porch overlooking a sunken garden, 2 bedrooms, 2 baths. Packed with charm & only $70,000. Why rent any longer? Call Steve at Clarke Realty, 555-7120.

Your Own Home

Finally, a home where you can be what you want & do what you want. Creative folks will love this 2 bedroom contemporary, with its rustic exposed-beam ceiling, wide windows & 2 generously-sized baths. Plenty of room to make your personal statement. For $89,000, why not take a look? Call Deena at Clarke Realty, 555-7120, today.

Live Your Dream

If you long for a home of your own, make that dream come true in this gorgeous 2 bedroom home. Hard to believe that for $98,000 you can have your own soothing spa, emerald lawn, 2 car garage & 2 full baths. Call Jay at Clarke Realty, 555-7120, to see this special property.

Start Smart

in this immaculate 3 bedroom, 2 bath home. Ideal for a family, it's got lots of living space, a great fenced yard, economical gas heat & best of all, it's close to schools. Offered at $76,000. Your monthly payments may be less than rent. Call Tim at Clarke Realty, 555-7120.

A Home of Your Own

For a first-time buyer, this home is perfect. Low down and low monthly payments. Pretty as a picture. With yellow siding, wide white shutters, a brick fireplace, 2 bedrooms & 2 full baths. A great way to begin for only $105,000. Call Bess at Clarke Realty, 555-7120, today.

Your First Home

is waiting. Try this stunning 3 bedroom, 2 bath contemporary offered at a bargain-basement price of $89,000. You can enjoy a stone fireplace, plant shelves, a kitchen greenhouse window & a relaxing lattice-covered terrace. Let your money work for you while you live in comfort. Call Jo at Clarke Realty, 555-7120, now.

Bargain Bungalow

Ready-made for first-time homebuyers, this simple cottage is full of surprises. Larger than it looks, this 2 bedroom, 2 bath charmer can be yours for just $76,000. To see it, call June at Clarke Realty, 555-7120.

Easy to Own

It's hard to believe that you can live in such comfort for so little. But this smacking clean 2 bedroom, 1 bath stunner is only $76,000. It can all be yours if you call Elizabeth at Clarke Realty, 555-7120.

Honeymoon Heaven

can be yours in this 1 bedroom gingerbread cottage off the main roads. You'll love the blooming wisteria in the spring, gently falling leaves in the autumn, rock-walled patio where you can watch the stars. A delight to live in, this homespun charmer is only $87,000. Hurry & call Fred at Clarke Realty, 555-7120, today.

Just the Two of You

will fit right into this charming cottage in a park-like setting. Quaint bay windows, antique fixtures, a spacious brick-lined veranda make this home special. You can't match it for the price. 2 bedrooms & 2 baths for only $87,000. Call Anne at Clarke Realty, 555-7120, today.

The Perfect Place to Start

Sprawling 1 bedroom home nestled against the banks of a rippling creek. At night, open the big French doors in the bedroom & listen to it run. The modernized, oak-cabineted kitchen makes cooking easy, while the tidy living room looks out to trees. Designed for 1 person, it's priced at just $92,000. See it today. Call Timothy at Clarke Realty, 555-7120.

AD TIP: Use testimonials: "Neighbors refer to it as a palace."

Canyon Creek Charmer for Less Than $90,000

Come see this 2 bedroom, 2 bath special in Canyon Creek. The minute you walk in the double doors, you'll love its lofty, open rooms, colorful tiled kitchen, romantic fireplace. You'll never have to worry about storage. With an attic & 2 car garage, there's plenty of room. All this for just $88,000. Call Jo Ann at Clarke Realty, 555-7120, today.

Beginner's Bargain

This is a hard-to-find home, priced under $90,000, with 3 bedrooms, 2 baths, a giant yard & huge family room. In a great school district. Don't miss this one! Call Susan at Clarke Realty, 555-7120, now.

The Price Is Right

for a first-time homeowner on a budget...only $76,000. But this 2 bedroom, 2 bath charmer is loaded. Maytag appliances, wool carpeting, built-in barbeque. If you want more for your money, call Paul at Clarke Realty, 555-7120, today.

The Ultimate Beginner Home

You couldn't pick a nicer place to begin. 3 roomy bedrooms, 2 full baths, a living room fireplace that'll warm your heart, bright kitchen, lushly landscaped yard. For only $87,000, make it yours today. Call Edward at Clarke Realty, 555-7120.

Just Beginning?

Then stop by this unique 2 bedroom, 2 bath home, built in the days of quality craftsmanship. From the smooth, cedar-lined closets to the polished bannister on the stairwell, it radiates charm & care. A miniature gem, it is reasonably priced at $92,000. Call Jonathen at Clarke Realty, 555-7120, now.

Character
At a Price You Can Afford

Charming 2 bedroom, 2 bath traditional in an established neighborhood. Offered at $87,000, it features Italian tile entry, gleaming hardwood floors & delightfully mature landscaping. Call Neil at Clarke Realty, 555-7120. Do it today.

4+ BEDROOMS

4 Bedrooms
$90,000

You can't beat the price for a home this large & in a good neighborhood, too. 2 stories, full basement, 3 full baths, wall-to-wall carpeting...it's a dream come true. Immaculate. Call Tim at Clarke Realty, 555-7120, to see it today.

For the Large Family

5 bedroom, 3 bath home on peaceful tree-shaded street. Walk through the white columns to an elegant entry with huge closets. Gather the family in the warm, wood-paneled den. Laze away the afternoon in a big hammock under the 100-year-old oak. Priced at just $92,000, this home offers old-fashioned value. To see it today, call George at Clarke Realty, 555-7120.

Big Family
Needed

to fill the 6 bedrooms of this sprawling ranch. Set on a rambling corner lot, it features a giant basement playroom, 3 car garage, 2 full baths & brand-new paint job. If you want lots of room for only $95,000, call Gina at Clarke Realty, 555-7120. Hurry.

4 Bedrooms
Hacienda Heights

If you want to live in one of the city's most prestigious areas & need lots of room, check out this charming Georgian shaded by elms. Rose-colored brick, with light blue shutters & a sweeping side porch. It's elegant & perfect for a large family. Offered at just $89,000. Call Fred at Clarke Realty, 555-7120, today.

4 King-Size Bedrooms

& lots of living space make this cedar ranch a real find. You'll love the price tag, too. Only $87,000 for nearly an acre of land, storage shed, maintenance-free floors, roomy kitchen, charming backyard playground & 3 full baths. Stake out your claim today. Call Henry at Clarke Realty, 555-7120.

Need Lots of Room?

Drive out to a home where there's room for you to breathe...a huge, rambling traditional in one of the area's best school districts. With the master bedroom downstairs & 3 others up, you can enjoy peace & quiet. From the kitchen's bay window, watch the kids play safely in your fenced yard. The 2 car garage has plenty of room for bikes & trikes. 3 full baths, too. Made for comfortable living, this home is just $95,000. To see it, call Neil at Clarke Realty, 555-7120.

Affordable 4 Bedroom Ranch

Room for everyone in this sprawling home just 20 min. from downtown. You'll love its charming country decor, with Early American accents & big brick fireplace. Room for a garden & pool, too. Can't beat the price—$98,000 for almost 4,000 sq. ft. & 3 full baths. Call Richard at Clarke Realty, 555-7120. Won't last.

6 Bedrooms
Only $102,000

Give the kids their own bedrooms in this well-crafted home. Set under towering elms on a corner lot. 3-3/4 baths, separate dining room, huge family room & 2 massive stone fireplaces. Over 2,400 sq. ft. Come see it today. Call Thomas at Clarke Realty, 555-7120.

Big,
Bright,
& Beautiful

If you love kids & plants, this house is made for you. Lots of light, cheery wall-coverings, 5 sumptuous bedrooms, 3-1/2 baths—even a garden where you can putter to your heart's content. Family priced at $105,000. Call Ricardo at Clarke Realty, 555-7120, today.

4 Bedroom
Colonial

The house you've been looking for—tasteful, well-designed brick home perfect for a large family. With big rooms, huge closets, a double fireplace, sun porch, separate dining room, eat-in kitchen & 3 full baths, you'll never feel cramped again. Best of all, it's only $100,000. Call Marie at Clarke Realty, 555-7120, to see it today.

LOTS OF EXTRA SPACE

Affordable & Roomy

If you like elbowroom, you'll love this 3 bedroom, 2 bath rambler on a quiet tree-lined street. Large rooms, wide staircase, lots of nooks & crannies for storage, there's even a huge attic for all your memorabilia. Priced at only $89,000, it's bound to sell quickly. Call Janis at Clarke Realty, 555-7120, today.

Cramped?
Need More Room?

Then step up to a home that's big & bright, with wide windows, 3 spacious bedrooms, a cheerful breakfast nook in the kitchen & large den. 2 full baths, too. Set under sky-high pines on an estate-like lot, it's priced at $88,000. Right now, call Tom at Clarke Realty, 555-7120.

A Lot of House
for Only $87,000

Live in a home with room to spare...a charming 1920's Victorian with high ceilings, large fireplace, huge closets, 2 full baths, graceful stairway & modern kitchen. Each of the 3 bedrooms is large enough for its own sitting area. Call Dana at Clarke Realty, 555-7120, today.

Enjoy King-Sized Comfort for
Only $87,000

Move into a home where you can spread out. A 3 bedroom, 2 bath ranch almost hidden beneath towering oaks & elms. You'll love the walk-in closets, giant basement, huge storage area in the garage & best of all, the open, airy feeling created by walls of windows. Call Randy at Clarke Realty, 555-7120, today.

A Texas-Sized Home
—You Can Afford

Been wondering about what to do with your growing family? Consider this 3 bedroom rambler set in rolling hills. With a low down & monthly payments that will surprise you, you can own a spacious, easy-care home. Full-wall closets, scads of cabinets, 2 baths, generously-sized rooms. Priced at only $97,000. Call Ian at Clarke Realty, 555-7120, now.

ROOM TO GROW

Room to Grow

If you're looking for a home today with room to expand tomorrow, consider this 2 bedroom, 2 bath charmer. Solidly built, with an open floor plan, situated on 1/2 acre lot. Features quality custom cabinets, Indiana limestone fireplace, mahogany doors & delightful redwood deck. At $98,000, it could be your key to the future. Call Jill at Clarke Realty, 555-7120.

Bring Your Builder

With a little work this 2 bedroom, 2 bath shack on an acre lot could be your gold mine. The setting is perfect...a clearing surrounded by pine trees & ancient oaks. Live on site while planning your dream house. At only $69,500, it is a great opportunity for someone with vision & a limited budget. Call Tom—Clarke Realty, 555-7120, to see this unique offering.

A Home to Grow Into

This modular house makes expanding easy... today it's 2 bedrooms but there is room & blueprints for 4. With all the latest conveniences, it offers tons of glass, redwood cabinets, plush carpeting, colorful Swedish fireplace & 2 full baths. To see if it's right for you, call Henry at Clarke Realty, 555-7120. Do it now.

Do You See a Larger Home in Your Future?

Then take a look at this dynamic 2 bedroom, 2 bath custom redwood built for growing. Its flexible floor plan was made for adding on. Enjoy the library loft, eat-in kitchen, open living area, cozy bedrooms. If you have an eye to the future, call Frank at Clarke Realty, 555-7120. At $87,000, this is bound to be snatched up soon.

Small House —Lots of Land

It's a unique opportunity. Tiny 2 bedroom, 1 bath cottage on gorgeous 1 acre lot. Surrounded by higher priced homes, it's only $76,000. Plenty of room to grow. Invest in your future today. Call William at Clarke Realty, 555-7120, to see this special home.

AD TIP: Don't be afraid to use long copy in your ads. Readers will read them—clients will love them.

PRICE/TERMS

FIXER-UPPER

A Sorry Sight

Older home needing tender touch of skilled handyman. Create value out of this neglected, but primely located home. 2 bedrooms, 1 bath, solid frame construction. It can be yours for only $67,000. Call James at Clarke Realty, 555-7120, today.

If You'd Rather Do It Yourself

then go ahead in this attractive 3 bedroom, 2 bath traditional home. Needs a little loving care, but what potential. Ivy covered walls, huge rocking chair porch, cheerful bedrooms. Couldn't ask for anything more at only $65,000. Call Ken at Clarke Realty, 555-7120.

For Do-It-Yourselfers

3 bedroom, 2 bath home full of promise. From the solid brick walls to the hardwood floors to the unique fireplace...the quality is there. See for yourself today. Call Tim at Clarke Realty, 555-7120. At just $60,000, you can't afford to pass this one up.

A Little Imagination Can Pay Big Dividends

If you have the creativity to see beyond the dust & grime, you'll find this 2 bedroom, 2 bath, a real gem. Polished redwood ceilings, brick hearth, lots of skylights & stained glass...needs work, but your labor will pay off handsomely. To make a great investment today, call Ben at Clarke Realty, 555-7120.

Bring Your Toolbox

This 3 bedroom ranch isn't for everyone but what a deal if you can do the work yourself. Just $75,000 gives you almost 3,000 sq. ft. of living space, 2 baths & a big yard, too. Call Marchella at Clarke Realty, 555-7120.

Probate Fixer

It's a little run-down, but for $68,000, who cares? 2 bedroom, 2 bath Spanish cottage with red tile roof, gigantic cactus-studded lawn, convenient to shops & schools. Call Henry at Clarke Realty, 555-7120. Bring your paintbrush!

> *AD TIP: The headline is the single most important part of any ad.*

Dirt Cheap

You get what you pay for but with a little muscle you can transform this cottage full of character into a cozy & comfortable home. 2 bedrooms, 2 baths, sun porch, shady trees, interesting rock room make it unique. But it'll take some work to really bring out the charm. At just $65,000, who's complaining? Get a deal. Call Noel at Clarke Realty, 555-7120.

Handyman's Dream

All this smart 3 bedroom, 2 bath ranch needs is a face-lift. Underneath it's in great shape. Walls of windows look out to a sweeping emerald lawn. The kitchen is made for family gatherings. Generously-sized rooms throughout. Can you believe it's only $90,000? In a great neighborhood, too. Call Mike at Clarke Realty, 555-7120, today.

Fantastic Fixer

Great opportunity for the right person. 2 bedroom, 2 bath cottage on acre of estate-like grounds. Glass walls overlook bubbling creek...soothing brick-walled patio. Special charm here but sadly neglected. See its promise today. Call Virginia at Clarke Realty, 555-7120. Better hurry.

Abandoned —Yet Picturesque

You'll fall in love with this storybook cottage, with 2 cozy bedrooms & 2 full baths upstairs, window-lined kitchen, sun porch for dining. Hard-to-find rolled roof...and mosaic tiled pathways leading into an overgrown garden. Will take some work, but there'll never be another one like it. Only $78,000. See it today. Call Marie at Clarke Realty, 555-7120.

Forgotten Home

This rambling 3 bedroom shows signs of neglect. But if you're handy, it's a bargain. For just $77,000, you get a family-sized living room, cheerful kitchen with eating area, separate dining room & 2 full baths. Don't miss the opportunity. Call Francine at Clarke Realty, 555-7120, to see this great buy today.

Spanish Fixer

You can take your time fixing this one up...the basics are solid. All that's needed are a few cosmetic touches & you'll have a stunner. 2 bedrooms, 2 baths, adobe fireplace, elegant tiled patio. Yours for just $68,000. Bargains like this don't come along every day. Call Veronica at Clarke Realty, 555-7120, now.

Try a Little Tenderness

on this 3 bedroom, 2 bath brick home set amid flowering shrubs & trees. Built in the 1940's, it needs some repairs & updating. But its quality can't be beat for $66,000. Hardwood trim, oak floors, pine cabinets. See it today. Call Jim at Clarke Realty, 555-7120.

Needs TLC

Great fixer in established neighborhood. 3 bedroom, 2 bath stucco with plenty of room to sprawl out. For only $77,000, what you see is what you get. If you're looking for a perfect family home at a rock-bottom price, call Eugene at Clarke Realty, 555-7120. Today.

> *AD TIP: Write your ads one day then put them down and read them the next.*

Fix & Save

Bring your toolbox to this 2 bedroom, 2 bath gem in a quiet neighborhood. Lattice-covered patio, rock walls, hand-carved mantel...lots of extras. Priced at just $76,000, you won't want to miss this! Call Adam at Clarke Realty, 555-7120. Hurry.

Forgotten Cottage

Not pretty but loaded with potential. 2 bedrooms, 2 baths, bookcases, flagstone patio, sunny eat-in kitchen...start with the basics & take it from there. Unique design that the artistic person will love. Only $77,000. Call Roger at Clarke Realty, 555-7120, now.

Rambling Wreck

Hard to believe that $70,000 will give you a 3 bedroom, 2 bath, 2,500 sq. ft. home. All you have to do is a little fixing. On a 1/4 acre lot, it offers a 2 car/door garage, spick & span laundry room, well-designed kitchen & ample closets. The rest is up to you. Call Tom at Clarke Realty, 555-7120, to see its possibilities.

French Fixer-Upper

With a little sweat equity you can transform this 2 bedroom, 2 bath French-style house into a charming home. Hardwood floors, built-in hutch, great old pine cabinets...they don't build them like this anymore! It can be yours for just $76,000. Call Marie at Clarke Realty, 555-7120, today.

Bring Your Paintbrush

when you move into this 3 bedroom, 2 bath ranch. Way below market at $76,000, it's an opportunity to put your personal stamp on a home with promise. Lots of room for the family. Great yard for gardening. Check this lovely home out today. Call Kimberly at Clarke Realty, 555-7120.

Neglected Home

It's sad when a 3 bedroom, 2 bath charmer like this goes to seed but all the better for you. For only $88,000 you can move into a rambling cedar ranch with huge brick hearth, 2 car garage, hand-made playground & wonderful cherry bannister. Will take a little work to turn it into your home but it'll be worth it. Call Harold at Clarke Realty, 555-7120, to see this remarkable value today.

Brick Ruin

The neighbors will love it when you move into this abandoned 4 bedroom charmer. Local eyesore but great value. 2,500 sq. ft. of comfortable living area, 2 stories, 2 full baths, spacious basement workshop where you can do all the fixing. Just $76,000. To see it today call Barbara at Clarke Realty, 555-7120.

Enjoy Hard Work?

Then you won't mind fixing up this rustic redwood 2 bedroom, 2 bath. By investing just $67,000 you can make thousands. Great view, towering trees, secluded setting. Lots of stone & glass. See it today. Call Henry at Clarke Realty, 555-7120.

Add Your Personal Touch

to this 3 bedroom, 2 bath suburban sprawler that's begging for attention. Create your own color schemes, select fixtures...the basic plumbing & electrical work is done but lots of touching up remains. That's why it's just $76,000. Wonderful opportunity for design-minded person. Call John at Clarke Realty, 555-7120, today.

You Finish

this natural wood-filled cedar contemporary. Framing & construction already done, needs floors, finishings & fixtures. Can't beat the price. Only $67,000 for 2 bedrooms, 2 full baths, huge garage, eat-in kitchen & enormous wooded lot. Make it yours today. Call Mike at Clarke Realty, 555-7120.

You Fix It

Imagine a knotty pine cabin sitting on a sweeping mountainside lot. 2 bedrooms & 1 bath with a wood-burning stove, brick hearth, pine cabinets in galley kitchen. Special home for special person. Needs lots of work, but do at your leisure. Only $80,000. Call Carolyn at Clarke Realty, 555-7120. Now.

See the Potential

in this 3 bedroom, 2 bath fixer situated in established, peaceful neighborhood. Tall trees guard its front gate, flowering shrubs fill the backyard. Delightful home, if you give it loving attention it lacks. At only $77,000 it's worth a look. Call Ken at Clarke Realty, 555-7120, today.

Great Fixer-Upper

For the handy person who likes to putter around the house, this 2 bedroom, 1 bath cabin is a magnificent opportunity. Heavy oak paneling on the walls, gigantic stone fireplace, glassed-in front porch. Will take some elbow grease, but could be very special. Only $76,000. Call Harold at Clarke Realty, 555-7120, now.

Do It Yourself

in this special 3 bedroom, 2 bath home, waiting for a handy person's touch. Once graceful & charming, it's in sad shape, needs paint, repairs, & lots of love. Terrific potential. In a neighborhood of high-priced homes it's only $60,000. Call Timothy at Clarke Realty, 555-7120, today.

Neglected Charmer

If you love lots of gingerbread trim, handmade cabinets, & sweeping staircases, this home was made for you. A run-down 2 bedroom, 2 bath Victorian near Center City hiding its charms beneath a coat of neglect. If you're the right person to bring them out again, call Tim at Clarke Realty, 555-7120. Only $60,000 & it's yours.

Fix-N-Save

If you're handy with your hands, this house can be a great money-maker. 3 bedrooms & 2 baths in an established part of town, with cedar siding, wood windows & a wonderfully tree-filled yard. Yours for just $70,000. Perfect for the wise investor. To see it today, call Mark at Clarke Realty, 555-7120.

BARGAIN PRICE

Waiting for a Bargain?

Then head straight for this 3 bedroom, 2 bath immaculate home, just around the corner from the high school. White clapboard, with plantation shutters & concealing landscaping. Best of all, it's bargain priced at $78,000. Hurry to see it. Call Roger at Clarke Realty, 555-7120, today.

For The Family With More Taste Than Money

This 3 bedroom, 2 bath ranch is a real find. Built with care, it blends convenience with charm. You'll love the dishwasher, laundry room & easy-care floors and the lazy Saturday morning breakfasts on the flower-filled patio. Located on a choice corner lot, priced at just $78,000. See it to believe it. Call Tom at Clarke Realty, 555-7120, now.

All-Brick Bargain

They don't build them like this anymore & this luscious 2 bedroom, 2 bath beauty is priced to sell. Casement windows, white brick walls, gorgeous rose garden...make it the home of your dreams for only $76,000. Owner anxious, so call Sue at Clarke Realty, 555-7120—today.

Champagne Taste, Beer Pocketbook?

You'll recognize the quality when you see it, but you won't believe the price. Charming 3 bedroom, 2 bath traditional in great school district for only $85,000. Close to shops & offices, set far back from street under huge shade trees. There's even a porch swing! Imagine your family in this top-notch home today. Call Tim at Clarke Realty, 555-7120.

Bargain Price

They don't get much lower than this... $72,000 for a California contemporary with plant shelves, giant windows, lots of sun, neutral decor. 3 bedrooms, 2 baths make it perfect. There's even room for a pool. Don't let this get away. Call John at Clarke Realty, 555-7120, now.

Unbelievable Buy

You couldn't build it for less...just $80,000 for a 3 bedroom, 2 bath home of classic design. Built to last, it features quality touches like a large brick-walled family room, ceramic countertops, imported wallcoverings & mirrored closets. Call Marcie at Clarke Realty, 555-7120.

RV Owner's Retreat

rock-bottom priced at $67,000. 3 bedrooms, 2 baths on a heavily wooded lot with redwood siding, shingled roof, secluded sleeping wing. Huge screened porch. Room for RV. Call Tim at Clarke Realty, 555-7120, today to see it.

Just Reduced!

Owner's found another home. Needs to sell quickly. Charming colonial with white-pillared porch, 3 bedrooms, 2 baths, brick veranda, totally upgraded kitchen & bath. Yours for just $76,000. Call Roger at Clarke Realty, 555-7120.

Priced to Sell—Fast

Can you believe only $80,000 will put you into a 2 bedroom, 2 bath, gray-shingled Cape Cod? Has glistening white trim, window boxes & all the charm you'd ever want? You'll love evenings by the toasty fire, cozy breakfasts in the country kitchen, the look of the slate entry floor. Will go quickly. Call Helen at Clarke Realty, 555-7120, today.

Unbelievable Bargain

Rambling, 3 bedroom, 2 bath home on a sprawling hillside lot for under $90,000. You'd never guess it had so many extras: dishwasher, trash compactor, disposal, efficient gas heat, central air. Live in style affordably. Call Timothy at Clarke Realty, 555-7120, today.

Bargain of the Year

Other homes in the neighborhood are selling for thousands more, but you can pick up this cozy 4 bedroom Dutch farmhouse for just $65,000. Great for growing family, with rumpus room, chandeliered dining area, 3 full baths & 2 car garage. Homegrown vegetable garden, too. Enjoy country in the city. Call Tom at Clarke Realty, 555-7120, today.

Price Reduced $5,000

It's like putting money in your pocket when you move up to this 3 bedroom, 3 bath canyon rustic. Live with nature amid its many trees. Watch the birds feed at your windows. Knotty pine walls make it warm & cozy while skylights bring in the sun. Waiting for a special family. Call Kim at Clarke Realty, 555-7120. At $100,000 there aren't many like this one.

Live The Way You've Always Wanted—for Less Than You Ever Dreamed Possible

Just $99,000 gives you the key to this 3 bedroom, 2 bath French provincial stunner in one of the best areas. From the bubbling hot tub in the secluded garden to the elegant French doors of the den, it's tasteful & refined. Call George at Clarke Realty, 555-7120, today.

Price Slashed

It's the deal you've been waiting for...a 2 bedroom, 2 bath contemporary ranch for less than $90,000. You'll love the paver-tiled entry, step-down living room, stone fireplace, dining room perfect for entertaining. See the decorator's touch in the custom wallcoverings & drapes. Call Fred at Clarke Realty, 555-7120.

Below Market

Value is what you get in this new 3 bedroom, 2 bath home on a circular drive. You'll feel like royalty when you walk through the white columned portico & cross the parquet foyer. In the living room, there's room for a grand piano. Dine beneath an antique chandelier. Live in style for only $98,000. Call Tom at Clarke Realty, 555-7120, today.

The Price Is Right

for one of the most popular models in Hidden Creek...the 3 bedroom Broadmoor home. Featuring a dramatic entry skylight, 2-story living room, 2 full baths, plush carpets & many upgrades. Over 2,750 sq. ft. Priced at $87,000, it's a bargain lover's delight. Call Sam at Clarke Realty, 555-7120, to see it today.

Looking for a Bargain?

Then head for the hills—Indian Hills. See this blue & white Cape Cod, with its all-brick fireplace, sweeping circular staircase, serene atrium, 3 good-sized bedrooms & 2 full baths. For just $77,000, you can live in comfort, convenience & style. Call Victoria today at Clarke Realty, 555-7120, for a real bargain.

What a Buy!

A Hollywood address at a terrific price. Just $60,000 moves you into this snug 2 bedroom, 1 bath Spanish stucco, with 2 tiled verandas, hand-carved wood trim & French doors galore. Quality to last a lifetime. Call Henry at Clarke Realty, 555-7120, now.

Divorce Sale

The court says "Sell" so the owners have cut the price on this 3 bedroom, 2 bath cedar home way below market. Natural woodwork, top-quality floors, a garden tub in the master bath. Over 2,200 sq. ft. It's the kind of home where you can add your personal touch. To see it today, call Francis at Clarke Realty, 555-7120.

Red Tag Special

on this sweeping 2 bedroom, 2 bath contemporary close to the university in its own little glen. Dramatic white walls, track lighting & floor-to-ceiling windows make the perfect showcase for your collections. A home for gracious & carefree living, offered at $87,000. To see it today, call Carl at Clarke Realty, 555-7120.

ATTENTION: Bargain Lovers!

If you've been looking for that perfect home, at a decent price, consider this 3 bedroom, 2-story in Country Club Heights. In immaculate shape, it features a charming sitting area, imported wall-coverings, gas fireplace, 2-1/2 baths & cozy country decor. Below market priced at $87,000, it's bound to sell quickly. Hurry and call Roger at Clarke Realty, 555-7120.

MUST SELL QUICKLY

Anxious Owner Wants Out

Make an offer on this exciting 3 bedroom, 2 bath ranch-style home, with split rail fencing & charming country decor. From brass lights to the peg & groove floor, it aims to please. Action-priced at just $86,000. Call Tom today at Clarke Realty, 555-7120.

Move in Tomorrow

This 2 bedroom stunner is ready & waiting for someone who wants style, pizzazz & luxury at a bargain price. You'll love the sizzling hot tub, walnut paneling, easy neutral decor & 2 tiled baths. For only $65,000, it's a great buy. Call Jo Ann at Clarke Realty, 555-7120.

Owner Packing

See this terrific 2 bedroom, 2 bath Spanish villa—unbelievably priced at just $87,000. Offers terra-cotta floors, adobe fireplace, tons of Mexican tile, even a hand-painted mural. Make it yours today. Call Anne at Clarke Realty, 555-7120. Hurry.

Need a Home Right Away?

Then start packing. This 4 bedroom beauty is priced for quick action. For just $90,000, you can enjoy the comfort of Karastan carpets, a built-in entertainment center, glass-walled dining area & luscious rose garden. 2 full baths, too. Hurry to see it today. Call Richard at Clarke Realty, 555-7120.

Owner Says "Sacrifice"

so here's your opportunity for a great deal. 2 bedroom, 2 bath Craftsman cottage with top-of-the-line appliances, 2 car garage, spacious veranda, bright & cheery kitchen. Only $65,000. In a good neighborhood, too. Call Jackson at Clarke Realty, 555-7120.

Emergency Sale

Owner says "sell fast." So the price on this 3 bedroom, 2 bath traditional brick is rock-bottom. Imagine, $75,000 will give you a solidly built, low-maintenance home that features a handmade brick hearth, bougainvillea-draped patio, quaint frontyard fish pond & custom drapes. Don't miss this one. Call Tim at Clarke Realty, 555-7120. Now.

HELP!
Fell Out of Escrow

Gorgeous Florida-style home on curving, tree-lined street. 3 spacious bedrooms, 2 luxurious baths, plant-filled lanai. Upgrades throughout. Unbeatable price of $79,000. Call Henry at Clarke Realty, 555-7120. This won't last.

Can You Move Fast?

Owner wants offer on this 3 bedroom, 2 bath traditional, located in one of the city's best school districts. Your kids will love its old apple tree, huge playroom, big country kitchen. Best of all, it's priced at just $87,000. Make a deal. Call Tim at Clarke Realty, 555-7120.

> AD TIP: *Avoid being cute and clever. Credible and convincing will sell more homes.*

Priced to Move

Can't go any lower on this 2 bedroom, 2 bath charmer framed by oak trees & elms. Step up to its lattice-work front porch, just right for rocking. Heavy antique wood trim, unique carved sideboard, warm heart of pine cabinets. Yours for just $76,000. It's sure to sell fast. Call Henry at Clarke Realty, 555-7120, today.

Owner Anxious

She's ready to move, are you? Can't beat the low, low price of this 4 bedroom, 3 bath brick. Room for horses, cats & kids...it offers comfortably-sized rooms, ceiling fans, central air, even a wood-burning stove. Only $87,000...so make your move today. Call June at Clarke Realty, 555-7120. Hurry.

WANTED:
Fast Sale

We've cut the price on this 3 bedroom, 2 bath custom home to just $87,000—far below its replacement value. Enjoy relaxing in its hot jacuzzi, serving drinks from the wet bar, reading in its loft study. Designed for comfort & convenience, it's a steal. Call Barbara at Clarke Realty, 555-7120. Do it now.

Desperate Seller Says "Dump It"

right into your lap for $99,000...a home you thought you never could afford. With 4 huge bedrooms, 3 full baths, custom-crafted cabinets, a soothing brick-lined spa, it radiates luxury. A bargain basement special...if you act quickly. Call Robert at Clarke Realty, 555-7120.

Distress Sale

Immediate sale required on this 4 bedroom, 3 bath cedar ranch in friendly family neighborhood. Move-in condition. Top-quality appliances, wool carpet, custom cabinets... couldn't ask for anything more at just $79,000. See it today. Call Brenda at Clarke Realty, 555-7120. Better hurry.

Seller Wants Out

Cut-rate price on 2 bedroom, 1 bath log cabin nestled on quiet lake just 15 min. from town. Glassed-in porch overlooks your own pier. Hardwood floors, rustic fireplace, open loft, galley kitchen...it's a bargain lover's dream. For just $35,000. Call Larry at Clarke Realty, 555-7120. Do it today.

Reduced for Fast Escrow

Thousands slashed off price of this 4 bedroom, 3 bath colonial, convenient to freeways & shopping. Easy-care white siding, forest green awnings & a sleek lawn create an elegant environment. Inside you'll be charmed by the cove ceilings, plaster walls, Early American accents. At $87,000, it's a real bargain. Call Marie at Clarke Realty, 555-7120 today.

FORECLOSURE

Bank Says "Dump It"

3 bedroom hacienda in Country Club Manor priced for quick sale. Just $75,000 gives you easy-care stucco construction, red tile roof, colorful Mexican tile, 2 full baths, an attic that will hold all your mementos. Better act quickly. Call George at Clarke Realty, 555-7120. Now.

Bankruptcy Special

desperate to sell charming 2 bedroom, 1 bath cottage on lake. From your huge screened front porch, watch the ducks swim & play. At night, cozy up to the massive stone fireplace. The gentle pine cabinets will warm your heart. So will the price. Just $55,000. Call Vera at Clarke Realty, 555-7120, today. Move quickly.

Forced Sale

of delightful 2 bedroom, 2 bath contemporary in booming neighborhood. Walls of windows bring in the sun. Gather your friends around the glowing streamlined Swedish fireplace. Entertain on the tile-floored patio. At $77,000 it's a real bargain. See it today. Call Elizabeth at Clarke Realty, 555-7120.

Bank Repo

This convenient & practical 1 bedroom home is priced for quick action. Just $55,000 puts you into a glass-walled A-frame, with labor-saving kitchen, full bath & comfortable patio for relaxing. Hard to find at any price. Call Henry at Clarke Realty, 555-7120, for details.

Foreclosure

Take advantage of cut-rate price on this 3 bedroom quality home. Located in prestigious Seward Circle, it features a whirlpool tub in the master bath, comfortable kitchen/family room with fireplace, walls of glass & a view. For only $88,000 it can't be beat. Call Yolanda at Clarke Realty, 555-7120, to see it today.

> *AD TIP: Show your ads to others — co-workers, family, friends — to make sure your meaning is clear.*

Public Announcement

The following property is ordered for immediate sale by the Bank of America:

A historical 3-story brownstone close to downtown. Features etched glass cabinets, sunny balcony off master bedroom, 2 more bedrooms & updated claw-foot bath. Antique lover's delight, it's priced to sell at just $78,000. Call Tim at Clarke Realty, 555-7120, today.

Bank Wants Out

so they've slashed the price on this 3 bedroom, 2 bath ranch. You'll love the privacy of the master bedroom suite, the comfort of the rock-walled living room. On an acre of land, too. Bargain price of $90,000. Call Vic at Clarke Realty, 555-7120, now.

Bankruptcy Forces Sale

of a luxurious 3 bedroom, 2 bath home close to Monterey Golf Course. Enormous eat-in kitchen opens to secluded patio. Walls of glass spill sunlight into the living room. Private & quiet bedrooms. Just $88,000. Call Ruth at Clarke Realty, 555-7120, today.

Bank Says "Sell"

this architect-designed professional home in park-like setting. 2 master suites upstairs, high-tech kitchen & living room below, it's open & airy. 2 baths, too. Custom quality for (would you believe?) just $80,000. Call Rick at Clarke Realty, 555-7120.

Stop Foreclosure

on this 4 bedroom, 3-1/2 bath rambler nestled on wooded lot. Easy-care vinyl floors, plushly carpeted family room, living room dominated by antique fireplace. 2,100 sq. ft. Grace & charm are yours for just $99,000. Can't beat it. Call Tom at Clarke Realty, 555-7120.

OWNER/SPECIAL FINANCING

Below Market Loan

waiting for you on this 2 bedroom, 2 bath frame cottage in terrific school district. Hardwood floors, Dutch tile fireplace, delightful screened porch & a spreading elm for less than you ever thought possible. $5,000 moves you in tomorrow. Owner will carry balance. Great deal on a cute house. Call Diane at Clarke Realty, 555-7120, today.

Low Monthly Payments

on this 3 bedroom, 2 bath traditional near Grover Park. It's roomy & open, with 2 stories, atrium, wall-to-wall carpeting & wonderful patio terrace. Assumable loan of $75,000 at below market rate. Call Tom at Clarke Realty, 555-7120, to find out more. Don't wait on this one.

Low Down

makes it easy to move into this striking 2 bedroom, 1 bath hidden on a heavily wooded lot. If you like bold contemporary colors & accents like a whirlpool tub, built-in storage, slick tile floors & brass fixtures, this home's for you. Owner will carry at full price of $59,500. Call Gene at Clarke Realty, 555-7120, today.

It Only Takes a Little...

down payment to move into this delightful cedar home near a top-rated high school. With 3 bedrooms, each child can have their own. Parents will love the secluded master suite. Outside, there's plenty of room to roam. 2 baths, too. You won't believe the low monthly payments. Call Richard at Clarke Realty, 555-7120, now.

Owner Will Carry

low interest mortgage on this roomy 3 bedroom, 2 bath home, full of history & charm. In one family for 6 generations, features huge windows, cozy breakfast nook, ceiling fans & hand-rubbed hardwood trim. A special home with great financing. Call Juan at Clarke Realty, 555-7120. Don't delay!

Seller Wants Small Down

& it's yours. Cozy 1 bedroom beachfront cottage in fast-growing community. From the moment you walk through its picket fence gate, you'll delight in its mellow charm. Aged wood floors, giant pine cabinets, clever custom touches. Full price only $76,000. Call Jim at Clarke Realty, 555-7120, to see it today.

Seller Will Carry

low interest loan on this 2 bedroom, 2 bath cedar contemporary high on a hill. Relax in its soothing spa, enjoy the wide open feeling of the 2-story living room, snuggle next to its massive stone fireplace. Just $87,000. With small down, move in tomorrow. Call Timothy at Clarke Realty, 555-7120, now.

Try a Low Down

& owner will carry on great 2 bedroom, 2 bath rambler. Full price of $78,000... easy to own. Stone walls, rose garden, sunny & bright bedrooms, a living room just right for family gatherings. Call Ginger at Clarke Realty, 555-7120, to see it today.

No Red Tape

on this 4 bedroom, 3 bath sprawler. Owner carries it all. Enjoy hassle-free living with wall-to-wall carpeting, separate laundry, easy to care for decor. Priced at just $87,000, make your deal today. Call Henry at Clarke Realty, 555-7120.

Name Your Terms

Owner will listen to any reasonable offer on this exciting 3 bedroom, 2 bath ranch. Split rail fences, country accents...it's a spread you'll want to brand your own. Just $90,000. Call Jo today at Clarke Realty, 555-7120.

Flexible Financing

Owner willing to carry loan on this great 2 bedroom, 2 bath. Cleverly designed to protect your privacy, it offers a terrific playroom, backyard sandbox, lots of storage...not to mention colonial charm. Offered at just $84,000. Hurry & call Tom at Clarke Realty, 555-7120, today.

> *AD TIP: Get inspiration from others — including the current homeowners.*

Worried About Getting a Loan?

Then try this 3 bedroom, 2 bath rustic 15 min. from Center City with owner financing. Sweeping vistas of rolling hills, all the latest appliances, charming flagstone patio...it's a dream come true. A price of just $80,000. Call Phil at Clarke Realty, 555-7120, to see it today.

Owner Is Flexible

on terms for this 4 bedroom, 2-1/2 bath prize, located in comfortable neighborhood. Easy-care siding, fully landscaped yard, huge 2 car garage...it's life the way you imagine it should be. For only $77,000, who can resist? Call Tony at Clarke Realty, 555-7120, to see it today.

Owner Will Carry 2nd

on the home you've always wanted but didn't feel you could afford. Stunning 2 bedroom, 2 bath hillside home, with warm wood accents, plush carpeting, secluded spa. Perfect setting for antiques. Offered at just $87,000...work out your own terms. Call Richard at Clarke Realty, 555-7120, to view this bargain.

Below Market Financing

on this 3 bedroom, 2 bath historic home. Carefully renovated by owner who's willing to finance loan. Whipped cream decor, bay window, polished oak bannister...immaculate. Full price $55,000. See it today. Call George at Clarke Realty, 555-7120.

Terrific Terms—For You

Owner will carry balance at below market rate on this 3 bedroom, 2 bath colonial, after reasonable down payment. Close to schools & shopping. In great shape. Only $88,000. Call Hal at Clarke Realty, 555-7120.

Low Monthly Payments

on this originally designed, tastefully decorated 2 bedroom, 2 bath contemporary. With its dramatic plant shelves, arched windows & gentle skylights, it's sure to bring out the artist in you. Be creative in the financing, too. Just $77,000, owner will carry. Call Brad at Clarke Realty, 555-7120. Hurry.

Generous Owner

willing to finance you on this sumptuous 3 bedroom, 2 bath home. In a great neighborhood with nearby community club, shopping mall. Conveniences galore. At only $88,000, one look is enough. Call Tim at Clarke Realty, 555-7120, to set it up.

ASSUMABLE LOAN

Looking for a Low Interest Rate?

Then check out this assumable 3 bedroom, 2 bath California-style home. Cool tile floors, sunny, cheerful kitchen, white decor. Great place to add your personal touch. Only $77,000. Call Tina at Clarke Realty, 555-7120, to see it today.

Assumable Loan

You'll save thousands & you'll love your lifestyle. 3 sunny bedrooms, 2 baths in a snug brick ranch, with cheery fireplace, antique pine mantel, dining room wainscoting. Full price of just $88,000. Don't pass this one by. Call Mike at Clarke Realty, 555-7120.

AD TIP: Be sure your copy is not only completely accurate, but also believable.

Low Interest Fixed, 28 Years

You couldn't make a better deal today. 3 bedrooms, 2 full baths, a view from the deck that will be a perpetual delight. Yours for just $86,000. Call Jim at Clarke Realty, 555-7120, today.

Great Assumable

on a gorgeous 2 bedroom, 2 bath ranch in the best area. Honey birch cabinets, wall-to-wall carpets, a patio that goes on forever. Priced at just $77,000 with a 25-year loan. Great deal. Call Tim at Clarke Realty, 555-7120, to see it now.

Take Over Loan

on this charming 1 bedroom cottage, snuggled in the hills outside the city. Old-fashioned brick veranda smothered by roses & glass kitchen cabinets make it special. Even better is the below market rate on a 27-year loan. With full price of $66,000, monthly payments less than rent. To see it fast, call Roger at Clarke Realty, 555-7120.

You Assume at
Below Market Rate

on this gracious, white-pillared colonial, with striped awnings, professionally landscaped lawn, 3 bedrooms, 2 baths. Live in style with low monthly payments on 25-year loan. Full price only $88,000. Call Tom at Clarke Realty, 555-7120, to see it today.

Your Chance to Take Over

loan on this 3 bedroom, 2 bath charmer. Cedar-shingled siding, shiny white trim, flower garden your friends will envy... it's made for easy armchairs & cozy evenings by the fire. Only $88,000. Call Marie at Clarke Realty, 555-7120, now.

LOW TAXES

Save on Taxes

Put money in your pocket—not the government's, when you own this 3 bedroom traditional home with a circular drive. 2 full baths, family-sized kitchen, 2 car garage, lots of room. A real money-saver at $88,000. Call Richard at Clarke Realty, 555-7120, to see it today.

Tax Bill Last Year—$300

Think of what you'll save by owning a home in the county with the lowest tax rate in the state. For just $76,000, you can move right into this 3 bedroom, 2 bath beauty, just 5 min. off the freeway. You'll love its island counter in the kitchen, huge family room & peaceful woods framed by ample windows. Call Tim at Clarke Realty, 555-7120, today.

Low, Low Taxes

on a 2 bedroom, 2 bath home high in the hills. Spectacular views from every window...cedar charm, fully modernized kitchen & bath. It's easy to live in & easy on your wallet. Just $87,000. Call Anne at Clarke Realty, 555-7120, to see today.

Save Money on Taxes

when you move into this 3 bedroom French provincial home just across the county line. Elegance is reflected in its vaulted ceilings, wood-framed windows, 2 spacious baths. Over 2,000 sq. ft. Yours for only $87,000. To see it today, call Elaine at Clarke Realty, 555-7120.

> *AD TIP: Price and location are the two most important home buying factors. The newspaper will place your ad by location but you should also include the price.*

Don't Give It
to the Government

You'll be surprised at how low taxes are in this charming 3 bedroom, 2 bath traditional home. Save hundreds every year while living in comfort & convenience on 1/2 acre all your own. Priced at just $87,000. Call Veronica at Clarke Realty, 555-7120, to see it today.

INVESTMENT VALUE

Below Value
Money-Maker

Gracious 3 bedroom, 2-story brick home. Priced at just $80,000...far below its value. See the quality custom decorating, curved staircase, breakfast bar kitchen & you'll know it's a great deal. 2 baths, too. Call George at Clarke Realty, 555-7120, to see this great bargain.

Outstanding Value

in this 3 bedroom, 2 bath Craftsman-style home with quaint dormer windows, rustic brick fireplace, glassed-in hutch. Custom-crafted in 1936, it's bargain priced at just $76,000. Irreplaceable value. Call Josie at Clarke Realty, 555-7120, to take a look today.

A Real Home
for Only $62,000

Hurry to see this dramatic 2 bedroom, 1 bath ranch with floor-to-ceiling windows, cedar shingle siding, brick planters & patio. A place to really feel at home. Call Harry at Clarke Realty, 555-7120, today.

Invest Now for a Big
Pay-Off Tomorrow

Imagine 2,000 sq. ft. of comfortable living in a top neighborhood for less than $150,000. It's hard to find...3 bedrooms, 2 baths, your own pool, a garden filled with flowering shrubs. For an outstanding value, call Freddie at Clarke Realty, 555-7120. Hurry.

What a Value!

Simple, well-built 1 bedroom cabin of enduring character & charm. Hearty wood walls, solid pine floors, craftsman-like touches throughout. Best of all, it's just $65,000. Don't let it get away. Call Ken at Clarke Realty, 555-7120. Now.

More for
Your Money

in this spacious 4 bedroom, 3 bath home priced far below market. Made for those who enjoy living well, it features a private upstairs balcony, imposing living room, warm oak-paneled family room & 2 car garage. Would you believe it's only $88,000? To see this terrific bargain, call Elizabeth at Clarke Realty, 555-7120.

Unbeatable Value!

You couldn't build it for this price. $78,000 gives you 3 comfortably-sized bedrooms, built-in barbeque, attractive cedar fence, custom wallcoverings & drapes. 2 baths, too. Terrific school just around the corner. Make your move today. Call Len at Clarke Realty, 555-7120.

Don't Read This Ad

unless you want to save $10,000. Because this 3 bedroom, 2 bath beauty is way below market. White brick exterior, French windows, covered patio overlooking a sunken garden...it's class at a bargain price. Call Roberta at Clarke Realty, 555-7120, to make it yours today!

Do You Recognize a Value When You See It?

Then hurry over to this 2 bedroom, 2 bath contemporary...a marvelous blend of style & comfort. Priced at just $75,000, it's full of upgrades like premium carpet, hand-built planters, custom tile & a sunlit patio perfect for Sunday brunches. To see it today, call Tina at Clarke Realty, 555-7120. Start packing!

Lowest Price in the Neighborhood

on a block of high-priced homes, this 3 bedroom cedar is a real stunner at $65,000. Spacious, comfortable rooms ...2 bright & cheery baths...a fenced yard your pets will love. Great for a growing family on a budget. Call Tim at Clarke Realty, 555-7120, to take a look today. Won't last long!

Great Value

You'll be thrilled at the price of this 3 bedroom, 2 bath home...just $77,000 gives you a window-lined atrium, huge bedrooms, lots of closet space & a workshop where any handyman would be happy. Call Roger at Clarke Realty, 555-7120, to see it today.

A Real Money-Maker

In the past year, the value of homes in this area has skyrocketed. But this cozy 2 bedroom, 2 bath charmer is being offered at an old-fashioned price. Just $56,000 & you're in a home with delightful dormer windows, planter boxes, aged & shiny hardwood floors. Make it yours today. Call Dean at Clarke Realty, 555-7120. Hurry.

A Smart Move

You'll live in style in this chic 3 bedroom, 2 bath contemporary for a price you can feel good about. Only $80,000 gives you mirrored walls, high-gloss floors, a shimmering patio full of sunlight. In a private setting, this won't last long. Call Marie at Clarke Realty, 555-7120, to see it today.

Enjoy the High Life for a Low Price

Take a 1/2 hour drive to this 3 bedroom, 2 bath ranch in the woods. You'll be surprised at the lifestyle that can be yours for just $85,000. A hot, bubbly spa to unwind in, family room with wet bar, luxurious walnut paneling in the living room. Call Ronald at Clarke Realty, 555-7120, today.

Looking for Value?

Then come see a home that radiates good taste, quiet charm & quality construction for less than $90,000. Set in secluded park-like grounds, behind gates, this 3 bedroom, 2 bath clapboard is rock-bottom priced. To see it today, call Tom at Clarke Realty, 555-7120. Do it now.

DON'T RENT—BUY!

Cheaper Than Rent

Enjoy low monthly payments on this 2 bedroom, 1 bath cottage, next to a gurgling little creek. From the glassed-in sleeping porch to the mellow pine cabinets & unique rock fireplace, it's yours to love. Can't beat the price. Just $61,000. Call Patricia at Clarke Realty, 555-7120, to take a look today.

Tired of Renting?

Then why do it when you can have monthly payments of less than $700 in this immaculate 3 bedroom home? Think of all the room you'll have...more than 1,500 sq. ft., 2 baths & a 2 car garage, too. Find out how easy it is to own. Call Sally at Clarke Realty, 555-7120, today.

Can You Pay Rent?

You can own this 1 bedroom ivy-covered, trellised cottage on a quiet, tree-lined street. In a neighborhood of gracious, older homes, full of gentle charm & it's yours for $70,000. Call Clara at Clarke Realty, 555-7120, today.

Less Than Rent

You won't believe the low monthly payments on this almost new 2 bedroom, 2 bath contemporary. Stylishly decorated, with a gas fireplace, roomy eat-in kitchen & pleasant redwood deck. Priced at only $76,000. Make your move today. Call Lee at Clarke Realty, 555-7120.

AD TIP: Read your ad aloud and make sure it flows well.

Why Rent?

when you can own a marvelous 2 bedroom, 2 bath home? For just $78,000, live in a Swiss-style chalet with pine cabinets, an impressive rock fireplace & window boxes filled with flowers. Have a real home. Call Linda at Clarke Realty, 555-7120, to view this charmer now.

Tired of Your Landlord?

Then move into this 2 bedroom, 2 bath stunner with privacy & convenience. A place you can be & do whatever you want to...from dabbing on an easel in the sunlit loft to lazing next to a glowing fire. At only $65,000 you can make it your place. Call Vivian at Clarke Realty, 555-7120, to see this beautiful home today.

Get Away From Your Landlord!

& live in a home where you call the shots. A 2 bedroom, 2 bath marvel of comfort & charm, close to jogging trails & shopping. With rich neutral decor, open & airy design, it's the perfect setting to express who you are. Priced at $70,000, it won't last long. Call John at Clarke Realty, 555-7120, to see it today.

Stop Throwing Away Your Money on Rent

Put it to work for you in this delightful 2 bedroom, 2 bath frame cottage. Grow a garden in the spacious backyard, rock away the evenings on the wide front porch, warm yourself by a fire in its brick hearth. The good life for only $89,000. Call Roger at Clarke Realty, 555-7120, to make it yours today.

Attention: Renters!

Don't miss the chance to own a home of your own...especially this 3 bedroom, 2 bath contemporary ranch in a terrific neighborhood. Priced at just $70,000, your monthly payments may be less than rent. To find out more, call Susan at Clarke Realty, 555-7120. Better hurry!

Unhappy With Renting?

Then make the smart move into a home of your own. Like this 2 bedroom, 2 bath, country-comfort traditional. 2 car garage, excellent storage, tasteful design. For just $65,000. Call Thomas at Clarke Realty, 555-7120, to find out how easy home owning can be. Now.

Sick of an Interfering Landlord?

Then stake out your own territory in this 2 bedroom, 2 bath colonial, secluded from the street. Full of traditional charm, it offers cherry cabinets, a limestone fireplace, crown moulding, park-like setting. Yours for only $65,000. Call Ed today at Clarke Realty, 555-7120.

It's Easier Than You Think to Own a Home...

especially this 3 bedroom, 2 bath stone cottage just off Fernwood Drive. Imagine your delight in its antique mosaic tile, hand-carved rock walls, the peaceful walled garden. At $70,000, it's easy to afford. Find out how you can do it by calling Harold at Clarke Realty, 555-7120, now.

Don't Rent—Buy!

Take a look at this 2 bedroom, 2 bath stucco, highlighted by red tile, blue shutters, gleaming hardwood floors & an old-fashioned kitchen that's tops in counter space & storage. Priced at just $66,000. To see it, call Geraldine at Clarke Realty, 555-7120, today.

Renters: Save Money on Taxes

by owning this 2-story, 2 bedroom contemporary, close to the beach. For just $76,000, you can enjoy floor-to-ceiling windows, 2 ceramic tile baths & a roof-top patio with an ocean view. Think of all the money you'll save. Call Tom at Clarke Realty, 555-7120, today.

Who Says You Can't Afford a Home?

They haven't seen this 3 bedroom, 2 bath ranch, priced at just $80,000. With the right down payment, it's less than rent. Plenty of room to sprawl out with large-sized family room, tasteful living room & big bedrooms. To see it today, call Regina at Clarke Realty, 555-7120.

Owning a Home Is Easy

but finding the right one is hard. That's why this 2 bedroom A-frame is so unique. For just $55,000, you get a cedar loft, charming plant-filled kitchen, massive living room & spectacular full bath. Built with care, it's for someone who'll own with pride. Call Mary Ann at Clarke Realty, 555-7120, if you'd like to see it today.

Renters Take Notice

With less down than you might expect, you can own this charming 2 bedroom, 2 bath colonial that offers a better lifestyle than any rental. Your monthly payments will be low & you'll get that money back when you sell. If you've been thinking about owning a home, there's no better time than now. Call Ronald at Clarke Realty, 555-7120, to see how you can do it today.

Dreaming of Your Own Home?

Make your dreams come true in this spick & span 3 bedroom, 2 bath brick bungalow. With just a little down, you can move in tomorrow. With the assumable low interest loan, the monthly payments are fixed for 25 years. The full price is only $60,000. We can help you do it if you call Leah at Clarke Realty, 555-7120. Don't wait until tomorrow. Call now.

If You Can Pay Rent...

then you can own this charming 3 bedroom, 2 bath Cape Cod under a canopy of trees. Realistically priced at $77,000, it offers ample closet space, a cozy kitchen nook, a rock garden & roses on a sweeping lawn. Desirable location, too. To find out more, call Marylou at Clarke Realty, 555-7120. Now.

At Last... Your Own Home

when you move into this 3 bedroom, 2 bath contemporary loaded with extras you don't see in rentals. Of quality construction, it's in mint condition. Priced at just $80,000, it's perfect for the family looking to own. Call Kenneth at Clarke Realty, 555-7120, to see if this is the one for you.

A Home of Your Own

If you're tired of renting, find out how easy it is to own this rustic gray, 2 bedroom California ranch on its own 1/4 acre. You'll have a dozen trees that belong just to you, a laundry room where you'll never need a quarter & a sleeping area that's set back from the street & 2 full baths. Life the way it's supposed to be for only $80,000. Call Tom at Clarke Realty, 555-7120, to see how you can finally own a home of your own.

Tell Your Landlord Good-Bye!

When you see this gorgeous 2 bedroom, 2 bath brick colonial, you won't believe it's less than rent. Just $3,000 moves you in. Low monthly payments and low interest, fixed for 26 years. It's better than renting because you'll be living in style. To find out more, call John at Clarke Realty, 555-7120. You'll want to start packing today!

Renters: Longing for Privacy?

Come home to a place where you'll really belong, a 2 bedroom, 2 bath contemporary where you can do as you please. Its easy neutral decor reflects your style. Enjoy the convenience of a kitchen with the latest appliances & a 2 car garage with room for everything. Priced at $76,000, it's the perfect way to begin. Call Fred at Clarke Realty, 555-7120, now.

AD TIP: Don't tamper with a good thing. If an ad gets a good response, run it until the listing is sold or the response slows down.

Why Rent When It's So Easy to Own?

When you consider how rents are rising, owning a home makes lots of sense. For just $80,000, you can live in this 3 bedroom ranch close to town. It offers conveniences most rentals don't—dishwasher, disposal, 2 full baths, plenty of storage space & the monthly payments are surprisingly low. To see it today, call Carl at Clarke Realty, 555-7120.

Renters: Want to Take More Control Over Your Life?

Discover security & freedom in owning your own home. Never worry about rent hikes, spare change for laundry, someone pulling into your parking place. For low monthly payments you can own a charming 2 bedroom, 2 bath home, with a delightful garden, brick patio & dramatic skylights. Priced at just $70,000, it's the perfect place to make your own. Call Norma at Clarke Realty, 555-7120, now.

TRADE

Owner Will Trade

cozy 2 bedroom, 1 bath cabin high in the Sierras for 1 or 2 bedroom home in Orange County. Just 5 min. from the ski slopes with rustic pine interior, handsome hand-hewn fireplace, spacious loft for guests. Offered at $70,000 or ???. Call Ted at Clarke Realty, 555-7120, today.

Willing to Trade

clean 2 bedroom, 2 bath contemporary in growing neighborhood for older 4 bedroom home. Walk to park, shopping, bus line. City convenience, with country feeling. Priced at $67,000 or ???. Call Tom at Clarke Realty, 555-7120, to make a deal today.

What Will You Offer For...

a spanking new 3 bedroom, 2 bath quality home on a choice corner lot? Sparkling tile entry, hardwood trim, charming eat-in kitchen. Only 20 min. from town. Appraised at $60,000, owner willing to trade for 2 or 3 bedroom city home. Call Dan at Clarke Realty, 555-7120 to see it today.

In the Mood to Trade?

Owner anxious to trade stylish 2 bedroom, 2 bath contemporary in woods for sophisticated urban home. Natural wood siding, tons of glass, feed the birds off the redwood deck. Country living at its finest. Priced at $65,000 or ???. Call Rick at Clarke Realty, 555-7120, today.

What Will You Trade For...

a comfortable 4 bedroom, 3 bath home that's hard to find under $100,000? Quality-built 5 years ago, it reflects the owner's exquisite taste & careful upkeep. Willing to trade for lakefront or penthouse...you name it. Call Donald at Clarke Realty, 555-7120, with your offer today.

> *AD TIP: If you're having trouble getting started with an ad, it's always a good idea to try starting from the middle or end and revise it later.*

STYLE

ARCHITECTURE

Art Deco Delight

You won't believe it 'til you see it...a carefully preserved, architecturally original art deco pad. 2 bedrooms, 2 sleek tiled baths, bold colors, exotic touches that spell individuality galore. Priced at just $90,000, it's an art lover's dream! Call Harriet at Clarke Realty, 555-7120, for a quick look.

Colonial Charm

fills this homespun 3 bedroom, 2 bath rambler convenient to freeways, schools & shops. From the Williamsburg siding to the rosy shutters, it captures a tradition of serenity & style that makes for gracious living. Priced at just $110,000. Call Joe at Clarke Realty, 555-7120, today.

Colonial Charm/ Contemporary Convenience

make a delightful blend in this rustic 3 bedroom, 2 bath with microwave, intercom, garage door opener, automatic sprinklers. For only $106,000 you can live in the style you adore with the convenience you're accustomed to. Call Vivian today at Clarke Realty, 555-7120, to see it.

Williamsburg Colonial

You can almost hear the horses trotting outside this delectable 2 bedroom, 2-story. Shaded by ancient oak trees, it offers wall-to-wall carpeting, ceramic tile kitchen & bath, garden-view dining through bay window. Real family home at only $102,000. Call Lennie at Clarke Realty, 555-7120, today.

Salt Box Styling

at a price you'll love. Just $103,000 will give you a weathered gray, New England-style home, with cheerful red shutters & tasteful brick walk. 3 good-sized bedrooms, country wallcoverings, 2 oak & brass baths. Call Elizabeth at Clarke Realty, 555-7120, to see it today.

Authentic Early American

just waiting for someone to bring out its polish & charm. 3 upstairs bedrooms, 2-1/2 baths, wainscoted living room, cove-ceilinged dining room...terrific potential for only $102,000. This one's a hidden beauty. Call Carrie at Clarke Realty, 555-7120, to make it yours today.

> AD TIP: *Never assume understanding. Spell out all but the most common abbreviations.*

Original Log Cabin

hiding beneath sharp cedar siding on this 1 bedroom lakefront home. You'll adore the interior log walls, ceiling fans, airy loft. Your own pier, too. For just $65,000 you can't beat it. Call Bob at Clarke Realty, 555-7120. Hurry.

Miniature Tudor Gem

You never thought you could afford it but here it is...a 2 bedroom, 2-1/2 bath English manor with half-timbers, plaster walls, elegant brick fireplace. Just $103,000. Call Cathy today at Clarke Realty, 555-7120, to see this unique property.

Historic Stone Cottage

From the roses trailing over the lattice to the ancient birdbath, this 2 bedroom, 2 bath home is made to charm. Glowing hardwood floors, spacious wood cabinets, nooks & crannies will bring a sparkle to your eyes. Small but delightful. Only $87,000. Call Mary at Clarke Realty, 555-7120, to see it today.

Storybook Cottage

Straight from a picture book, it features a rolled roof, casement windows, rustic brick patio, colorful window boxes. 2 bedrooms, 1 spacious bath all for just $95,000. Call Tim at Clarke Realty, 555-7120, for a happy ending.

Country Chalet

Your refuge from the city's hustle. Soothing 2 bedroom, 2 bath A-frame with lattice work shutters, secluded spa, open & airy "great room" for family relaxing. Just 10 min. from downtown. Only $100,000. Call Jo Anne at Clarke Realty, 555-7120, to see this home's rustic splendor.

Old-World Charmer

Beer steins & cuckoo clocks would fit right in here...with its gleaming dark wood trim, cozy dining nook, delightful casement windows. Discover a bit of the old country, right inside the city. 2 bedrooms, 2 baths for only $92,000. Call Tony at Clarke Realty, 555-7120, & get ready for a treat!

Cotswold Cottage

with a garden that'll be the apple of your eye. Curl up next to the ancient brick fireplace. Go to sleep in one of 2 bedrooms under cozy upstairs eaves. Breakfast in a room lined with French windows. For $100,000...it can be your fairy tale come true. 2 baths, too. Call Doreen at Clarke Realty, 555-7120, to begin the story.

1930's Classic—$97,000

From the heavy, cross-beamed ceiling in the dining room to the huge butler's pantry in the kitchen to the rocking chair front porch...this 3 bedroom, 2 bath home was built for spacious & comfortable living. Of a quality only found in custom homes today. Call Jay at Clarke Realty, 555-7120, to see it today.

Vintage Charmer

Two elm trees shade its wide front veranda, while stained glass windows decorate the living room. If you treasure tradition, you'll love this cozy 2 bedroom, 2 bath frame cottage. Priced at just $99,000. To see it today, call Norma at Clarke Realty, 555-7120.

AD TIP: Be sure you tell your readers what to do in order to respond to your ad. Don't assume they'll call you unless you ask them to.

Authentic Adobe—$92,000

with the clean lines, gleaming red tile roof & open-air feeling of the old Southwest. 2 bedrooms, 1-1/2 baths nestled on 1/4 acre of cactus, rocks & stones. A home of character. Call Gregory at Clarke Realty, 555-7120, today.

Southwest-Inspired

Painted with the desert's colorful brush...rustic hand-tiled accents...3 large bedrooms...2 full baths. Breathe easy in style & comfort. Easy price, too. Just $105,000. Call Ken at Clarke Realty, 555-7120, to see it today.

Rustic Pueblo

with all the charm you'd ever want. Spanish-styled cabinets, wrought iron trim & smooth earth-tone tiles. Low, low maintenance. 2 bedrooms, sunlit bath. Yours for just $92,000. Call Mike at Clarke Realty, 555-7120. Now.

Enjoy California Living in Chicagoland

in this sunny & bright 3 bedroom, 2 bath sprawler designed for free-flowing living. Entertain your friends in the redwood patio's used-brick spa. After work, relax next to the 2-way fireplace, watch TV in the airy loft. Comfortable living at a price you can afford. Just $98,000. Call Karl at Clarke Realty, 555-7120, today.

House of Glass

makes the great outdoors part of everyday life in this dramatic 2 bedroom, 2 bath contemporary. Watch the squirrels play from the comfort of your living room. Go to sleep with stars shimmering through the skylight. Only $88,000. Call Victor at Clarke Realty, 555-7120. Be prepared to love it.

ATMOSPHERE

Homespun Charm

abounds in this 3 bedroom, 2 bath traditional home, surrounded by poplar & willow trees. From the shiny copper kitchen to the delicately stenciled walls to the random plank floors...it's a home where you can hang your heart. Only $87,000. Call Donna at Clarke Realty, 555-7120, to see it today.

The Price Is Old-Fashioned Too

Nooks & crannies fill this 2 bedroom Victorian. Intriguing accents like an outdoor refrigerator, built-in ironing closet, 2 updated baths, lots of old-fashioned detailing. The price is old-fashioned, too. Just $77,000 & you can move in tomorrow. Call Ty at Clarke Realty, 555-7120, to take a look.

Home With a Heart

You'll love the cheery foyer, with its unique wallcoverings & brass fixtures. The combination kitchen/family room with its glowing fireplace & brick walls. The 3 bedrooms, 2 baths, each special & charming. Ready-made for a family, this home is just $88,000. Call Pattie at Clarke Realty, 555-7120, today.

Johnny Appleseed Stopped Here

Well, someone planted the huge apple tree that shades this old-time, white frame charmer. 3 good-sized bedrooms, one with fireplace. Oak-floored living room with picture windows framing delightful view. Cheery kitchen where whole family can dine. 2 full baths, too. Only $89,000. Call Henrietta Smith at Clarke Realty, 555-7120, today—& bring a bucket for the apples.

Step Back in Time

when you enter this charming yellow cottage, with rock walls & flowers galore. Pull up your rocking chair to the massive stone fireplace. Fill the huge kitchen windows with plants. Enjoy serene meals in a dining room overlooking your yard. 2 bedrooms, 2 baths, 1,600 sq. ft. for only $90,000. Call Marie at Clarke Realty, 555-7120, to see it today.

Love Antiques?

Then this 3 bedroom, 2 bath home is the perfect showcase for them. 2 stories, with lots of warm wood paneling, hardwood floors, sun spilling through charming French windows. Artistically decorated, waiting for your personal touch. Just $100,000. Call Tom at Clarke Realty, 555-7120, to see it today. Bring your measuring tape!

Small Town Charmer, Small Price

Quality construction that's been well cared for with lath & plaster walls & ceilings you don't find in newer homes. 2 bedrooms, 1-1/2 baths in secluded setting only a few blocks from downtown. Priced at just $90,000. Call Jim at Clarke Realty, 555-7120, to take a look.

Old Town Cottage

Old-world styling in 3 bedroom, 2-story home with a sense of history. Modernized galley kitchen with skylights...2 ceramic tiled baths...antique, polished floors...high ceilings. Enjoy the peace of the past for only $98,000. Call Tony at Clarke Realty, 555-7120, today.

Nostalgic About the "Good Old Days?"

Then bring them back in a newer home built to remember the past. You'll love chatting with neighbors on the wide front porch...the floor-to-ceiling living room window that shows off your Christmas tree...the 3 bedrooms with full-wall closets & quiet, plush carpeting. Made for living today, in the style of the past. Only $86,000. Call Mary Jane at Clarke Realty, 555-7120, to see it now.

Bold & Brassy

Sassy 2 bedroom, 2 bath contemporary loaded with brass fixtures...bold colors...made for someone who takes life on the run. Low maintenance, all the kitchen time-savers you can imagine... little to do but enjoy. Only $95,000. Call Ron at Clarke Realty, 555-7120, for a look today.

City Chic

Urban sophisticates will love this smart 2 bedroom in the heart of downtown. Behind the brick exterior, the feeling is open & modern...with exposed-beam ceilings, galley kitchen, track lighting & spacious bath. Only $88,000. To see it today, call Rick at Clarke Realty, 555-7120.

See What Pride of Ownership Means

in this tasteful 3 bedroom home thoughtfully upgraded with custom closets, Malibu lights, automated sprinklers, full security system, whirlpool tub. All for only $90,000. Call Timothy at Clarke Realty, 555-7120, now.

Crisp &
Clean

Spanking clean, almost new 3 bedroom ranch. Made for easy family living, it features a huge den, 2 complete baths, great workshop/garage. Realisticly priced at just $99,000. Call Tommie at Clarke Realty, 555-7120, & see it today.

Light
& Airy

You'll love the way light spills down through the living room skylight...dances in through the kitchen's greenhouse window & drenches the spacious patio. The 3 bedrooms are open & bright...the 2 baths gleam with tile. Priced at just $87,000. Call Ken at Clarke Realty, 555-7120, today.

Cute &
Cozy

You'll love to snuggle in this charming bungalow hiding behind flowering shrubs. Hang your lace curtains in its delightful wood windows. Display your bone china in its glass cabinets. Bring a brass bed for each of the 2 bedrooms. A wonderful place for the right person. 2 full baths, too. Ring John at Clarke Realty, 555-7120, to take a peek.

Sleek &
Sophisticated

If you're looking for a contemporary home with plenty of pizzazz, try this 2 bedroom, 2 bath stunner. Smart checkerboard tile, gleaming white cabinets, glass-block walls & windows. Plus a patio where you can relax in peace. Great price, too. Only $89,000. Call Ned at Clarke Realty, 555-7120, to see it today.

Garden Lover's
Delight

Bring your watering can to this 2 bedroom, 2 bath brick home with flowers that bloom all year long. There's a shed to store your tools & giant work shelf you'll love. The house is great too. Lots of windows. Hardwood floors. White plaster walls to show off your greenery. In great shape! To see this beauty, call Tim at Clarke Realty, 555-7120, today.

Do You Have
a Green Thumb?

Then head over to this 3 bedroom, 2-1/2 bath rambler with brick planters & lush concealing landscaping. Enjoy the scenery from your splendid redwood deck. Or through the full-wall windows in the spacious living room. A house with garden-like grounds for only $98,000. Call Tom at Clarke Realty, 555-7120, now.

A Tropical Paradise

The California feeling begins in the atrium, where giant plants abound. Free-flowing design is carried out to open sunlit rooms of comfort. 3 bedrooms, 2 baths...for the relaxed lifestyle you love. Just $87,000. Call Henry at Clarke Realty, 555-7120, to make it yours.

Sun Lover?

Then come to a home that's made for you. A stylish 2 bedroom, 2 bath with skylights, rooftop patio for tanning & steamy spa. Only $92,000. Call Tom at Clarke Realty, 555-7120, today.

AD TIP: Have you been perfectly honest? Don't mislead your readers just to get them to call.

SPECIAL FEATURES

KITCHENS

Farm-Style Kitchen

Get ready to rustle up a hearty breakfast in this 3 bedroom, country-cozy home. The large kitchen looks out over your own spread of land. Big house, too. With 2 full baths, giant den & 2 car garage. Priced at just $90,000. Call Harvey at Clarke Realty, 555-7120, & get cooking!

A Gourmet Cook's Dream

Built-in care & style in this home, made for those who love to entertain. With an elegant galley kitchen. Serve your guests on the brick veranda, or dine beneath a brass chandelier. Enjoy after-dinner drinks next to the handsome fireplace. A 2 bedroom, 2 bath gem for just $89,000. Call Judy at Clarke Realty, 555-7120, to see it today.

Copper Kettle Kitchen

will bring a smile to your face—it's so warm & inviting. From the shiny copper trim to the brick breakfast bar, it's a room where your family will love to gather. If you're looking for a comfortable 3 bedroom, 2 bath home, filled with charm, for just $90,000, call Tina at Clarke Realty, 555-7120. Don't wait on this one.

Country-Fresh Kitchen

Imagine soup bubbling on the handsome cast-iron stove...sit in the rocker & watch your vegetable garden grow. This country-style kitchen is the heartbeat of this 3 bedroom rambler, on a spacious cul-de-sac lot. There's also a brick-walled den, 2 complete baths & picture window living room. Yours for just $90,000. Call Mike at Clarke Realty, 555-7120, today.

High-Tech Kitchen

to suit your contemporary lifestyle. You'll love its up-to-the-minute appliances, gleaming metal cabinets, great stainless steel accents & 2 stylish baths. This 2 bedroom, 2-story home represents the latest in design & taste, at just $95,000. To check it out today, call Jo at Clarke Realty, 555-7120.

A Cook's Delight

A kitchen designed for convenience & practicality with ceramic counters, solarium floors, top-of-the-line appliances. You'll love the versatility of serving either outdoors or in the spacious dining room. Imagine a 2 bedroom, 2 bath house that didn't cut corners when it came to the more important things. Offered at just $90,000. Call John at Clarke Realty, 555-7120, to take a look.

A Light
& Airy Kitchen

with a window where you can watch the sun setting over the river. You'll enjoy ease & comfort in this 3 bedroom, 2 bath home, where you can hear the sounds of birds calling & waves gently lapping. Old-fashioned charm, at an old-fashioned price of $88,000. Call Larry at Clarke Realty, 555-7120, today.

Country
Kitchen

You'll feel right at home popping an apple pie into its big oven. Designed for baking, eating & relaxing, this family-size kitchen fits right in with this 3 bedroom, 2 bath home's easy style. If you like gingham, soft armchairs & a roaring fire at night, come see it today. Only $87,000. Call Barbara at Clarke Realty, 555-7120, now.

Hang Your Pots Here

from the ceiling of a country kitchen that will charm you. With its pine dining nook, mellow antique cabinets & all the counter space you'll ever need. After dinner, relax in the oak-paneled living room, where a potbellied stove keeps you warm. For just $90,000, you can own a 2 bedroom, 1 bath cabin in one of the prettiest settings around. Call Karla at Clarke Realty, 555-7120, today.

Clean Glass

You'll love its clean & contemporary look, a solid glass-block wall that lets light flood in...with walls that curve gently around your dining table. Special 2 bedroom, 2 bath house, with hardwood floors, antique fireplace & artistically landscaped lot. Many extras for only $87,000. To see it today, call Jean at Clarke Realty, 555-7120.

FIREPLACE

Snuggle Up Next To...

a roaring fire in this cozy 2 bedroom, 2 bath home. Enjoy the fire's glow on the fine wood panels in the living room... warm up some hot chocolate in the roomy kitchen. You'll love this home's quaint dormer windows, flagstone patio & gentle charm. To see it today, call Sue at Clarke Realty, 555-7120.

Dutch Tile
Fireplace

in this very special 3 bedroom, 2 bath home. A bit of Europe in the custom window coverings, gleaming wood trim, planter boxes full of flowers. Offered at just $88,000. See it today. Call June at Clarke Realty, 555-7120.

Like to Roast
Marshmallows?

Then get ready for a treat. This comfortable 2 bedroom, 2 bath home features a huge antique brick fireplace with its own wood box & gas starter. Perfect for long winter evenings. You'll also love the spacious, eat-in kitchen, roomy bedrooms & 2 car garage. All this & a wooded lot for just $88,000. Call Fred at Clarke Realty, 555-7120, to see it today.

By the
Fire's Glow...

you can relax & unwind after a hard day's work. Pull down a book from the built-in shelves framing the fireplace. Grab a snack in the comfortable, window-lined kitchen. Made for easy living, this 2 bedroom, 1 bath cottage is only $84,000. To see this charmer today, call Tom at Clarke Realty, 555-7120.

2 Fireplaces!

That's right. Your family will love evenings next to a crackling fire in the living room of this sprawling 3 bedroom, 2 bath ranch. Later retire to the master bedroom with a fireplace all your own for more intimate moments. Nestled under pines & giant oaks. Priced at just $87,000. Make a point of seeing it today. Call George at Clarke Realty, 555-7120.

Potbellied Stove

is only one of the charming features of this 3 bedroom, 2 bath home. Surrounded by towering elms & flowering shrubs, it offers a country-style kitchen, family room with fine wood paneling & wonderful garage workshop. Only $82,000. To see it today, call Ken at Clarke Realty, 555-7120.

Chestnuts Roasting by an Open Fire...

in the magnificent stone fireplace of this 2 bedroom, 2 bath cottage. Tradition lovers will cherish its heart of pine cabinets, gingerbread porch & cozy upstairs bedrooms with window seats. Just $83,000. Call Lennie at Clarke Realty, 555-7120, to see this unique home. Do it now.

Tennessee Stone Fireplace

Old-world style craftsmen built this stunning fireplace one stone at a time. Its beauty makes it the focal point of this 3 bedroom, 2 bath rambler, conveniently close to town. Spacious, classically-styled rooms make the perfect backdrop for any decor. Lots of conveniences, too. Priced at just $88,000. Call Veronica at Clarke Realty, 555-7120 today.

White Brick Fireplace

sets the mood of this 3 bedroom, 2 bath California-style home. Contemporary & striking with features that will warm your heart. Maytag appliances, central air, Karastan carpeting, custom-built redwood patio drenched by sun. Great home with a great price. Just $85,000. To see it today, call Sue at Clarke Realty, 555-7120.

Antique Fireplace

You'll marvel at the intricacy of its hand-carved mantel created by an old-world craftsman. Watch the fire glow on its rosy red bricks. This 2 bedroom, 2 bath home is full of warmth & charm, with breakfast nook in the sunny kitchen, hardwood floors & heavy pine cabinets you couldn't buy today. A delicious reflection of the past, priced at just $75,000. Hurry & call Jenny at Clarke Realty, 555-7120. This won't last.

DINING ROOM

Garden-View Dining

Dine amid the flowers in this comfortable 3 bedroom, 2 bath home with a glass-walled dining room overlooking your sunken patio. In a private setting, just 10 min. from town, you can enjoy the feel of country living with all the city conveniences. Only $92,000. To see it today, call Greg at Clarke Realty, 555-7120.

AD TIP: As ad expert David Ogilvy says, "You can't save souls in an empty church." People must read an ad before they will respond. So make sure your ads count.

Unique Rock
Dining Room

Not many homes have a dining room like this one...with a wall carved straight out of the mountain by a long-ago craftsman. The rest of this 2 bedroom, 2 bath home reflects that same long-ago care: knotty pine cabinets, unusual '50s flooring, a galley porch framed by windows. Only $86,000. Call Kim at Clarke Realty, 555-7120, to see it today.

Dine on the Green

in this spacious 3 bedroom. Enjoy windows looking out over an expansive lawn. That soothing view is yours from almost every room of this colonial charmer...you'll love the way the tasteful neutral decor blends with the outdoor colors. There's room for a horse, pets & lots of kids. 2 full baths, too. Just $90,000. Call Tim at Clarke Realty, 555-7120, to take a look today.

For Your
Dining Pleasure...

a sunlit solarium dining room perfect for wrought iron & flowers. You'll enjoy its easy-care floor, custom curtains, delightful colors. Just like the rest of this 2 bedroom, 2 bath cottage...made to please. Tasteful upgrades throughout. Priced at just $80,000, definitely worth a look. To see it today, call George at Clarke Realty, 555-7120. Hurry.

Dinner for 12?

No problem in this 3 bedroom ranch. Fixing a gourmet meal is easy in its smart & roomy kitchen. Other special features include 2 complete baths, giant 2 car garage & softly lit patio where your guests will love to relax. Only $89,000. Call Paul at Clarke Realty, 555-7120 today. Get the invitations ready!

MASTER BEDROOM SUITE

Your Own
Sitting Room

A place to get away from it all & unwind. That's what you have in this 3 bedroom, 2-1/2 bath ranch, with a master bedroom suite with retreat designed to protect your privacy. Your kids will have their space, too, in the large family room, sprawling fenced yard & generously-sized bedrooms. Your escape for just $90,000. Call Veronica at Clarke Realty, 555-7120, to see it today.

Suite Living

That's the style in this roomy, 2 bedroom traditional with a master suite that will delight you. With 2 full-wall closets & a bath that's an efficiency expert's dream. Other features include an eat-in kitchen, 2 car garage & natural, easy-care landscaping. Only $93,000. Call Vernon at Clarke Realty, 555-7120, today.

Need Space
of Your Own?

Then come home to this 3 bedroom, 2 bath colonial with a master suite that's everything you've dreamed about. Sunny & bright sitting area, walk-in closets, whirlpool tub. You'll love the rest of the house, too: an ample living room, separate dining room, convenient laundry, step-saving kitchen. Just $95,000. To make it yours today, call Richard at Clarke Realty, 555-7120.

AD TIP: Write more copy than you need then cut out unnecessary words.

Two Suites for the Price of One

If you're interested in sharing a home, consider this dramatic contemporary... featuring 2 spacious master suites & 2 full baths situated on opposite ends of the huge light-flooded living room. No need to worry about privacy. Kitchen is small, but with top-of-the-line appliances. Breakfast bar, too. All this for only $93,000. To see it today, call Kenneth at Clarke Realty, 555-7120.

Escape at Home

to a master bedroom suite you'll adore. With sunny French windows. Private patio (with room for a spa). Delightful garden tub & all the closet space you could ask for. It's your escape in a 3 bedroom home you'll love...with half-paneled walls, beamed ceilings, fireplace to keep you toasty warm. Character & charm throughout. Only $99,000. Call Ken at Clarke Realty, 555-7120, today.

A Hideaway in Your Own Home

The master suite in this 3 bedroom ranch is situated for privacy. Walk through double doors onto your secluded patio. Relax in its greenhouse tub. Also features cheery kitchen, walnut-paneled den, 2 full baths & ivy-covered brick patio. On lot sprinkled with giant oaks, it's just $99,000. To see it today, call Richard at Clarke Realty, 555-7120.

The Suite Life

belongs to you in this stunning 2 bedroom contemporary with a master bedroom suite you'll adore. Well laid out with its own sitting area, gigantic closets & tasteful, expansive bath. You'll also love the home's slate entry, upgraded carpets, fireplace & lushly landscaped yard. Only $89,000. To take a look today, call Ed at Clarke Realty, 555-7120.

Your Private Place

It's all yours...a secluded sitting area, double doors opening to a walled garden, generous closets, well-designed bath for 2. Your master bedroom suite in a 3 bedroom, French country home. Other special features are bleached wood floors, plank shutters & light oak cabinets. A home of imagination for only $90,000. Call Jo at Clarke Realty, 555-7120, now.

A Suite Just for You

in this sprawling 3 bedroom ranch. Your own bedroom with a private sitting area, ample closets, a bath with room for both of you. A special place in a special home, offering 2 full baths, wall-to-wall carpeting, light & bright kitchen, 2-car garage. Priced at just $92,000. To take a look, call Ned at Clarke Realty, 555-7120.

Get Away From It All

in a master suite designed for your comfort & convenience. Create your own sitting area, enjoy custom-made closets, relax in the hot tub just through your garden doors. 3 big bedrooms, 2 full baths, ceramic tile kitchen, basement workshop & a lawn dotted with ancient oaks. Just $96,000. To see this great escape, call Val at Clarke Realty, 555-7120.

LARGE GARAGE

Attention: Handypersons!

Have the garage workshop you've been dreaming of in this terrific 3 bedroom home. No need to work on the house, it's in mint condition. 2 complete baths, gigantic family room, eat-in kitchen...save your spare time for hobbies. Priced at just $90,000. To see it today, call Tom at Clarke Realty, 555-7120.

Are You a Pack Rat?

Then you'll love the garage of this spacious 2 bedroom, 2 bath home. Plenty of room for years of memorabilia. Lots of elbowroom in the house, too, with its window-walled den, fireplace-graced living room & breakfast bar kitchen. Bright & airy feeling. Only $93,000. To take a look today, call Jim at Clarke Realty, 555-7120. Better hurry.

Three Cars?

Then bring them home to this 3 bedroom traditional with a huge garage. It's like the rest of the house...sprawling & comfortable. You'll love the hand-built brick fireplace, warmly paneled den, 2 complete baths. Plus a yard with room to roam. All for just $97,000. Call Fred at Clarke Realty, 555-7120, to see it today.

Custom-Built Garage

That's right—a garage lined with custom cabinets to store everything you've never had a place for. That kind of care is reflected throughout this 2 bedroom charmer featuring French windows, 2 complete baths, stained glass accents & skylights. Priced at just $90,000. Call Henry at Clarke Realty, 555-7120, today.

Need a Bigger Garage?

& a bigger house, too? Then take a minute today to see a spacious 3 bedroom home with plenty of room to roam. You'll love its genuine "great room," 2-1/2 baths, kitchen with lots of space for cooking & eating. A real family home at a family price of just $95,000. Call Anne at Clarke Realty, 555-7120, now.

AD TIP: If you see a word used over and over again in your real estate classifieds, avoid it. Use a thesaurus to come up with different words to say the same idea.

SPECIAL ROOMS

Is Photography Your Passion?

Then enjoy the luxury of a real darkroom in this delightful 2 bedroom, 2 bath California ranch...with walls of windows that spill sunlight into your living room...a private walled patio where you can bathe in the rays...skylights through which you can see the clouds. Priced at just $88,000. Call Brad at Clarke Realty, 555-7120, today.

Room for Guests

in this comfortable, 3 bedroom, 3 bath home. Features a bedroom/sitting area with its own entrance. Perfect for in-laws. You'll love the home's quiet quality, with upgraded carpet, plantation shutters, cool & easy colors. Nestled on 1/4 acre lot. Only $89,000. Must see! Call Travis at Clarke Realty, 555-7120.

Home + Office

Perfect for the self-employed, this 3 bedroom traditional offers a cozy, wood-paneled office facing the street. Even has its own entrance. Rest of the house is private...white clapboard with spacious rooms, 2 baths, sunny eat-in kitchen. Old-fashioned price of just $93,000. To take a look today, call John at Clarke Realty, 555-7120.

Like To Sew?

Then take a peek at a room with a wall of specially built shelves & nooks where you can keep everything straight. In a great 3 bedroom, 2 bath house. Hardwood floors, curved bannister, top-quality carpet, tasteful wallcoverings. A gentle home made for gentle people. At a gentle price of $90,000. To see it today, call Eugene at Clarke Realty, 555-7120.

A House +
Greenhouse, too!

Plant lovers will delight in this old-fashioned greenhouse, where you can indulge your green thumb all year round. It adjoins the kitchen of this rambling, 3 bedroom, 2 bath farmhouse...featuring old barn planking, porcelain fixtures, nooks & crannies galore. Just 10 min. from the heart of town. Priced at only $89,000. To take a look today, call Sam at Clarke Realty, 555-7120.

ENERGY EFFICIENT

Looking to Save on Utility Bills?

Then stop by this 2 bedroom, 2 bath contemporary home, with solar hot water & an energy-efficient gas furnace. Thick insulation & total weatherstripping will also cut your bill. In the winter, enjoy the living room's heatilator fireplace. In summer have towering oaks for shade. 2 cords of firewood thrown in. Just $95,000. To see a real money-saver, call Jim at Clarke Realty, 555-7120.

Want to Save Money?

Then let the sun do your heating in this solar-heated 3 bedroom, 2 bath on a convenient wooded site. Walls of thermopane windows hold in the warmth while you relax by a native stone fireplace in the living room. Plenty of room for firewood in oversized 2 car garage. Cool price of just $89,000. To see it today, call Caroline at Clarke Realty, 555-7120.

> AD TIP: *Tracking the source of your responses will help you plan an effective strategy and save you money.*

High Fuel Bills Got You Down?

Then own a 3 bedroom, 2 bath home made to hug in the heat. With super insulation, triple-glazed windows, solar hot water...it's a great way to save hundreds of dollars. You'll like the house, too... butcher block countertops, clean lines, a simple heat exchanger fireplace. Simple price, too. Just $90,000 & it's yours. Call Ken at Clarke Realty, 555-7120.

No Drafts Here...

Want to get away from those annoying drafts? Move into a smart-looking, 2 bedroom, 2 bath contemporary that will always keep you warm. Tons of insulation under white, white walls. Double pane windows frame a leafy view. Gas efficient furnace in workshop basement. A home where you can live in comfort for just $97,000. Call Nancy at Clarke Realty, 555-7120, to take a look.

Looking for Energy Efficiency?

Then own a 3 bedroom brick home with all the extras...a toasty heat-exchanger fireplace beneath an antique mantel, solar heater that pours hot water into 2 ceramic baths, estate-sized lot with trees to cut for wood. Get back to the basics in comfort for only $85,000. Call Ken at Clarke Realty, 555-7120, today.

ROOM FOR ENTERTAINING

If You Love to Party...

then live in a home made for it. A 3 bedroom, 2 bath ranch 5 min. from the city. For just $89,000, you get a spacious family room with wet bar, sit-down dining room & romantic brick patio. The kind of home your friends will love to visit. To see it today, call Jim at Clarke Realty, 555-7120.

Enjoy Entertaining?

Then come see this sprawling, 3 bedroom, 2-1/2 bath traditional just minutes from downtown. You'll love the elegant dining room, relaxed family room, convenience-packed kitchen. You'll adore this neighborhood's tall trees, secluded homes & peaceful feeling. Priced at just $97,000. Call Henrietta at Clarke Realty, 555-7120, to see today.

Do You Have a Lot of Friends?

Then bring them over to party in the hot, bubbly spa of this luscious 3 bedroom. Hidden behind a lattice fence, you'll love lounging on its redwood deck. Bring out the snacks from your galley kitchen. Freshen up in the 2 baths. Live a luxurious lifestyle for a sensible price. Just $90,000 & it's yours. Call Adam at Clarke Realty, 555-7120, to see it today.

Your Own English Pub

comes with this 2 bedroom, 2 bath hillside home. Set on a wide, fully landscaped lot, it offers contemporary convenience & old English charm. Your friends will love its heavy dark beams, rough-hewn cedar finish, beveled mirror. The perfect spot to party...only $90,000. To take a look today, call Jim at Clarke Realty, 555-7120.

Entertainer's Delight

If you enjoy company, you'll love this easy-care 3 bedroom, 2 bath home. Made for entertaining, it features a gourmet kitchen, elegant dining area, family room with massive stone fireplace & expansive lawn for ball games. Priced at just $96,000. Call John at Clarke Realty, 555-7120, to take a look today.

Company Coming?

Then welcome them in a home made for casual entertaining. A free-flowing California contemporary with downstairs bedroom & bath perfect for overnight guests. Enjoy drinks on the flower-filled deck. Or chatting at the kitchen bar while cooking. Relax in the soothing spa with its picture-postcard view. 3 bedrooms, 2 baths for just $95,000. To see, call Roger at Clarke Realty, 555-7120, today.

Are You a People Person?

Then you'll enjoy entertaining in this comfortable 3 bedroom traditional. From its wide closets to the 2 tastefully decorated baths to the family room with its huge brick fireplace...this is a place your friends will feel right at home. You'll love the country-fresh kitchen, too. At a great price—just $87,000. Stop by today. Call Loni at Clarke Realty, 555-7120.

The Perfect Singles Pad

You couldn't have designed it better...a 1 bedroom contemporary with shining tile, airy loft, classy gray carpet, expansive bath. Enjoy the warmth of a crackling Swedish fireplace...the romance of a lattice-covered patio. All the latest appliances. Yours for $87,000. Call Tom at Clarke Realty, 555-7120, today.

Entertain With Flair

in this exciting 3 bedroom, 2 bath home just down the block from the city tennis courts. You'll love its tasteful, mirrored dining room, huge kitchen, flickering fireplace in the family room. The brick patio is a great place to picnic. Only $94,000. To see this special home, call Marie at Clarke Realty, 555-7120, now.

A Home Your Friends Will Love

& you will too. Sprawling 2 bedroom, 2 bath ranch with cedar shingles & white wood trim surrounded by giant trees. From the window seat in the living room to the cheery dining nook off the kitchen, it's made for casual living. Lots of conveniences, too. Only $89,000. To see today, call Ned at Clarke Realty, 555-7120.

ONE-LEVEL

No Steps

in this gracious 3 bedroom, 2 bath ranch resting beneath a canopy of trees. Designed for easy living with wide doorways, wheelchair ramp & thoughtful conveniences. Priced at just $95,000. To see today, call Jo at Clarke Realty, 555-7120.

No More Stairs

Live in easy 1-level comfort in this gleaming 2 bedroom home. You'll love its conveniences, everything within reach. Specially adapted bath, too. Extra touches like living room fireplace, sun-spotted patio & wide, wide closets. Only $94,000. Call Henrietta at Clarke Realty, 555-7120, to take a look.

Need a One-Story Home?

Then take a look at this long & lean 3 bedroom, 2 bath home with hallways where the sun streams in. All rooms are big & wide, with easy-to-reach cabinets & extra conveniences. Gorgeous natural landscaping, low maintenance. All for just $88,000. Call Ken at Clarke Realty, 555-7120, today.

Tired of Climbing Stairs?

Then live in 1-story splendor in this gracious 3 bedroom, 2 bath home. Designed to bring in the light & trees, filled with natural wood trim, wall-to-wall carpet, totally updated kitchen. In terrific location. Priced at just $98,000, this is sure to sell quickly. Call Frank at Clarke Realty, 555-7120, today.

Not a Single Step

in this secluded 2 bedroom, 2 bath ranch, bordered by a split rail fence. From the geraniums on the window sills to the generously sized flagstone patio, it's a home made for taking it easy. You'll love the dramatic rock wall in the living room...sun-speckled dining room... efficient kitchen. Only $90,000. To see today, call Jay at Clarke Realty, 555-7120.

PORCHES/PATIOS/SPAS

Bring Your Rocking Chair!

Enjoy crickets chirping as you watch the sun slowly sinking from the front porch of this Victorian beauty. Newly restored, it features delightful gingerbread trim, hardwood floors, etched glass cabinets. 2 wonderful dormered bedrooms, 2 charming baths. Minutes from downtown. Only $88,000. To take a look today call Judy at Clarke Realty, 555-7120.

Sip Iced Tea

on the veranda of this spacious 2 bedroom southern-style home. Luxuriously draped in ivy & surrounded by rustling oaks. Close to shops & schools, it offers a dreamy family-style kitchen, paneled den & 2 ceramic baths. All for just $95,000. Stop by today. Call Fred at Clarke Realty, 555-7120.

A Sun Porch
Made for Plants

Have your own gorgeous conservatory where you can breakfast, watch TV, or just relax amid nature's splendor, in this comfortable 3 bedroom Dutch colonial. With 2 full baths, eat-in kitchen & chandeliered dining room. A must-see at $97,000. Call Henry at Clarke Realty, 555-7120, today.

A Candlelight Dinner

Enjoy romantic moments on the bougainvillea-covered brick patio of this charming 2 bedroom, 2 bath home. Surrounded by high walls, listening to a gentle fountain splash, it's your own little world. After dinner, relax by a glowing fire. A sparkling home, in top shape, with all the conveniences, for just $90,000. To bring the romance back into your life, call Jack at Clarke Realty, 555-7120, today.

Enjoy Sunbathing?

Then you'll love this 3 bedroom, 2 bath contemporary with an extra-wide patio. Attractive redwood planking keeps it cool while beds of flowers add color & life. Inside enjoy the modern look of fresh white walls & neutral carpeting, plus all the conveniences. Great location, too. Only $90,000. To see it today call Ted at Clarke Realty, 555-7120.

A Very Private Spa

is waiting for you on a hidden patio surrounded by shrubs just steps from the master bedroom. If you value privacy, you'll love this 3 bedroom, 2 bath home. Desirable corner lot, features solid plaster walls, exposed-beam ceilings, wonderful fireplace. Just $88,000. Call Nancy at Clarke Realty, 555-7120 to see it today.

Like to BBQ?

Then get the charcoals ready...there's a Texas-style brick BBQ waiting for you on the patio of this 3 bedroom, 2 bath home. Set up a picnic table on its huge, velvety lawn. With a spacious kitchen & sprawling living room, there's plenty of elbowroom. Just $92,000. To see today, call Tom at Clarke Realty, 555-7120.

A Cool Porch
for Hot Summer Nights

You'll practically live in the giant screened porch of this 3 bedroom, 2-story traditional. Made for indoor-outdoor living, it's fully carpeted & looks out onto a forest of trees. You'll love the rest of the house, too...classic lines, 2 full baths, see-through fireplace. Only $91,000. Call John, today, at Clarke Realty, 555-7120.

Tahiti in
Your Own Backyard

Set up your lounge chair on the flagstone lanai of this open & airy 2 bedroom, 2 bath home. Live in tropical splendor with walls of windows overlooking lush landscaping. Easy-care kitchen, plush carpets, rosy-rock fireplace. Just $90,000. To see it today, call Paul at Clarke Realty, 555-7120.

A Steaming Spa

is bubbling on the upstairs porch of this 3 bedroom, 2 bath home. Entertain your guests in its bubbly comfort, while overlooking sparkling city lights. A free-flowing home with wall-to-wall carpeting, white brick wall, atrium entry. Can you believe just $95,000? Call Rick at Clarke Realty, 555-7120, today.

An Old-Fashioned Porch Swing

is waiting for you on the columned porch of this 1940's frame home. Solidly built, with lots of custom touches, this 3 bedroom, 2 bath sprawler features a huge picture window, beamed ceilings, butler's pantry & heavy oak staircase. Just 10 min. from downtown. Priced at only $82,000. Call Caroline at Clarke Realty, 555-7120, today.

Enjoy the Great Outdoors

from the inviting redwood deck of this 2 bedroom, 2 bath cottage. Entered through French doors with a breathtaking view of the mountains, it's shaded by giant trees. Enjoy the warmth of a wood-burning stove, knotty pine paneling, hardwood floors. A delightful home for just $80,000. To see it, call George at Clarke Realty, 555-7120, today.

A Touch of Hawaii

in the lush tropical patio of this sunlit 2 bedroom, 2 bath beauty. You'll adore its professional landscaping, redwood construction, lots of glass & stone. Call Jo at Clarke Realty, 555-7120. Only $96,000.

A Peaceful Patio

stretches along the entire length of this 3 bedroom ranch with full-wall windows opening to it from every room. Shaded by a lanai, shielded by brick walls, it creates a private setting in the middle of the city. Kitchen with breakfast bar, master suite, 2 full baths. Comfortable living for just $88,000. Call Mary Ann at Clarke Realty, 555-7120, today.

Miss the Old-Fashioned Front Porch?

Enjoy yesterday's charm with today's conveniences in this near-new 3 bedroom traditional. From the front porch cornices to the walk-in pantry, it features the best of the past...but with upgrades like a dishwasher, 2 car garage, top-quality flooring, gas fireplace, 2 baths. Offered at only $88,000. To see it today, call June at Clarke Realty, 555-7120.

LANDSCAPING

Rose Garden

Get a beautiful garden with this splendid 3 bedroom, 2 bath California ranch. It features ceramic tile floors, galley kitchen, raised hearth fireplace & rows of French windows where you can watch the roses grow. Great schools. Only $97,000. To smell the roses today, call Jonathan at Clarke Realty, 555-7120.

Plants Galore

surround this 3 bedroom California Craftsman, creating a very private & natural setting. Enjoy them from the wide front porch perfect for rocking chairs. From the kitchen, walls of glass look onto your own miniature forest. A delightful home, featuring 2 baths, beamed ceilings & living room fireplace, for only $95,000. To see it today, call Nick at Clarke Realty, 555-7120.

> *AD TIP: Write more than one headline and then choose the best.*

2 Acres of Trees & Flowers

surround this 2 bedroom cottage with private road & barn. Perfect for folks who enjoy the country feeling with all the city conveniences. Offers solar hot water, cedar siding, generous eat-in kitchen, 2 full baths. Lots of land for $90,000. Call Fred at Clarke Realty, 555-7120, today.

Park-Like Setting

with towering pines, spreading oaks & emerald lawn around this 3 bedroom, 2 bath Cape Cod just 20 min. from town. You'll adore its many shutters, screened porch, graciously-sized rooms. A quality home for only $88,000. To see it today, call Gina at Clarke Realty, 555-7120.

Nature's Handiwork

creates the perfect setting for this 1 bedroom pine home. Giant rocks, trees, wonderful cactus garden. Enjoy the view through the French windows. You'll love the efficient kitchen, cool tile floors & built-in bookcase. All for just $87,000. Call Ted at Clarke Realty, 555-7120.

POOL

Keep Fit in Your Own Pool

at this 3 bedroom ranch on a cul-de-sac. Sunny & bright, with fine wood paneling in the den, cheery kitchen nook & 2 full baths—this home was made for enjoyment. To see it today, call Lisa at Clarke Realty, 555-7120.

AD TIP: Write as if you were talking to a friend.

California-Style Living for Only $99,000

Are you ready for a more relaxing, healthier lifestyle? Get into the swim of things in this 3 bedroom, 2 bath home. Take a leisurely dip in the pool...enjoy the convenience of a changing room off the spacious kitchen...watch the fun from the fireplace-warmed den. To see, call Melissa at Clarke Realty, 555-7120.

Skinny-Dipper's Delight

Totally private, sun-warmed pool comes with this secluded home. Just steps from the master bedroom, it's surrounded by high brick walls. You'll love the rich, full landscaping, modern conveniences, 3 big bedrooms, 2 full baths. Priced to sell at $98,000. Call Mary Jane at Clarke Realty, 555-7120, to see it today.

A Lap Pool Just for You

It's hard to tell where the garden ends & pool begins at this delightful 2 bedroom, 2 bath home. Made to blend in with the flower-filled setting, this pool is great for exercise or relaxing. The house has sunny, spacious rooms; handmade fireplace; gleaming kitchen. Just $92,000. To see a home that suits your lifestyle, call Ed at Clarke Realty, 555-7120, now.

A Black-Bottom Pool

Something you've always dreamed about —a home with a pool, can be yours for only $95,000. It's the kind of pool rarely seen with a 2 bedroom home...lushly landscaped with redwood decking made to soak in the sun. Home features skylights, big kitchen, 2 car garage & 2 full baths. Call Jim at Clarke Realty, 555-7120, today.

CONDITION

WELL CARED FOR

Model Perfect —Just Listed

This 3 bedroom stunner sits on a winding street bordered by flowers & mature trees. In tip-top shape, it offers vaulted ceilings, gas fireplace, plant shelves & dramatic arched windows. 2 baths & 2 car garage, too. At $95,000, this won't last long. Call Victor at Clarke Realty, 555-7120, today.

Fussy Buyer's Dream

If you want a home that reflects lots of care & pride, come see this 2 bedroom showplace. From the gleaming hardwood floors to the spick & span French windows & self-cleaning ovens, it absolutely shines. Only $89,000. Call Jordan at Clarke Realty, 555-7120, today.

Perennial Perfection

describes this sparkling 2 bedroom, 2 bath cottage, jam-packed with custom touches. Things like hand-polished cherry cabinets, carved wood dining nook & brick sidewalks. All kept up with love & care. Priced at just $77,000, it's a bargain hunter's dream. Call Nancy at Clarke Realty, 555-7120, to see it today.

Better Than New

3 bedroom, 2 bath ranch situated in convenient Marble Hills. Tasteful upgrades throughout. Mirrored walls & closets, Victorian-style bath, custom-crafted workshop, chandeliered dining. On a secluded corner lot. At only $89,000, it's ready for you to make your move. Call Tom at Clarke Realty, 555-7120, today.

Spick & Span

Cute 2 bedroom, 2 bath cottage surrounded by darling white picket fence. See pride of ownership in the fresh new paint, glowing tile, wall-to-wall carpeting, delightful stenciling. A home of character & charm at a ready-to-move-in price of only $77,000. See it today. Call Jamie Lee at Clarke Realty, 555-7120.

Love & Care

are the hallmarks of this luscious 3 bedroom traditional brick home a few blocks from the university. Carefully maintained, it features old-style charm with all the latest conveniences. You'll love its rocking chair porch, dormered bedrooms, 2 spacious baths. Move in tomorrow for just $90,000. Call Ted at Clarke Realty, 555-7120, today.

> *AD TIP: Ask for action at the close of your ads.*

Nothing to Hide Here

This 3 bedroom, 2 bath rambler is in perfect shape. You can tell by the shiny slate floor entry, glowing hardwoods, spick & span eat-in kitchen. Shaded by a spreading elm in a friendly family neighborhood. Only $87,000. See it for yourself. Call Lee at Clarke Realty, 555-7120.

Lovely to Look At...

& delightful to live in. 2 bedroom, 2 bath Cape Cod in absolutely mint condition. Nestled behind towering trees on a quiet street, its gentle charm reflects years of quality care...from the mellow pine kitchen cabinets to the antique tile fireplace & sparkling wood trim. All you have to do is move in. Priced to go quickly at $78,000. To see it today, call Marie at Clarke Realty, 555-7120.

Don't Touch Anything...

this 3 bedroom sprawler is perfect. You'll love its immaculate tile floors, easy-care natural landscaping, whisper-soft carpeting. Lots of conveniences like 2 huge baths, automatic sprinklers, Malibu lighting, updated kitchen. Yours for just $92,000. Call Ned at Clarke Realty, 555-7120, today.

Ms. Clean Lived Here...

You'll appreciate the care that went into this shining 2 bedroom, 2 bath home. Nothing to do but enjoy it. From the gigantic walk-in kitchen pantry to the lattice-covered brick veranda to the cozy upstairs bedrooms...it's better than new. You just don't find this kind of quality in homes today—at least not for $88,000. To see this special property, call Julie at Clarke Realty, 555-7120, today.

A Well-Kept Tradition

If you long for a slightly grander lifestyle in a home that reflects the graciousness of the past, come see this 3 bedroom, 2 bath brick in a quiet neighborhood. You'll be delighted by the arched doorways, glassed-in bookcases, coved ceilings, sweeping staircase. Carefully maintained over the years, this home is offered at yesterday's price of $87,000. To see it today, call Ken at Clarke Realty, 555-7120.

Neat & Tidy

Lots of room in this sunny 2 bedroom, 2 bath traditional perched on a hillside. See it today & fall in love with its spick & span hardwood floors, highly polished kitchen cabinets, meticulously manicured English garden. Old-world charm at an old-fashioned price of just $86,000. Call Henry at Clarke Realty, 555-7120, now.

A Pristine Gem

Rambling 3 bedroom home surrounded by nature's finest. Just 5 min. from downtown with trees, flowers, even a fountain. Nothing to do but enjoy the scenery—this home is in tip-top shape. Big bedrooms, 2 baths, sun porch, eat-in kitchen. Only $98,000. To see it today, call Jimmy at Clarke Realty, 555-7120.

Make It Easy on Yourself

All you have to do is arrange your furniture...that's easy in this 3 bedroom, 2 bath beauty with its wide open floor plan. Spend evenings in front of a roaring fire in the massive stone hearth. Or relax on the lattice-covered lanai. Easy living at the easy price of $92,000. Call Ken at Clarke Realty, 555-7120, today.

Nothing to Do But...

move into this spacious, 2 bedroom, 2 bath Spanish hacienda. Thick adobe walls, Mexican tile accents, gleaming copper kitchen. A little gem that glows with love & pride. Offered at just $95,000. To see this lovely home today, call Leonard at Clarke Realty, 555-7120.

MAINTENANCE-FREE

Live It Up!

in a 2 bedroom, 2 bath home where all you have to do is enjoy. Top-of-the-line appliances, brand-new roof, sparkling wall-to-wall carpeting. Extra touches like kitchen skylights, garden tub, 2 car garage. A home made for people who like to take it easy. Affordable price of just $91,000. Make your move today. Call Fred at Clarke Realty, 555-7120.

Hate Hassles?

Then move into this delightful 3 bedroom, 2 bath home built to suit your style. Easy-care, quality carpeting, newly remodeled kitchen & bath, natural landscaping. Over 2,000 sq. ft. Hassle-free price of just $85,000. To see it today, call Peggy at Clarke Realty, 555-7120.

Forget the Lawn Mower

You won't need it in this sunny 2 bedroom home with a forest of trees & wildflowers. Extras like tile counters, 2 ceramic baths & wall-to-wall carpeting. Only $82,000. Call Martin, today, at Clarke Realty, 555-7120.

Relax & Enjoy Life

in this easy-care 3 bedroom home with a warm wood-paneled playroom, giant garage, 2 full baths, naturally landscaped fenced yard that's practically maintenance free. Great school just around the corner. Just $96,000. Call Barbara at Clarke Realty, 555-7120, today.

Peace of Mind

is yours in this almost new 3 bedroom ranch built for people who have better things to do than housework. Filled with up-to-the-minute conveniences like microwave oven, automatic sprinklers, timed outdoor lights. Also offers generously-sized rooms, 2 baths, 2-car garage. Realistic price of $96,000. Call Virginia at Clarke Realty, 555-7120, now.

Maintenance-Free

Spread-out 3 bedroom ranch with attractive cedar shingles, split rail fence & unique brick work. You'll really appreciate extra touches like the sunny laundry room, 2 ceramic baths, vacuum system & central air. Just $98,000. Call George at Clarke Realty, 555-690, today.

Tired of Repair Bills?

Then get away from them in this almost new 2 bedroom, 2 bath California ranch. Energy-efficient gas furnace, central air, top-of-the-line appliances & fresh country decor, it's tailor-made for people who want to take life easy. Priced to go at $80,000. To see it, call Virginia at Clarke Realty, 555-7120.

Like a Worry-Free Home?

Then move into this smart, cedar-sided A-frame, built to last for years. Never needs painting. Brand-new roof. Gleaming natural trim. Maintenance-free yard. 3 bedrooms, 2 baths. Worry-free price of $85,000. Call Mary at Clarke Realty, 555-7120, to see it today.

Carefree Living

in this 2 bedroom, 2 bath home tucked against a hillside. You'll love its gleaming tile floors, hardwood cabinets, rosy-stone fireplace. A home where you can live with ease—just 5 min. from the city tennis courts. If you have more to do in life than home repairs, call Alan at Clarke Realty, 555-7120, today. Only $85,000.

For the Fun of Life

3 bedroom ranch made for fun. From the family-sized kitchen to the pool-room sized den to the yard big enough for pool & playground. Top-quality appliances, imported wallcoverings & high-grade flooring make it easy. 2 baths, too. To see this special home today, call Jo at Clarke Realty, 555-7120.

Have the Lifestyle You Deserve

in this maintenance-free, easy-care 2 bedroom, 2 bath home. You'll love the lush plant-filled atrium, sparkling top-quality floors, dramatic Swedish fireplace with white brick wall. Just $92,000. Call Lisa at Clarke Realty, 555-7120, today.

AD TIP: Use specifics rather than generalities.

Take the Time to Smell the Flowers

that surround this luscious, garden-style 2 bedroom, 2 bath home. Plenty of time to putter here...there's practically no maintenance. From the flagstone patio to the top-quality kitchen cabinets & double-glazed windows, this home was designed to give you time to do what you love most. If you'd like to experience a relaxing lifestyle for just $92,000, call Tim at Clarke Realty, 555-7120, today.

Have the Time You Need

in a 3 bedroom home you'll adore. Because this stately brick traditional has been carefully upgraded to free you from care. Brand-new roof, furnace, top-of-the-line appliances...it's life the way it was meant to be. Tastefully decorated, too, with charming pair of baths, study & sunny screened porch. Yours for just $95,000. To see it today, call Denise at Clarke Realty, 555-7120.

Family House

If you have a houseful of children you'll love this 4 bedroom contemporary. With its rough-&-tumble playroom, durable wool carpeting, sunny & bright wood-paneled bedrooms & 3 baths, it was made for family living. There's even a workshop. Family priced at $96,000. Call Dee at Clarke Realty, 555-7120, today.

Take It Easy

in the home you deserve. A maintenance-free 2 bedroom, 2 bath Florida-style contemporary that lets the sun & fresh air in. You'll love its easy-care yard, worry-free floors, spacious & bright closets, skylit bath. Easy price of $89,000. See it today. Call Susan at Clarke Realty, 555-7120.

QUALITY WORKMANSHIP

Own the Best for Just $94,000

If you're looking for style & quality on a budget, come see this dreamy 2 bedroom. Built with a care that's hard to find, it offers French doors, custom cabinets, luxurious bath. Tucked away on a cul-de-sac, it's new on the market. To see it today, call Ken at Clarke Realty, 555-7120.

Quality Conscious?

Then here's the home you've been looking for...a stunning cedar chalet hidden in the woods. Top-of-the-line appliances, airy loft, massive stone fireplace. You'll adore the wood-paneled bedroom. Quality throughout at just $90,000. See it for yourself. Call Loni at Clarke Realty, 555-7120, now.

Top-of-the-Line

The good taste & superb quality of this 2 bedroom home will surprise you—especially at a price of just $98,000. You'll fall in love with the greenhouse tub, custom decorating, ceramic countertops, handsome oak fireplace. Great location, too...just 10 min. from Lockheed. To see this special home today, call June at Clarke Realty, 555-7120.

> AD TIP: *Feel free to mention brand names in your ads. Capitalize on all the advertising major companies do to promote their products.*

Come Inside & You'll Be Surprised...

at what a little imagination can do. This 3 bedroom, 2 bath home tucked away in Rolling Hills breaks the mold. Upgrades galore...slate entry to glass-walled atrium ...to antique mouldings throughout. Custom features at ready-made price of just $96,000. See it today. Call Elaine at Clarke Realty, 555-7120.

Built With Pride

This 3 bedroom, 2 bath traditional near the Medical Center radiates thoughtful quality. You'll appreciate special touches like the elegant double-doored den, handcrafted trim & sunny brick veranda. A handsome home you'll be proud to own. Only $95,000. To see it today, call Frank at Clarke Realty, 555-7120.

Appreciate the Finer Things?

Then you'll love this dramatic 2 bedroom, 2 bath contemporary with sheets of glass overlooking the city lights. White, white walls...track lighting...spiral staircase with loft...the perfect home to show off the things you treasure. Built with care...only $95,000. Call Henry at Clarke Realty, 555-7120, today.

For the Special Person

Handcrafted 1 bedroom home snuggled in the woods 15 min. outside town. Knotty pine interior, wood-burning fireplace, glowing hardwood floors. Quality materials, thoughtful construction. Only $80,000. To take a look, call Virginia at Clarke Realty, 555-7120, now.

Here's a
Winner

Stunning 3 bedroom home built with outstanding quality. You can't match the distinctive solid oak beams, unique carved fireplace, wonderful swirling bannister. A home with a heart & 2 full baths for only $90,000. Close to town, too. For a look today, call Annie at Clarke Realty, 555-7120.

If You Care
About Quality...

then come see this friendly 3 bedroom, 2 bath Cape Cod built by Johnson & Smith. It's the sought-after Springvale model, valued for its easy floor plan & first class upgrades. Special touches like island cooking center, 2-1/2 car garage, superb carpeting, hand-hewn fireplace, custom fixtures. A home you'll treasure for only $95,000. Call Ken at Clarke Realty, 555-7120, today.

Why Not a
First Class Home?

Especially when it's bargain-priced at just $98,000. You'll love its 3 spacious bedrooms, 2 baths, Italian tile floors, French doors opening to a brick patio. The perfect home for many moods. Convenient location, too. To see it today, call Regina at Clarke Realty, 555-7120.

AD TIP: Avoid being cute and clever. Credible and convincing will sell more homes.

UNIQUE APPEALS

HISTORY

An Old
Carriage House

Unique home under canopy of trees, high on a ridge overlooking the city. Once belonged to neighboring estate...now it can be yours for just $99,000. 2 sunny bedrooms & baths, eat-in kitchen, stone fireplace in living room. To see this one of a kind home today, call Noreen at Clarke Realty, 555-7120.

Circa 1912

Originally a weekend cottage for the rich, this simple cedar-shingled home today is close to everything. Buried in a forest of trees, its patio gives you a view as clear & untouched as it was long ago. Updated kitchen & bath, 2 bedrooms, gorgeous rock fireplace. Just $95,000. Call Ken at Clarke Realty, 555-7120, to take a look.

Carpenter-Owned

You'll know the minute you walk in & see the polished redwood finishes. Special things like a glossy wood ceiling, handmade window frames, cedar cathedral hallway. 2 bedrooms, 2 car garage. This home can be yours for just $88,000. Call Vi at Clarke Realty, 555-7120, now.

Builder's
Own Home

You'll love this charming 3 bedroom. Located on one of the choicest lots in Tundra Hills, it offers a splendid brick patio, atrium-like dining area, classy white brick fireplace & secluded bedroom wing. 2 full baths. Priced at $99,000. Make it yours today. Call Mike at Clarke Realty, 555-7120.

Interior Decorator's
Dream Home

Stunning 2 bedroom, 2-1/2 bath contemporary featuring skylit loft, sleek oak kitchen & closet space galore. Custom wallcoverings & drapes in pale pastels reflect today's freshest look. Loaded with upgrades. Indulge yourself in sophistication for only $97,000. Call Betty at Clarke Realty, 555-7120, today.

AWARD-WINNING

Award-Winning
Roses

Rose lovers will have ready-made winners in the spacious rear garden of this delightful 2 bedroom frame cottage. Sunny, bright rooms. Minutes from downtown. Only $86,000. To see today, call Lori Beth at Clarke Realty, 555-7120.

Architectural Winner

Own a home that's been professionally recognized for the quality of its design. Built by Rogers & Kammer, this sought-after Boudine model features the "great room" concept, with a glass-walled garden, ceramic tile floors, unique rock fireplace & wonderfully efficient kitchen. 3 bedrooms, 2 baths, just $89,000. To see, call Jay at Clarke Realty, 555-7120.

Featured in
Gary Post Tribune

Perhaps you saw this snug 2 bedroom home & its marvelous garden in the local paper. Featured a few months ago, it's a delightful blend of color & light with flowers that bloom year-round. An open & airy loft spills light into the combination kitchen/living room. You'll love the spacious redwood-decked bath & convenient full-wall closets. At $98,000, this won't last. Call Margie at Clarke Realty, 555-7120, today.

Award-Winning
Energy Efficiency

in this special solar-heated home just 25 min. from the city. Save big on utility bills with triple-glazed windows, thick insulation, padded carpeting, heatilator fireplace. Enjoy efficiency in 3 bedroom, 2 bath comfort. Only $90,000. Call Leo at Clarke Realty, 555-7120, today.

A Prize-Winning Beauty

Architect Fred Jones won an award for this compact 2 bedroom, 2 bath contemporary that maximizes space while creating a light, airy feeling. High-tech accents, spiral staircase, glamorous glass-block walls. First class quality at just $87,000. To see this unique home today, call Jim at Clarke Realty, 555-7120.

CELEBRITY OWNED OR VISITED

Jimmy Carter
Slept Here

in the graciously appointed guest bedroom of this 4 bedroom farm-style rambler. Country buffs will love its charming decor, chair mouldings, great big brick hearth. 2 generously-sized baths & family-sized kitchen. Only $95,000. Take a look today. Call Tony at Clarke Realty, 555-7120.

Elizabeth Taylor's First
Hollywood Home

At the edge of Beverly Hills you'll find this charming 2 bedroom, 2-1/2 bath Spanish villa. Cradled on a hillside, it features French windows, gleaming hardwood floors, a bougainvillea-draped patio & a history other homes can't touch. For only $99,000. To see it today, call Richard at Clarke Realty, 555-7120.

Michael Jackson's
Boyhood Home

Where the legend began...in this sprawling 4 bedroom, 3 bath rambler in a quiet neighborhood. From its big sleeping porch to the roomy kitchen & terrific fenced yard, it's a home made for a growing family. Make it part of your family's legend today. For only $98,000. Call Jackson at Clarke Realty, 555-7120, to see it now.

> *AD TIP: Take your reader on a tour of the house, rather than just listing it's rooms or amenities.*

Share a Memory With Frank Sinatra

when you move into this solid 3 bedroom, 2 bath home owned by one of the singer's closest friends. He's shared many happy moments here & so can you. You'll love the rich, dark wood detailing ...wide front porch with a swing, stained glass accents throughout. A home made for memories. Priced at only $97,000. To see it today, call Linda at Clarke Realty, 555-7120.

Live in Iacocca Style

in the 4 bedroom, 3 bath white clapboard home where one of this country's top businessmen grew up. Enjoy long summer evenings on its shady front porch. Relax by the brick hearth's roaring fire. Arrange your library on its built-in bookcases. It's a home your family will love ...for only $99,000. Think of what you can tell your friends. Call Mimi at Clarke Realty, 555-7120, today.

Eddie Murphy's First House

We all have to start somewhere & Eddie's first house was this tasteful 3 bedroom, 2 bath traditional in a family neighborhood. Elegant touches like floor-to-ceiling French windows, stone veranda, gleaming oak floors. A home you'll be proud to own for $152,000. Call Fred at Clarke Realty, 555-7120, to see it today.

Vic Damone Lived Here

That's right. This tropical retreat just a few blocks from celebrity row was once owned by Vic Damone. Stunning vistas of sky & sea from every room of this 3 bedroom, 2 bath California contemporary. Small but grand...Just $150,000. To see it today, call Clarence at Clarke Realty, 555-7120.

AD TIP: After you've written your headline, body and close, check your ad. Does it grab your attention? Offer any benefits? Lead you to make an immediate response?

CHAPTER TWO

MID-RANGE HOMES

LOCATION

COUNTRY

Your Refuge
From the City

If you're tired of city hassles but love the convenience, come see this 3 bedroom, 2-1/2 bath on a heavily wooded lot just 25 min. from town. Features living room big enough for a grand piano, sunny & open country kitchen, sprawling bedrooms & 2 delightful baths. Over 2,500 luxurious sq. ft. Life at its finest for only $140,000. Call Ron at Action Realty, 555-6960, now.

A Forest
of Trees

Rustic 3 bedroom charmer of brick & stone with walls of windows to bring in the view. Cooks will love the extravagant kitchen. The family will adore the walnut-paneled den & 2 full baths. A quiet spot priced at just $135,000. Call Jim at Action Realty, 555-6960, today.

At the End of a
Country Road

sits an old-fashioned, yellow clapboard 4 bedroom home. Put a swing on the wide front porch...start a fire in the antique hearth...relax under the 100-year-old oaks. Thoughtfully updated on 1/2 acre all its own. All for only $125,000. To see it today, call Natasha at Action Realty, 555-6960.

An Acre
of Woods

cradles this old-style 3 bedroom, 2 bath charmer. Weathered barn siding, copper weathervane make it unique. Built just 5 years ago, it blends the finest of the old with the best of the new. If you're looking for a comfortable home with flair for less than $140,000, call Jim at Action Realty, 555-6960, today.

Country
Comfort

fills this gracious 3 bedroom 2-story traditional. Located just 20 min. from downtown, it's set on a gigantic, wooded lot. Country fans will love its cozy decor with custom wallcoverings, oak trim & whisper-soft carpets. 2 Victorian-style baths. Priced to sell at just $135,000. Call Ken at Action Realty, 555-6960, today.

Green Peace

If you enjoy peace & quiet, come home to this 2 bedroom rustic secluded in the woods 10 miles outside town. It offers natural wood floors, skylights, walls of windows & a patio that goes on forever. Only $125,000. Take a drive today. Call Mike at Action Realty, 555-6960.

> *AD TIP: Advertising can be expensive so make every word count.*

Forest
Atmosphere

Trees stretching to the sky, wildflowers, birds...all surround this rambling 3 bedroom Cape Cod. Conventional from the street, along the back run walls of glass. 2 baths, lots of upgrades. Only $145,000. To see a great home in a wonderful environment, call Ted at Action Realty, 555-6960, today.

A Home With
a History

Sprawling 2 bedroom, 2 bath cabin built with 1920's quality, thoughtfully modernized for 1990's living. You'll adore the rough plank floors, knotty pine cabinets, exposed-log ceilings. Character & quality for only $130,000. Take a look today. Call Kenneth at Action Realty, 555-6960.

Country Living
Without the Drive

It's hard to find—a spacious 3 bedroom home almost hidden in trees yet only minutes from town. With its brick walls, solid oak floors & double pane windows, this home will last forever. A tasteful home with 2 full baths for just $145,000. Call Vi at Action Realty, 555-6960, now.

A Winding
Stream

curves outside this delightful 2 bedroom, 2 bath country home. Enjoy its gentle murmur while you rest in front of the stone fireplace...putter in the vegetable garden...cook in the country kitchen. A pleasant home on 1/4 acre for only $135,000. To see it today, call Timothy at Action Realty, 555-6960.

Old-Fashioned
Family Homestead

Imagine putting up a Christmas tree in the high-ceilinged, wood wainscoted living room. Or roasting chestnuts in the giant rock hearth. Or making snowmen in your own woods. A 3 bedroom, 2 bath country homestead for only $150,000. To see it, call Carl at Action Realty, 555-6960.

Your Own Forest
of Maples

waits outside the back door of this 3 bedroom, 2 bath ranch. Its huge bay windows let you enjoy the autumn colors. The charming split rail fence lends a country feel. You'll appreciate all its city conveniences, too. Just 30 min. from town. Only $140,000. Call Kim at 555-6960, today.

Wooded
Hideaway

The retreat you've been waiting for—a dramatic 3 bedroom, 2-1/2 bath cedar contemporary set in a sunlit forest clearing. Soaring ceilings, classic lines, walls of windows. A quality home designed for those who appreciate the unique. 45 min. from the city. Only $145,000. Call Fred at Action Realty, 555-6960, today.

Bird Watcher's
Paradise

Get out the binoculars when you come to this 3 bedroom, 2 bath ranch on a private 1/4 acre mountainside lot. Enjoy the view from its many windows, outdoor patio, or from the master bedroom balcony. Made for indoor-outdoor living. Priced at just $144,000. To see it, call Marybeth at Action Realty, 555-6960.

Pine Cones & Chipmunks

are your closest neighbors in this wonderful 2 bedroom ranch. Country folks will love its rustic cedar siding, bright & sunny rooms, spacious redwood deck. 2 full baths, too. A home to hang your heart in for just $125,000. Call Tom at Action Realty, 555-6960.

WATERFRONT

Unspoiled Shoreline

just steps from this sprawling 3 bedroom, 1-3/4 bath home. Perfect for long walks at sunset, evening barbecues or just watching the waves. Sun-lovers will enjoy this home's bright & spacious rooms, shiny tile floors & huge brick patio. Lots of square footage for just $145,000. Call Ned at Action Realty, 555-6960, today.

10 Steps to Sand

from the front door of this charming 2 bedroom, 2 bath beach cottage. Surrounded by a white picket fence, it features a delightful breakfast nook, sun porch & hardwood floors. Ready-to-move-in price of $120,000. Call John at Action Realty, 555-6960, now.

Riverfront Sanctuary

You'll feel right at home in this tranquil 3 bedroom, 2 bath Southern beauty. From the luxurious carpeting to the columned porch & elegant French doors, it creates a lifestyle you'll love. Peace for just $135,000. Call George at Action Realty, 555-6960, to see it today.

By the Old Mill Stream

is an ancient stone house overflowing with yesterday's charm & today's conveniences. Open the balcony's double doors & watch the sun-sparkled ripples. Sit on the huge screened porch & hear the crickets chirp. With 3 bedrooms, 2 baths, thick trees, it's a custom delight. Only $150,000. Call Nancy at Action Realty, 555-6960, today.

Walden Pond

Thoreau would've loved this peaceful home...3 bedrooms, 2 baths on a pond where ducks swim & frogs play. Serenity abounds inside with spacious rooms, sunny eat-in kitchen, sprawling patio where you can enjoy nature's beauty. Priced at just $135,000. To see it today call Jimmy at Action Realty, 555-6960.

Watch the Ships

from the living room of this stunning lakefront home. Designed for low maintenance with 2 big bedrooms & 2 giant baths, it features open ceilings, Swedish fireplace, high-tech galley kitchen. Only $140,000. Call Hank at Action Realty, 555-6960, today.

Whitewater View

is yours from every room of this 3 bedroom house of glass. Let the waves lull you to sleep. Take a dip before breakfast. Come home to a spiral staircase, Italian tile floors, artist-designed fireplace. Life the way you've always wanted it to be for just $160,000. See it today. Call Leslie Anne at Action Realty, 555-6960.

Picture Yourself Living at the Ocean...

having coffee on the beach or taking a quick dip. You can in this cozy 2 bedroom, 1-1/2 bath beach cottage. Weathered siding, white trim, shingled roof... it's charming on the inside, too. Affordable beach living at only $135,000. Take the plunge today. Call Tom at Action Realty, 555-6960.

Steps to Surf & Sun

If you've always wanted to be a beach bum, do it in style. This glamorous 3 bedroom, 2 bath home offers sparkling tile floors, sheets of windows, 3 balconies. Loaded with upgrades. Convenient outside shower, too. Priced to move fast at $160,000. Call Hank at Action Realty, 555-6960, now.

Your Own Bass-Stocked Pond

comes with this elegant 3 bedroom, 2-1/2 bath traditional just 15 min. from the city. Enjoy the sporting life in sophistication & style. Brick walls, crown mouldings, graceful curving staircase. A great price at $165,000. To see it today, call Frank at Action Realty, 555-6960.

Fish in Your Own Backyard

Imagine the fun you'll have with a little lake just steps from your sprawling 3 bedroom, 2 bath ranch. Watch the kids play through the kitchen greenhouse window—or from the wide brick patio filled with flowers. You'll love the workshop/garage with room for lots of fishing poles! 2 baths, too. Great price of just $150,000. Call Mike at Action Realty, 555-6960, today.

Got a Boat?

Then dock it at the pier of this 3 bedroom, 2 bath California ranch. Perched on the lakeside, it gives you the feeling of the country close to the city. You'll enjoy its atrium, floor-to-ceiling windows, sophisticated white brick fireplace. Priced to sell at $140,000. Call Regina at Action Realty, 555-6960, to see it today.

Beach Charmer

You'll love the widow's walk on its second story...the windows that look out to the sea...the mellow wood that's relaxing & warm. A 2 bedroom, 2 bath home of charm & grace for only $135,000. See it today. Call Susan at Action Realty, 555-6960.

Lakefront Pad

Dramatic, sophisticated 1 or 2 bedroom home designed for the professional. High-tech accents, airy library loft, ceramic counters & baths. Steps from the pier. Only $150,000. Call Timothy at Action Realty, 555-6960.

Private Island Hideaway

Unique cedar-built island home with an open & cheerful floor plan. 3 bedrooms, 2 baths, almost hidden by towering trees & flowering shrubs. Thoughtful touches like garden tub, built-in bookcases, giant garage. Just $155,000. Call Nancy at Action Realty, 555-6960, now.

AD TIP: *Highlight benefits rather than features.*

HILL

Just a
Step Above...

Stunning 3 bedroom, custom-designed home high on a hill. Sunlight spills through its large windows, master bath features elegant Jacuzzi. Stained glass accents gigantic kitchen. Down-to-earth price of just $145,000. Drive up today. Call Ken at Action Realty, 555-6960.

Hillside Haven

2 bedroom, 2 bath contemporary with a backyard as big as your imagination & a view as big as all outdoors. You'll love the hammock on the redwood deck, airy kitchen with its comfortable breakfast bar, handmade stone fireplace. Realistic price of only $145,000. Call Virginia at Action Realty, 555-6960, today.

High in the
Hills

above the traffic & smog you'll find this secluded hideaway. A 3 bedroom, 2 bath cedar chalet that gives you time for the things you want to do. Lots of natural wood. Only $135,000. Call John at Action Realty, 555-6960, now.

A Hill for
Sledding

comes with this gorgeous 3 bedroom, 2 bath colonial set amid trees, above the city. Enjoy a wood-burning stove in the den, room for a vegetable garden, a kitchen that's perfect for baking. Your kids will love the winter fun. Priced at just $150,000. Call Ned at Action Realty, 555-6960, today. This won't last.

Head for
the Hills

Move up to a 3 bedroom, 2 bath home where you can watch the squirrels gather hickory nuts from your trees. See the sun set in all its splendor. Have plenty of space for the family to sprawl in comfort. A traditional style home, with 3 car garage, for only $143,000. To see it today, call Will at Action Realty, 555-6960.

Live Where You Belong—
at the Summit

It's the home you've worked so hard for. A hilltop showplace that shines with success. Features tiled pool with view to the sumptuous master suite, 4 bedrooms, 3 baths. Quality throughout. Listed at just $150,000. Move up in the world. Call Jim at Action Realty, 555-6960, today.

Peak
Performance

in this long & luscious 3 bedroom, 2 bath stunner set among rolling hills. Top-of-the-line appliances, high-grade brick & stone exterior. A home you'll appreciate for its beauty & value as well as comfort. Rock-bottom priced at $145,000. Call Victor at Action Realty, 555-6960, now.

At the Top
of the Hill

you'll find a top-quality home. 3 bedrooms, 3-1/2 baths, designed to blend with nature. Look out to your own trees & enjoy the warmth of a massive stone fireplace. Fix family meals in the large kitchen. Just 15 min. from town. To see it today, call Patrick at Action Realty, 555-6960.

No Smog Here

Enjoy fresh air above the smog in this delightful 2 bedroom, 1-3/4 bath hilltop home. You'll adore its intricate, Victorian-style trim, trellised patio, built-in dining room hutch. Cozy comfort with a terrific view for only $135,000. Don't let it slip away. Call Tim at Action Realty, 555-6960, today.

A Home in the Mountains

The home you've dreamt of. An old-fashioned Ponderosa-style ranch on a private road. Enjoy its wide & roomy front porch where you can watch the clouds & sky. 4 bedrooms, 2 baths & a style all your own for just $145,000. It's worth a 40 min. drive. Call Tommy Lee at Action Realty, 555-6960.

Be King of the Hill

in this majestic 3 bedroom, 2-1/2 bath home high in the hills skirting the city. Luxury appointments throughout, sizzling spa, gas fireplace, central air & Jenn-air range. Classy decor, too. Pauper-priced at $135,000. Call Jennifer at Action Realty, 555-6960.

The High Life

is yours in this sophisticated 2 bedroom, 2 bath home high above the city. Entertainers will adore the spacious living room with its chic white fireplace. For more relaxed gatherings, try the oak-paneled family room with its convenient wet bar—or the hot & bubbly spa on the redwood deck. A home to enjoy for only $144,000. Call Ted at Action Realty, 555-6960, to take a look today.

AD TIP: In your closing, try for an immediate response.

Above the Rat Race

Your mountain retreat far from the maddening crowd. A quiet, secluded 2 bedroom cedar in a forest glen. Only 25 min. from the city, it feels far removed. Natural wood floors, massive fireplace, tree-shaded patio where you can relax in peace. Priced at just $125,000. Make your escape today. Call Brian at Action Realty, 555-6960.

The World Below You, The Sky Above You

Enjoy feeling free in your own hillside home. Rambling 3 bedroom, 2-1/2 bath rustic with an engaging courtyard, skylights, generous veranda. Your nearest neighbor is an acre away. Watch the trees change with the seasons for only $160,000. To see it today, call Jean at Action Realty, 555-6960.

Sky-High Style

For the sophisticate who enjoys wide open spaces, a soaring 2 bedroom contemporary with gleaming white walls, colorful tile accents & rustic landscaping. Lots of sunlight & fresh air. High in the hills, only 15 min. from downtown. Just $130,000. Call Dennis at Action Realty, 555-6960, today.

DESERT

Sagebrush & Wildflowers

make a pretty setting for this delightful desert home. Stucco-built with long low lines, it features a Mexican tile patio, sliding glass doors & handmade adobe fireplace. 2 bedrooms, 2 full baths set on an acre of land. Just $125,000. See it today. Call Peter at Action Realty, 555-6960.

The Sky Goes
on Forever

from the sprawling veranda of this long & lean desert ranch. Watch the sunset pour through your wide windows & paint the living room in pastels. Enjoy the coolness of adobe, the splash of ceramic tile. 3 bedrooms, 2 baths, with a view you'll adore. Only $140,000. To take a look today, call John at Action Realty, 555-6960.

The Simple Life
—Desert Style

in this cool, easy-care home on a little hill that captures every breeze. 3 bedrooms, 2 baths, eat-in kitchen, 2 car garage, shaded patio. Landscaped by Nature herself. Yours for just $134,000. Call Mike at Action Realty, 555-6960, now.

A Desert Classic

Streamlined 2 bedroom, 1-3/4 bath home in harmony with nature. Walls of windows bring the outdoors in, while thick stucco walls & shiny tile floors keep you cool. Soothing inner courtyard with gentle fountain & flowers—the perfect place to breakfast. Priced at just $150,000. See it today. Call Roger at Action Realty, 555-6960.

Your Home in the Sun

Imagine cool whitewashed walls. A clay tile patio brimming with flowers. A master bedroom with French doors opening to a brick-walled spa. A kitchen any gourmet cook would love. 2 bedrooms, 2 full baths. Come home today. Just $123,000. Call Jonathan at Action Realty, 555-6960.

GOLF

Your Best Shot

Enjoy luxurious golf course living in this stunning 3 bedroom, 2-1/2 bath Spanish villa. Relax in high-ceiling splendor with glass doors open to the soothing view. A gracious & tasteful home with many upgrades, for only $145,000. Call Roger at Action Realty, 555-6960, today.

Fore!

Get ready to tee off when you live in this dreamy 2 bedroom, 2 bath home. You'll love its wide plantation shutters framing a soothing greenbelt view. Curl up in front of a crackling fire. Relax in the spa off the master bedroom. Quality you can't duplicate at the price. Only $143,000. Call Ken at Action Realty, 555-6960, today. Don't forget your clubs!

Life on the Green

the way you've always imagined it. In a gentle Williamsburg-inspired colonial skirting one of the town's most prestigious golf courses. 4 gracious bedrooms & 2 kid-sized baths. A kitchen you will love. Move-in price of $145,000. Call Vi at Action Realty, 555-6960, now.

Like to Golf?

Your golfing buddies will envy you in this splendid 3 bedroom, 2 bath home right on the green. Imagine living where every room looks out onto a greenbelt view. With imported wallcoverings, unusual limestone fireplace, 2 ceramic tile baths. Unbeatable location for $150,000. Call Jo at Action Realty, 555-6960, now.

Bring
Your Putter

when you move into this breathtaking 2 bedroom, 2 bath overlooking Everglades Country Club—one of the area's most elite golf courses. Built of redwood, stone & glass, it's free-flowing, open, sunny. Easy landscaping never needs mowing. Enjoy the good life for only $134,000. Call Brenda at Action Realty, 555-6960.

Is Golf Your Passion?

Then indulge it in this charming 2-story, 3 bedroom Dutch Colonial right on the greenbelt. Park your cart on its velvety rear lawn. Entertain in the unique pub-style family room. You'll love the 2 spacious baths, generous eat-in kitchen, ample closets. A home with class for under $160,000. Call Teddy at Action Realty, 555-6960, today.

Life That Fits You
to a Tee

in this stylish contemporary 2 bedroom. Golf whenever you like just outside your back door. Living is easy in this low-maintenance home which features floor-to-ceiling windows, exposed beams, professional landscaping. At an unbelievable price of just $139,000. Call Tom at Action Realty, 555-6960. Better hurry.

Championship Golf Course

borders this sumptuous 3 bedroom Georgian with a graceful curved staircase, chandeliered dining room, impressive crown moulding. 2-1/2 baths, too. A home you'll love & find very convenient. Just $147,000 gets you in the swing of it. Call Leslie Annabelle at Action Realty, 555-6960, now.

Overlooks 17th Fairway

You'll never tire of the view from this 2-story, 4 bedroom traditional where you can gaze at acres & acres of soothing green. Enjoy the view from your hand-built brick patio. Or while dining in the bay-windowed nook. Or as you watch a fire glow in your rosy brick fireplace. 2 full baths. Only $155,000. To see it, call Ted at Action Realty, 555-6960.

Country Club Living
for Only $140,000

It's the lifestyle you love but never thought you could afford. Almost new 3 bedroom, 2 bath home backing right on the golf course. You'll delight in details like an upstairs balcony, mirrored closets, rough-hewn cedar family room. All just seconds from the first tee. Priced for quick sale, so call Jim at Action Realty, 555-6960, today.

RECREATION/LEISURE

Hunt & Fish
in Shangri-la

A little piece of paradise, carved out of the woods just for you. With a rustic, A-frame log cabin with sunlit loft & gentle rippling pond just yards from your front door. 5 acres to hunt to your heart's delight. If you love the outdoors this house is a dream come true for just $125,000. Call Rick at Action Realty, 555-6960, today.

AD TIP: Use headlines that create self-interest and avoid ones that merely provoke curiosity.

Hunters' Hideaway

Secluded 2 bedroom, 2 bath cabin in the woods. At night, warm yourself by the wood-burning stove or turn on the efficient gas heat. See the stars in all their glory. A quiet spot for outdoor fun. Only $130,000. Call Gina at Action Realty, 555-6960, to see it today.

Wilderness Retreat

Snug 2 bedroom, 1 bath cottage deep in the mountains, beneath silvery birches & rustling oaks. A home where you can get away from it all. If you'd like a rustic life in a breathtaking setting, with just a few modern conveniences, call Jenny at Action Realty, 555-6960. Only $120,000 & it's yours.

Tennis, Anyone?

We're serving up a 3 bedroom, 2 bath home any tennis pro will love. Just steps from one of the city's finest clay courts— a secluded family retreat featuring stone walls, French windows & sparkling pool. Stables within walking distance. Only $160,000. If you have refined taste & a great backhand, call James at Action Realty, 555-6960, now.

Grab Your Racquet!

Move to a home where you can play to your heart's delight on your own tennis court. It's unusual to find such luxury in a reasonably priced home. But this 3 bedroom, 2-1/2 bath French-style charmer & court is just $155,000. To get in a few sets fast, call Timothy at Action Realty, 555-6960, today.

AD TIP: Your ad copy should sustain, not divert, the attention your headline succeeded in getting.

Built for Fun!

If you like golfing, tennis, boating & riding, this home was made for you. Set in a terrific recreation area, it's the perfect spot for sports-loving families. 4 bedrooms, 2 baths, with a garage big enough for toboggans, a fireplace where you can roast marshmallows, a yard with room for a horse. Only $165,000. To see this stunner today, call Fred at Action Realty, 555-6960.

A World of Fun Is at Your Doorstep

If you're an outdoor person, consider this 2 bedroom, 1-1/2 bath contemporary. With jogging trails behind the house, hiking trails nearby & a lake 10 min. away, it's a great location for sports-lovers. Priced for action at just $130,000, this prize won't last long. Call Jim at Action Realty, 555-6960, today.

Like to Water Ski?

Then move into a 2 bedroom ranch where the water is at your doorstep. You'll love its blend of convenience & charm, with a rock wall fireplace, cedar shingles, picture windows galore. Best of all, there's a dock where you can park your speedboat year-round. Fun in the sun for only $130,000. Call Henry at Action Realty, 555-6960, today.

Head for the Slopes

when the snow falls, get cozy in one of the area's most charming ski cabins. A gingerbread & knotty pine delight just 5 min. from the lifts. Spacious loft with room for friends plus 2 bedrooms, 2 full baths. Efficient gas furnace & handsome stone fireplace keep you toasty. Relax in style for just $115,000. Call Frank today at Action Realty, 555-6960.

Ski Chalet

Your family will love this dramatic A-frame with a wall of glass that lets you watch the snow fall. Stunning floor-to-ceiling stone fireplace to enjoy from the natural wood galley kitchen. With 3 bedrooms, 2 baths, there's no need to sacrifice privacy. Just minutes from the slopes. A hot deal for a cool season at just $129,000. Call Sam at Action Realty, 555-6960, now.

CONVENIENCE

Commuter Blues?

Find the cure in this charming 3 bedroom, 2 bath on a shady tree-lined street. You'd never guess offices, shops & schools are just around the corner. Carved wood trim & old-fashioned windows add a delicate touch. Updated kitchen & baths add modern flair. Character without the commute for just $140,000. To see it today, call James at Action Realty, 555-6960.

Traffic Got You Down?

Then enjoy the freedom of living just minutes from downtown in this 2 bedroom, 2 bath traditional. With its thick brick walls, upkeep is easy. You'll have plenty of time to prune the rose garden... watch a fire in the marble hearth...cook in the gourmet kitchen. Gracious, convenient living for only $135,000. Call Tim at Action Realty, 555-6960, today.

AD TIP: Don't cloud your ads with every detail about the listing. Concentrate on the major benefits a home buyer will achieve.

Move to Where the Action Is

just steps away from fine restaurants, museums, art galleries. Lovers of elegant living will appreciate the quality of this 3 bedroom, 2 bath home. Gleaming hardwood floors, French doors, walled garden, ceramic counters. A touch of class for only $140,000. See it today. Call Henry at Action Realty, 555-6960.

Want a Terrific School District?

Then you won't want to miss this handsome 3 bedroom, 2-1/2 bath colonial so close to the best schools your kids can walk. It's the kind of home you'll want to stay in a long, long time. Berber carpets, thermopane windows, Jenn-air range, lots of extras you'll love. 2 baths, too. Only $150,000. To see a great buy, call Tony at Action Realty, 555-6960, now.

5 Minutes From Mall

Shopping is easy when you live in this convenient 3 bedroom, 2 bath New Orleans-style home just blocks from the city's largest mall. Plenty of room to show off your goodies in the spacious, window-studded living room, comfortably-sized bedrooms or charming eat-in kitchen. Big yard, small price of $135,000. Call Ann at Action Realty, 555-6960.

Two Blocks From Medical Center

You'll love the easy lifestyle of this sunny Florida-style home with 2 huge bedrooms, 2 full baths. Natural landscaping for easy-care. Top-quality flooring, easy-to-reach oak cabinets. All you have to do is tend the plants in the sun-splashed atrium. 5 min. walk to Medical Center. Easy price of $127,000. To see it today, call Jo at Action Realty, 555-6960.

A Real Time-Saver

If you don't like to waste a minute, see this 3 bedroom, 2 bath contemporary close to offices, shops, restaurants. Packed with conveniences like gas fireplace, drip watering system, relaxing spa jetted tub. At only $143,000, this one won't waste time on the market. Call Ken at Action Realty, 555-6960, now.

Downtown Delight

Old-time Victorian charmer just 10 min. from city center. At night, sit on the spacious veranda & watch the twinkling skyscrapers. Or brew a pot of tea on the old-fashioned cast-iron stove. You'll love the sloping eaves of its 3 bedrooms, 2-1/2 baths. A convenient, character-filled home for just $139,000. Call Elizabeth at Action Realty, 555-6960, now.

Want a Good Education for your Children?

Then give them the best education in the city. Move into this sprawling 3 bedroom, 2 bath ranch in the superb Colima school district. Terrific basement playroom, fireplace-warmed den, cheerful eat-in kitchen. Fenced yard big enough for pool or playground. At $145,000, isn't your child's education worth it? Call Carol at Action Realty, 555-6960, to see it today.

Live Near the University

in this elegant 3 bedroom, 2 bath Georgian surrounded by a private hedge. You'll love the marble hearth in the bookcase-lined library. The classic kitchen, overlooking a sunken garden. Steps from concerts, lectures & classes. Only $150,000. To see this fine home today, call Veronica at Action Realty, 555-6960.

Park Your Car Here

& put away the keys. You won't need them in this 2 bedroom, 2-1/2 bath downtown stunner. Classic adobe lines with walls of windows, splashes of tile, wonderful garden. 2 car garage, too. Top location at bottom-level price of $134,000. Check it out today. Call Sam at Action Realty, 555-6960.

Come Home for Lunch

to a sprawling 3 bedroom, 2 bath ranch behind a split rail fence. It's hard to believe you can find country style so close to everything. You'll adore its sunny, skylit kitchen, private master suite. Living room with double doors that open to a luxuriously landscaped patio & yard. Only $142,000. If you'd like to spend more time at home, call Ned at Action Realty, 555-6960, today.

Watch the Ducks at the Park

Your kids will love living next door to Griffith Park. For fun, feed the ducks or visit the playground. You'll enjoy it, too. Because you'll be living in a spacious 3 bedroom, 2 bath home with every convenience you can imagine. Like a sun-drenched screened porch, 2 car workshop/garage, basement playroom/laundry. Only $152,000. Call Jim at Action Realty, 555-6960.

In the Heart of the City

you'll find a home that's tasteful & elegant. Classic 2 bedroom, 2 bath just off Main Street. Refined atmosphere created by full-length windows, gourmet kitchen, wrought iron balcony off master bedroom. Exquisite & convenient living for only $145,000. Stop by today. Call Barbara Ann at Action Realty, 555-6960.

Top-Rated Schools
Within Walking Distance

No need to worry about the kids' education when you move into this stunning 3 bedroom, 2-1/2 bath contemporary... you'll know they're getting the best. Your family can relax in the generous-sized den with its full-wall brick fireplace or chat with friends in the creamy pastel living room. Lowest price in neighborhood—only $143,500. Better hurry. Call James at Action Realty, 555-6960, today.

Live Near Swan Lake

You're just minutes from the ballet in this charming, traditionally styled 2 bedroom home. Shaded by a sweeping elm, it features a designer kitchen, gleaming hardwood floors, glass cabinets, 2 custom baths & 2,500 sq. ft. Upgrades throughout. Only $134,500. To see it today, call Henry at Action Realty, 555-6960.

Just Steps to Everything

If you're tired of driving, why do it? Live in this delightful 2 bedroom Victorian close to shops, schools, offices. You'll enjoy puttering in its wonderful brick-walled garden...relaxing in the sun-spattered living room...snoozing in the delicately-styled bedrooms. A rare Victorian jewel for just $123,000. Be good to yourself. Call Tom at Action Realty, 555-6960, today.

10 Minutes From Boeing

Come home to a genuine tree-shaded family neighborhood just a few blocks from work. Sprawling traditional home with room for everything. 4 bedrooms, 2-3/4 baths, wide front porch, eat-in kitchen, massive living room fireplace. Old-fashioned style at cut-rate price of $132,000. Call George at Action Realty, 555-6960, today.

A Choice Location

when you live in this 3 bedroom, 2 bath brownstone just minutes away from concerts, fine dining & boutiques. Or spend the evening at home, curling up in front of a flickering fire, watching the stars from your expansive redwood deck. A quality home in a terrific location for just $151,000. Call June at Action Realty, 555-6960, now.

Why Commute?

when you can have all the pleasures of country living right inside the city. Set on a 1/2 acre lot, this 3 bedroom ranch looks out to trees, bushes, squirrels. Just 5 min. from city hall. Lots of upgrades, too. To see it today, call Karl at Action Realty, 555-6960. Better hurry.

NEIGHBORHOOD

Small Town Charmer

With its lath plaster walls & hand-trowelled ceilings, this 2 bedroom, 2 bath beauty is vintage charm. Surrounded by a white picket fence, it offers the best in gracious living, combined with thoughtful updating. You'll love its gleaming sun porch, old-fashioned lush flower beds. Just $134,000. To see it today, call Pearl at Action Realty, 555-6960.

Take a Sunday Afternoon Stroll

through this charming neighborhood, with its white clapboard homes, spacious lawns, big trees. You'll enjoy life in this generous 5 bedroom Victorian. Sheltered by a 100-year-old oak, it offers 3-1/2 baths, mahogany-paneled den, stained glass living room accents. A great buy at $144,000. Call Ken at Action Realty, 555-6960, today. This won't last.

The Old Neighborhood

is getting spruced up & you can take advantage of it in this historic 3 bedroom, 2-1/2 bath brownstone. Special touches like marble floors, beveled glass, hand-crafted window seats make this a unique home. Priced at just $134,000. See it today. Call Jill at Action Realty, 555-6960.

A Prestige Address for Under $155,000

Desperate owner is willing to sacrifice gorgeous 4 bedroom, 3 bath home in best area. You'll love its huge sheets of glass, glamorous rock-walled terraces, impressive stone fireplace. Quality throughout. Priced at $153,950. Better hurry. Call Carl at Action Realty, 555-6960, today.

The Good Life

awaits you in this exclusive 3 bedroom, 2 bath home on a graceful residential circle. Begin the day in the sunny solarium-style breakfast room. Relax in the soothing spa off the master bedroom. Play with the kids on the expansive emerald lawn. Offered at just $152,000, this home is surrounded by higher-priced properties. To see it today, call Dean at Action Realty, 555-6960.

The Prettiest Street in Town

Sought-after 2 bedroom on charming street of restored Victorians. Its gingerbread trim, carved cabinets & trellised, rose-decked patio will steal your heart. A value at only $134,000. To see it today, call Rhonda at Action Realty, 555-6960.

AD TIP: Target your ads for the type of prospect you're seeking.

You'll Love This Address

& the price, too. Only $144,000 gives you a charming Spanish villa in the best part of town. 3 bedrooms & 2 baths, with white adobe walls, spotlights, colorful tile floors...reflections of your carefree lifestyle. To see it, call Sue at Action Realty, 555-6960.

Executive Family Neighborhood

The perfect spot to raise a family. Generous 3 bedroom, 2 bath ranch on 1/4 acre. Ceramic tile kitchen big enough for family feasts. Warm wood-paneled den great for evening fun. Just $159,000. Call Vivian at Action Realty, 555-6960, now.

A New England-Style Village

Live amid the splendor of the past in this friendly 3 bedroom, 2 bath Salt Box. Recreated with exciting architectural detail, it offers Karastan carpets, gleaming hardwoods. Only $155,000. Call Rich at Action Realty, 555-6960, today.

If You Treasure Tradition...

you'll enjoy living in this lovingly restored home, located on one of the city's most famous historical streets. White shutters, Wedgewood blue siding, diamond-paned windows. It's as pleasing to the eye as it is to the pocketbook. Only $145,000. To see this special home today, call Ron at Action Realty, 555-6960.

Young Family Neighborhood

Give your kids the childhood they deserve in this comfortable 3 bedroom, 2-1/2 bath traditional, with friendly neighbors, good schools, lots of playgrounds. You'll appreciate its ample closets, big family room, sunny & cheerful eat-in kitchen. Just $142,000. Call Edward at Action Realty, 555-6960.

A Friendly Lifestyle

is yours in this charming 2 bedroom, 1 bath cottage. Located in an established neighborhood of quality homes, it features an English garden, bay windows, brick patio & glowing hardwood trim. Only $131,000. Make new friends today. Call Samuel at Action Realty, 555-6960.

The Right Neighborhood at the Right Price

If you thought it would take years to move up to prestigious Gold Coast row, think again. This 3 bedroom Georgian manor is offered at just $153,000, far below market value. It's your chance to live in style...with an impressive, intricately carved fireplace; chandeliered dining room; manicured lawn. Call Joe at Action Realty, 555-6960. Make your move now.

An Elegant Address

is yours when you move into this stunning 3 bedroom, 2-story. Pass through its iron gate & gaze at the roses through the floor-to-ceiling French windows. Enjoy the gleaming ceramic-tiled gourmet kitchen. A home that will make you the envy of your friends for only $139,000. Call Jean at Action Realty, 555-6960, today.

Longing to Live on Lake Shore Drive?

Then do it in this affordable yet superbly crafted 3 bedroom, 2-1/2 bath home. Hard to believe its quality touches: criss-crossed beamed ceilings, antique crystal fixtures, beveled mirrors. At $162,000 it's sure to move fast. Call Lennie at Action Realty, 555-6960, today.

Prestigious Moore Creek Only $152,000

In a neighborhood of higher priced homes, this 4 bedroom, 2-1/2 bath Dutch Colonial is a bargain. You'll enjoy its huge sleek lawn perfect for croquet. The stunning living room, with a tile fireplace designed by an artist. The posh master bedroom, with its cozy sitting area & secluded spa. Better move fast. Call Ken at Action Realty, 555-6960, now.

Detroit's Finest Neighborhood

The home you've been waiting for at a price you can afford. Just $154,000 gives you an exclusive address & a 3 bedroom, 2 bath home loaded with special features. Whirlpool tub, trash compactor, automatic sprinklers, gas barbecue. Live in style now. Call Frank at Action Realty, 555-6960.

Exclusive Artistic Community

If you enjoy an ambiance of creativity & comfort, see this darling 2 bedroom, 1-1/2 bath home. Entered through a private, flower-filled courtyard, it features Italian tile floors, hand-painted murals, classic French doors. A special spot for just $144,000. Call Geraldine at Action Realty, 555-6960, today.

Cove Island Road —$140,000

Live on a gently curving road lined with stately homes, for an unbelievable price. You'll adore this home's 3 big bedrooms, 2 custom baths, family-sized kitchen, warm & cozy den. No reason to wait. Call Brenda at Action Realty, 555-6960, to see this great value today.

Live With the Elite

on prestigious Mulhouse Row. For just $145,000 you can own a charming French Normandy home, with 3 generously-sized bedrooms & 2 full baths. Set on a sweeping lawn, it features top-of-the-line appliances, secluded brick patio, 3 car garage. Call Fred at Action Realty, 555-6960. Do it now.

PRIVACY

Secluded Splendor

Enter a different world through the double doors of this Oriental-style home. Built around a Japanese garden, it offers 3 bedrooms, 2 baths, sliding walls of glass, unique stone fireplace, cheerful tile kitchen. Over 2,500 sq. ft. of opulence for just $165,000. To see this special property, call Ted at Action Realty, 555-6960, now.

Love Nest

Snuggle up next to a crackling fire in this charming 2 bedroom, 2 bath home. You'll adore its warm rosy red bricks, lush brass fixtures, hand-painted tile accents. Perched on its own little hill just 5 miles from town, it overlooks romantic city lights. Only $143,000. Call Carl at Action Realty, 555-6960, today.

Your Private Haven

Elite home with 4 bedrooms, 2-3/4 baths in a secluded setting. Room for kids, horses, dogs. Lavish stone floors, St. Charles kitchen, Dutch tile fireplace. Magnificent bookcase-lined study. All for just $157,000. Call Jim at Action Realty, 555-6960, now.

Escape to Comfort

in this posh 3 bedroom, 2 bath home amid rolling sand dunes. Your family will love its warm woods, expansive windows, picture-perfect view. Plenty of room to spread out with 3,000 sq. ft. & a yard that goes on forever. Make it yours today for just $161,000. Call Tina at Action Realty, 555-6960.

A Family Haven

This 4 bedroom, 2 bath on its own acre has something for everyone. Over 2,800 sq. ft. with private rooms for teenagers. Playground for toddlers. Kitchen with counter space galore. Huge garage/workshop. Your kids can grow up with horses, gardens, the real joys of life. Great buy at $155,000. Call Jon at Action Realty, 555-6960, today.

Hidden in the Hills

you'll find this redwood & stone 3 bedroom, 2 bath 2,400 sq. ft. home with breathtaking views. Floor-to-ceiling windows in almost every room, hand-hewn fireplace, Maytag appliances, walk-in closets & pantry. See it today. Only $145,000. Call Roger at Action Realty, 555-6960.

Rustic Retreat

This 3 bedroom, 3 bath beauty is a delight. With exposed-beam ceilings, wall-to-wall stone fireplace, terra-cotta tiles, a rich blend of wood & glass. Spectacular scenery, too. Just $152,000. If you're looking for something different, call Eddie at Action Realty, 555-6960, now.

AD TIP: Read other classified ads — especially those from top producers.

Make This Home
Your Haven

It's the perfect place to unwind. 3 big bedrooms, 2 luxury baths, a bubbling spa on a private patio. You'll love its attractive cedar shingles, gabled roof, charming country decor. Only 10 min. from town. Just reduced to $133,600. Call Frank at Action Realty, 555-6960, today.

3 Acres of
Privacy & View

For those with independent spirits...a home with room for everything that makes you different. Artist-designed & decorated, with unusual stonework, walls of windows, all the latest conveniences. Lots of fresh air & sunshine, too. Only $157,000. For a one of a kind home, call Fred at Action Realty, 555-6960, now.

If You Like
Privacy...

you'll relish this 4 bedroom, 2 bath, 2,100 sq. ft. French country home, just 10 min. from downtown. Set far back from the street, it overlooks its own wooded ravine. Plaster walls, bleached floors, custom cabinets. Only $162,000. To make it yours, call Judy at Action Realty, 555-6960, today.

Get Away
From It All

in this dramatic 3 bedroom, 2 bath contemporary with white walls, pastel trim, gleaming hardwood floors. It's a city-style refuge, just 5 min. from the freeway. You'll adore its sky-high ceilings, tasteful design, luxurious kitchen, secluded setting. Just $157,000. See it today. Call Veronica at Action Realty, 555-6960.

Hard to Find,
But Worth a Look

Marvelous home, screened by trees, on an elegant street. Charming wrought iron balconies, French windows, a brick veranda where a gentle fountain plays. 3 bedrooms, 2 baths...all spacious & exquisitely decorated. Make it your private retreat for only $160,000. Call Ken at Action Realty, 555-6960, today.

Come Inside...
You'll Be Surprised

when you see this 4 bedroom, 2 bath ranch built around one of the prettiest courtyards you'll ever find. Tons of brick, stonework, plants galore. Enjoy spacious rooms, ample closets, a kitchen awash in skylights. A very special home for just $170,000. Call Mary Ellen at Action Realty, 555-6960. Better hurry.

Hillside Haven

Very private 2 bedroom, 2 bath home reached by a long, tree-shaded drive. Invisible from the street, it looks out to a panoramic city view. Elegant brick floors, marble countertops, hand-hewn hearth. Hot spa bubbles on secluded patio. Unique opportunity for the right person. Only $155,000. To see it today, call Henry at Action Realty, 555-6960.

Independence at Last

Finally a home where you have room to breathe. With 2 acres of trees that all belong to you. Enjoy crackling fires in one of two huge stone fireplaces. Cook in the designer kitchen. You'll love this 3 bedroom, 2 bath beauty, with all the space you need to be yourself. Great value at just $167,000. Call Ken at Action Realty, 555-6960, now.

SAFETY & SECURITY

Estate-Like Walls

surround this miniature mansion tucked away in the city. Georgian columns, brick walks, French doors. 3 bedrooms, 2 baths. Enjoy high-ceiling splendor with a marble hearth & huge kitchen. Only $150,000. Call Tim at Action Realty, 555-6960, today.

Through Iron Gates

enter this private guarded community where you can live with peace of mind. Splashy 2 bedroom California contemporary, accented by cool pastels, tile fireplace, flower-filled veranda where you can putter to your heart's delight. Easy living at easy price of $140,000. Call Hank at Action Realty, 555-6960, today.

Snug & Secure

That's how you'll feel in this friendly 3 bedroom Cape Cod located in an exclusive, guarded community. Charm abounds with its copper kitchen, 2 ceramic baths, handsome brick fireplace. On large, lovely lot with willow trees & small stream. Bargain priced at just $155,000. Call Deena at Action Realty, 555-6960, now.

Limited to a Few

Enjoy utter peace of mind in this sunny 2 bedroom stucco villa, situated in a carefully planned & guarded community. Surrounded by rolling hills, this home is built around a delightful inner courtyard with trees, flowers & birds. Lovely red tile roof & blue shutters. Just $143,000. For security & style, call Jonathan at Action Realty, 555-6960, today.

By Invitation Only

Not everyone gets to visit Hidden Hills & even fewer have the opportunity to live here. Behind its gates you'll find this romantic hacienda, with 3 bedrooms, 2 baths. You'll adore its rich woods, jewel-like stained glass, soothing tile floors. Plenty of room. Live in utter security for only $167,000. Call Mike at Action Realty, 555-6960, now.

VIEW

On a Clear Day

you can see the entire valley from the stunning wraparound deck of this 3 bedroom, 2 bath contemporary. High on a hillside, its walls of windows catch the sun making the creamy pastel decorator touches sparkle. Free-flowing design with cheerful eat-in kitchen, private spa, huge family room. Just $147,000. To see the view today, call Jim at Action Realty, 555-6960.

Enjoy Spectacular Sunsets

from the bougainvillea-draped tile patio of this secluded Spanish charmer. Almost hidden by tall trees & flower-studded bushes, it blends old-world style with contemporary convenience. 3 big bedrooms, 2 full baths, a brass hearth you'll adore. Only $145,000. Stop by for today's sunset. Call Ted at Action Realty, 555-6960, now.

AD TIP: Avoid words that people don't use. Not everyone is William F. Buckley.

Picture-Perfect
View

Soft clouds, sparkling blue sea, colorful boats. Enjoy the view from this hillside Italian villa with 2 bedrooms, 2 baths. Overflowing with charm, from the floor-to-ceiling windows to its own miniature tower. A home you'll love with a price-less view for just $137,000. Call Tim at Action Realty, 555-6960, to take a look today.

Carpet of
City Lights

beneath this stunning 3 bedroom, 2-1/2 bath contemporary high in the hills of Buckhead. You'll enjoy its ever-changing & fascinating view through expansive windows. You'll also enjoy a luxury-sized living room, spacious redwood deck, sleek black & white kitchen. The home of your dreams for only $154,000. Don't miss it. Call John at Action Realty, 555-6960, now.

Overlook
the Park

from the spacious balcony of this old-world home. Rich mahogany woods, French windows, polished brass accents. 3 bedrooms, 2 baths—all generously sized. Best of all, everywhere you look there's a soothing view of trees & flowers. Enjoy it for only $150,000. Call Jim at Action Realty, 555-6960, today.

Count the
Stars

from the spacious patio of this sprawling 3 bedroom ranch. Bright & sunny kitchen, 2 artfully designed baths, stone walls in family room. A comfortable home with a touch of luxury—for just $149,000. Call Victor at Action Realty, 555-6960, now.

180-Degree
View

is yours in this dramatic 2 bedroom, 1-3/4 bath contemporary. Nestled high above the city, it looks out to the sea. Enjoy spectacular sunsets while dining in the tile kitchen. Or relaxing next to its oversize brick fireplace. Or lounging in the hot spa on the cedar deck. A 1,600 sq. ft. home you'll adore, with a view to the horizon, for only $152,000. Call Denise at Action Realty, 555-6960.

This View
Is It!

Stunning panorama of city lights twinkles beneath this 3 bedroom cedar home, just 20 min. from town. Rustic log interior, unusual stone fireplace, huge rumpus room, 2 baths. Enjoy the view from either of 2 decks. For the feel of outdoor living at just $147,000, call Ken at Action Realty, 555-6960, now.

A View That Goes
on Forever!

from this distinctive 3 bedroom, 2 bath white brick that overlooks the entire valley. Its never-ending patio is great for entertaining. So is its secluded, sizzling spa. Contemporary styling with unusual flair for only $156,000. Call George at Action Realty, 555-6960, today. Better hurry.

Unspoiled
View

from this rustic 3 bedroom log home just 10 miles from the city. On a small knoll, it looks out for miles. Lots of stone, brick, fine woods. All the latest conveniences, too. Only $157,000. To see its beauty, call Kenneth at Action Realty, 555-6960, now. Won't last long.

Spectacular
Point of View

Jutting out of a mountainside, you'll find this 3 bedroom home. Wide windows let you see for miles from every room. Free-flowing floor plan, with spacious rooms, 2 baths, quality materials. Yours for just $155,500. A forever view that's sure to sell quickly. Call Lennie at Action Realty, 555-6960, today.

Your House
of Glass

You needn't worry about anyone throwing stones. This long & rambling 4 bedroom, 2-1/2 bath contemporary is secluded on almost an acre of woods. Enjoy the incredible view from the leafy patio, bay-window dining nook, or sunlit, brick-floored living room. A bargain at only $154,000. To see it today, call Danny at Action Realty, 555-6960.

Panoramic View
Just $140,000

At last, an affordable house with a priceless view, just min. from downtown. You'll love this home's easy comfort with 3 big bedrooms, 2 full baths, cheerful eat-in kitchen, warm wood-paneled den. Almost every room has a view. Yours for only $137,500. Call Ken at Action Realty, 555-6960, today.

Scenic
Splendor

surrounds this cheerful 4 bedroom, only 30 min. from downtown. You'll adore its towering cactuses, giant rocks, terrific sunsets. Plus a warm & inviting house that offers a huge family room & spacious kitchen. See it today. Only $138,000. Call Kim at Action Realty, 555-6960.

Above the
Lights

sits a rambling 3 bedroom with expansive windows, 2 patios & a delightful view. At sunset, watch the lights sparkle beneath your feet. In the morning, see the sun's rosy glow. Enjoy whisper-soft carpeting, hardwood floors, the seclusion of a master bedroom suite. Can you believe just $144,000? Call John at Action Realty, 555-6960, now.

AD TIP: After you've written your ad copy, do what the reporters do and start cutting out excess words.

SIZE

STARTER HOMES

Start in Style

If you're looking for your first home, consider this stylish 2 bedroom contemporary. With vaulted ceilings, natural wood beams, skylights, sinfully luxurious bath. Convenient to everything. Easy to own price of just $123,000. FHA or VA financing available. To see it today, call Will at Action Realty, 555-6960.

Dream Home

Only a few miles from downtown but it feels worlds apart. Come home to indulgence. From the soothing spa off the master bedroom to the walls of glass that bring in city lights, this sophisticated, 3-level home is waiting for someone special. High-tech kitchen, top-of-the-line appliances, and quality throughout. Only $135,000. Call Bill at Action Realty, 555-6960, to see it today.

Charming First Home

Delightful 2 bedroom cottage behind white picket fence. You'll fall in love with its intricate Victorian trim, sun-drenched lattice porch, mellow pine cabinets. Bring your wicker furniture & wind chimes. This home is priced to sell at just $126,000. Call June at Action Realty, 555-6960, for a look.

A Home You'll Be Proud to Own

On a winding street, you'll find this wonderful 3 bedroom traditional. Solid brick walls, graciously-sized rooms, 2 full baths, ready for a growing family. Terrific school district, too. Make your first home one you'll want to keep. At $128,000, it's certainly worth a look. Call Lenny at Action Realty, 555-6960, today.

Start Off Right

in a 2 bedroom, 2 bath contemporary you'll love to live in. A home for the '90s with its slick mosaic tile & patterned brick patio. Enjoy open & airy rooms, arched windows, plant shelves & 2 car garage. Just $129,000. To see it today, call Betty at Action Realty, 555-6960.

Just Right!

Comfortable 2 bedroom home with tender touches like gingerbread trim, sunny screened porch, fabulous garden. Generously-sized rooms make it easy to arrange furniture, while there's plenty of space for all your knickknacks. Light & bright, priced at only $130,000. Call Roger at Action Realty, 555-6960, today.

AD TIP: Try to paint a vivid portrayal of the home you're advertising. This will inspire your prospects to call.

A Classy Way to Start

You'll fall in love with this dramatic 2 bedroom, 2 bath home minutes from downtown. From its spiral staircase to the window-lit loft to the sleek modern cabinets, it's packed with sophistication. Pastel accents show off the latest looks to perfection. Terrific value at $129,000. To check it out today, call Carl at Action Realty, 555-6960.

Honeymoon Delight

You'll never want the honeymoon to end in this charming 2 bedroom cottage. Sitting beneath a canopy of trees, this delightful home features gleaming hardwood floors, glass cabinets, antique mantel, quaint window seats & a relaxing spa on a quiet brick patio. Sweetheart price of $128,000. Take a peek today. Call Geena at Action Realty, 555-6960.

If You're Ready to Retire...

consider this easy-care 3 bedroom home in one of the area's finest neighborhoods. With big rooms & 2 baths, you can always welcome guests. They'll love the big stone patio. You'll love the convenient kitchen, separate laundry, workshop/garage. Bargain-priced at $130,000. See it today. Call James at Action Realty, 555-6960.

Have the Kids Moved Out?

If you're looking for a smaller home, see this quality-packed 2 bedroom. Designed for worry-free living, it features the finest appliances, plus all the upgrades you can imagine. Enjoy walls of windows, plant shelves, cozy dining nook & snuggle-up fireplace for just $132,000. 5 min. to Medical Center. Call Kenneth at Action Realty, 555-6960, today.

4+ BEDROOMS

Give Each Kid Their Own Room

Space won't be a problem in this rambling 4 bedroom colonial. 3 baths make mornings easy while giant eat-in kitchen, sprawling walnut-paneled den & expansive sloping lot are great for family fun. 3,400 sq. ft. house for little price of $145,000. To see it today, call Jim at Action Realty, 555-6960.

Need 4 Bedrooms?

Then live in this charming French home just 2 miles from downtown. From the delicately latticed windows to the rolled roof & bleached floors, it radiates refined style. 3 baths, too. Take a look today. Call Ned at Action Realty, 555-6960.

4 Bedroom Traditional

Perfect family home—big red brick with white shutters, sitting proudly on top a hill. Your kids will play happily on its huge lawn, while you'll be thankful for the cheerful eat-in kitchen, terrific den, 2 baths & lots of closet space. Great schools within walking distance. At $152,000, won't last long. Call Betty at Action Realty, 555-6960, today.

4 Bedrooms —$150,000

The home you've been waiting for at a price you can afford. 3 teen-sized bedrooms plus secluded master suite with retreat. Features top-quality carpets, new paint, backyard playground & warm, cozy fireplace in a den you'll all adore. Call Ted at Action Realty, 555-6960, to see it today. Bring the kids!

4 Big
Bedrooms

Give your kids the privacy they deserve in a home you'll love. With classic kitchen perfect for family meals, mellow wood-paneled den & study nook overlooking the tree-filled yard. 2 spacious baths, 3 car garage (over 1,900 sq. ft.). A home you'll cherish for only $155,000. Stop by today. Call Ruth at Action Realty, 555-6960.

Large Family?

Then you'll really appreciate the space of this sparkling 5 bedroom California Craftsman. Plenty of nooks & crannies, big basement, attic...not to mention the sunny eat-in kitchen & a living room that goes on forever. Can you believe just $157,000? To see this unique home, call Ken at Action Realty, 555-6960, now.

Lots of Kids?

Then come to a home made with kids in mind. Sprawling 3 bedroom, 2-1/2 bath ranch on its own 1/4 acre, just 10 min. from town. Big yard, large rooms, top-quality flooring, mellow hardwoods, French windows, closet space galore. Only $160,000. You won't want to miss it. Call Nick at Action Realty, 555-6960, today.

Need a
Separate Floor?

If you're longing for privacy, see this 4 bedroom colonial nestled on a cul-de-sac. Lower level master suite features sitting area & fireplace. Other bedrooms upstairs. Thoughtful touches like ceramic countertops, copper accents, gorgeous gray barn siding. A beauty for just $149,500. Call Lennie at Action Realty, 555-6960, today.

Brady Bunch
Home

Give the whole family a present with this delightful 5 bedroom traditional home under an awning of trees. White brick with blue shutters, a patio knee-deep in flowers. For the kids, bedrooms big enough to play in, above-ground pool & garage to hold all their bikes. Just $165,000. Bring the kids today. Call Elizabeth at Action Realty, 555-6960.

For Your Family

A 4 bedroom home in one of the finest areas. Enjoy the luxury of 3 ceramic tile baths. Relax in the warm, walnut-paneled den with its rosy brick fireplace. Chat with your neighbors from the rocking chair front porch. A traditional home with flair—for only $159,500. Visit today. Call Henry at Action Realty, 555-6960.

The Home
Your Family Deserves

Rambling 4 bedroom, 2 bath ranch with lots of room. Copper kettle kitchen, gleaming hardwoods, polished oak floors, glass-front fireplace make it warm & intimate. Circled by leafy trees. Pretty as a picture for just $162,500. Check it out today. Call Debbie at Action Realty, 555-6960.

Perfect for
the Large Family

Texas-sized 5 bedroom home on quiet street. Steps to terrific schools. You'll love its open & airy feeling, with a "great room" trimmed in mahogany, cheerful kitchen, sun-drenched eating area, 3 full baths. 3,500 sq. ft. Great deal at just $158,000. To see this spacious home today, call Henrietta at Action Realty, 555-6960.

For the Growing Family

4 bedroom traditional with a nursery next to the master bedroom. Your kids will love their bright, open rooms with extras like window boxes & walk-in closets. You'll enjoy the living area with its whisper-soft carpets & French windows. Fenced yard & 2 baths, too. See it today. Call Leena at Action Realty, 555-6960.

More Than 3 Kids?

Then move into a home with elbowroom. A 5 bedroom stunner with sweeping veranda. Gracious pillars mark the entrance while the generous living room opens to a brick patio. Family-sized kitchen, beamed dining room. A home with a heart (& 3 baths) for just $167,000. Make it yours today. Call Jim at Action Realty, 555-6960.

Give Your Kids What They Deserve

In this sprawling 4 bedroom patio home, each of your children can enjoy an airy, bright bedroom with ample closets & plenty of space for studying. Downstairs you'll enjoy the living room's walls of windows & charming fireplace. Generously-sized kitchen, 2 baths. A lot of house for $159,000. Call Ned at Action Realty, 555-6960, today.

AD TIP: Don't ruin your ad by using too many abbreviations. Studies have shown that too many abbreviations confuse readers.

LOTS OF EXTRA SPACE

Need Room for Relatives?

Then move into a home where you can live in peace. Generous 4 bedroom, 3 bath colonial in an established neighborhood. Guests will have their own entrance & bath. You can bake plenty of pies in the country kitchen then munch them on the spacious brick patio. The upgrades will delight you. A home to love for just $157,000. Call Joseph at Action Realty, 555-6960, today.

Room for Two Families

Everyone will love this generous contemporary, with 2 full-sized master suites & 4 other bedrooms. Relax in the soaring living room, with windows stretching up to the sky. Or gather around the dramatic copper fireplace. Brick walls, terra-cotta floors, 3 baths. A home to share for just $189,000. Call Joseph at Action Realty, 555-6960, now.

Square Footage Galore

You won't believe the room inside this 4 bedroom, 2-1/2 bath home—over 4,000 sq. ft. From the 2-story living room to the charming eat-in kitchen, it feels airy & bright. Spacious bedrooms in their own wing. Plus 30' x 15' outdoor patio, with abundant brick planters. You can finish the basement, too. Only $155,000. Call Jack at Action Realty, 555-6960, today.

Texas-Sized
Ranch Home

Come see this sprawling 4 bedroom ranch. From the cedar shingles to the white wood trim, it's straight out of a picture book. Tasteful touches like stone walls, island kitchen, walk-in closets, 3 full baths. For $187,000, it is hard to believe. Call Kenneth at Action Realty, 555-6960, today.

Great House to
Share With Relative

You couldn't ask for anything more...4 bedrooms, 3 baths, downstairs suite perfect for relative. Plenty of sunshine & fresh air throughout. Your kids will love the giant fenced yard overlooked by the kitchen's tall windows. Fireplace, den, loads of upgrades. Just $187,000. Call Kim at Action Realty, 555-6960, now.

Inner Space

This is it, a charming 3 bedroom, 2 bath home that stretches on forever. With arched doorways, walls of glass, vaulted ceilings, you'll never feel cramped. Artfully designed outdoor living room, too. Special house for just $156,000. Call Fred at Action Realty, 555-6960, today.

Room to
Roam

You'll never feel cramped in this marvelous 3 bedroom, 2 bath home with over 2,000 sq. ft. Enjoy sun-splashed meals in the delightful ceramic kitchen. Relax by the lofty stone fireplace. Snooze in the hammock under the giant birch tree. Texas-sized home for only $157,000. To see it today, call Ken at Action Realty, 555-6960.

To Each
His Own...

Imagine the kids' delight when each has his own room in this 4 bedroom, 2 bath stunner. You'll love the free-flowing contemporary design, easy-care tile kitchen, giant garage/workshop. Huge yard perfect for family ball games. A home you'll want to stay in forever. Only $149,000. Call Mike at Action Realty, 555-6960, today. This won't last.

10 Rooms
—Count 'em

It's true...10 wonderful rooms for you to do with as you please. Nestled on estate-like grounds just 20 min. from town, this gracious home shows a few signs of age, but for only $165,000...it's a bargain. Victorian-style trim, charming porch draped in flowers, 2 sunny bay windows, 3 baths. Call Ted at Action Realty, 555-6960, now.

ROOM TO GROW

Explore the
Possibilities

in this delightful cedar-sided home, secluded in a forest glen. Now with 2 bedrooms, it's easy to expand to 4. In the meantime, enjoy majestic stone fireplace, natural beams, shiny hardwood floors, kitchen greenhouse window. Charming home, with much potential. Rock-bottom priced at $147,000. To see it today, call Nell at Action Realty, 555-6960.

AD TIP: *Write fast and edit later.*

Something to Grow On

Hidden by trees, this 2 bedroom, 2 bath home sits in a spectacular natural setting. Although it needs some work, you'll adore the flagstone patio, knotty pine cabinets, floor-to-ceiling windows. Room to expand, too. At $134,000, it's ideal for someone with vision & creativity. If that's you, call Joel at Action Realty, 555-6960, today.

Looking to a Larger Home Someday?

Then start here in a cozy 2 bedroom, 2 bath cottage on a 1/4 acre lot. Solidly built of brick, its free-flowing floor plan makes expanding easy. Special touches like marble hearth, glass cabinets, hardwood floors. A delightful home for just $137,000. Call Ruth at Action Realty, 555-6960, now.

A Property You'll Appreciate

In it's heyday, this 2 bedroom, 2 bath beauty was a gem. Now it needs a little work. But when you're done, you'll have a spectacular home. Built of cedar, with generous glass & stone, it offers 2 decks, an atrium & oak kitchen cabinets. And plans for another 2 bedrooms & bath. Only $131,000. To see it, call Neil at Action Realty, 555-6960.

Thinking of Expanding in the Future?

Then make a smart move to a home where you can live in comfort—now. Charming 2 bedroom traditional in an exclusive area, with a delightful stream running through the yard. You'll love its huge screened porch, arched doorways, plaster walls. On 1/4 acre of trees, birds & flowers...plenty of room for later expansion. Only $132, 000. Call Ken at Action Realty, 555-6960, today.

PRICE/TERMS

FIXER-UPPER

Are You Handy
Around the House?

Make money with your talent in this sadly neglected, but charming 2 bedroom cottage. A little fixing & you'll have a gem, with a country garden, etched glass cabinets, hardwood floors. On its own acre. $145,000. Call Tod at Action Realty, 555-6960.

Fix &
Finish

Someone with vision will snap this up: 2 bedroom cedar cottage, with picture windows, 3 sets of French doors, rosy brick fireplace, solid oak cabinets. Attractive rock-terraced yard. Only $120,000. Better hurry. Call Art at Action Realty, 555-6960, now.

What a Fixer!

It's an opportunity you seldom see. Rambling 3 bedroom, 2 bath fixer. Set on a rock-studded hillside, it offers almost 2,000 sq. ft. of living area...but needs finishing. Gorgeous stone fireplace, solid cherry cabinets, sturdy stockade fence. Only $142,000. See the possibilities for yourself. Call Terry at Action Realty, 555-6960, today.

Fix It Up for
Little Down

Desperate owner wants out of 2 bedroom Spanish villa. Make his loss your gain. Solid stucco construction, spacious floor plan, sadly neglected interior. But at night, you can gaze down on a sea of city lights. Lovely terraced yard. Full price of just $121,000. FHA/VA. Better hurry. Call Tom at Action Realty, 555-6960, now.

Your
Fixer-Upper

3 bedroom, 2 bath home packed with possibilities. From the glass-walled sun porch to the double fireplace—the maple kitchen to the quaint dormer bedrooms. Charm galore, but needs touching up. Yours for just $123,000. See it today. Call Rich at Action Realty, 555-6960.

Fixer With a
View

You'll see the possibilities immediately—white clapboard, shingled roof, wide eaves shading a spacious porch. 3 bedrooms, 2 baths, set on a bluff overlooking the sea. A peaceful place you can take your time fixing up. All the basics work. Just $135,000. If you want a priceless view, call Tim at Action Realty, 555-6960.

Want a
Great Fixer?

Then see a home with a heart. Roomy 3 bedroom, 2 bath traditional only minutes from downtown. You'll love its glowing mahogany moulding, unusual fireplace, beveled lights. An elegant home, fading from lack of care. Yours for just $133,000. Call Roger at Action Realty, 555-6960, today.

Bring Your
Toolbox!

You'll need it in this 2 bedroom rustic next to a bubbling brook. Lots to do, but imagine waking up to the sun streaming through the trees. Breakfasting on a rock terrace all your own. Watching the sunset through lattices that create an outdoor living room. Surrounded by forest, yet close to town. Only $123,000. Call Judy at Action Realty, 555-6960, today.

Neglected
Victorian

This delicate downtown charmer is waiting for attention. Traces of past grandeur in its wrought iron gate, brick walled garden, beveled glass accents. 3 graciously-sized bedrooms, 2 generous baths. Much work to be done. But just $125,000. Bring back the elegant past today. Call Lee at Action Realty, 555-6960.

Run-Down
Ranch

set in rock-strewn cactus country 6 miles outside town. A bargain at just $134,000 & you get almost 3,000 sq. ft. Massive stone fireplace, kitchen that'll feed an army, living room with heavy oak beams. 3 bedrooms, 2 baths. To see it today, call James at Action Realty, 555-6960.

One of a Kind
Fixer

A custom home built in the '50s, this long & lean 5 bedroom contemporary shows signs of neglect. But beneath the dust & dirt, you'll find 3 mosaic tile baths, white brick fireplace, solid oak cabinets. Quality under cover. Won't last at $134,000. Call Jim at Action Realty, 555-6960, to take a peek today.

Abandoned
Craftsman

One of this city's finest historical homes, fallen into ruin. You'll love the cove-ceiling living room lined with bookcases & a crackling fireplace. 4 bedrooms, 2 baths perfect for a handy family. Just $137,000. To see it, call Josie at Action Realty, 555-6960.

Elegant
Eyesore

On a street of well-kept, stately traditional homes, this 3 bedroom, 2 bath traditional is embarrassing but a great opportunity. Solid brick walls on a lawn dotted by cherry trees. Spacious floor plan with room for privacy & entertaining. The kitchen is a chef's delight. With a little work, you'll be proud to own this home. Only $139,000. Call John at Action Realty, 555-6960, today.

New But
Neglected

All this 3 bedroom, 2 bath contemporary needs is a little touching up. But see what it offers: spacious & sunny living room, oak-paneled den, skylights in the kitchen, loft study, secluded sleeping wing. Lots of potential for only $144,000. To stop by today, call Henry at Action Realty, 555-6960.

Here's a Fixer-Upper for You

This sad Cape Cod desperately needs attention. 4 bedrooms, 2 baths, 1/2 acre of weeds. If you can ignore the peeling paint & dirt, you'll see its charm. Spacious, classic lines with a brick fireplace, sweeping staircase, window-lined sleeping porch. Only $133,000. Call Len at Action Realty, 555-6960.

BARGAIN PRICE

Bargain Beauty

It's hard to believe you can own this gorgeous 3 bedroom, 2 bath traditional for only $144,000. Surrounded by estate-like properties, it features an entertainment-sized living room, private bedroom balconies, designer kitchen & 1/4 acre of rolling hills. Tasteful decor, too. Call Jim at Action Realty, 555-6960, today.

Low Price

Incredible value in breathtaking 2 bedroom, 2 bath home just 10 min. from town. Circled by towering pines & flowering shrubs, its huge windows bring the outdoors in. You'll love its slate fireplace, cheerful breakfast nook, airy loft. Bargain price of just $135,000. For a real deal, call Steve at Action Realty, 555-6960, now. Better hurry.

Are You a Bargain Hunter?

Then you must see this 3 bedroom, 2 bath beauty. Set on a gracious lawn, its unique New Orleans style is charming. Enjoy breakfasting on any of its 3 balconies, luxuriating in the rosy glow of its antique fireplace, wandering in the fabulous flower garden. Just $155,000. Discover it for yourself. Call Joe at Action Realty, 555-6960.

Price Reduced $10,000

If you've been looking for a 3 bedroom bargain, this is it. A lazy, sprawling ranch with cul-de-sac privacy. You'll love its 11 ft. bow window overlooking a huge yard, spacious bedrooms, combination kitchen/family room with warm brick walls & gentle fireplace. 2 baths, 3 car garage. A lot of comfort for only $134,000. To see it today, call Tim at Action Realty, 555-6960.

Terrific Bargain

We've slashed the price on this 2 bedroom cedar home way below market. For just $129,000, you can own its captivating blend of natural wood, light, stained glass. Totally updated kitchen, newly renovated bath, redwood deck where you'll love to entertain. Set in a forest of trees. See it today. Call Action Realty, 555-6960 & ask for Geri. Now.

Baker St. Bargain

If you've been waiting for a bargain in a great neighborhood, see this delightful 3 bedroom, 2 bath traditional full of character & charm. From the stained glass windows to the sweeping staircase, it's one of a kind. Custom touches you couldn't duplicate at the price—just $154,000. Stop by today. Call Teddy at Action Realty, 555-6960, now.

It's a Bargain!

You'll love this opportunity—only $135,000 puts you in an almost new California contemporary packed with upgrades: whirlpool tub, plant shelves, arched windows, 3 sunny & bright bedrooms, 2 custom baths. Super schools, too. A delightful find you'll want to see. Call Trudy at Action Realty, 555-6960, today.

Rock-Bottom Price

Imagine a spacious lawn with bonsai accents...huge living room with 2-story windows...terra-cotta tile floors...4 very private bedrooms, 2 fully modern baths. All for $125,000. See yourself there today. Call Vi at Action Realty, 555-6960.

Privacy Priced Right

If you've been searching for a home that offers value & privacy, see this stunning 3 bedroom, 2 bath contemporary in an excellent neighborhood. Long & low from the street, it's built around a lush garden courtyard with a steamy spa. Wide windows, plush carpets, dramatic Swedish fireplace. Comfort & style you can afford. Just $143,000. To see it today, call Jay at Action Realty, 555-6960.

Yesterday's Price on Today's Home

One of Jamesion & Rogers' most popular models, this 3 bedroom, 2 bath Tanglewood home features the finest in modern living. You'll know by the delightful French windows flanking the fireplace... stunning plant shelves...graceful curving stairway. Today's conveniences at yesterday's price of just $142,000. To see for yourself, call Jimmy at Action Realty, 555-6960, today.

The Right Price

You'll love this charming 2 bedroom, 2 bath home, especially when you see the price. Only $134,000 & you can enjoy quiet quality with crown mouldings, gleaming hardwood floors, an elegant entrance courtyard & over 2,100 sq. ft. of living space. You can't afford to pass this one up. Call Gina at Action Realty, 555-6960, today.

Budget Price

You can't find many 4 bedroom, 3 bath homes at this price. Just $144,000 & your family can live in style. Sweeping redwood decks, giant screened porch. Up-to-the-minute kitchen with breakfast bar & dining nook. Over 2,000 sq. ft. Call Richard at Action Realty, 555-6960, now. This one won't last.

Price Reduced

Owner needs fast sale on delightful 3 bedroom, 2 bath brick home close to the university. You'll love its wide shutters, classic lines, double fireplace that warms the living room & sun porch. Big attic & basement, too. Priced at $138,000, it's way below market. To see this gem today, call Hal at Action Realty, 555-6960.

Below Appraisal

It's the bargain you've been waiting for. $123,000 gives you an open & airy 2 bedroom, 2 bath contemporary in a secluded setting. Special touches like marble vanities, whirlpool tub, custom cabinets. Make it yours today. Call John at Action Realty, 555-6960, now.

Love a Bargain?

Then head for this 3 bedroom, 2 bath ranch in the hills. Just $130,000 gives you a home with a vast oak fireplace, gigantic eat-in kitchen, spacious & private bedrooms, ample closets. All nestled behind gates on a huge lot. You won't believe it until you see it. Call Fred at Action Realty, 555-6960, now.

> *AD TIP: Don't tamper with a good thing. If an ad gets a good response, run it until the listing is sold or the response slows down.*

Sacrifice Price

Antique lovers will adore this charming 2 bedroom, 2 bath cottage in the historical district. With its gleaming mahogany trim, shiny hardwood floors, lots of hand-painted extras, it glows with years of care. Can you believe just $122,500? Call Josie at Action Realty, 555-6960, to see it today.

Unbelievable Price

Just $127,000 & you own a 3 bedroom, 2 bath home your family will love for years to come. With its imposing brick fireplace stretching along an entire wall, solid oak floors, airy kitchen with cherry cabinets, it has something for everyone. Room for a pool, too. To see it today, call Elaine at Action Realty, 555-6960.

Budget Stretcher

A home that will please your heart & your wallet. Just $131,000 gives you this 3 bedroom, 2 bath New England-style brick on quiet tree-lined street. You'll love its classic floor plan: bedrooms upstairs, downstairs a marvel of comfortable living space. Pleasant yard, too. Call Nel at Action Realty, 555-6960, to see it.

Priced to Please

Just $137,000 & you own a home as pretty as a picture. Sprawling 4 bedroom Craftsman with elegant drive, towering shrubs, brick walkways. Inside you'll love its arched doorways, ceramic tile kitchen, 2 custom baths. See this wallet-pleaser today. Call Nick at Action Realty, 555-6960, now.

AD TIP: Put the biggest benefit in the headline or beginning of the ad.

Top Quality, Low Price

Only $146,000 gives you a gracious 4 bedroom Southern-style home with white pillared porch, floor-to-ceiling windows, petite balconies, sprawling kitchen. Lots of luxury for a little price. Call George at Action Realty, 555-6960, today.

MUST SELL QUICKLY

Sale Fell Thru —Sellers Have Moved

Need quick action on charming 3 bedroom traditional just 8 min. to downtown. Nestled on an oversized wooded lot, it features a family room with fireplace, full basement, paved circular drive, 2 baths & 2 car garage. Must-sell price of $128,000. To take a look, call James at Action Realty, 555-6960, now.

Priced to Move Fast

Grab the opportunity of a lifetime...2 bedroom, 2 bath brick home under a canopy of trees. Extras include hardwood floors, hand-built fireplace, charming eat-in kitchen. Will go fast at $125,000. Call Shari at 555-6960, Action Realty, today.

Owner Wants Out!

Anxious owner needs family for gracious 4 bedroom, 3 bath colonial. You'll love its rear awnings, island kitchen, walk-in closets, expansive emerald lawn. Offered on first come, first served basis at $134,500. Call Carlyle at Action Realty, 555-6960, to see this bargain today.

Desperate & Must Sell

3 bedroom, 2 bath contemporary is ready to move at $134,000. Incredible price for over 2,000 sq. ft. of luxury with private master bath, sprawling redwood deck, cook's dream kitchen. Snap it up. Call Ken at 555-6960, Action Realty, now.

Start Packing!

Mortgage payments are adding up on this 4 bedroom, 2-1/2 bath Victorian & desperate owner wants to deal now. Unique home with intricate wood accents, brass fireplace, sunny & roomy kitchen. Heartwarming price of just $131,000. Call Ted at Action Realty, 555-6960, to see today.

Needs Fast Sale

You won't believe your luck when you see this stunning 2 bedroom contemporary. For just $129,000, you can own a dramatic, top-quality home, with a garden tub, steamy spa, heatilator fireplace. Better hurry. Call Fred at 555-6960, Action Realty, today.

Need a Home Quickly?

Then consider this rambling 3 bedroom, 2 bath ranch in terrific family neighborhood. Your kids will love the backyard pool, while you enjoy the conveniences of an upgraded kitchen, brick-walled family room, 2 car garage. Ready-to-sell price of just $129,500. To see it today, call June at Action Realty, 555-6960.

Vacant Beach Beauty

Owner falling into debt on this sprawling 3 bedroom, 2 bath beach beauty. Situated on double lot, it features a warm & lazy sun porch, orchard stone fireplace, secluded master balcony. Action priced at $133,000. Call Frank at Action Realty, 555-6960, now.

Need Quick Sale

on charming, almost new 3 bedroom, 2 bath in best area. Enhanced by mature landscaping, delightful bay windows, solid oak woodwork & 2 car garage, it's bound to go fast at $128,000. Call Joe at Action Realty, 555-6960, today.

Let's Make a Deal
—Fast

Need quick action on top-quality 2 bedroom, 2 bath brick bungalow in finest school district. You'll love its white picket fence, casement windows, charming stone patio. Built to last for just $128,000. Make your move today. Call Richard at Action Realty, 555-6960.

Move In Fast

Bring your chintz to this sunny 4 bedroom, 3 bath ranch! Pull up some overstuffed chairs to the majestic stone fireplace. Arrange the dining table by the 12 ft. bay window. Character abounds in brick floors, cedar siding, elegant rock veranda. Unbelievable value at $135,000. Call June at Action Realty, 555-6960, today.

Owner Desperate

and this house is priced to sell! For just $132,000, you can own this gracious 4 bedroom, 2 bath, 2,100 sq. ft. white pillared colonial. Set on a sweeping lawn, it offers bright & cheerful kitchen, warm wood-paneled family room, living room perfect for entertaining. Call Roger at Action Realty, 555-6960, for a steal of a deal today.

AD TIP: Long ads are fine, but make sure they are still tightly written. Remember, in classified ads you're paying by the word.

Need a Home
in a Hurry?

Then run over to this rambling 3 bedroom, 2 bath ranch, just 5 min. from downtown. Model-perfect, with shining redwood trim, spacious & sunny windows, lush & mature lawn. Priced to move fast at $128,000. Hurry & call Regina at Action Realty, 555-6960, now.

Help!
Owner Has Another!

Here's your chance to reap a tidy profit with this charming 3 bedroom, 2 bath contemporary priced way below market. Elegant accents like slate fireplace, cultured marble vanities, ceramic counters, set it apart. Shaded by 100-year-old oaks. Make it yours today. Call Kim at Action Realty, 555-6960. Better hurry!

Must Sell
Today

Owner is down to wire on marvelous 4 bedroom, 3 bath Victorian. Your antiques will shine in these high-ceilinged, darkwood trimmed rooms. Lots of windows spill in the sun, professionally landscaped lawn. Can you believe just $131,000? Hurry over. Call Brenda at Action Realty, 555-6960, right now.

FORECLOSURE

Near Foreclosure

Just $145,000 gives you an acre of woods all your own & a majestic 3 bedroom Tudor-style home. Gleaming hardwood floors, wide staircase, ancient fireplace. Make it your showplace today. Call Virginia at Action Realty, 555-6960.

Foreclosure Pending

on this free-flowing 3 bedroom, 2 bath California contemporary snuggled next to a winding stream. A real money-saver with tile floors, southwestern accents, sheets of windows. At $132,000, far below value. Call Ruth at Action Realty, 555-6960, today.

Bank Orders Sale

Terrific 3 bedroom, 2 bath family home for an unbelievable price. Party-sized family room with stone fireplace, bay-windowed living room, redwood deck surrounded by trees. Try $128,500. Better move fast. Call Fred at Action Realty, 555-6960, before it's gone.

Lender Says "Sell"

Rock-bottom price on this graceful 4 bedroom, 2 bath ranch home in prestigious Portola Hills. You'll love its circular driveway, pillared porch, open & airy feeling. Lush landscaping, too. Yours for just $131,000. Better see it today. Call Jim at Action Realty, 555-6960. Hurry.

Ready for a Bargain?

Delightful 2 bedroom, 2 bath redwood rustic in sun-spattered forest glen. Only $121,000 gives you rich blend of wood, stone, tile. Couldn't duplicate at the price. Call Sharon at Action Realty, 555-6960, if you're ready for a bargain.

Lender Forces Sale

Don't miss this opportunity—$119,000 & you can own one of the most elegant Victorian homes in the city. With 4 bedrooms, 2 baths. You'll be charmed by its high ceilings, 2 antique fireplaces, delightfully modern kitchen. Call Nick at Action Realty, 555-6960, today.

Last Chance
Before Foreclosure

Owner about to lose dreamy 3 bedroom, 2 bath beauty in choice setting. Copper kettle kitchen, unique oak mantel, garage/ workshop. A find at any price. But just $124,000? See it & believe it. Call Jim at Action Realty, 555-6960, now.

Lender Wants Out

Willing to sacrifice stunning blue & white, 4 bedroom colonial in prestige area. Thick wool carpeting, top-of-the-line tile, custom decor in pastels you'll love. Action priced at $130,000. Call Tina at Action Realty, 555-6960, for an incredible deal.

Bank Will
Sacrifice

Unique opportunity to own upscale 3 bedroom, 2 bath contemporary for way below market. Sophisticated, high-tech decor with spiral staircase, 2-story living room, secluded bedrooms. A must-see at $134,500. Call Ken at Action Realty, 555-6960, today.

For Sale by Lender

Give your family a spacious 3 bedroom country home, full of intimacy & warmth, for less than you ever dreamed possible. Just $133,500 & you own almost an acre of land, 2 fireplaces, gourmet kitchen. The impossible dream come true. Call Mary Ellen at Action Realty, 555-6960, now.

> *AD TIP: After someone finishes reading your ad, they should say to themselves, "That sounds like a nice house to live in."*

OWNER/SPECIAL FINANCING

Owner Will Carry
Below Market

Stunning 3 bedroom, 2 bath ranch in the hills for only $133,000. Owner financing could save you thousands. Quality-crafted home with oak-paneled family room, sunny eat-in kitchen, wonderful 3 car garage. Better move fast. Call Richard at Action Realty, 555-6960, today.

Owner Willing
to Carry

custom 3 bedroom, 3 bath French provincial home in an exclusive neighbor-hood. You'll love its gleaming white accents, charming tile fireplace, sparkling bright kitchen. Low, low price of just $133,500 & owner will take back 2nd. Enjoy worry-free living today. Call Jim at Action Realty, 555-6960, now.

No Qualifying

Owner will carry delightful 2 bedroom, 2 bath cottage with bay window, ceramic kitchen, quaint nooks & crannies. Mint condition. Just $124,500. Won't last so call Gil at Action Realty, 555-6960, fast.

Hassle-Free
Home Buying

because owner is willing to carry below market loan on 3 bedroom, 2 bath tradi-tional. Solid brick walls, box hedges, colorful window boxes. Not to mention glowing hardwood floors, high ceilings, designer kitchen. At $141,000, it's a home you'll love with financing you can afford. Call Kenneth at Action Realty, 555-6960, before it's gone.

Only a Little
Money Down...

moves your family into this luscious 3 bedroom, 2 bath cedar home hidden by trees. You'll adore the bleached wood, exposed beams, mellow pine kitchen. Plus 2 car garage. Owner financing makes the $134,000 price tag very affordable. To see it today, call Lonnie at Action Realty, 555-6960.

EZ
to Own

With owner willing to carry low interest loan, this 4 bedroom, 2 bath New England Salt Box is a bargain. Gently weathered gray siding, ice blue shutters ...it's full of taste & charm. Your kids will love its big family room & play-sized yard. Only $142,500. Better act fast. Call Tommi at Action Realty, 555-6960, now.

Owner Will
Help You

own this charming 3 bedroom, 2 bath traditional by carrying low interest loan. Perfect for entertaining, it features a spacious brick veranda, warm cherry breakfast nook, attractive wood-burning stove. Only $135,500. To see this bargain today, call Joe at Action Realty, 555-6960.

Great
Terms

With owner willing to carry, you can make a deal on this 3 bedroom, 3 bath beauty. Reached by a gently curving, tree-lined street, it's private yet very convenient. Upgrades like gas fireplace, kitchen grill, whirlpool tub. Only $129,500. Name your terms. Call Edward at Action Realty, 555-6960, now.

For a Little Down,
You Get a Lot

Dreamy 3 bedroom, 2 bath home with continental flair belongs to you. Extras like colorful awnings, white brick fireplace, 3 car garage. $143,500 & owner willing to carry. See a sweet deal today. Call Kim at Action Realty, 555-6960. Hurry.

Can't Get
a Loan?

Forget the red tape. Owner will carry you on this stunning 4 bedroom, 2 bath clapboard home. Nestled behind flowering bushes, it's open & sunny, with spacious rooms & classic lines. Terrific neighborhood. Just $134,500. Don't miss your chance. Call Frankie at Action Realty, 555-6960, today.

Below-Market
Financing

You'll save thousands of dollars when you own this gracious white colonial home. With 4 bedrooms, 2 baths, there's breathing room for everyone. Plus wonderful brick patio decked with flowers. Can you believe just $143,600? Owner will carry. Great opportunity. Call Ken at Action Realty, 555-6960, today.

Owner
Financing

can move you into this wonderful 3 bedroom, 3-story contemporary perched on a hillside. You'll love the below market loan. Not to mention the sophistication, quality & panoramic view that'll belong to you. Unbeatable at $145,600. Call Linda at Action Realty, 555-6960, today.

EZ
Terms

Charming 3 bedroom, 2 bath French country home will bring out the artist in you, with its whitewashed walls, bleached floors, flower-splashed patio, 2 elegant baths. Priced at just $145,000, you can be creative in the financing too, because owner will carry. To see it today, call Roger at Action Realty, 555-6960.

Do You Have a
Low Down Payment?

Then you can own this stunning tri-level contemporary built of redwood, stone & glass. 2 bedrooms, 2 baths, "great room" that'll take your breath away. Panoramic view, too. Priced at only $149,000, with owner willing to finance. See this budget-pleaser today. Call Len at Action Realty, 555-6960, now.

Less Down Than
You Might Expect

moves you into this rambling 4 bedroom, 2 bath country home in the city. You'll adore its white clapboard siding, trellised patio, skylight-filled kitchen. Comforts galore for just $145,000. With owner willing to carry, it's easy. Be the first to call Henry at Action Realty, 555-6960. This won't last.

Looking for
Nothing Down?

Then try this 3 bedroom, 2 bath California ranch in a friendly family neighborhood. Designed for easy living, it features all wool carpets, mahogany doors, stunning stone fireplace. Only $134,500. With owner willing to finance. Better hurry & call Joe at Action Realty, 555-6960, today.

Let's Talk
Terms

You can deal on this 4 bedroom, 2 bath stunner because owner will carry. Priced at just $145,000, it offers the comfort of a screened porch, the elegance of a formal dining area, the coziness of a brick-walled family room with roaring fireplace. 2 car garage, too. For a real deal, call Jo at Action Realty, 555-6960, today.

Just a
Small Down...

moves you into a charming 3 bedroom traditional in the heart of Old Town. You'll love its shiny hardwood floors, gleaming oak trim, mellow pine cabinets. Lush trees & shrubs on sprawling lawn. Only $133,000. Call Ali at Action Realty, 555-6960, today. Don't miss this!

Owner
Is Easy

on financing this sumptuous 3 bedroom, 2 bath ranch in excellent neighborhood. Willing to carry all or part at full price of $135,000. Built of brick, this home features picture windows, cheerful eat-in kitchen, workshop/garage & gigantic emerald lawn. Great place to raise kids. To take a look today, call Mike at Action Realty, 555-6960.

Below Market
Interest?

That's what you get on this elegant 3 bedroom traditional because owner will finance. You won't believe your good fortune when you see its marble vanities, ceramic counters, walls of sunny French windows. Upgrades galore at bargain price of just $145,000. Call Fred at Action Realty, 555-6960, today.

ASSUMABLE LOAN

Take Over Low Interest Loan

With just a little down you can take over below market loan on newer 3 bedroom, 2 bath contemporary on estate-sized lot in prestigious Rolling Hills. Full price just $136,000. For quick action, call Jewel at Action Realty, 555-6960, today.

Low Interest Fixed 25 Years

Great terms on like-new 4 bedroom, 2 bath colonial near university. With small down you can have all the comfort & convenience you've ever wanted. Full price only $127,500. Hurry over. Call Hank at Action Realty, 555-6960, now.

Your Chance to Assume

below market loan on 3 bedroom, well cared for rambler in executive family neighborhood. With low, low down you can have the home of your dreams today. One look & you'll go for it at $134,500. Call Diane at Action Realty, 555-6960.

Terrific Assumable

We don't think you'll find a lower rate than the one on this sprawling, sparkling 4 bedroom, 2 bath ranch. On a heavily wooded lot in one of our finer neighborhoods. Full price just $133,000. To see it today, call Jim at Action Realty, 555-6960. Don't let this one slip away.

Below Market Assumable

Enjoy yesterday's charm in this delightful 3 bedroom, 2 bath Victorian. Nostalgic touches, thoughtfully updated, shaded by towering trees. With low down, take over low interest loan. Full price only $126,000. To take a peek today, call Henry at Action Realty, 555-6960.

Great Terms

Can you believe below market rate, fixed, 25 years on a 4 bedroom family ranch in an elite area? Full price just $144,000. Newer, well cared for home with eat-in kitchen, room to roam den, tasteful living room. See it to believe it. Call Jim at Action Realty, 555-6960, today.

It's Yours, Far Below Market Rate

Sensational 3 bedroom, 2 bath hillside sprawler with 2 car garage. It's everything you'd ever want in a family home. With low down, the full price is only $139,500. Be the first to call Steve at Action Realty, 555-6960.

$9,000 —Takeover

You'll feel good when you've settled into this 3 bedroom, 2 bath rambler—not just for all the comforts it offers—but because of your low monthly payments. With a great assumable, low down, full price is only $138,500. See it today. Call Hilary at Action Realty, 555-6960, now.

Super Assumable

Make the smart move into this charming 2 bedroom, 2 bath traditional, packed with upgrades on a secluded wooded lot. With little down, you can assume terrific low interest loan. Full price just $127,500. Call Noel at Action Realty, 555-6960, today. Be ready to move fast.

Can't Qualify?

Then save money by assuming below market loan on this fabulous 4 bedroom, 2 bath colonial. Located in elite area, it features sunny eat-in kitchen, warm & rambling family room, secluded bedrooms. Only $147,000. Better hurry on this one. Call Jeannie at Action Realty, 555-6960, now.

You Save Thousands

by assuming below market loan on this stunning 3 bedroom, 3 bath hillside ranch. You'll love its walls of windows, unique stone fireplace, dramatic kitchen, huge garage. With small down, it's yours for just $143,000. Make a real deal today. Call Lee at Action Realty, 555-6960.

Assumable Low Interest Loan

Great loan can be yours on terrific 2 bedroom, 2 bath sprawler in historic area. Filled with skylights, stained glass, totally upgraded. Bargain price of $131,000. Hurry & call Gina at Action Realty, 555-6960, today.

AD TIP: Put personality into your ads. Then your buyers will know right up front what kind of agent they'll be working with.

Assume Low Interest Loan

You'll love the low monthly payments on this delightful 3 bedroom ranch. Sprawling rooms, rosy brick fireplace, huge redwood deck, garage/workshop, add luxury to practicality. With small down, it's yours for just $141,000. Once in a lifetime opportunity. Call George at Action Realty, 555-6960, fast.

Want a Low Interest Loan?

Then assume at below market rate on this stunning 2 bedroom, 2 bath contemporary close to the hospital. Perched on a hill, hidden by boulders & cactus, you'll enjoy its cool Southwest decor. Full price just $142,000. Won't last long so call Jim at Action Realty, 555-6960, now.

Looking for Low Interest?

Then head for this sunny & bright 3 bedroom, 2-1/2 bath ranch. With a small down, you can assume below market loan. Enjoy low monthly payments in a home your whole family will love. Terrific neighborhood, too. Full price only $139,500. Be the first to call Dee at Action Realty, 555-6960, about this deal.

LOW TAXES

Tax Bill —Only $300 a Year

Savings mount up when you live in a home with a low, low tax rate. Especially a home as well cared for as this 4 bedroom, 2 bath cedar. Hidden in a forest glen, it offers the joy of country living with all the city conveniences. Just $145,000. Why wait any longer? Call June at Action Realty, 555-6960.

Save Big on Taxes

when you live in this charming 3 bedroom, 2 bath home just over the county line. You'll appreciate its seclusion & quality while enjoying terrific tax benefits. Priced at only $143,000, it's sure to sell quickly. Call Jim at Action Realty, 555-6960, to take a look today.

Looking for Low Taxes?

Then head for this rambling 3 bedroom, 2 bath ranch. You'll save hundreds on taxes while enjoying a fenced acre of land, private sizzling spa, handyman's dream workshop. All for just $139,500. To see it today, call Ken at Action Realty, 555-6960, now.

Hate to Pay Taxes?

Then move into this tax-saving 2 bedroom, 2 bath beauty in suburban Northridge. A quality home with trellised patio, warm brick family room, 2 car garage... it's in a community with one of the lowest tax rates in the state. Priced at just $139,000. Call Linda at Action Realty, 555-6960, to find out how you can save.

A Tax Haven for You

You'll love this secluded 2 bedroom, 2 bath charmer built around a soothing inner atrium. Cool tile floors, quality upgrades, walls of windows. Lowest tax rate in area. Can't beat the value for $137,000. Call Carl at Action Realty, 555-6960, now.

AD TIP: Try to avoid vague generalaties.

INVESTMENT VALUE

Super Value —Small Price

That's what you get in this luscious 3 bedroom, 3 bath contemporary, snuggled on an acre of woods. Tons of upgrades you'll appreciate at a price far below their value—just $129,500. Don't miss out. Call Kimberly at Action Realty, 555-6960, now.

Terrific Value!

You won't believe your good luck when you own this 3 bedroom, 2 bath cedar ranch. Hard-to-find touches like sprawling stone patio, terra-cotta tiled kitchen, impressive rock fireplace. Low price of only $143,000. Call Jim at Action Realty, 555-6960, now.

This House Isn't for You...

unless you'd like to save thousands. Because at $154,000, it's priced far below its value. If you want 3 bedrooms, 3 baths in a luxury home with your own acre of woods, call Tim at Action Realty, 555-6960, today. Better hurry.

Your Chance to Make Money

Live in comfortable 3 bedroom, 2 bath home in excellent area at a bargain price. Just $145,000 gives you double fireplace that warms living & family rooms, private master suite, rosy wood-filled kitchen. Call Joseph at Action Realty, 555-6960, to see it today.

A Money-Maker for You

If you appreciate life's finer things, you'll adore this stunning 4 bedroom, 2-1/2 bath French provincial. Exquisitely decorated with 2,800 sq. ft. of custom upgrades you'll love. Best of all, it's an excellent value at just $155,000. To take advantage of a golden opportunity, call Kim at Action Realty, 555-6960, today.

Extraordinary Value

radiates throughout this long & luscious 4 bedroom, 2 bath hacienda. Quality stucco construction, with red tile roof, spacious courtyard, professional landscaping. Unbelievable price of just $145,000. To see it today, call Johnny at Action Realty, 555-6960.

Profitable View

the moment you move into this dramatic 2 bedroom contemporary. It's worth far more than the $134,500 price tag. Upgrades alone worth thousands...not to mention the panoramic view. See for yourself. Call Fredrick at Action Realty, 555-6960, today.

Can You Recognize a Bargain When You See It?

Then rush right over to this 4 bedroom, 2-3/4 bath New England colonial... packed with luxury & surrounded by higher priced homes. If you want charm & value for only $137,500, call Suzanne at Action Realty, 555-6960, today.

AD TIP: Watch out for words that have potential double meanings. Back side might easily be taken to mean rear end instead of backyard.

Gold Coast Bargain

Here's your chance for a Gold Coast address at an incredibly low price. Just $145,000 moves you into a quality former model home with gleaming hardwood floors, elegant floor-to-ceiling windows, a graceful curving staircase. Once in a lifetime opportunity. Call Frank at Action Realty, 555-6960, now.

Super Value

in a 4 bedroom, 2 bath rambling ranch your family will love. For just $134,500, you can enjoy a gigantic cedar-fenced yard, sprawling family room with fireplace, sunny & bright eat-in kitchen. Way under market. Call Sue at Action Realty, 555-6960, & bring the kids out today.

You Won't Believe

the quality you get in this delightful 3 bedroom, 1-3/4 bath cedar A-frame—for just $135,500. Upgrades like whirlpool bath, greenhouse window, full-wall stone fireplace. Grab it up today. Call LeAnne at Action Realty, 555-6960, fast.

Lowest Price in the Neighborhood

For just $145,000, you can own a home you'll love forever. A gracious, 4 bedroom white brick provincial with matching side verandas, 2 private balconies & a French country kitchen/ family room you'll never want to leave. Better act quickly. Call Joe at Action Realty, 555-6960, now.

Own a Money-Maker

You'll adore this charming 2 bedroom, 2 bath historical home on a delightful tree-shaded street. All the nostalgic touches you want, plus modern conveniences. Far below value at $142,000. Call Linda at Action Realty, 555-6960, today.

Top Quality, Low Price

It's hard to find such a well built 3 bedroom home—especially for under $140,000. In an executive family neighborhood, this brick beauty offers a professionally landscaped lawn & 2 car garage. Sure to sell quickly at $138,500. Be the first to call Denise at Action Realty, 555-6960.

Exceptional Value

in a canyon home you'll adore. 3 sunny & bright bedrooms, 2-1/2 elegantly appointed baths, country kitchen perfect for pie baking. Breathtaking view. Priced to move fast at $135,500. Call Kim at Action Realty, 555-6960, now.

DON'T RENT—BUY!

Longing for a Home of Your Own?

Then stop throwing your money away on rent & see this gorgeous 3 bedroom Cape Cod, situated on its own little peninsula. With owner willing to finance, it's easy to own. Just $132,000, & you can enjoy a lifestyle better than any rental for not much more. Call Jim at Action Realty, 555-6960, today.

Why Rent When Owning Is So Easy?

Especially with below-market owner financing on this 2 bedroom, 2 bath gem. Elegantly designed, with white brick walls, tile patios & a kitchen you'll adore —it's a renter's dream come true. Full price just $129,500. To see it today, call Barbara at Action Realty, 555-6960.

Don't Settle for Less... Than a Home of Your Own

If you've been renting, consider the benefits of owning this gracious 3 bedroom, 3 bath home in an excellent neighborhood. You'll have privacy, comfort, conveniences most rentals don't offer. Best of all you can decorate it as you please. Offered at just $134,500. Call Jim at Action Realty, 555-6960, to see how easy owning a home can be.

Renters: Want a Great Tax Deduction?

Why give your hard earned money to Uncle Sam when you could be putting it to work in your own home? Especially this charming 3 bedroom, 2 bath redwood home, snuggled under treetops. Built with a quality you never find in rentals. Only $132,000, with special financing available to first-time buyers. To find out more, call Jim at Action Realty, 555-6960, now.

If You Rent, You Can Own

Owning a home is easier than you might think. Especially when it's this 4 bedroom, 2 bath Craftsman. Bargain priced at just $135,000, it features wide, spacious rooms & its own fruit orchard. Perfect for a growing family. To see if it's right for you, call Ted at Action Realty, 555-6960, today.

AD TIP: If you are having trouble getting started with an ad, it is always a good idea to try starting from the middle or end and revise it later.

TRADE

Like to Make a Deal?

on this stunning 2 bedroom, 2 bath lakefront home with its own pier. Appraised at $145,000, owner willing to trade for 3 bedroom closer to city. Call Lee at Action Realty, 555-6960, for this unique chance.

Let's Trade

What would you offer for charming Victorian-style farmhouse just 30 min. from town? Old-fashioned gingerbread trim, 2 acres of land, brand-new gas furnace. Priced at just $126,000. Owner will trade for ????. Call Brandy at Action Realty, 555-6960, today.

Like to Swap?

You'll love this dramatic 3 bedroom contemporary with a city-light view. Spacious loft, spiral staircase, high-tech kitchen. Appraised at $145,000, owner willing to trade for same size, character home. Call Jennifer at Action Realty, 555-6960, for a real deal.

A Fair Exchange

is what the owner of this sumptuous 2 bedroom, 2 bath cedar chalet is after. If you'd like to live in the woods just 30 min. from town...with all the city conveniences, think about a trade. Appraised at $134,500. Call Jim at Action Realty, 555-6960, if you're ready for a change.

Owner Willing to Trade

delightful 3 bedroom, 2 bath ski cabin for home closer to city. Priced at $127,000, this unique home features dramatic Swedish fireplace, loft with plenty of room for guests, comfortable eat-in kitchen. Call Elizabeth at Action Realty, 555-6960, today.

> AD TIP: As ad expert David Oglivy says, "You can't save souls in an empty church." People must read an ad before they will respond, so make sure your ad counts.

STYLE

ARCHITECTURE

Heritage Home

Own this 3 bedroom, 2 bath historic home in the exclusive Oak Springs neighborhood. It offers many original touches: beveled glass, mosaic floors, hand-carved cherry bannister. Plus all the contemporary conveniences. All for just $156,000. Call Jim at Action Realty, 555-6960, to see it today.

New England Charm

fills this delightful 3 bedroom, 3 bath Salt Box in prestigious community. You'll love its wood cornices, copper kettle kitchen, wonderful country decor. Affordably priced at only $143,500. To see this charmer today, call Henry at Action Realty, 555-6960.

New England Colonial

You'll feel like royalty every time you descend its grand staircase. With 4 bedrooms, 2 baths, it's an exceptionally large colonial nestled on 1/4 acre of grounds. Everything your heart desires. Only $158,000. To see this stunning home today, call Ray at Action Realty, 555-6960.

AD TIP: *Don't be afraid to use long copy in your ads. Readers will read them and clients will love them.*

Currier & Ives Classic

It doesn't take much imagination to picture Christmas in this charming home. 4 bedrooms, 2-1/2 baths, high ceiling splendor with full-length windows & delightful touches of wood. A home you'll love for only $155,000. Call Gina at Action Realty, 555-6960, to see today.

Turn of the Century Charmer

Bring your wicker to this lacy Victorian. The wide veranda is ready & waiting. You'll adore the original stained glass, intricate oak staircase, tastefully updated eat-in kitchen. A home with heart for only $149,000. Call Hillary at Action Realty, 555-6960.

Vintage Victorian

The best of the past combined with the flair of the new. You'll love its skylights & floor-to-ceiling windows, blending beautifully with rich woods. To see this one of a kind home, call Ginger at Action Realty, 555-6960, now. Only $156,500.

Frank Lloyd Wright Inspired

Enjoy the prairie-style look with its long & open rooms in this dramatic 4 bedroom, 2 bath home. Secreted in its own little forest, it offers a sunlit kitchen, library, 2 car garage. Exciting individuality for only $149,500. Call Steve at Action Realty, 555-6960.

French Farmhouse

You'll love the feel of the old country in this almost new French-style home. 3 bedrooms, 2 baths...with storybook rolled roof, bleached plank floors, casement windows. Wonderful neighborhood for kids. Only $142,500. Make it yours. Call George at Action Realty, 555-6960.

French Country Charm

Delightful home featuring bleached woods, cool tile floors, a custom-crafted kitchen that's warm & homey. With 3 bedrooms, 2 baths, there's room for everyone. Even a rolling fenced yard your pets will love. Just $149,000. Call Lee at Action Realty, 555-6960, today.

Tudor Beauty

From the roses lining the brick walk to the antique copper-hooded fireplace, this 3 bedroom, 2-1/2 bath home is one of a kind. You'll adore its half-timbers, heavy beamed ceilings, glowing woods. In established neighborhood of quality homes. Only $151,000. To see for yourself, call Lyn at Action Realty, 555-6960.

Your English Manor

The home you've been dreaming about...elegant half-timbered styling, sitting proudly on a sweeping emerald lawn. Curl up with a book next to its grand stone fireplace...dine in the gourmet kitchen...tend the flowers in the carefully manicured garden. 3 bedrooms, 2-1/2 baths. Offered at $149,000, this won't last long. Call Fred at Action Realty, 555-6960, today.

The Mood of the Mediterranean

Playful, sunny, boldly splashed with color—this artistic 3 bedroom home is waiting for someone special. Enjoy strolling under its arched walkway...relaxing on the tile veranda...watching glorious sunsets through sheets of windows. Only $148,000. Call Ken at Action Realty, 555-6960, now.

Garden Villa

Romance fills this gentle 3 bedroom, 2 bath stucco home cradled on a lush hillside just 10 min. from downtown. Soft fountain plays in entry courtyard, while lavish patio stretches along rear. Secluded, bubbly spa off master bedroom. Genuine charm for just $139,000. To see it, call Florence at Action Realty, 555-6960.

Georgian Grace

You'll feel elegant in this stylish, almost new 4 bedroom traditional. It's so grand, with its massive living room, walnut-paneled den, shiny ceramic kitchen. High stone walls encircle a very private & velvety yard. Yours for only $146,000. Call Debbie at Action Realty, 555-6960, to see it today.

Historic Rancho

You'll love the way the breezes sweep past this long & low 4 bedroom, 3 bath ranch. Quality upgrades throughout, plus 2 acres all your own. Great family home only 25 min. from town. Can you believe $146,000? Call Edna at Action Realty, 555-6960, to make it yours today.

Santa Fe
Style

The artist in you will adore the cool pastel look of this rambling 3 bedroom adobe home. In a setting studded with cactus & giant boulders, with curved fireplace, wood accents, colorful tiles. All for only $145,000. If you're looking for something special, call Fred at Action Realty, 555-6960, today.

Perfect Pueblo

Unique 3 bedroom stucco in mint condition set on its own acre of desert. Watch the sky light up with color through its wall of windows. Quality throughout with custom touches you'll love. In terrific school district. Just $143,000. Call Fred at Action Realty, 555-6960, to see it today.

Custom Cedar

If you want to live in the city but love the country, try this stunning 3 bedroom, 2 bath cedar home. Nestled on an acre of pine trees, it's open & airy with natural exposed beams, terra-cotta tiles, sleek Swedish fireplace. Just 10 min. from town. Only $137,000. Call Len at Action Realty, 555-6960, to see this unique home today.

Contemporary
With Pool

Sleek & sophisticated, this 3 bedroom, 2-1/2 bath contemporary offers cul-de-sac privacy on a 1/4 acre of grounds. Architecturally unique, it features a sun-splashed loft, tiled designer kitchen, 3 balconies with views you'll adore. Gorgeous free-form pool. Unbelievable price of just $139,000. To see it today, call Greg at Action Realty, 555-6960.

Stunning
Contemporary

You'll feel apart from the world in this hillside dream with 3 levels of comfortable living. Airy accents blend with rich woods to create a one of a kind environment. Upgrades throughout. Only $150,000. To see all the special touches for yourself, call Jim at Action Realty, 555-6960, today.

ATMOSPHERE

Rustic Charmer

It'll grab your heart—long & rambling redwood with lots of stone & brick. 4 bedrooms, 2 baths, dramatic copper kitchen. Set on an acre of land all your own. Only $149,000. To see this unique property, call Kenneth at Action Realty, 555-6960, now.

For a
Special Family

Our first house...it was small so we pushed out walls to make room for our growing family & added an alcove lined with French windows & a crackling fireplace. To keep the bedroom wing quiet, we put down the best carpeting we could find. The rest of the house gleams with Italian tile floors. Only spot we haven't touched is the kitchen. It's small enough to save you steps—& while you wash the dishes, you can watch the roses grow in your big backyard. We've filled the house with love & now it's time to turn it over to someone else. If you'd like a 4 bedroom house that's really been a home, offered at $198,000, in a terrific school district, call Pauline at Action Realty, 555-6960, today.

Distinctive & Different

On a graceful winding street, you'll find this stately 4 bedroom, 3 bath traditional. Custom-built in 1945, it reflects the quality of the past with the conveniences of the present. You'll love its huge columned veranda, sunny family room, gigantic kitchen. Only $145,000. To see it today, call Jim at Action Realty, 555-6960.

A Touch of Charm

If you're an antique buff, you'll adore this splendid almost new Victorian. With 3 bedrooms, 2 baths, it faithfully reproduces the elegance & charm of that era, from the rocking chair front porch to the attic perfect for rainy day playing. Only $152,000. Call Vera at Action Realty, 555-6960, today.

Lovely to Look at, Delightful to Live In

3 bedrooms, 3 baths...full of light & space. You'll feel elegant in the gracious living room, comfortable in the rambling family room. Traditional styling, with walls of windows looking out to a 1/4 acre of grounds. Just $155,000. To see for yourself, call Linda at Action Realty, 555-6960, today.

One of a Kind

Splendid 3 bedroom, 3 bath home nestled in its own grove just 10 min. from town. Very private, with double decks looking out to panoramic view. Top-quality construction, unique stone fireplace. Just $150,000. To see something special, call Denise at Action Realty, 555-6960, now.

Better Home & Garden

Tasteful 2 bedroom, 2 bath home hidden by a high brick wall. You'll love its gracious French styling & elegantly manicured English garden. Can you believe only $156,000? Call Mike at Action Realty, 555-6960, to see this gem today.

Modern & Dramatic

If you like open & airy living, you'll adore this stunning 3 bedroom, 2 bath tri-level. Special touches like skylight in master bedroom, gleaming tile floors, bold contemporary fireplace, and a 2 car garage. Only $145,000. Call Nancy at Action Realty, 555-6960, to see it today.

Your Shangri-la

The home you never thought you'd find. 3 bedroom, 2 bath paradise with walls of windows, stunning inner atrium, conveniences galore. Hidden behind lush landscaping on secluded cul-de-sac. A very private place for just $149,000. To see it today, call Josephine at Action Realty, 555-6960.

Rambling Rustic

Bring the whole family when you come to see this 4 bedroom, 2 bath quality ranch...there's something for everyone. With a huge white board fenced yard, cozy wood stove in the family room, charming French country kitchen, it radiates warmth & comfort. Just $157,000. To visit today, call Gina at Action Realty, 555-6960.

Yesteryear Charm

fills this tranquil 3 bedroom, 2 bath city home secluded behind wrought iron gates. You'll adore the old apple tree in the front yard, bougainvillea-draped patio, sun-splashed kitchen. A genuine treasure at $143,500. Call Victor at Action Realty, 555-6960, today.

Executive Dream Home

Party & play in this sumptuous 3 bedroom, 2 bath ranch. Wide, spacious rooms make it perfect for your entertaining. Your kids will love the backyard playground & delightful pool. A dream come true for only $151,000. Call Elena at Action Realty, 555-6960, now.

Garden Delight

This charming 2 bedroom, 2 bath home features a garden that's the envy of the neighborhood. Enjoy the flowers through the bay windows or in the country kitchen's greenhouse window. Handy shed, too. Just $147,000. If you love to garden, call Mia at Action Realty, 555-6960.

Handcrafted Charm

Custom-built in 1945, this tasteful 3 bedroom, 2 bath offers comfortable living in a quality setting. Upgrades like unique tile floors, butler's pantry, high ceilings will delight you. So will its fine neighborhood. All for just $142,000. To see it today, call Jo at Action Realty, 555-6960.

House Beautiful

Peaches & cream decor fills this delightful 4 bedroom, 2 bath brick beauty. You'll adore its full windows, whisper-soft carpets, elegant custom wallcoverings. Set on a spacious lawn with towering oaks, it's just $145,000. To see today, call Vi at Action Realty, 555-6960.

The Good Life

belongs to you in this sprawling 4 bedroom, 2 bath contemporary in terrific family neighborhood. Just minutes to community center. Come home to wall-to-wall comfort in a peaceful setting. Only $152,000. To start on the good life, call Jay at Action Realty, 555-6960, now.

Old Gas Post Lantern

marks the entry to this utterly charming 3 bedroom, 2 bath country home in the city. Winding brick walks, abundant skylights, unusual stonework create an exciting look. Just $153,000. To see a far from ordinary home today, call Ken at Action Realty, 555-6960.

Limited Edition

This sprawling 3 bedroom, 3 bath home is one of a kind. Your family will love to gather in the cozy kitchen/den next to the crackling fireplace. Or under the magnolias shading the redwood deck. A true family oasis for just $152,000. Call Henry at Action Realty, 555-6960, today.

Designed With Pride

Grand stone fireplace, gleaming hardwood floors...in this almost new 3 bedroom, 2 bath Cape Cod. Cradled on a wooded site, it features a shiny copper kitchen, central air & 2 car garage. Only $145,000. Call Fred at Action Realty, 555-6960, today.

A Reflection of Your Lifestyle

That's how you'll feel when you step into this dramatic 2 bedroom, 2 bath quality home. The slate fireplace gleams with care...the ceramic kitchen glows with pride...the landscaped lawn shows a professional's care. Just $152,000. Call Mike at Action Realty, 555-6960, today.

SPECIAL FEATURES

KITCHEN

Julia Child Would Love...

the thoughtfully designed gourmet kitchen of this gracious 3 bedroom, 2 bath traditional home. With generous ceramic counters, double oven & microwave—it's a cook's dream. Wonderful oak eating nook, too. Give yourself a home where you can indulge in one of life's greatest pleasures. Only $152,000. Call Jim at Action Realty, 555-6960, today. Bring your recipe file!

Designer Kitchen

Entertain friends while you're cooking in the sumptuous kitchen of this dramatic 2 bedroom, 2 bath contemporary. You'll adore its hand-painted tiles & up-to-the-minute conveniences. Then dine by a crackling fire in a living room with a view that will take your breath away. Class & comfort for just $151,000. Call Ted at Action Realty, 555-6960, now.

Brick & Copper Delight

Your family will love this farm-style, sun-splashed kitchen with room for everyone...almost as much as they'll enjoy the rest of this 3 bedroom, 2 bath ranch. From the wood-burning stove in the family room to the plant-filled front porch, it's packed with country charm. Only $149,000. To see this fine family home today, call Jim at Action Realty, 555-6960.

Kitchen-Lover's Heaven

If you're a serious cook, come see this delightful 4 bedroom, 2 bath traditional home. You'll happily spend hours in its skylight & stained-glass-filled kitchen featuring only the finest appliances. The rest of your family will appreciate the generous walnut-paneled den, secluded sleeping wing & huge workshop/garage. Just $155,000. Call Hank at Action Realty, 555-6960, now.

Kountry Kitchen

You'll enjoy whipping up a farm-style breakfast in the charming kitchen of this 3 bedroom, 2 bath, 2,700 sq. ft. ranch. Fits right in with the cozy, wood-warmed look you'll love. Set on its own 1/4 acre, this home is a bargain at $149,000. Call Greg at Action Realty, 555-6960, & get the griddle going!

FIREPLACE

Cuddle Up By...

the cozy timbered fireplace that warms the master bedroom of this elegant 2 bedroom, 2 bath home. Live in luxury with French doors, private atrium, charming kitchen/family room. Gently priced at $150,000. Make it yours, call Josie at Action Realty, 555-6960.

Let the
Fire's Glow

warm your family's evenings in this 3 bedroom, 2 bath ranch. Relax next to its massive Tennessee stone fireplace in the walnut-paneled den. Or under the cheerful brass chandelier in the country kitchen. Watch the stars come out above your spacious redwood deck. All for only $147,000. Call Jimmy at Action Realty, 555-6960, today.

Enjoy
Fireside Chats

in this dramatic yet intimate living room dominated by a classical white fireplace. Elegance & grace fill this outstanding 3 bedroom, 2 bath home situated on a wooded lot. Only $155,000. To see it today, call Ken at Action Realty, 555-6960.

Unusual
Stone Fireplace

is the focal point of this soaring 3 bedroom cedar chalet tucked away on a hillside. You'll adore its mellow pine cabinets, 2 spacious baths, gleaming hardwood floors. For just $135,000, it's worth the 1/2 hour drive from town. Call Tim at Action Realty, 555-6960, today.

Old-Fashioned
Wood Burner

helps create the charm of this near new 2 bedroom, 1,500 sq. ft. log home. But then there's the solid cherry cabinets, rocking chair front porch, backyard vegetable garden. Quality throughout. Just $142,000. If you'd like to see this country-fresh but city-smart home, call Fred at Action Realty, 555-6960, now.

A Flickering Fire

will light up your evenings in this 3 bedroom, 2 bath custom home. Nestled on a wooded lot, it'll charm you with its bleached wood floors, spacious ceramic kitchen, unique family room. A home to love for just $144,000. Call Jim at Action Realty, 555-6960.

Orchard
Stone Fireplace

You'll love the roaring fires you can build in the massive stone fireplace of this comfortable 3 bedroom, 2 bath ranch. Enjoy its warmth in the fine wood-paneled den or cheerful island kitchen. For only $142,000, this home is packed with charm. To see it, call Theodore at Action Realty, 555-6960.

Dramatic
Danish Fireplace

makes evening entertaining easy in this long & luscious 2 bedroom, 2 bath contemporary. Whip up classic meals in its gourmet kitchen, serve drinks to your guests on the redwood patio while they enjoy the view. At just $137,000, this home is an entertainer's dream. Call Fred at Action Realty, 555-6960, to see it.

Fireside
Comfort

fills this wonderful 3 bedroom, 3 bath traditional on a quiet, tree-shaded street. You'll love the built-in bookcases flanking the marble hearth, floor-to-ceiling kitchen cabinets, sweeping staircase & 3 fireplaces. Quality you can't find today, for only $142,000. To see for yourself, call Ken at Action Realty, 555-6960.

Hang Your Stockings Here!

Your kids will love this old-fashioned hearth, perfect for Christmas pictures. It's only one of the many special features of this charming 4 bedroom, 2 bath traditional home in a terrific school district. Yours for bargain price of $149,500. Call Ned at Action Realty, 555-6960, today.

DINING ROOM

Have Delightful Dinners

on the trellised patio of this charming 2 bedroom stucco villa nestled on an acre of lush grounds. Hidden from the street, you can enjoy the gentle music of its fountain, soft lights, fragrant gardenias. A home of many moods for just $142,500. To see this special spot, call Timothy at Action Realty, 555-6960.

Distinctive Dining

Your guests won't be surprised if they're served by a butler in this elegant 3 bedroom, 2 bath Georgian. Chandeliered dining, walnut-paneled study, generous French windows...a home where you can live out your fantasies. Only $151,000. Call Jim at Action Realty, 555-6960, to take a look at this fine home today.

A Gazebo for Dining

White gauze frocks & flower-filled vases will fit right in, in this delightful backyard gazebo, next to this charming 3 bedroom, 2 bath Victorian. Gleaming hardwood floors, antique stained glass, walk-in pantry...wonderful home all for just $141,000. To see it today, call Nancy at Action Realty, 555-6960.

Dine in Splendor

by the light of a chandelier in this regal 3 bedroom, 2 bath traditional. You'll love its high ceilings, heavy dark beams, shiny oak floors. Gracious living for only $135,000. Call Fred at Action Realty, 555-6960, for a look today.

Company Coming for Dinner?

Entertaining is easy in this rambling 4 bedroom, 3 bath ranch. Guests will love its relaxing redwood deck with a view of the hills. Easily serve 12 in the spacious dining room. Later enjoy a fire's rosy glow in the finely paneled family room. Just $151,000. Call Kimberly at Action Realty, 555-6960, to see it today.

MASTER BEDROOM SUITE

Escape From Your Kids

in the privacy of the luscious master bedroom suite of this elegant 3 bedroom, 2 bath traditional. Lovely seclusion, stately double doors, luxurious bath. A home you'll be proud to own. Only $145,000. To see it today, call Geraldine at Action Realty, 555-6960, today.

Your Private Suite

is waiting in this sumptuous 4 bedroom, 2-1/2 bath rambler set on a gracefully curving street. Tastefully designed for privacy, it offers fireplace-warmed den, sunny eat-in kitchen, spacious workshop/garage. What more could you ask for at just $155,000? Call Ned at Action Realty, 555-6960, today.

> *AD TIP: Never write down to your readers.*

Secluded
Suite

You'll fall in love with it. French doors opening to a steamy spa, flower-decked patio, 2 walk-in closets, garden tub—in a 3 bedroom, 2 bath home that will delight you. Just $151,000. See it for yourself. Call Johnny at Action Realty, 555-6960, today.

Parental
Retreat

It's your escape—a sun-splashed master suite with delightful sitting area, spacious bath, walk-in closets. Your family will enjoy this 4 bedroom, 2-1/2 bath traditional offering all the comforts you can imagine. Only $154,000. Call Leonard at Action Realty, 555-6960.

Looking for a
Master Suite?

Then head for this stunning 3 bedroom cedar contemporary high in the hills. Very secluded with master suite opening to a balcony overlooking dramatic 2-story living room. Special home for just $149,000. Call Nick at Action Realty, 555-6960, now.

Suite
Hideaway

You can get away from it all in the charming master bedroom suite of this comfortable 3 bedroom ranch. Cuddle up in front of its toasty fireplace, unwind in its whirlpool bath. Luxury in a home your family will adore. Just $147,000. Call Jim at Action Realty, 555-6960, for a private showing today.

AD TIP: Use the same "tone" throughout your entire ad.

Spacious
Suite

can be your private retreat in this 3 bedroom, 2 bath, 2,700 sq. ft. home. Far removed from the generous kitchen, delightful brick-walled family room & convenient workshop/garage, it's perfect for relaxation & reflection. Even has its own walled garden. Only $149,000. Call Ted at Action Realty, 555-6960, today.

Luxurious
Suite

Little touches make this 2 bedroom, 2 bath cedar special. Like the master suite with its own fireplace, sitting area, wonderful garden bath. You'll appreciate the quality of this home, located in an executive family neighborhood. Just $142,000. Call Nick at Action Realty, 555-6960, to view this special home today.

Your Own
Suite

If you long for peace & quiet, consider this gracious 3 bedroom, 2 bath traditional. Quality features like brick fireplace, ceramic kitchen, 2 car garage. Best of all, it offers delightfully secluded master bedroom suite with its own spa. Privacy & convenience at a "suite" price of only $149,000. Call Steve at Action Realty, 555-6960, today.

Indulge
Yourself...

in a home with a master bedroom suite you'll love. Rich carpeting, elegant tile fireplace, gorgeous whirlpool bath...a dream come true. You'll enjoy the rest of this 3 bedroom, 3 bath beauty, too. Perched high on a hill, it offers a cheerful kitchen, wood-paneled family room, 2 car garage. Just $159,000. Call Fred at Action Realty, 555-6960, now.

LARGE GARAGE

Like to Tinker?

Do it in style in the spacious heated garage/workshop of this splendid 4 bedroom, 2 bath ranch. With 3 bays, there's plenty of room. When you're done, enjoy the crackling fire in the cozy den or supper in the country kitchen. Just $141,000 puts you in a home made for family living. Call Joey at Action Realty, 555-6960, now.

Enjoy Carpentry?

Then you won't want to miss this terrific workshop, set up in a roomy 2 car garage. Custom cabinets for all your tools. You'll be proud to own this delightful 3 bedroom, 2 bath home... with its warm brick hearth, redwood accents, solid oak cabinets. Just $145,000. To see it today, call James at Action Realty, 555-6960.

Park Your Cars in a Carriage House

Give your cars a stylish home in this fantastic old brick carriage house, waiting at the end of a long curving drive. You'll enjoy the home that comes with it... elegant 4 bedroom, 2 bath Georgian with crown moulding, high ceilings, tasteful wood trim. Beauty at its best for $157,000. Call Fred at Action Realty, 555-6960, to make it yours today.

More Than 2 Cars?

Then give them the home they deserve. A wonderful 3-bay garage in a stunning 3 bedroom, 2 bath ranch. You'll love its well-designed workshop, farm-style kitchen, terrific family room & peaceful bedroom wing. All for only $148,000. Call Gregory at Action Realty, 555-6960, to see it today.

Store the Big Toys Here

No more family fights over all the cars in the driveway...this 3 car garage has room for everything, even snowmobiles! 3 bedroom, 3 bath home is spacious & comfortable with bay windows, oak paneling, kitchen any cook would love. Nestled on a secluded 1/4 acre, priced at just $152,000. Drive out today. Call Linda at Action Realty, 555-6960.

SPECIAL ROOMS

Your Own Aviary

Bird-lovers will adore the wonderful aviary of this rambling 4 bedroom, 2 bath ranch. Watch your feathered friends from the generous brick patio hidden by shrubs —or through the kitchen's delightful greenhouse window. Packed with charm, this secluded home is yours for only $148,000. Call Greg at Action Realty, 555-6960, to see this unique home.

Need a Darkroom?

No more messy kitchen developing. Enjoy the luxury of your own darkroom in this stunning 2 bedroom, 2 bath California contemporary, owned by a Sports Illustrated photographer. Built for lasting enjoyment, this home offers arched windows, ceramic eat-in kitchen, sun-spotted plant shelves. Only $146,000. Call Joe at Action Realty, 555-6960, today. Bring your camera!

AD TIP: Never assume understanding. Spell out all but the most common abbreviations.

Grow Orchids Here!

Enjoy blossoming orchids as the snow falls in the delightful greenhouse of this elegant 3 bedroom, 2 bath home. Made for tasteful, luxurious living, it features gleaming hardwood floors, beveled mirrors, a grand staircase you'll adore. Just $149,000. Call Tim at Action Realty, 555-6960, & make your flowers happy.

Need an Office at Home?

Then come see this wonderful 3 bedroom, 2 bath ranch with a homey office facing the street. You'll have plenty of privacy for meeting clients, while your family enjoys the Early American comforts of a rosy brick hearth & gleaming copper kitchen. Only $156,000. Call Jim at Action Realty, 555-6960, today.

Keep Fit
in Your Own Gym

If you're a fitness buff, you'll love the gym in this sprawling 2 bedroom, 2 bath contemporary. Mirrored walls, railings, mats...you'll never have to worry about staying in shape. Enjoy the designer kitchen, fireplace-warmed family room, spacious lawn, too. A gym (& home) for just $145,000. Call Carl at Action Realty, 555-6960, for a workout today.

ENERGY EFFICIENT

Save Money Here

You won't realize how much money you've been wasting on utilities until you move into this solar-heated 3 bedroom cedar home. Open & airy with walls of glass, beamed ceilings, knotty pine cabinets. Simplicity for just $153,000. Call Mike at Action Realty, 555-6960, to start saving today.

Cut Fuel Costs

by living in this gorgeous 3 bedroom, 2 bath home on a wooded lot just 20 min. from town. With thermopane windows, thick insulation, toasty heatilator fireplace, it'll withstand winter's coldest blows. 3 cords of wood, too! All for only $152,000. Call Victor at Action Realty, 555-6960, to get a head start on winter.

Peak Energy Efficiency

is what you get in this charming 2 bedroom, 2 bath ranch in one of our finest areas. You'll love its thick plaster walls, double pane windows, top-of-the-line furnace & central air. Not to mention extras like the Dutch tile fireplace & delightful window seats. Yours for only $155,000. Call Kenneth at Action Realty, 555-6960, today.

Stay Warm Here...

in this sprawling redwood chalet hidden in the woods just outside town. With solar heating & hot water, you'll save a bundle. Enjoy 3 wood-beamed bedrooms, stained glass windows, spacious deck where you can feed the deer. Just $145,000. Call Ned at Action Realty, 555-6960, to see it today.

Good Cents

If you want to save on fuel bills, consider this gracious 3 bedroom, 2 bath, almost new home. With its top-of-the-line energy saving appliances, you'll save hundreds while enjoying French doors, stylish brick patio, dreamy country kitchen. Only $152,000. Call Roy at Action Realty, 555-6960, for a look today.

AD TIP: Use testimonials: "Neighbors refer to it as a palace."

ROOM FOR ENTERTAINING

Entertain in Style

in this elegant 3 bedroom, 2 bath Georgian set on its own little hill just outside town. You'll love its gourmet kitchen, chandeliered dining room, bookcase-lined family room. Just $158,000. Call Fred at Action Realty, 555-6960, to see it today.

Planning to Party?

Then do it in style, in this fantastic 3 bedroom, 2 bath California contemporary your friends will love. Whether it's relaxing in the very secluded spa, cuddling up next to a roaring fire or snacking in the stained glass-accented kitchen, there's plenty to keep you busy. Only $145,000. Call Ted at Action Realty, 555-6960, for a look today.

Love a Party?

Then you'll adore this rambling 3 bedroom, 3 bath brick home perfect for entertaining. With its stunning kitchen, oak-trimmed dining room, relaxing walnut-paneled den, ivy-covered patio, it's a home your friends will love. Great neighborhood, too. Just $143,000. Call Jean at Action Realty, 555-6960, today.

You'll Be the Envy of Your Friends

when you live in this stately white colonial just 2 miles from downtown. With 4 bedrooms, 2 baths, it offers room to entertain plenty of friends. Big living room for grand piano, fireplace-warmed family room, velvety lawn perfect for croquet. All for only $159,000. Call Richard at Action Realty, 555-6960, to visit today.

Made for Entertaining

Details make this 3 bedroom, 2 bath home distinctive...the steamy spa hidden by high brick walls; cool, tree-shaded veranda; tasteful library with wet bar. Touches you'll appreciate whenever you entertain. Just $149,000. Call Dick at Action Realty, 555-6960, & get the invitations ready today!

Lots of Friends?

You'll want to invite all of them to this stunning 3 bedroom, 2 bath California contemporary. Enjoy the romantic, spotlit patio; dramatic living room; cheerful ceramic kitchen with all the upgrades you desire. Great place to visit—better place to live. Just $147,000. Call Kimberly at Action Realty, 555-6960, to make it yours today.

Elegant Entertaining

is yours in this gracious 4 bedroom, 2 bath home. Serve 10 course meals in the splendid dining room with its own fireplace. After dinner, relax in the walnut family room, or on the stunning redwood deck with a view as big as the valley below. Only $154,000. Call Sal at Action Realty, 555-6960, to see it today.

For You & Your Friends

Delightful 4 bedroom, 3 bath Victorian charmer where everyone will feel at home. Nestled under an awning of trees, this gingerbread fantasy offers a rocking chair front porch, sun-spattered oak living room, cheerful & bright kitchen. Yours for just $148,000. Call Theodore at Action Realty, 555-6960, to see this unique home today.

Expecting Guests?

That's no problem in this spacious & comfortable 3 bedroom, 3 bath home. Private guest suite makes overnight stays easy. You'll appreciate the generous eat-in kitchen, sprawling family room, big yard for football. Big enough for all your friends. Just $158,000. Call Noel at Action Realty, 555-6960, to see it today.

Expected to Entertain?

Then do it in style in this dreamy 3 bedroom, 2 bath executive home. Gather your guests under its elegant patio awnings, dine in chandeliered splendor, relax by the roaring fire in the marble hearth. Good taste for only $150,000. Call Jenny at Action Realty, 555-6960, today.

Entertainer's Paradise

You couldn't pick a finer home...3 bedrooms, 2 baths with a gentle fountain playing in its lush inner courtyard. Enjoy the ease of slate floors, the sophistication of a Swedish fireplace, the joys of a private spa. Yours for just $148,000. To see this secluded home today, call Jimmy at Action Realty, 555-6960.

Welcome Your Friends

in this sprawling 4 bedroom, 3 bath country-style home. Located on a choice corner lot, it blends homespun charm with contemporary convenience. You'll love its cherry breakfast nook, sunny brick patio, great workshop/garage. Unbeatable price of $144,000. Bring the gang today. Call Roger at Action Realty, 555-6960.

AD TIP: Highlight benefits rather than features.

Great Party House

Imagine a 15' x 21' living room warmed by a fieldstone fireplace & opening onto a lovely deck—with a gourmet kitchen only steps away. Soaring ceilings open to secluded sleeping wing with 3 comfortably-sized bedrooms, 2-1/2 baths. Perfect home to throw a party. Just $138,000. Call Jim at Action Realty, 555-6960, to see it today.

Out-of-Town Guests?

You won't have to worry when you're living in this generous 3 bedroom, 2 bath ranch. Built around a private courtyard, you'll have plenty of room for friends. You'll love the huge windows spilling in the sun, country-fresh kitchen, warm & intimate den. Only $149,000. Call Sue at Action Realty, 555-6960, for a look.

Perfect for Entertaining

You'll love throwing a party when you live in this stunning 3 bedroom, 2 bath contemporary in a prestigious neighborhood. Gourmet kitchen makes cooking easy, while your friends relax in the brick-walled family room. On more formal occasions, enjoy the bay-windowed dining room. All this for $155,000. Call Vera at Action Realty, 555-6960, today.

ONE-LEVEL

Long, Luscious & Not a Single Step!

If you're looking for a 1-story home with a comfortable lifestyle, try this spacious 3 bedroom, 2 bath ranch. Walls of windows look out to your own fenced acre. Enjoy a grand stone fireplace, cheerful island kitchen, 3 car garage for $145,000. Call Jo at Action Realty, 555-6960, now.

Totally Accessible Home

It's what you've been dreaming about—a charming 2 bedroom, 2 bath traditional just 5 min. from the Medical Center. Lush natural landscaping, easy-care kitchen, convenient tile floors. Designed with you in mind...just $145,000. Call Roger at Action Realty, 555-6960, today.

No Stairs to Climb

You will find this 3 bedroom, 2 bath home a gem. All on one level, it features the finest carpeting & appliances. Plus an open & airy floor plan that's perfect for plants. Yours for $136,000. Call Jim at Action Realty, 555-6960, today!

Easy One-Level Living

You'll love the wide & spacious rooms in this 2 bedroom, 2 bath stunner. Not to mention the thoughtfully designed kitchen & elegantly spacious hallways. On a choice wooded lot, it's a home to suit everyone's needs for only $143,000. Call Kelly at Action Realty, 555-6960, today. Tomorrow might be too late.

For People With Special Needs

Come home to an almost new dramatic contemporary filled with the latest conveniences. It offers the warmth of an orchard stone fireplace, beautiful rose garden off the 2 bedrooms, cheerful sun-filled kitchen, luxury of 2 spacious baths. Just 20 min. from Medical Center. For $144,500, you can't afford not to look. Call Lu at Action Realty, 555-6960, now.

AD TIP: Don't advertise all of your listings. Put in one or two in each price range and location to attract prospects.

PORCHES/PATIOS/SPAS

Bubbling Spa & Fountain

are yours when you move into this wonderful 3 bedroom, 2 bath ranch. You'll love the way the spacious living room opens into the outdoor patio lush with plants & charming lattice walls. Perfect spot to unwind after a hard day's work. Just $149,000. Reward yourself today. Call Ned at Action Realty, 555-6960.

Bring the Romance Back Into Your Life

in this storybook 3 bedroom, 2-3/4 bath Victorian reached by a winding path. You'll fall in love with the stunning brick-walled patio splashed with colorful flower beds & the softly lit flagstone terrace. End your special moments relaxing by the master bedroom's flickering fireplace. Just $154,000. Call Jim at Action Realty, 555-6960, to rekindle the romance in your life today.

Long, Cool Porch

stretches forever at this inviting 3 bedroom, 2 bath Cape Cod. Bring your rocking chair & watch the gorgeous sunsets over the fields. A classic, almost new home, with country decor you'll adore. Wonderfully natural lot. Only $152,000. Call Tina at Action Realty, 555-6960, to see this beauty today.

Feel the Cool Ocean Breeze

brushing against your cheeks on the wide open rooftop patio of this 4 bedroom, 2 bath stucco home. Just a few blocks from the beach, it features pastel colors you'll love. Plus special touches like 2 adobe fireplaces, red tile roof, huge kitchen. Just $146,000. To stop by today, call Reginald at Action Realty, 555-6960.

Secluded
Sunbathing

No peeping Toms here. The splendid patio of this 3 bedroom, 2 bath ranch is totally private. Nestled on 1/4 acre of grounds, this charming home features a massive brick fireplace, gleaming hardwood floors, copper kettle kitchen. Terrific price of $152,000. To see it today, call Kim at Action Realty, 555-6960.

Hidden Spa

Just off the master bedroom of this stately 4 bedroom, 3 bath Georgian, there's a surprise. A lush patio, filled with plants & flowers, surrounding a steamy spa. On more formal occasions, entertain in the elegant living room, warm walnut-paneled den or gleaming tile kitchen. All for just $155,000. For great value in an executive neighborhood, call Timothy at Action Realty, 555-6960, & find out about it today.

Sunny Solarium

Bring your plants to this glass-walled delight...focal point of a charming 2 bedroom, 2 bath Victorian. If you like gingerbread trim, cozy fireplaces & brass accents, this home's for you. See it today. Only $145,000. Call Frank at Action Realty, 555-6960.

Spa
With a View

You'll love entertaining in this huge hot tub with a view stretching to the ocean. Almost new 3 bedroom, 2 bath contemporary with all wool carpet, ceramic counters, sumptuous fireplace. Only $150,000. For a look today, call Jim at Action Realty, 555-6960.

Old-Fashioned
Screened Porch

Spend relaxing evenings listening to the crickets & watching TV in an outdoor living room. Attractive 3 bedroom, 2 bath ranch secluded on a cul-de-sac just 20 min. from town. Offers a cheerful eat-in kitchen, rambling den, 2 car garage. Only $153,000. Call Fred at Action Realty, 555-6960, today.

Relax on
the Front Porch

of this charming one owner New England Salt Box. With 3 bedrooms, 2 baths, it's packed with old-fashioned touches & modern conveniences. In a terrific family neighborhood where people look out for each other. Only $145,000. For a real deal, call Jim at Action Realty, 555-6960.

Bring Your
Wicker & Plants!

You'll fall in love with the wide gingerbread porch of this old-fashioned 3 bedroom Victorian in an established neighborhood. Lots of stained glass, carved woods, sunny kitchen. Just $142,000. To see it today, call Tina at Action Realty, 555-6960.

Watch the
World Go By

from the lazy rocking chair porch of this sprawling 4 bedroom, 3 bath traditional. In a neighborhood of gracious trees & winding streets, it's full of peace & comfort. Gleaming hardwoods, 2 massive fireplaces. Only $154,000. Call Mary at Action Realty, 555-6960, to see this oasis today.

Life the Way It Used to Be

If you like wide front porches, crumbling brick patios & glorious bougainvillea, consider this one of a kind 3 bedroom, 2 bath Craftsman. Needs some sprucing up but it's full of delightful character. In a rapidly appreciating neighborhood, too. Bargain-priced at $135,000. For a look today, call Vi at Action Realty, 555-6960.

Elegant Spanish Courtyard

In this 3 bedroom, 2 bath stucco charmer, life revolves around the marvelous inner courtyard. Reached through French doors from every room, it's a tropical paradise. Cool tile, splashing fountain, bright flowers. Home & garden for just $142,000. See it today. Call Kim at Action Realty, 555-6960.

Sky-High Patio

Watch the city lights twinkle from the rooftop veranda of this massive 4 bedroom, 2 bath home. Set on a sweeping lawn, it offers a circular staircase, dramatic windows, arched doorways. Wonderful neighborhood. Only $159,000. Call Sheila at Action Realty, 555-6960, today.

LANDSCAPING

Bonsai Beauty

Serenity surrounds this quiet 2 bedroom, 2 bath Cape Cod on a secluded street. With its simple Japanese garden & 6 elegant bonsai trees, it's an Oriental oasis. Enjoy classic lines, hardwood floors, gleaming kitchen. Just $143,000. Call Steve at Action Realty, 555-6960, today.

Let Nature Be Your Decorator

when you live in this stunning 3 bedroom, 2 bath redwood home set high in the hills. Gnarled trees, shrubs & rocks create a breathtaking setting you can enjoy through an expanse of windows. Rustic luxury for $148,000. Call Jim at Action Realty, 555-6960, today.

Showcase Garden

1/2 acre of formal gardens, rich in color & beauty, lies behind this prestigious 3 bedroom, 2 bath traditional. Complementing the garden's quality is the home's marble hearth, Jenn-air range, French doors. Offered at just $149,000. To stroll the garden today, call Ted at Action Realty, 555-6960.

Your Own Orchard

You'll adore this spick & span 3 bedroom colonial with its rustic oak fireplace, gleaming hardwood floors, spacious 2 car garage. Surrounding it is a sumptuous citrus orchard with lots of orange, lemon & lime trees. Reap a bountiful harvest for just $143,000. Call Jim at Action Realty, 555-6960, today.

Love Flowers?

Then feast your eyes at this rambling 3 bedroom, 2 bath canyon rustic. From the outdoor patio sprinkled with impatiens to the elegant balcony with bonsai trees to the rear terraces studded with cactus, it's a nature lover's delight. On a 1/4 acre, it's yours for $152,000. To see the flowers today, call June at Action Realty, 555-6960.

> *AD TIP: Use headlines that provoke a reader's self-interest not just his curiosity.*

100 Pine Trees
All Your Own

You'll never need to worry about buying a Christmas tree when you own this 3 bedroom, 2 bath beauty—you'll have 100 just outside your door. Enjoy the fresh scent of pine needles on the redwood deck or through the walls of windows in the comfortable family room. Country living just 10 min. from the city. Only $149,000. To take a whiff today, call Jim at Action Realty, 555-6960.

Pluck a Peach

from the mouthwatering orchard of this newer 4 bedroom, 2 bath farm-style home. Country folks will love its rustling trees & friendly birds, while city slickers can enjoy the ultimate in modern conveniences. A home for everyone at just $151,000. Grab this peach today. Call Lisa at Action Realty, 555-6960.

100 Year Old
Oak

shades the brick walkway of this charming 3 bedroom, 2 bath heritage home. It's filled with nostalgic delights, yet thoughtfully updated. From its wide front porch to the sweeping staircase, it's a home to treasure. Just $148,000. Call Jim at Action Realty, 555-6960, to see the best of yesterday today.

Tropical Oasis

It's your little piece of paradise, a glass-filled Florida-style home hidden in its own tropical jungle. Each of the 3 bedrooms looks out to the lush landscaping, while the sunny family room opens to an incredible patio. With 2 baths, giant kitchen, 2 car garage, it's a bargain at $151,000. For a trip to the jungle today, call Sue at Action Realty, 555-6960.

Pick Your Own
Pecans

Sprawling pecan tree is only one of the old-fashioned charms of this delightful 2 bedroom, 2 bath traditional in a wonderful neighborhood. Knotty pine cabinets, wood-filled family room, elegant built-in bookcases create an atmosphere of ease & warmth. Yours plus all the pecans you can eat for $145,000. Call Henry at Action Realty, 555-6960, to grab a few today.

POOL

Pool Party!

Invite your friends over for a splash in the delightful pool of this stunning 2 bedroom, 2 bath contemporary. Located on a choice corner lot, it offers a gleaming ceramic kitchen, fireplace-warmed den & roomy workshop/ garage. Comfort & luxury for $141,000. Call Jim at Action Realty, 555-6960, to take a dip.

Gorgeous
Natural Pool

You'll love the way nature creeps right up to the edge of this beautiful black-bottom pool. No harsh tiles or cold concrete... bushes & flowers surround its shimmering beauty. 3 bedroom, 2 bath contemporary home offers the finest in indoor-outdoor living. Many upgrades. Only $159,000. Call Josephine at Action Realty, 555-6960, today.

AD TIP: Tracking the source of your responses will help you plan an effective strategy and save you money.

138

Like to
Swim Laps?

Then do so in privacy at your own convenience, in the luxurious pool of this 3 bedroom, 2 bath garden villa. With high block walls, a classic Georgian hearth, gleaming designer kitchen. This secluded home is bargain-priced at $158,000. To see, call Kim at Action Realty, 555-6960.

The Best Exercise
in the World

is waiting for you at this exciting 4 bedroom, 2 bath ranch. Your own free-form pool, heated by the sun & surrounded by flowers. Enjoy pool-side meals in the kitchen or dining room. Later relax by the family room's flickering fireplace. A home to keep you in shape for $149,000. Call George at Action Realty, 555-6960, to see it today.

Grecian
Pool

waits for you in the rear garden of this long & luscious 3 bedroom stucco charmer. Let the water invite you through the French windows lining the terrace. When you're done, shower in one of the 3 full baths. An elegant home in an executive neighborhood for $158,000. Call Fred at Action Realty, 555-6960, today.

Pretty
Pool Home

Good taste fills this delightful 3 bedroom, 2 bath French country home with window boxes, bleached floors, whitewashed cabinets. Even the pool is pretty, nestled in a color-splashed garden with gleaming mosaic tile. Only $146,000. Call Richard at Action Realty, 555-6960, to see this picture-perfect home today.

End Your Day
With a Splash

when you come home to this exciting 3 bedroom, 2 bath contemporary. You'll love its open & airy design with delightful brass & copper accents. Best of all, the huge patio steps down to a wonderful black-bottom, gas-heated lap pool. Excitement & fitness for $149,000. See it today. Call Victoria at Action Realty, 555-6960.

Swim
& Sun

at your leisure in this dramatic 4 bedroom, 2 bath California contemporary. Your kids will love the huge pool with its terrific deck. You'll appreciate the floor-to-ceiling windows overlooking the water. Automatic pool cover for extra safety. Fun in the sun for only $157,000. Call Jo Ann at Action Realty, 555-6960, to start enjoying this fun home now.

CONDITION

WELL CARED FOR

House Beautiful

You'll appreciate the love & care that went into this stunning 3 bedroom, 2 bath French provincial. Thoughtful touches like Jenn-air range, white brick gas fireplace, easy-care floors. Nothing to do but relax on the ivy-covered veranda. Easy living for $152,000. Call Ted at Action Realty, 555-6960, today.

Better Home & Garden

Tradition-lovers will appreciate the gentle updating of this rambling 4 bedroom, 2 bath Craftsman. In the same family for 50 years, it reflects unusual taste & quality. Set on a winding, tree-shaded street, it's just $160,000. For a look today, call Henry at Action Realty, 555-6960.

Picture-Perfect

You'll adore this charming 2 bedroom, 2 bath cottage with all its fanciful touches. Pastel trim, whitewashed walls, gleaming bleached floors...impeccable condition. A real beauty for $146,000. Call Sally at Action Realty, 555-6960, to take a peek.

Wall-to-Wall Comfort

Your family will enjoy this sprawling 3 bedroom, 2 bath ranch in perfect condition. Nothing to do but move into its delightful redwood-trimmed rooms. Architecturally designed on an acre lot, it blends smoothly into the surrounding hills. A special home for $153,000. For a look today, call Ken at Action Realty, 555-6960.

Plenty of TLC

is reflected in this gorgeous 3 bedroom, 2 bath rambler. You'll love its sun-filled eat-in kitchen, massive rock-walled family room, tastefully elegant living room. In a wonderful family neighborhood. Ready-to-move-in price of just $137,000. Call Tim at Action Realty, 555-6960, today.

Are You a Fussy Buyer?

Then head over to this 3 bedroom, 2 bath colonial in an excellent neighborhood. It shines with care...from the terra-cotta tiles on the 2 fireplaces to the gleaming crown moulding. Meticulously manicured lawn, too. Yours for $145,000. Call Gina at Action Realty, 555-6960, now.

The Home
You Deserve

You'll love living in this quality 4 bedroom ranch with expansive windows that overlook a wooded ravine. Quiet luxury in its polished wood ceilings, hand-built stone hearth, spacious wraparound decks. Top condition. Only $156,000. Call Jim at Action Realty, 555-6960, to see this gem today.

Mint Condition
Just Listed

This stunning 3 bedroom, 2 bath traditional won't last...it's so clean it shines. From the slate floors to the flagstone patio, it's sure to please everyone's eye. Striped awnings, rosy brick fireplace, stained glass windows. A sparkler for just $156,000. Call Ken at Action Realty, 555-6960. Better hurry!

For the
Discriminating Buyer...

Quality 4 bedroom, 2-1/2 bath colonial in sought-after neighborhood. You'll recognize pride of ownership in its gleaming mouldings, shiny hardwood floors, sparkling French windows. Set on estate-like grounds. Only $154,000. To make it yours, call Suzanne at Action Realty, 555-6960, today.

Picky, Picky, Picky

If you're a fussy buyer, head over to this 3 bedroom, 2 bath brick beauty. You won't find a thing wrong. From the old-fashioned sash windows to the top-of-the-line appliances, it's all in perfect working order. Hard-to-find condition for just $145,000. Call Fred at Action Realty, 555-6960, for a look-see today.

Ready & Waiting

You can stop looking, after you see this charming blue & white French home on a winding street. With 3 bedrooms, 2 baths & a generously-sized living area, it offers privacy & luxury. Just $151,000. To see for yourself, call Tim at Action Realty, 555-6960, now.

Your Family
Deserves the Best...

so give it to them in this meticulous 4 beroom, 2 bath cedar ranch. Nestled on its own natural acre. It offers gleaming white trim, stockade fencing, lots of upgrades. Tip-top shape for only $156,000. If you want the best, call Linda at Action Realty, 555-6960, today.

Ready to Move?

Then see this spick & span 3 bedroom, 2 bath ranch sure to turn heads. With its charming tree-lined walkways, delightful awnings, hand-painted tile kitchen, it's a creative person's dream come true. Priced for quick sale at $145,000. Call Kerry at Action Realty, 555-6960, today.

Forget the
Cleaning Crew

This 4 bedroom custom cedar home is spotless. With its shiny natural woods, knotty pine cabinets, unusual stone fireplace, it's as pretty as a picture. Surrounded by unspoiled natural beauty... yours for $143,000. For a look today, call Jim at Action Realty, 555-6960.

> *AD TIP: Read your ad aloud and make sure it flows well.*

A Perfect "10"

Jewel-like 3 bedroom, 2 bath Mediterranean in mint condition. From the colorful tile portico to the elegant flower-decked balconies, it's waiting for the discriminating buyer. Secluded on a hillside with a forever view, just $146,000. To see, call Ted at Action Realty, 555-6960.

MAINTENANCE-FREE

Hate Housework?

Then why do it when you can live in this sun-filled 2 bedroom California contemporary that's so easy to care for? Ceramic counters, whisper-soft carpets, central vacuum system. Natural landscaping, too. For $152,000, isn't it worth a try? Call Tim at Action Realty, 555-6960, for a look today.

Forget the Housework

This shining 3 bedroom, 2 bath beauty will be spick & span in no time. With its easy-care floors, abundant natural brick & stone, high-tech kitchen, you've got little to do but enjoy life. A hassle-free house for only $145,000. Call Jim at Action Realty, 555-6960.

Built for FUN!

Whether you have 1 child or 5, you can do a lot of living in this sprawling 3 bedroom ranch. Featuring only the finest materials, it can withstand anything. You will love its walls of windows, easy neutral decor, soothing views. Just $151,000. To see it today, call Barbara at Action Realty, 555-6960.

No Yard Work!

Think of all the time you'll save in this intriguing Oriental home, set far back from the street & surrounded by nature's beauty. Sell the lawn mower, slip into its spa, feel your troubles disappear. Relaxing open floor plan, too. Just $152,000. For a look today, call Jim at Action Realty, 555-6960.

Hassle-Free Home

If you're tired of leaky roofs, broken furnaces & running faucets, move into this delightfully worry-free home. A sprawling 3 bedroom, 2 bath contemporary beauty in an executive neighborhood. Features only the finest fixtures & appliances. Priced at $149,000. If you want to save thousands on repair bills, call Sue at Action Realty, 555-6960.

Do Yourself a Favor

Stop spending your time fixing up your house & move into a home where it's all been done—beautifully. You'll adore this 3 bedroom, 2 bath traditional tucked away in the heart of an exclusive area. With gas fireplace, brick walls, ceramic kitchen. Finally, you can enjoy life. For only $143,000, can you afford not to take a look? Call at Action Realty, 555-6960, today.

Like More Time for Fun?

Then give yourself this stunning 3 bedroom, 2 bath contemporary snuggled into a hillside just outside town. No yard to mow. No wood to polish. Just clean, simple high-tech accents you'll love. Priceless view, too. Just $144,000. You'd better act fast. Call Jim at Action Realty, 555-6960, now.

Minimum Maintenance

Long & luscious 3 bedroom, 3 bath stucco home. Perfect for a young family or retirees, it features a naturally landscaped yard, sumptuous wool carpeting, automatic sprinklers, romantic Malibu lights. If you want more time in your life, call Ken at Action Realty, 555-6960, today. For $140,000, it's worth a look.

For Family Fun

Your kids will love this roomy 5 bedroom, 3 bath Dutch colonial. With its playground, sandbox & fenced yard, there's always something to do. You'll love how easy it is to care for...with quality upgrades & features most other homes don't offer. Just $149,000. To see today, call Jo at Action Realty, 555-6960.

A Reflection of Your Lifestyle

If you have more to do in life than fix up your house, come see this dramatic 3 bedroom, 2 bath Colorado contemporary. Natural rock walls never need painting. Carefree brick floors never need polishing. Filled with skylights, you'll love its style. Only $149,000. For a look today, call Steve at Action Realty, 555-6960.

QUALITY WORKMANSHIP

Enjoy Custom Features at a Reasonable Price

If you're looking for quality, consider this spacious 4 bedroom, 2 bath ranch. Close to schools, freeways & shopping, it offers French doors & windows, handbuilt planters, Italian tile floors, rosy brick hearth, walk-in closets, luscious carpets, 2 patios & a professionally landscaped corner lot. Just $160,000. Call Dee at Action Realty, 555-6960.

Blue Chip Home

You'll adore all the upgrades in this delightful 3 bedroom, 2 bath traditional...with its custom cherry cabinets, shiny hardwood floors, unique stone terrace. In an excellent family neighborhood, with super schools. All for just $147,000. Call Ned at Action Realty, 555-6960, today.

Beauty at Its Best

You'll be impressed by this 3 bedroom, 2 bath home's gracious white brick walls, striped awnings, manicured hedges. Even more impressive is its gleaming copper kitchen, stylish see-through fireplace, walk-in closets galore. Just $152,000 & you'll be the envy of your friends. Call Jim at Action Realty, 555-6960, now.

Blue Ribbon Special

On the prettiest street in town, you'll find this delightful 4 bedroom, 3 bath white clapboard home. Glistening with fresh paint & green shutters, it offers the finest in family living. For just $151,000, you get an airy screened porch, gleaming tile kitchen, wonderful oak staircase. To see for yourself, call Jim at Action Realty, 555-6960.

Quiet Quality

radiates throughout this stunning 3 bedroom, 2 bath California contemporary. From the dramatic stained glass entry to the terra-cotta tile patio, it's filled with upgrades you'll adore. Convenient executive neighborhood. For a look today, call Lee at Action Realty, 555-6960.

AD TIP: Avoid being cute and clever. Credible and convincing will sell more homes.

Only the Finest...

belongs in this stately 3 bedroom, 2 bath Georgian manor. With its 9 ft. ceilings, crown mouldings, elegant English garden, it's a masterpiece of superb taste. Secluded behind a private hedge, it can be yours for $149,000. Call Ann at Action Realty, 555-6960, today.

Carpenter's Home

Built by a custom craftsman for his own family, this 4 bedroom, 2 bath colonial offers exceptional beauty. You'll recognize the fine workmanship in its matched walnut paneling, ornate carved banisters, gleaming cherry hutch in the spacious kitchen. Secluded beneath towering pines, it's a step above the average for just $152,000. Call Ted at Action Realty, 6555-6960, today.

Doctor's Home

Only the finest fills this luxurious 4 bedroom, 2-1/2 bath home resting on an estate-sized lot. You'll appreciate the quality of the den's walnut paneling, the solid cherry cabinets in the kitchen, the style of its solarium dining room. A home designed to please for just $155,000. To see it today, call Annabelle at Action Realty, 555-6960.

Post World War II Quality

They don't build them like this any-more...a 1947 cedar Craftsman with 4 bedrooms, 3 baths. Wide front porch is perfect for a swing. It offers gleaming hardwood floors, sun-filled rooms, picture windows galore. Unbeatable quality for only $152,000. To take a look today, call Kim at Action Realty, 555-6960.

Come Home to the Best

when you live in this long & luxurious redwood ranch. With 3 bedrooms, 2 baths, it's hidden in the hills just 15 min. from town. Watch the sun sparkle through its many windows. Enjoy quiet evenings on the peaceful patio. A top-notch home you'll cherish for $153,000. For a look today, call Carol at Action Realty, 555-6960.

AD TIP: If you are having trouble getting started with an ad, it is always a good idea to try starting from the middle or end and revise it later.

UNIQUE APPEAL

HISTORY

Former Playground
for the Rich

It's a once in a lifetime opportunity. Luxury cottage built in the '40s by a rich family as a weekend retreat. Now this 2 bedroom, 2 bath stunner is close to the city but it still radiates old-fashioned charm. All the quality you'd expect...on a stunning 1/2 acre lot. Just $145,000. Call Joe at Action Realty, 555-6960, today.

Converted
Mill House

If you're an antiques buff, you'll love living in this massive stone mill with a water wheel that still works. Wide exposed-beam ceilings, weathered bricks, charming fireplace. With 2 bedrooms & an oversized bath. Only $147,000. For a look today, call Jim at Action Realty, 555-6960.

Live in a
Lighthouse

If you're drawn to the sound of waves crashing on rocks or the shimmer of sun on the sea, take a 45 min. drive to this magnificent home. Converted 10 years ago, it offers 3 bedrooms, a warm & sun-splashed kitchen & a 360 degree view you will never tire of. Just $152,000. Watch the waves today. Call Karen at Action Realty, 555-6960.

Artist's Haven

Deep within the woods, 20 min. from town, there's a luxury cabin owned by an artist. A splendid 3 bedroom log home filled with skylights, knotty pine cabinets, gleaming hardwoods, paintings & murals that can never be replaced. Just $145,000. To see it, call Jennifer at Action Realty, 555-6960.

Renovated Barn

You'll love the open & airy feeling of this antique New England-style barn converted into a wonderful 3 bedroom, 2 bath home. The owners left all the special touches that make this home unique, while adding the conveniences that make life comfortable. Only $154,000. To see what careful renovation can do, call Ted at Action Realty, 555-6960.

AWARD-WINNING

Live in an
Award-Winning Community

in this attractive 3 bedroom, 2 bath cedar ranch where you can walk to tennis courts, stables & swimming pool. You'll enjoy its plant shelves, track lighting, magnificent brick fireplace, thoughtfully landscaped lot. Just $145,000. To see it today, call Jonathan at Action Realty, 555-6960.

Architecturally Acclaimed & Affordable!

You'll love the way this 3 bedroom, 2 bath ranch feels. Sumptuous skylights bring in the sun, cool tile floors reflect the light, tasteful tile accents add warmth & charm. Renowned for its easy floor plan, this flower-filled home is only $154,000. Call Sue at Action Realty, 555-6960, for a look today.

You Saw It on the Cover of California Magazine

but you never thought that someday it could be yours. Stunning 2 bedroom jewel on heavily wooded lot. Exceptional design with loft bedrooms opening to treetops, circular stairway winding down to eat-in kitchen, sun-strewn living room/studio. Outstanding home for $150,000. Call Jo at Action Realty, 555-6960, now.

Prize-Winning Garden

You'll appreciate the years of tending that went into this showcase garden. Enjoy the perennial splashes of color from the huge patio of your French-style 3 bedroom, 2 bath home. Unique & exotic blossoms galore. Only $156,000. To see stunning beauty, call Miguel at Action Realty, 555-6960, now.

National Historical Landmark

You'll see from the plaque on the door that this is more than a house...it's a home with history. Throughout the 3 bedrooms & 2 baths, you can feel the warmth of woods, the sparkle of crystal & the glow of an antique fireplace. On a quiet, well-established street under shady elms. Just $145,000. Call Timothy at Action Realty, 555-6960, to journey into the past today.

CELEBRITY OWNED OR VISITED

Kris Kristofferson Is Selling His House!

This is your chance to own a celebrity home in a terrific family neighborhood. With 3 bedrooms & 2 baths, its special features include a walnut-paneled den, recording studio, tasteful designer kitchen. A home you'll love for $158,000. Call Lu at Action Realty, 555-6960, now.

The Roger's Home

One of this city's first families is putting their grandmother's home on the market. A 2 bedroom, 2 bath Victorian that gleams with tender care. You'll love the ivy-covered porch, shiny mahogany living room, marble hearth & spacious updated kitchen. A gem for $156,000. Call Kim at Action Realty, 555-6960.

Own a Home on the Hope Ranch

This is a once in a lifetime opportunity...marvelous 3 bedroom, 2 bath home on the famous Hope Ranch. Built for the foreman in 1934, quality shows in its solid hardwood floors, shiny cherry cabinets, massive brick fireplace. On 1/2 acre all its own, this unusual home is only $153,000. To see it today, call Ken at Action Realty, 555-6960.

Millionaire's Guest House

Built for well-loved friends, this 2 bedroom charmer is new to the market. Among its many special features are inlaid floors, glass cabinets, superb carved staircase. On estate grounds for only $148,000. Call Kim at Action Realty, 555-6960, today.

146

CHAPTER THREE

PRESTIGE HOMES

LOCATION

COUNTRY

The Best of
Both Worlds

Enjoy the beauty of the country in city-style comfort in this 5 bedroom, 3 bath traditional home. Just 25 min. from town, it's cradled in one of the most spectacular settings you can imagine. Offers the finest in craftsmanship & care. Just $225,000. Drive out today. Call Jim at Elite Realty, 555-7970.

Country Roads
Take You Home

to this luxurious 4 bedroom, 3 bath Tudor on its own acre. It's just a 1/2 hour ride through unspoiled scenery to this charmer with leaded glass windows, unique brick patio, 2 handsome fireplaces. Only $300,000. Call Ned at Elite Realty, 555-7970 today.

Board Your BMW
in the Country

at this magnificent estate just 40 min. from town. Escape to a 5 bedroom, 5 bath home filled with every conceivable luxury: gourmet kitchen, hand-carved mantels, marble floors, 4 car garage, your own pool. A home you'll love for $450,000. Bring your BMW out today. Call Leo at Elite Realty, 555-7970.

When Was the Last Time
You Saw a New Home
Lost Amid the Trees?

If you love nature's beauty, come home to this sprawling, 5 bedroom, 4-1/2 bath cedar contemporary, hidden in the woods just 35 miles from town. Reached by a private winding drive, its skylights & walls of glass frame a forest view. Slate floors, fieldstone fireplaces, lovely redwood deck...life at its finest for only $275,000. See the trees today. Call Fred at Elite Realty, 555-7970.

Improve Your Lot
in Life

by moving into this delightful 6 bedroom, 5 bath white clapboard charmer on 2 acres all your own. You'll adore its old-fashioned sun porch, bright & cheerful copper kitchen, warm wood trim & floors. Plus all the trees & flowers you'd ever want. In a community of fine estates, just $289,000. To see it today, call Sue at Elite Realty, 555-7970.

Country Escape

Come home to a 4 bedroom, 3 bath French country charmer, with a delightful little stream meandering through the yard, ancient shady oaks, song birds, chipmunks, deer. Only 35 min. from town. Soothing bleached wood floors, relaxing stone fireplace, peaceful patio open to the woods. Just $276,000. Escape today. Call Jim at Elite Realty, 555-7970.

Comfort in the Oaks

Driving home through the trees you can see the lights sparkling in this elegant 5 bedroom, 3 bath brick manor. Secluded in its own forest glen, it offers a Jenn-air range, Berber carpets, mahogany trim. Only 40 min. from the city, it's a must-see at $300,000. Call Julie at Elite Realty, 555-7970, now.

Country Living At Its Best

If you've had a secret longing to live in the country, come see this charming 6 bedroom, 3 bath Dutch colonial. Built like an old-fashioned farmhouse, it's packed with the latest conveniences. You will love its peg & groove floors, 15 ft. fireplaces, delightfully warm decor. But don't let its style fool you. This home is almost new & in perfect shape. All for just $274,000. For a look today, call Kim at Elite Realty, 555-7970.

Unique Country Estate

Designed for the individualist, this sumptuous stone home blends into 5 acres of surrounding countryside. 4 bedrooms, 3 baths, filled with artistic touches like hand-painted murals, brick floors, mosaic tiles. If you'd like something different for $325,000, call Jim at Elite Realty, 555-7970, to see today.

Be a Country Squire

If you've always wanted to live like a lord, do it in this 7 bedroom, 4 bath Georgian new on the market. You'll love its elegant gates, winding drive, herring-bone brick patios. Not to mention all the tasteful touches inside. An acre of gorgeously landscaped grounds for only $375,000. Fulfill your fantasy today. Call Kim at Elite Realty, 555-7970.

For the Armchair Farmer

Authentic 6 bedroom, 5 bath Early American farmhouse tastefully upgraded for today. Original wood floors, paneling, windows, blend beautifully with the brick & copper kitchen, sun-drenched solarium, 3 car garage. Set on 6 acres that long ago were a family farm. Make it your homestead for just $255,000. Call Jean at Elite Realty, 555-7970, now.

Green Acres

An oasis of serenity, this 5 bedroom, 3 bath contemporary melts into the acre of woods that surrounds it. Enjoy the warmth of cedar paneling, openness of exposed beams, delight of a gourmet kitchen. 25 miles from town, it's yours for only $200,000. Call Kenneth at Elite Realty, 555-7970, today.

Your Own Manor

Enjoy country seclusion just 20 min. from the city in this wonderful 6 bedroom, 4 bath English traditional. With its classic lines & elegant flair, it's worthy of your finest treasures. Gleaming hardwoods, leaded windows, stained glass cabinets, luxury throughout. All for just $333,000. Drop by today. Call Ted at Elite Realty, 555-7970.

Gentleperson's Estate

Let this charming 5 bedroom, 3 bath brick mansion bring the glory of the past back into your life with its gracious white columns, elegant porch, 2 fireplaces warming the family room. Resting on an emerald acre of lawn, this almost new home offers yesterday's style & today's comforts. Just $325,000. To visit, call Jenny at Elite Realty, 555-7970, now.

Scarlett O'Hara Would've Loved It...

4 massive columns, a palatial front porch, elegance & taste throughout. Glorious 4 bedroom, 3 bath Southern home on 7 acres was built for gracious entertaining & comfortable family living. One of a kind for just $289,000. To see for yourself, call Mary Anna at Elite Realty, 555-7970, today.

WATERFRONT

Crab & Fish From Your Own Pier

You'll love living in this warm & sprawling 5 bedroom, 3 bath home next to its own lake. Just 20 steps from your back door, tie up a row boat at your own pier & relax. You'll enjoy the sun-sprinkled country kitchen, vast stone fireplace, rough hewn cedar living room, glorious rocking chair porch. Special home for only $235,000. Call June at Elite Realty, 555-790, now.

Lakeside Estate

Elegant 2-story Georgian brick home set on rolling hills next to a sparkling lake. Stone veranda where you can watch the sunset, 4 comfortably-sized bedrooms, 4 roomy baths. A home you'll be proud to own for $245,000. To see it today, call Kimberly at Elite Realty, 555-7970.

> AD TIP: *Have you been perfectly honest? Don't mislead your readers just to get them to call.*

Swan River Masterpiece

Imagine a lazy river running through your yard. Open the double French doors of your private balcony & let its music lull you to sleep. Or enjoy the river from the terrazzo patio of your 5 bedroom, 4 bath New Orleans-style sweetheart. A home to treasure for $304,000. Call Jim at Elite Realty, 555-7970, to see it today.

On the Sand

You'll have the beach on your doorstep in this stunning 5 bedroom, 4 bath white contemporary. Walls of glass cast gentle sunset rays onto whitewashed floors, natural wood beams, glowing rock fireplace. 3 levels for family privacy, a lot as big as your imagination. See this beauty today. Only $255,000. Call Sue Ellen at Elite Realty, 555-7970.

Bring Your Boat!

& dock it at the slip of this gorgeous 4 bedroom, 4 bath Mediterranean villa. You will love walking along its arched porch. Breakfasting on the flower-filled patio. Entertaining your friends in the elegant living room. Feel the caress of ocean breezes for just $367,000. Call Bill at Elite Realty, 555-7970, for a look today.

Riverfront Wilderness Ranch

Hard-to-find luxury home on the river. 5 bedroom, 5 bath cedar ranch filled with over 3,500 sq. ft. of comfort. Secluded on 5 acres, this home is surrounded by unspoiled natural beauty. Enjoy the wildlife through the wraparound walls of windows or from your private redwood deck. A pristine paradise for $355,000. Call Josie at Elite Realty, 555-7970, to see it today.

Beauty &
the Beach

Sun-lovers will adore this dramatic 4 bedroom, 4 bath contemporary with its private strip of sand. Skylights, high ceilings, tile floors create an open and airy feeling. The Southwestern decor reflects the latest styles. Upgrades galore. Just $377,000. Call Sue Ellen at Elite Realty, 555-7970.

On the
Water

You couldn't ask for a finer beach home than this luxuriously appointed, tastefully decorated European villa. It features thick stucco walls, hand-hewn beams, promenade porch. Comfort and elegance for $400,000. Call Kim at Elite Realty, 555-7970, to see it today.

Your Own
Lake

Custom cedar home nestled in hills next to pretty little lake. Your kids can learn to sail while you catch the evening supper. 4 bedrooms, 4 baths with a fantastic natural wood-filled "great room" where family will love to gather. 3 car garage, too. Only $301,000. Call Vi at Elite Realty, 555-7970. Bring your fishing pole!

Waterfront House
of Glass

Sophisticates will fall in love with this 3 bedroom, 4 bath contemporary in fast-growing executive neighborhood. French doors open to the ocean view. Inner atrium adds drama & excitement. Hidden from the street by high hedge, this unique home is just $345,000. To see a terrific view today, call James at Elite Realty, 555-7970.

Idyllic
Island Retreat

It's a home most people only dream about. Rambling 5 bedroom, 6 bath ranch hidden on its own little island. Polished redwood, huge stones, warm red bricks create warmth & intimacy, French windows bring in stunning natural beauty. You'll love its gourmet kitchen, 3 car garage, boat house. Just $445,000. Make your dream come true. Call Trane at Elite Realty, 555-7970, now.

View of
Spouting Whales

will be yours from this exciting 3 bedroom, 4 bath contemporary sitting on the sand. Built for high drama, this luxurious home offers a free-flowing floor plan with sprial staircases, designer kitchen, 3 car garage. Ocean view from every room. Yours for just $325,000. See the whales. Call Kenny at Elite Realty, 555-7970.

Hear the Surf

throughout this charming '50s beach cottage on an acre of sand dunes just 25 miles from town. You'll recognize its quality by the mosaic tile floors, hand-hewn fireplaces, elegant sun porch. 3 bedrooms, 4 baths just $266,000. Mint condition. Call Nancy at Elite Realty, 555-7970, today.

Your Private
Beach

is waiting for you just steps outside this delightful 5 bedroom, 4 bath ranch. On a small bluff overlooking the ocean, it offers your own pool, sauna, cabana, ceramic tile kitchen & 3 fireplaces. All for $298,500. To see it today, call Jeannie at Elite Realty, 555-7970.

Lakeside Luxury

You'll love to entertain in this magnificent lakeside retreat with Georgian-styled living room, banquet-sized dining room, lap pool overlooking the beach. With 5 bedrooms and 4 baths having guests is easy. Just $398,500. To see high style, call Jo at Elite Realty, 555-7970, now.

HILL

Hilltop Showplace

Your private road leads to this magnificent stone & glass estate surrounded by rugged mountain scenery. View of the city from almost every room of this 5 bedroom, 6 bath manor. All the conveniences & luxury you can imagine for just $425,000. Call Teddy at Elite Realty, 555-7970, now.

If You've Reached the Top, Live There

in this sprawling 6 bedroom, 6 bath executive retreat with a panoramic view. Window walls, skylights, private patios, inner atrium. Magnificent seclusion only 25 min. from town, for $399,000. If you are on your way up, call Tim at Elite Realty, 555-7970, today.

Be on Top of the World

in this exciting 5 bedroom, 4 bath redwood home high in the hills. Enjoy the beauty of nature while living in open & airy rooms with 3 fireplaces & upgrades galore. Very private setting, just 30 min. away. Call Fred at Elite Realty, 555-7970, for a trip to the top today.

Lavish Ozark Empire

Majestic estate home in park-like grounds just 45 min. from town. Secluded on its own mountain peak, this stunning manor offers 6 bedrooms, 5 baths, plus all the diversions you desire: pool, spa, tennis, billiard room, elegant garden. Only $550,000. Call Henry at Elite Realty, 555-7970, today.

Your Ivory Tower

Unique, ivory-colored contemporary sitting on a hilltop. Dramatic tri-level design with fireplace-dominated "great room," sheets of glass, 3 spacious bedroom suites, forever view. All for $299,000. If you want something special, call Alice at Elite Realty, 555-7970, today.

Palace in the Sky

Unusual 5 bedroom, 4 bath English Tudor high in the hills. Enjoy fabulous sunsets from the soothing spa on its private patio. Relax by one of the 3 mammoth brick fireplaces. Spectacular scenery, luxurious comfort. $475,000. Call Ken at Elite Realty, 555-7970, now.

Top of the World View

from this unique circular home with 6 bedrooms, 5 baths. Built 5 years ago on a mountaintop just outside town, it offers a panoramic view. Unusually large yard for hill property. Offered at $350,000. Call Josephine at Elite Realty, 555-7970, to drive up today.

AD TIP: Get in plenty of emotional appeal.

Hilltop
Spanish

You'll love the rustic feeling of this 4 bedroom, 3 bath charmer, resting in secluded splendor just 25 min. from town. With its lovely Spanish arches, thick stucco walls, tasteful tile accents, it's the perfect showcase for your favorite things. Delightful courtyard with bubbling fountain. Only $298,000. Call Sue at Elite Realty, 555-7970, today.

On the Bluff

overlooking a sapphire sea, you'll find this elegant white brick ranch. 4 sunny bedrooms, each with its own bath. Colorful striped awnings, huge flower-filled patio by the sea, refreshing pastel decor. Yours for $350,000. See it today. Call Jim at Elite Realty, 555-7970.

Hilltop Seclusion

You'll never want to leave this rambling 4 bedroom, 4 bath rustic built with 1940's care. Reached by its own winding road, it sits high in the mountains surrounded by nature's beauty. Enjoy its cheerful eat-in kitchen, 2 fireplaces, huge 3 car garage. Just $388,000. For a look today, call Sam at Elite Realty, 555-7970.

Mountaintop Marvel

Sumptuous retreat offering breathtaking mountain vistas. Literally walls of windows, every convenience you can think of, quiet luxury throughout the 7 bedrooms, 6 baths. Incomparable value at $466,000. Call Halley at Elite Realty, 555-7970, to see this unique property.

AD TIP: *Write more than one headline and then choose the best.*

Put the City
at Your Feet

when you live in this dramatic 7 bedroom, 6 bath contemporary in the hills just outside town. You'll love watching the sparkling city lights from the very secluded spa on your flower-filled redwood deck. Enjoy the luxury of wool carpets, Jenn-air range, greenhouse windows, myriad skylights. Yours for $412,000. See this quality home today. Call Fred at Elite Realty, 555-7970.

Your Own
Eagle's Nest

5 bedroom, 3 bath Colorado contemporary open to mountain vistas. Located on estate-sized lot filled with fragrant pines, this 7-year-old home offers a custom designer kitchen, double wraparound decks, elegant slate floors, 3 car garage. Only $305,000. Picture yourself there today. Call Jo at Elite Realty, 555-7970.

High on a
Windy Hill

You'll find this stunning 4 bedroom, 4 bath California ranch nestled behind a mile of white board fencing. Secure, private, spectacular. With a solar-heated pool, stable, 4 car garage. Views & seclusion for $350,000. To see it today, call Sue at Elite Realty, 555-7970.

A Little Above the
Rest of the World

is how you'll feel in this delightful 5 bedroom, 6 bath Spanish villa sitting on a mountaintop, just minutes from the city. Its quality & taste are reflected in its 2 ceramic kitchens, 3 lofty fireplaces, dramatic library lined with dark woods. A real home for just $445,000. Call Ron at Elite Realty, 555-7970, today.

DESERT

Desert Paradise

Come home to a fabulous desert oasis, a spacious 4 bedroom, 5 bath retreat amid red rocks & splashes of wildflowers. You'll love this stucco's long, cool lines, elegant terra-cotta tiles, breezy verandas, double French windows. Just 45 min. from the city. Only $345,000. For luxury in the sun, call Ted at Elite Realty, 555-7970, today.

Spectacular Desert Sunsets

can be yours from this long & low ranch on an acre of cactus-studded desert. Enjoy the view from the cool, whitewashed living room with its curved adobe fireplace. Or while dining in the eating nook of the cheerful tile kitchen. Or beside the sapphire blue free-form pool. A 4 bedroom, 3 bath bargain at $325,000. Call Ken at Elite Realty, 555-7970, today.

Adobe Palace in the Desert

If Santa Fe is your style, see this classic pueblo 30 min. from town. The ultimate in good taste & luxury, it features 4 king-size bedrooms, 3 full baths, entertainment-ready living & dining areas. Hand-painted tiles & murals throughout. A must-see at $395,500. Call Julie at Elite Realty, 555-7970.

Magnificent Desert Retreat

Sun-lovers will adore this bright & airy 5 bedroom, 4 bath contemporary, with its cool tile floors, wide sweeping staircase, windows that show off the desert's fantastic colors. Priced at $325,000, it's life at its finest. See for yourself. Call June at Elite Realty, 555-7970, now.

Stunning Desert Beauty

surrounds this low & rambling 5 bedroom, 4 bath stucco designed for an artist. Sun splashes in through full-length windows. Warm woods add charm. Unique home on 2 acres with arches, stained glass, 3 car garage. All for just $375,000. Call Jim at Elite Realty, 555-7970, to see this gem today.

GOLF

Park Your Golf Cart Here

just outside the French patio doors of this sumptuous 5 bedroom, 4 bath classic. On Pine Crest Country Club golf course, it overlooks acres of green. After golfing, enjoy the handsome walnut library, elegant sculptured dining room, warm & bright kitchen. Gracious home in choice location for $325,000. Call Tim at Elite Realty, 555-7970.

Pro Golf Course

You'll love living so close to the green in this charming 4 bedroom, 3 bath cedar ranch. Tastefully decorated with brick floors, warm wood trim, many upgrades. Acre of velvety lawn studded with trees. A wedge-shot from the second tee. Just $275,000. Call James at Elite Realty, 555-7970, now. Don't forget your clubs!

Enjoy a Golf Course View

from almost every room of this stunning 5 bedroom, 4 bath traditional overlooking the 8th fairway. Convenient for golfers, great for families, this classically-styled Georgian offers superb schools, top-of-the-line appliances, 4 car garage, enormous lawn. Only $375,000. Discover its serenity for yourself. Call Kim at Elite Realty, 555-7970, today.

Needed: Golf-Lovers

looking for stylish, comfortable 3 bedroom, 4 bath home right on this area's most elite course. Quiet luxury, big windows, lush landscaping, modern conveniences. If you're looking for $315,000 worth of quality on the green, call Ted at Elite Realty, 555-7970, today.

Tee Up

just steps from the front door of this rambling 5 bedroom, 4 bath redwood rustic right on the course. You'll love its towering pines, peaceful atmosphere, elegant features. Lots of brick, stone & rock. Only $295,000. Call June at Elite Realty, 555-7970, today.

Your Best Shot

is this magnificent golf course home on Dayton Country Club...Classic English styling with its own turret, casement windows, circular drive. 5 bedrooms, 6 baths...all luxuriously spacious & elegant. Just $399,000. To see it today, call Ken at Elite Realty, 555-7970.

Premier Golf Course Home

In an estate neighborhood, you'll find this French Normandy chateau built with quality & superb taste. 4 bedrooms (each with balcony), luxuriously large living room, many marble accents. Best of all, there's room for your golf cart in the 3 car garage. Just $425,000. Call June at Elite Realty, 555-7970, today.

AD TIP: Be sure to tell your readers what to do in order to respond to your ad. Don't assume they will call you unless you ask them to.

Your Own Putting Green & Sand Trap

comes with this 5 bedroom, 4 bath rambler on 2 acres in an executive family neighborhood. With more than 3,500 sq. ft. of comfort, it offers cedar shingles, copper kitchen, rosy brick fireplaces. Just $310,000. For a super home, call Jim at Elite Realty, 555-7970, today.

Golf Course Living at Its Finest

5 bedrooms, 4 baths on prestigious Far Oaks Country Club, that you'll enjoy playing. When you're done, relax in the secluded master bedroom spa—or start a fire in the unique fieldstone fireplace. Traditional charm with great value, for $299,000. See it today. Call Kim at Elite Realty, 555-7970.

If You Love to Golf...

then why not do it every day? It's easy when you live in this 4 bedroom, 5 bath Spanish villa just steps from the course. Enjoy splendid stucco comfort with all the luxuries you can imagine. All for just $325,000. To take a look today, call Jim at Elite Realty, 555-7970.

RECREATION/LEISURE

Rare Wilderness Showplace

Teddy Roosevelt would've loved it... sprawling luxury log home in thick woods 25 miles from town. With 5 bedrooms, 5-1/2 baths, it has its own pond for fishing, forest for hunting. Make every day a vacation for just $355,000. Call Jimmy at Elite Realty, 555-7970, today.

Jog to the Beach

from this stunning 5 bedroom, 4 bath California contemporary resting in sand dunes. Open to sun, sea & sky, its airy, light design brings nature close. Cool pastel decor, lots of tile, textured walls & floors. Just $256,000. Call Ken at Elite Realty, 555-7970, to see it today.

Work Out in Your Own Gym

when you live in this splendid 4 bedroom, 5 bath Georgian home with cul-de-sac privacy. Perfect for fitness buffs, it features gourmet kitchen, French windows, stunning brick patio, mirrored workout room. Minutes to jogging trails. Yours for $325,000. Call Ken at Elite Realty, 555-7970, for a look today.

Tennis Estate

You'll feel elegant in this wonderful 6 bedroom, 5 bath brick traditional set on an acre of park-like grounds. Enjoy morning workouts on your own tennis court. Or play at night under the lights. Every imaginable luxury. All for only $315,000. To see for yourself, call Joe at Elite Realty, 555-7970.

Your Private Dock

awaits your boat at this magnificent lakefront house of glass. With 5 bedrooms, 4 baths, it offers the ultimate in waterfront relaxation & recreation. Only $402,000. Call Lin, Elite Realty, 555-7970, now.

AD TIP: Watch out for real estate jargon in your ads. It will lose your readers.

Grab Your Racquet

& head for this stunning Mediterranean villa overlooking its own exquisite tennis court. Filled with flowers, sun & warm woods, this 4 bedroom, 5 bath haven has a grand living room, solarium dining, prize-winning greenhouse. Offered at just $395,000. If you're ready to play, call Steve at Elite Realty, 555-7970, today.

Fish & Game Haven

It's hard to find such a luxurious retreat so close to the city but just 45 miles from town you can enjoy this sumptuous 4 bedroom, 5 bath cedar with its own forest, bass-stocked lake & hiking trails. Your private paradise for just $398,500. Call Linda at Elite Realty, 555-7970, and test your pole today.

Sportsman's Paradise

You'll love to entertain friends in this magnificent hunting lodge. 5 bedrooms, 4 baths, plus rustic log loft for extra guests. Gourmet kitchen makes meals easy while mammoth fireplace sheds rosy glow over rock walls. Style, charm, relaxation for $375,000. Call Elizabeth at Elite Realty, 555-7970, now.

Enjoy Racquetball?

Then why not have your own indoor court? You can in this delightful 4 bedroom, 5 bath contemporary charmer in the area's finest neighborhood. Designed for easy family living, this home features all wool carpet, dramatic double fireplace, unusual glass-block walls. Keep fit for just $398,000. Call Juanita at Elite Realty, 555-7970, now.

For the Fun of Life

Rambling 6 bedroom, 5 bath rustic in sun-speckled clearing surrounded by forest. Wonderfully large eaves, huge old-fashioned windows, abundant charm. Just minutes to lakes, hiking trails, ski slopes. Only $387,000. Call Ken at Elite Realty, 555-7970, for a look today.

CONVENIENCE

The Feel of Country Living Without the Drive

Your own haven...4 bedroom, 4 bath country-style cottage nestled on acre of trees, flowers, shrubs. Nature's beauty will delight you through the French windows & doors or from the greenhouse window in the copper kettle kitchen. Just 5 min. from the city for $395,000. Call Ken at Elite Realty, 555-7970, today.

Estate Living in the City

Imagine living in a stately brick colonial with 4 large bedrooms, 4 full baths. An almost new home built to create its own tradition, with 3 fireplaces, crown moulding, sparkling chandelier. On park-like grounds near downtown. Just $391,000. For life the way you'd like it to be, call Josh at Elite Realty, 555-7970, now.

Looking for a Quality Home in Super School District?

Then head over to this gorgeous 5 bedroom, 4 bath French country home in Indian Ridge. Give your children a quality eduction while you enjoy bleached plank floors, oak cabinets, sprawling family room with 2 fireplaces. Lots of charm for $405,000. For a taste of France, call Rose Ellen at Elite Realty, 555-7970, today.

Enjoy University Atmosphere

in a warm & gracious home any family would love. With 5 bedrooms, 4 baths, this red brick colonial offers a handsome oak staircase, fireplace-warmed den, delightful family room or study overlooking a rolling lawn. Just $295,000. Call Jim at Elite Realty, 555-7970, to see it today.

Manhattan Style & Convenience

in this hard-to-find brownstone just blocks from downtown. Built to last in the 1800's, it's been richly restored with cleverly hidden modern conveniences. On 3 levels, it offers 4 bedrooms, 3 baths, & a brick-walled garden where you'll love to relax. Only $285,000. For a look today, call Lil at Elite Realty, 555-7970.

Downtown Dream

Sandwiched between skyscrapers, this unique contemporary stands out. Originally built for a corporate executive, its 4 bedrooms, 5 baths meet the highest standards of quality and convenience. Rooftop patio where you can enjoy the skyline. Just $450,000. Call Karl at Elite Realty, 555-7970, to see this urban fantasy come true.

Forget the Freeways

when you live in this old-fashioned, gated 5 bedroom, 4-1/2 bath estate just 10 min. from downtown. You never thought you could have trees, birds, sunshine combined with Victorian grace so close to the city. It offers gingerbread, stained glass, elegant woods for just $375,000. For a trip to the past today, call Sue at Elite Realty, 555-7970.

How Would You Like to Be Close to Work?

You can, when you live in this exciting 4 bedroom brownstone just steps from the medical center. Warm woods, etched glass, 3 fireplaces...it's a study in good taste & quiet quality. Only $401,000. To see it today, call Jennie at Elite Realty, 555-7970.

Center City Convenience

Stunning 4 bedroom, 3 bath contemporary with walls of glass offers the finest in city living. Close to boutiques, superb restaurants, the symphony. Enjoy a loft library, circular stairway, glass-block kitchen. A must-see for sophisticates, just $387,000. Call Cesar at Elite Realty, 555-7970.

Want Top-Notch Schools?

Elegant 5 bedroom, 4 bath French traditional in the highest ranking school district. With white brick, red awnings & an emerald lawn, it offers marble hearths, custom gourmet kitchen, family room gleaming with hardwoods. All this for just $415,000. Call Ali at Elite Realty, 555-7970, to give your kids the best.

NEIGHBORHOOD

Beverly Hills Charmer

You'll love your address almost as much you'll enjoy living in this sprawling English manor. With 8 bedrooms, 7-1/2 baths, there's room for the family & guests. Plus tennis court, spa, pool, 4 car garage & two-lane bowling alley. Life at its best for $650,000. Call Jolie at Elite Realty, 555-7970, now.

Executive Row

It's the lifestyle you deserve...stunning 5 bedroom, 4 bath home in an elite area. Secluded on an acre of manicured grounds, this columned colonial offers an entertainment-sized living room, banquet-perfect dining room, all the luxuries a family could desire. Only $415,000. Give yourself a treat. Call Jim at Elite Realty, 555-7970.

Country Club Comfort

You'll love living so close to the Oak Hills Country Club. Enjoy golf, tennis, swimming just 5 min. from home. And what a home you'll have—an almost new 5 bedroom, 6 bath ranch filled with warm woods, French windows, tons of upgrades. Just $345,000. To see it today, call Sue at Elite Realty, 555-7970.

Blue Chip Address

belongs to you when you move into this elegant Georgian estate on Pine Ridge Drive. 6 spacious bedrooms, 4 full baths, packed with luxury. Sprawling 3 acre lawn, too. Only $398,000. Call Ted at Elite Realty, 555-7970, to visit today.

Malibu Trend Setter

At last, a home as individual as you are. Built by a world traveler, this 3 bedroom contemporary features architectural accents from faraway places. Like the one of a kind brass hooded fireplace & hard-to-find Colombian tiles. Right on the sand, just $425,000. Call June at Elite Realty, 555-7970, to see it today.

AD TIP: Use headlines that create self-interest and avoid ones that merely provoke curiosity.

Discover
Elmwood

with its small town atmosphere & big city convenience, when you live in this gracious Victorian mansion. Built by an oil baron, it offers inlaid hardwoods, 3 marble hearths, gingerbread porch. With all the latest conveniences. Just $415,000. Come visit today. Call Muhammad at Elite Realty, 555-7970.

Enjoy Your
Success

in this elegant 5 bedroom, 4 bath clapboard nestled beneath sprawling elms & towering oaks. Gleaming hardwood floors, sun-splashed designer kitchen, wonderfully wide porch. Tastefully upgraded, it's yours for $387,000. Call Joe at Elite Realty, 555-7970, to move up now.

Prestige Home
in Premier Location

There's no finer address in town. Stately 5 bedroom, 4-1/2 bath traditional, flanked by matching porches & sky-high pines. You'll love its shiny wood floors, elegant chair rail mouldings, warm & wonderful family room. Only $400,000. Call Ken at Elite Realty, 555-7970, now.

Shoreline Drive
Prestige

belongs to you when you live in this jewel-like 4 bedroom, 5 bath Mediterranean. Owned by a designer, its pastel-tinted decor reflects the finest taste. You will love its bleached floors, emerald tile roof, whitewashed walls. Creative landscaping, too. Just $415,000. Make your move up today. Call Mary Beth at Elite Realty, 555-7970.

Vintage
Victorian Row

You've seen them a million times—the pastel fantasies perched along the hill. Now one of them can be yours. Delightful 4 bedroom, 5 bath charmer with intricate gingerbread trim, rocking chair front porch, more than a touch of class. A Victorian dream come true for $395,000. See it now. Call Bo at Elite Realty, 555-7970.

PRIVACY

Mountain Escape

Live the Lincoln lifestyle in luxury in this sumptuous 5 bedroom, 4 bath log cabin sprawled across a mountain. Sunrises, sunsets, wild deer—watch them through your sparkling windows. No neighbors to disturb you. You're all alone on 7 peaceful acres. Just $425,000. To look at this special home today, call Ruth at Elite Realty, 555-7970.

Artists, Writers,
Lovers

Secluded French retreat with delightful rolled roof, dormer windows, 2 brick patios...totally shielded from street by towering shrubs. 4 bedrooms, 3 baths, tastefully decorated. Ideal setting for those inspired by beauty & ambiance of contentment. Only $395,000. For a look, call June at Elite Realty, 555-7970, now.

AD TIP: The first question to ask yourself before writing an ad is, "What kind of person is most likely going to buy this home?"

Do You Treasure Your Privacy?

Then consider this elegant 6 bedroom, 5 bath English manor with a mile-long drive under a canopy of trees. Solid brick construction, with gleaming hardwood floors, grand staircase, floor-to-ceiling leaded glass windows. Just $415,000. Call Ken at Elite Realty, 555-7970, for a look today.

Rim of the Park

Stunning 5 bedroom, 4 bath California ranch new on market. In one family for 2 generations, it overlooks the park's towering trees and bubbling brook. Enjoy shiny hardwood floors, French doors, airy & open rooms. Acre of velvety lawn. Only $398,000. To see it today, call Jim at Elite Realty, 555-7970.

Silent & Secluded

If you crave privacy, consider this 4 bedroom, 3-1/2 bath cedar ranch resting in the foothills. Built on a grand scale, yet intimate & warm. Enjoy a panoramic natural view from your hidden spa or spacious flower-filled deck. Breakfast in the kitchen's nook with its wall-to-wall windows. Just $367,000. Call Ken at Elite Realty, 555-7970, today.

Wooded Executive Retreat

In a prestigious neighborhood, you will find this 5 bedroom, 4 bath contemporary dream. Surrounded by towering trees, it sits on its own acre hidden from view. You'll love its walls of windows, quality touches, feeling of being apart. Offered at $355,000. Call Malcolm at Elite Realty, 555-7970, today.

The Ultimate Haven

Relax in this 5 bedroom, 4 bath brick home with its bubbly spa, whirlpool tubs, generous patio & gas BBQ. Big enough for friends, intimate enough for quiet evenings alone. Complete security system, 3 fireplaces & 3 car garage. Yours for $402,000. For a peek today, call Sue at Elite Realty, 555-7970, now.

Ranch Retreat

If you've always fancied yourself a cowboy but can't give up city comforts, see this rambling 5 bedroom, 4 bath redwood retreat. Offers inspired clean lines with colorful Santa Fe touches. Its 3 Texas-size acres let you live your dream for only $365,000. Call Deanna at Elite Realty, 555-7970, today.

Your Shangri-la

If thoughts of a tropical paradise entice you, why not give in? It'll be easy when you see this long & luscious 4 bedroom, 3 bath California-style beauty. Skylights & greenhouse windows let the sun stream in. Exotic plants fill the huge indoor atrium. Full deck is perfect for basking. Escape to paradise for only $387,000. Call Sue at Elite Realty, 555-7970, for your first trip today.

Hilltop Hideaway

Good taste radiates throughout this mint 5 bedroom, 4 bath hilltop ranch. Priceless 360 degree view. Enjoy towering mountains from the secluded rear patio, twinkling city lights from the window-lined living room. Privacy & luxury for just $400,000. Call Stephanie at Elite Realty, 555-7970.

A World of Privacy

Live a lifestyle few can attain in this spectacular 5 bedroom, 4 bath contemporary cradled on an acre of hillside. Naturally landscaped pool, 3 car garage, wide-open vistas & all the extras you can imagine. Land in the lap of luxury for $425,000. Call Roy at Elite Realty, 555-7970, now.

24 Acres & Independence

If you've never really been comfortable in the city, come out to fresh air & rolling hills. To a 4 bedroom, 3 bath ranch. You can sit on a quiet veranda & count the stars at night. Or relax next to a roaring fire built with wood from your own trees. A home you & the kids will love...just 30 min. from town. Only $398,000. See it now. Call Ruth at Elite Realty, 555-7970.

Heavenly Haven

Secluded behind gates on a full acre, this splendid 5 bedroom, 6 bath traditional offers a tennis court, pool, spa, garden and a magnificent city view. Quality upgrades throughout, modular security. $435,000. For a look today, call Frankie at Elite Realty, 555-7970.

Romantic Retreat

If you love romance, you'll adore this 5 bedroom, 6 bath Mediterranean villa, with bougainvillea-draped patios, dancing fountain, spectacular ocean view. 2 acres of gardens & flowers...just $389,000. Call Ruth at Elite Realty, 555-7970, & let the fantasy begin.

Do You Want to Be Alone?

Then do it in style in this rambling weathered gray ranch 15 miles from town. Secluded on 5 acres of sagebrush & wild flowers, this stunning home offers 5 bedrooms, 4 baths & a host of luxuries. Rough it in sumptuous comfort for $415,000. Call John at Elite Realty, 555-7970, and see this spread now.

SAFETY & SECURITY

Gated Luxury

You'll feel like royalty when your sedan purrs through the wrought iron gate. Drive along winding roads to your 5 bedroom, 4 bath estate. Sleek emerald lawn, custom cabinets, gleaming wood floors, 3 car garage. Safe & secluded splendor for only $425,000. Call Carolina at Elite Realty, 555-7970.

Gate Guarded Splendor

You'll love living in this fabulous guarded community, cradled on rolling hills. Your 4 bedroom, 5 bath California ranch offers the finest in open, airy living, with 2 white brick fireplaces, wonderfully warm kitchen/family room, plant-filled patio. Just $395,000. For a special look today, call Ken at Elite Realty, 555-7970.

Enjoy Estate Privacy

in a secure, gate guarded community of prestige homes. You'll adore this 4 bedroom, 3 bath French Normandy with its elegant chandelier, double French doors, tasteful rose marble hearths. A secluded acre of manicured lawn. Just $385,000. Call Leo at Elite Realty, 555-7970, now.

Wrought Iron Gates

guard entrance to fabulous 5 bedroom, 4-1/2 bath English manor. Tasteful accents like cobblestone drive, lofty brick fireplace, warm wood-paneled kitchen. On a half acre with formal garden. All for just $415,000. Call Randy at Elite Realty, 555-7970, for a look today.

By Your Request

You'll never have to worry about strangers knocking at your door again. In this exclusive guarded community, entrance is by invitation only. Quiet serenity abounds in this spacious 4 bedroom, 3 bath Colorado contemporary with fieldstone fireplace, 2 brick patios, wall-to-wall windows. Just $402,000. See it today. Call Jim at Elite Realty, 555-7970.

VIEW

Your Personal Point of View

Dramatic 4 bedroom, tri-level hugging a hillside. Walls of windows open to wilderness sanctuary. Watch the deer & birds from the comfort of your spacious rock-walled living room. After breakfast in the cheerful eat-in kitchen, feed the birds from your sky-high patio. Your own eagle's nest for $376,000. Call Vi at Elite Realty, 555-790, to see the view today.

Watch the Ships

from the 30' x 15' balcony of this stunning 5 bedroom, 3 bath traditional, high on the bluffs. Enjoy cool ocean breezes, spectacular sunsets, murmuring waves. A lifestyle all its own for $375,000. To see, call Jim at Elite Realty, 555-7970, today.

Ocean View by Day— City Lights at Night

Enjoy both from this long & rambling 5 bedroom, 4 bath contemporary, secluded on a cul-de-sac. Delightful rear stone patio looks out to sun-sparkled waves. Relaxing redwood hot tub offers view of city lights. Only $398,000. Call June at Elite Realty, 555-7970, today.

Priceless View

Spectacular 4 bedroom, 4 bath circular home built exclusively for the view. Hundreds of sq. ft. of glass bring in nature's beauty. Tons of rock, stone & brick create a haven of comfort for $405,000. Call Sue at Elite Realty, 555-7970, today.

Only for Those Who Love...

a fabulous ocean view. Enjoy gorgeous sunsets or graceful sailing ships through the arched windows of this stunning 5 bedroom, 3 bath contemporary. Stained glass windows, full length deck, fieldstone fireplace. Just $389,000. Call Jack at Elite Realty, 555-7970.

Ocean & Mountain View

Enjoy the best of both worlds in this rambling 4 bedroom, 3 bath cedar ranch, nestled in the hills. You'll love its long, clean lines, with artistic touches like imported tiles, inlaid floors, curved brick walls. Only $410,000. To see the view today, call Jim at Elite Realty, 555-7970.

View to the Horizon

You'll be awed by every sunset in this 5 bedroom, 4 bath pueblo home designed for indoor-outdoor living. Tiled patios, sparkling fountain give an air of serenity. Only $412,000. Call Bo at Elite Realty, 555-7970, today.

View to Catalina

Built on a sprawling 1/2 acre, this 4 bedroom, 3 bath Florida-style ranch is sunny & bright. Filled with skylights, plant shelves, arched windows, mirrors. Great outdoor living area, too. A happy home in perfect shape for only $395,000. Call Sue at Elite Realty, 555-7970, today.

Ansel Adams Would've Loved...

the scenery surrounding this spectacular hillside retreat. Built of redwood with walls of glass, its view stretches to infinity. 5 king-size bedrooms, 5 full baths. The ultimate in luxurious living. Just $415,000. See it today. Call Ken at Elite Realty, 555-7970. Bring your camera!

Soothing Greenbelt Views

await you from almost every room of this 5 bedroom, 4 bath downtown brownstone. You'll love its character & charm, with elegant 1800's touches & contemporary rooftop spa overlooking Central Park. Unusual opportunity for $395,000. Call Nancy at Elite Realty, 555-7970, to see it today.

Your Private Lookout Point

Imagine sipping cocktails as you watch the city lights come on. Waking up to gorgeous sunrises streaming in through a wall of windows. Entertaining on a stone patio with breathtaking views. It can all be yours in this magnificent 3 bedroom, 2-1/2 bath home, surrounded by serenity & natural beauty. Offered at $405,000. Call Annabelle at Elite Realty, 555-7970, to see it today.

Skyline View

If you're a fan of city lights, enjoy them from the balcony of this adorable 5 bedroom, 4 bath French chateau. You'll love the marble floors, bleached wood cabinets, beveled glass. Elegance & drama for $415,000. Come by today. Call Ken at Elite Realty, 555-7970.

360 Degree View

Enjoy panoramic views from this 5 bedroom, 3 bath hideaway only 20 miles from town. In unique natural setting high on a hill, it offers vistas worthy of professional photographers. Crafted from cedar, stained glass & glowing hardwoods, it's specially priced at $425,000. Call Sue at Elite Realty, 555-7970, today.

Walls of Glass

bring spectacular outdoor scenery into this cool & soothing 4 bedroom, 3 bath contemporary retreat. If you like stone, rock, brick & glass, you'll love the feel & texture of this custom home. Offered at $375,000. To see this unique home today, call Marcy at Elite Realty, 555-7970.

Bird's-Eye View

belongs to you from dramatic glass-walled living room of this 5 bedroom, 3 bath California traditional. Bright & open, with skylights, terraces & indoor atrium, it's a quality home that's sure to please any family. Only $375,500. See for yourself. Call Fredrick at Elite Realty, 555-7970, today.

AD TIP: Try to paint a vivid portrayal of the home you're advertising. This will inspire your prospects to call.

SIZE

4+ BEDROOMS

Room to S-P-R-E-A-D Out

If your family likes privacy, consider this charming cedar-shingled ranch. Secluded on an acre of flowering shrubs, it offers 5 Texas-size bedrooms, 4 full baths. Delightful eat-in kitchen, redwood ceiling in living room, potbellied stove in family room. Just $310,000. Call Diana at Elite Realty, 555-7970, today.

Historic Home—6 Bedrooms, 8 Baths on 4.92 Acres

Quality & tasteful touches of the past are reflected in this delightful 1891 Victorian lovingly kept throughout the years. Modern baths & gourmet kitchen have been skillfully integrated with its unique charm & gentle luxury. Yesterday's value can be yours today for $310,000. Call Tim at Elite Realty, 555-7970.

Quality Family Home

If your family needs more room, consider this sprawling California ranch. 3 bedrooms, downstairs sauna, luxurious upstairs master bedroom with fireplace. Exposed beams create light & airy feeling, heightened by oversize glass doors that open to nature's preserve. Just $350,000. Your family deserves the finest. Call Kim, Elite Realty, 555-7970, now.

Big Enough for Two Families

Don't miss this spectacular 5 bedroom, 4 bath beauty. It's perfect for 2 families, with double master suites, 2 kitchens & a 3 car garage. Only $355,000. See it today. Call Kim at Elite Realty, 555-7970.

4 Bedroom Suites

It's the ultimate rambling farm-style clapboard with combination bedroom/ sitting areas & baths. Perfect for large family that likes plenty of privacy. Charm galore with shutters, hardwood floors, polished cherry staircase. Just $312,000. Call Lisa at Elite Realty, 555-7970, now.

Family-Pleasing Ranch

If you could design a perfect home for a large family, would it have a huge playroom, wonderful fenced yard, delightful eat-in kitchen, 4 bedrooms & 4 baths? If that's what you'd like then see this Early American ranch today. Only $278,000. Call Helen at Elite Realty, 555-7970.

Give Your Family the Best

Magnificent 6 bedroom, 6 bath English Tudor. Handcrafted 3 years ago, it offers the finest in contemporary conveniences, blended with old English charm. Manicured lawn, curved driveway, free-form pool. Only $475,000. Call Kim at Elite Realty, 555-7970, for a bit of Britain.

6 Bedrooms, Great Neighborhood

come with this warm & comfortable colonial, located in a prestigious neighborhood. Your kids will love the dormer windows, spacious attic, cozy play areas. You'll love its wool carpet, upgraded materials, sunny & sprawling lawn. For $315,000, isn't it worth a look? Hurry & call Ted at Elite Realty, 555-7970, now.

5 Bedroom Georgian Manor

You'll feel like the king of the castle in this stunning 5 bedroom, 4 bath manor. Special touches like extra-wide hallways, stained glass windows, gleaming copper kitchen, 2 fireplaces, 3 car garage. Offered at $375,000. Call Henrietta at Elite Realty, 555-7970, today.

Private Children's Wing

in this rambling 4 bedroom, 3-3/4 bath colonial charmer, nestled on a tree-filled lot. White clapboard, yellow shutters, awnings, brick walks, old-fashioned summer porch. A delight to look at & a pleasure to live in. Just $395,000. See for yourself. Call Calvin at Elite Realty, 555-7970, today.

For the Large Family

Ponderosa-style ranch with plenty of room to roam. With 6 bedrooms, 5-1/2 baths, gourmet kitchen, rock-walled fireplace, acres of white board fencing. A real treat for $315,000. Call Victor at Elite Realty, 555-7970, to see it today.

Executive Family Home

in the best area...sprawling 5 bedroom, 4 bath contemporary built with the finest materials & taste. 2 white brick fireplaces, gorgeous stone walls, quality slate floors. On 1/2 acre just one block from Elite Country Club. $398,000. For a look today, call Sue at Elite Realty, 555-7970.

4 Big Bedrooms in the Country

Give your kids the experience of country living, with animals, a garden & lots of fresh air. This old-fashioned style homestead offers big sunny rooms, 3 baths, sweeping staircase. You'll love the window-filled, eat-in kitchen with its superb rocking chair porch. Take it easy for $315,000. Call Ken at Elite Realty, 555-7970.

Large Brownstone

Ideal for the large family living in the city, with 5 bedrooms, 3-1/2 baths, generously-sized "great room." 9' ceilings add drama, while wrought iron staircase & French windows create charm. Delightful home in terrific neighborhood for $315,000. Call Barbara at Elite Realty, 555-7970, for a look today.

Perfect for the Waltons

with its gnarled apple tree, wide & inviting front porch, bushes bursting with flowers. Life the way it used to be in this 6 bedroom, 4 bath country retreat just 10 miles outside the city. Enjoy fresh air, sunshine & Mother Nature for $255,000. Call Joe at Elite Realty, 555-7970, today.

EXTRA SPACE

A Home With Room to Play

If you have an active family, drive out to this 4 bedroom, 4 bath contemporary packed with fun. Billiard room...home gym...graceful pool...plus upgrades like Jenn-air range, gaslit rock fireplaces, thermopane windows. Just $255,000. Call Sue at Elite Realty, 555-7970, now.

Room, Room & More Room

Let your imagination run wild in this tasteful 5 bedroom, 4 bath hillside charmer. With 12 rooms & 3,400 sq. ft., there is plenty of area for creativity. High ceilings, vintage windows, 3 fireplaces, shingle roof...just $315,000. To see a big & beautiful home, call Betty at Elite Realty, 555-7970, today.

Give Grandma Her Own Suite

with her own fireplace, in this delightful 6 bedroom, 4 bath Georgian manor. You will love its classic French windows, gleaming oak floors, shiny copper kitchen & 4 fireplaces. Just $345,000. See it now. Call Margarita at Elite Realty, 555-7970.

12 Room Mansion

Vacant for the past year, this old-fashioned estate needs some sprucing up. But it'll be well worth it. Unusual stonework, grand staircase, statue-decorated veranda. Old-world elegance on a full acre for $300,000. Call Daniel at Elite Realty, 555-7970, to see this diamond in the rough today.

5,000 Square Feet

If you've always wanted room to ramble, come to this delightful 5 bedroom, 4 bath California ranch. With its wide window walls, skylights, 3 patios & screened porch, you'll never feel closed in again. Plenty of space for workshop & storage in 3 car garage. Big lawn, too. Small price of $298,000. To see it today, call John at Elite Realty, 555-7970.

Giant Georgian

You'll be thrilled when you walk into this elegant 1920 classic, with sun spilling down its circular staircase. Through the arches waits a tasteful living room with 2 fireplaces. 10 ft. ceilings in the airy 4 bedrooms, 3 baths. Cradled on 1/2 acre of trees, this superb home is listed at $325,000. Call Nichole at Elite Realty, 555-7970, to take a look today.

Colossal Colonial

You'll love Christmas in this 5 bedroom, 4 bath blue & white colonial secluded on a cul-de-sac. Put the tree in the 2-story bow window, hang your stockings on the handsome oak mantel. Velvety lawn, too. Only $315,000. Call Henrietta at Elite Realty, 555-7970, today.

Big & Beautiful

Sun flows into this free & open 4 bedroom, 3-1/2 bath Colorado contemporary, with natural wood beams, plank floors, plenty of room to breathe. On quiet, tree-lined street in executive neighborhood. Just $345,000. To see it today, call Vic at Elite Realty, 555-7970.

PRICE/TERMS

FIXER-UPPER

For a Fix-It Person

If you have more taste than money, see this ramshackle mansion in a great neighborhood. Pry the boards off the windows & discover graciously proportioned, high-ceilinged rooms. Pull the weeds outside & you'll find 1/2 acre of once lush lawn. 12 rooms in all...$295,750. What you see is what you get. For real value, call Jim at Elite Realty, 555-7970, now.

Diamond in the Ruff

Sad looking golf course home has great potential—you can tell by the floor-to-ceiling windows, slate floors, solid oak cabinets. 4 bedrooms, 3 baths...perfect for the family willing to invest a little of themselves. Bargain-priced at $215,000. Call Ted at Elite Realty, 555-7970.

Abandoned Estate

If you don't mind creaking doors, sagging floors & overgrown fountains, see the possibilities in this once gracious estate home. With 4 bedrooms, 2-1/2 baths, on fenced 1/2 acre, its classic lines & faded elegance still hold charm. Priced to sell fast at $255,000. Hurry & call June at Elite Realty, 555-7970, now.

Bring Your Boots

You'll need them to wade through the years of debris in this once stunning 4 bedroom, 4 bath Greek Revival classic. Superbly styled in 1923, it's been terribly neglected. But for just $315,000, you can have a home worth thousands more. Call Tim at Elite Realty, 555-7970, & bring back the long ago elegance.

Eyesore Estate

You'll wonder how people could've lived like this—but you'll be grateful they did. For just $215,000, you can own a once splendid 5 bedroom, 6 bath colonial circled by magnificent oaks & silvery birches. In an exclusive neighborhood, this home, in time, can be a family showplace. If you don't mind hard work, call Ted at Elite Realty, 555-7970, right now.

Neglected Tennis Estate

If you're a tennis nut, consider this once charming estate with its own court. Abandoned last year, the 4 bedroom, 3 bath cedar ranch house needs lots of work...but you can reward yourself with a round of tennis or a dip in its sparkling pool. Much potential for just $255,000. See for yourself. Call Ken at Elite Realty, 555-7970, today.

TLC Will Save You $$$

This is your chance to move up in the world fast. Run-down Beverly Hills estate, with 5 bedrooms & 3 baths on 1/4 acre. Bring your toolbox because this home needs some work...but you're getting one of the finest addresses in the country. Only $300,000. For a once in a lifetime opportunity, call Julie at Elite Realty, 555-7970, today.

Abandoned 4 BR

Once dramatic contemporary with 4 baths on acre of stunning natural landscaping. Needs paint, electrical, & plumbing. But you can live in it now. Golden chance for $312,000. Call Barbara at Elite Realty, 555-7970, today.

Needs Your TLC

If you enjoy a challenge, see this seaside New England-style home with 4 bedrooms, 3 baths. Once a quality residence, it's fallen into disrepair. Skylights, refinished floors, a few new windows could do wonders. Just $295,000, surrounded by estates. Call Juanita at Elite Realty, 555-7970, today. Better hurry!

Former Showplace

You'll never guess a wealthy family lived here...until you see the 2 gleaming marble hearths, imported Italian tile & handcrafted cherry cabinets. Needs some polishing, but this 5 bedroom, 4 bath villa is a great bargain. Just $300,000. Create your own dynasty. Call Steve at Elite Realty, 555-7970, today.

AD TIP: Make sure that the seller reviews and is comfortable with your ad before placing it.

Fixer on 1/2 Acre— Potential Estate

Victorian fans will adore the lacy gingerbread on the front porch of this once regal 1893 home. With 4 bedrooms, 3 baths, its past beauty is hinted at in the oak & cherry staircase, dark rich trim, elegant windows. Layers of dirt & grime, but what a bargain at $287,000. Call Vivian at Elite Realty, 555-7970, to own a piece of the past today.

See the Possibilities

in this sadly neglected, recently abandoned 1956 contemporary. Art deco lovers will adore its unique touches, while families will appreciate its 4 big bedrooms, each with own bath. Classic styling with long rows of windows & many natural stones. It'll take work, but at $212,000, it's worth seeing. Call Mike at Elite Realty, 555-7970, now.

Abandoned Rustic

Your chance to own a home with history —splendid family ranch for generations now fallen into neglect. Enjoy the warmth of wood-filled rooms, brightness of a sun filled kitchen, comfort of 5 bedrooms, 4 baths. 2 wonderful acres. Even with its problems, this is a charming brick home. Just $225,000. To see it today, call June at Elite Realty, 555-7970.

Blue & White Rustic

It's hard to find a fixer with so much appeal, but this delightful 4 bedroom, 4 bath Dutch Colonial radiates warmth. Window seats, brick walkways, fantastic summer porch. Scrape away the dirt & you're in for a surprise. Terrific neighborhood. Only $200,000. Call Fredrick at Elite Realty, 555-7970, today.

Rustic Ruin

Once charming redwood rambler, accented by oak & brass, now smothered by leaves & debris. Bring your contractor because this 4 bedroom house needs work. But for $200,000, it's hard to find an empty lot in this neighborhood. See for yourself. Call Sandy at Elite Realty, 555-7970, now.

BARGAIN PRICE

Bargain Estate

If you love a bargain, rush right over to this 4 bedroom, 4 bath estate in a choice neighborhood. Hard-to-find quality, nestled on 1/2 acre, with solid brick construction, 3 fireplaces, 4 car garage. Just $215,000. Call Suzanna at Elite Realty, 555-7970, to make it yours today.

Live High for Less

You'll adore this first class 4 bedroom, 4 bath custom contemporary high in the hills. Surrounded by spectacular scenery, it offers Jenn-air range, Berber carpets, magnificent brass fireplace. Genuine bargain at $245,000. See it today. Call Ken at Elite Realty, 555-7970.

Elegant & Affordable

If you're looking for a golf course home under $215,000, this is it. Stunning 1965 contemporary with full-wall windows, 3 fireplaces, slate floors, marble vanities. Cradled on an acre of towering trees. Call Anne at Elite Realty, 555-7970, to hurry over today.

Attention: Bargain Hunters

At $213,000, this antebellum-style mansion is priced for quick sale. 4 bedrooms, 4 baths. Marble accents, French windows, full-length veranda, ornate iron work, gourmet kitchen. Thousands below market. Take advantage today. Call Freddy at Elite Realty, 555-7970.

Below Market Value

Desperate owner needs action on gorgeous 4 bedroom, 5 bath Colorado contemporary, with 2 fieldstone fireplaces, miniature citrus orchard, gleaming oak floors. Quiet quality on lovely acre lot for $245,000. Call Jani at Elite Realty, 555-7970, to make your move today.

Price Drastically Reduced

on a charming Spanish villa smothered in tropical landscaping. If you love thick adobe walls, colorful tile floors, hand-built fireplaces, massive wood beams, this 5 bedroom, 3-1/2 bath retreat is for you. Way below market at $275,000. To see, call Beth at Elite Realty, 555-7970.

Reduced Thousands

You'll love the deal on this terrific 4 bedroom, 5 bath tri-level in an exclusive area. Original bronze fountain in courtyard, dramatic 2-story living room with panoramic view, tasteful & elegant high-tech kitchen. Just reduced to $213,000. Wait 'til you see it! Call Noel at Elite Realty, 555-7970, today.

AD TIP: Target your ads for the type of prospect you're seeking.

Must-Sell Price

Be ready to move on this exciting 4 bedroom, 3 bath Cape Cod, built with all the luxury you can imagine. Wool carpets, custom-crafted window nooks, copper & brick kitchen...the country look you love at a very affordable $204,000. Hurry & call Kenneth at Elite Realty, 555-7970, before it's too late.

Divorce Forces Sale

Stunning peaches & cream 4 bedroom, 3 bath rambler in prestigious area. Exquisite custom touches like walk-in butler's pantry, dressing suites, see-through white brick fireplace, make it elegant. Super schools make it practical. Just $234,000. Hurry on this one. Call Willie at Elite Realty, 555-7970, today.

High-Class Bargain

This unusual 4 bedroom, 3 bath contemporary radiates excitement. Sleek black & white tile kitchen, dramatic hooded living room fireplace, sharp pastel spa on mosaic deck. Quality you couldn't ordinarily touch for $225,000. See it today. Call Kimlee at Elite Realty, 555-7970, now.

Designer Home, Great Price

You'll love entertaining your friends in this 5 bedroom, 3 bath French stunner. Perfect taste shows in its luxurious carpets, sparkling casement windows, elegant tile patio. Even the kitchen decor is superb. Yours for only $234,000. Call Ted at Elite Realty, 555-7970, today.

Champagne Taste on a Budget?

Then come home to this luxurious 4 bedroom, 5 bath California ranch snuggled in the foothills. Superior craftsmanship in its custom windows, brick floors, gleaming slate fireplaces. Not to mention the stained-glass-filled kitchen & acre yard. Quick-sale priced at $213,000. Call Jim at Elite Realty, 555-7970, fast.

Probate Sale— Sacrifice Price

Heirs want out of rambling 4 bedroom with den & 3-1/2 bath brick colonial resting behind wrought iron gates on velvety 1/2 acre. You'll adore its fan windows, lovely sun porch, cheerful eat-in kitchen. Quality home in elite area for $235,000. Call Ted at Elite Realty, 555-7970, today.

Unbeatable Bargain

You couldn't build this 4 bedroom, 4 bath contemporary ranch for $256,000. You'll appreciate the care that went into this home, with its solid cherry cabinets, skylights, terrific workshop/garage. Executive friendly neighborhood, too. Call Linda at Elite Realty, 555-7970, for a look today.

Searching for a Bargain?

Then head right over to this historic 4 bedroom, 3 bath stone home, tucked away next to a gurgling creek. Under a canopy of trees, it offers stained glass windows, hand-carved woods, thoughtfully modernized gourmet kitchen. Ridiculously priced at $240,000. Call Ann at Elite Realty, 555-7970, today.

Below '81 Sales Price

Owner needs out of charming 3 bedroom, 3 bath cedar-shingled traditional. On acre of trees, bushes & flowers, it's perfect for a growing family. Wonderful warm wood-paneled den, delightful eat-in kitchen, huge play area. Priced to go at $222,000. Bring the kids today. Call Fred at Elite Realty, 555-7970.

Bargain Delight

Warm & intimate 4 bedroom, 5 bath country-style home, with walls of windows looking out to rose garden. Built of solid brick & featuring its own miniature tower with spiral staircase leading to master bedroom or study. Just $215,000. For a special treat, call Susan at Elite Realty, 555-7970, today.

Below Market Manor

You'll feel terrific when you move into this elegant half-timbered English Tudor. For only $225,000, you get a home worth thousands more. Antique mantels shipped from London, hand-carved staircase, a library right out of the movies. See for yourself. Call Ken at Elite Realty, 555-7970, now.

Save Thousands Here

Delightful yellow clapboard home with 4 bedrooms, 5 baths. Graced by tall trees, this country charmer offers warm woods, rosy brick fireplaces, many luxuries. Just $234,000. To see this money-maker, call Vivianna at Elite Realty, 555-7970.

AD TIP: Feel free to mention brand names in your ads. Capitalize on all the advertising major companies do to promote their products.

Beautiful Bargain

Perfect for a magazine cover. Low & rambling cedar with flowers draped across a trellised patio, circular brick driveway, airy front sun porch. Touches of charm show in 5 bedrooms, 4 baths, gracefully proportioned rooms. Wonderful neighborhood. Just $213,000, see for yourself. Call Rahamini at Elite Realty, 555-7970, today.

MUST SELL QUICKLY

Owner Desperate— Already Bought Another

Hurry to see this charming French country home loaded with upgrades. 4 bedrooms, 5 baths offering the warmth of hand-painted tiles, bleached floors, walnut cabinets. Delightful forest-like setting just 5 min. from town. Priced to go fast at $212,000. Call Jim at Elite Realty, 555-7970, to view it now.

Owner Needs Action

on sophisticated 3 bedroom, 4 bath contemporary with view of city lights. Enjoy 45' deck with sizzling spa, high-tech kitchen, custom workshop in 3 car garage. Private winding drive. Just $200,000. For a look today, call Sue at Elite Realty, 555-7970.

Reduced to Sell Immediately

Better move fast on this delightful 4 bedroom, 4 bath brick traditional just 5 min. from University Medical Center. No expense was spared on this magnificent home with a splashing fountain out front. Due to transfer, doctor must sell quickly. Priced below replacement at $225,000. Call Tim at Elite Realty, 555-7970, now.

Better Move Fast

on stunning 5 bedroom, 4 bath California Craftsman in prestigious neighborhood. Enjoy beveled glass windows, heart of pine cabinets, built-in bookcases & china hutch. Old-fashioned quality at yesterday's price of $211,000. Call Jim at Elite Realty, 555-7970. Don't miss out.

Builder's Close-Out

Developer wants quick action on lovely 4 bedroom, 3 bath Spanish villa. Arched balconies, soothing tile courtyard, mountain view. Great schools within walking distance. Way below value at $211,000. Call John at Elite Realty, 555-7970, if you're ready to move.

Immediate Sale Required

on magnificent 6 bedroom, 5 bath manor in top area. On an acre of manicured grounds, this sumptuous Tudor offers the finest luxuries imaginable, coupled with abundant warmth & charm. Bargain beauty at $245,000. Hurry & call June at Elite Realty, 555-7970, today.

Must Sell Fast

Glorious ocean view contemporary with walls of windows overlooking sand & surf. Giant glassed-in patio, top-of-the-line upgrades. Cool & refreshing colors. 4 bedrooms, 3 baths. All for $301,000. Call Sue at Elite Realty, 555-7970, today.

Can You Act Fast?

Then hurry over to this wonderful historical home surrounded by estates. Antique lovers will adore its giant eaves, roofed driveway, elegant gate. Kids will love its nooks & crannies, spacious attic, large yard. 4 bedrooms, 5 baths for $203,000. Call Ken at Elite Realty, 555-7970, now.

Owner Needs Help

Paying 2 mortgages—must sacrifice 4 bedroom, 2-3/4 bath brick traditional in excellent area. Couldn't ask for better quality, with old-fashioned hardwood floors, gleaming updated kitchen, spacious summer porch. For $213,000, better act fast. Call Fred at Elite Realty, 555-7970, now.

Need Fast Escrow?

Then rush over to this custom 4 bedroom, 3 bath ranch in superb school district. Charm galore with French doors, bay window dining, decorator-perfect country kitchen. Stone walls & terraced gardens, too. Fast price of $202,000. Call June at Elite Realty, 555-7970, now.

Sale Fell Through—
Owner Moved

from this wonderful stone home, resting high on a hill, with a panoramic valley view. Thick walls, rocking chair front porch, sunny & bright 5 bedrooms. Lots of custom upgrades you'll love. At $213,000, this won't last. Call Randy at Elite Realty, 555-7970, quickly.

Owner Needs $$$ Now

so he's ready to deal on this almost new 4 bedroom, 5 bath colonial cradled in its own little woods. Island kitchen, greenhouse window, custom brick patio, huge screened porch. Plus birds, deer, squirrels, flowers...all for $215,000. It'll go fast. Call Vi at Elite Realty, 555-7970.

AD TIP: Price and location are the two most important home buying factors. The newspaper will place your ad by location but you should also include the price.

Just Listed Again, Fell Out of Escrow

Desperate owner needs ready-to-move family for terrific 4 bedroom, 4 bath traditional home on cul-de-sac. White brick, yellow shutters, columned porch, sloping lawn overlooking wooded ravine. Tons of upgrades. Bargain-priced at $225,000. Call Dick at Elite Realty, 555-7970, now.

FORECLOSURE

Lender Foreclosure

on stunning 4 bedroom, 5 bath rock-walled home in prestigious area. Enjoy the finest in materials, coupled with abundant comforts. Gently sloping 1/2 acre lot. Much privacy. Just $415,000. Call Ken at Elite Realty, 555-7970, today.

Victorian Foreclosure

Need quick action on 1894 historical home shaded by ancient oaks. If you love gingerbread trim, antique fireplaces, upgrades hidden in old-fashioned cabinets, hurry over. At $402,000, this 5 bedroom, 4 bath home is priced far below it's value. Call Fred Lee at Elite Realty, 555-7970, today.

Bankrupt Estate

Wonderful 1959 contemporary on acre of rolling lawn in executive neighborhood. Incredible value for 3 bedrooms, 4 giant baths, flagstone patio, hardwood floors, breathtaking vistas. Couldn't build it for $215,000. Hurry & call Michelle at Elite Realty, 555-7970, before it's gone.

Save the Foreclosure

on this landmark historical home high on a hill. Lovingly restored with quality upgrades, yet retains original charm. 6 bedrooms, 5 baths, all gleaming with rich woods & glass. A bargain at $305,000. Call June at Elite Realty, 555-7970, now.

Fabulous Foreclosure

Entertainer's dream. 5 bedroom, 3-1/2 bath, dramatic low-slung contemporary designed to catch everyone's eye. Wide, spacious rooms with magnificent architectural accents...luxurious pool...1/2 acre garden. Yours for only $325,000. Better move fast. Call Sue at Elite Realty, 555-7970, today.

Court Orders Immediate Sale

of this impressive 4 bedroom, 2-3/4 bath traditional brick, a tribute to excellent taste & fine quality. You'll love its high ceilings, huge summer porch, generously-sized kitchen, 3 car garage. A home for comfortable living on 1/2 acre. Just $275,000. Call Roger at Elite Realty, 555-7970, now.

Bargain Foreclosure

It's hard to find 4,000 sq. ft. for less than $275,000...but this rambling 4 bedroom, 3-1/2 bath rustic is it. Charm abounds in its polished redwood ceilings, delightful balconies, wide open windows. Heavily wooded lot adds privacy. If you're looking for a terrific bargain, call Mary at Elite Realty, 555-7970, fast. This won't last.

Foreclosed Estate

Wrought iron gates welcome you to this superbly crafted 5 bedroom, 4 bath traditional. Built of stone, rock & brick, it features gracefully proportioned rooms, stunning gourmet kitchen, solarium dining, 3 handsome antique fireplaces. On professionally landscaped 1/2 acre, it is yours for only $405,000. Move fast. Call Bob at Elite Realty, 555-7970, now.

Bankrupt Owner Needs Out

of delightful family home. 5 bedrooms, 3-1/2 baths & upgrades you'll love. Basketball court, black-bottom pool, sizzling spa, walnut-paneled den...designed for family fun. Just $425,000. Give your kids a treat today. Call Joe at Elite Realty, 555-7970.

Bank-Owned Estate

Bank wants out of this 2,800 sq. ft. executive retreat just 10 miles from town. Magnificent Tudor with 5 bedrooms, 4 baths, quality touches throughout. Acre of beautifully landscaped grounds. Priced far below value at $475,000. See it yourself. Call Fred at Elite Realty, 555-7970.

OWNER/SPECIAL FINANCING

Low Down Payment

on this adorable 5 bedroom, 4 bath ocean view home. Wide & airy with white exposed beams, indoor pool, slate floors, giant lawn. Best of all, owner will carry below market rate. A great buy at just $300,000. Call Joe at Elite Realty, 555-7970, to make a deal today.

Less Down Than You Might Think...

moves you into a home that's the envy of the neighborhood. Giant stone sprawler with 5 bedrooms & 6 baths, perched on a hill. Gorgeous hardwood floors, tons of built-ins, glamorous etched glass. Priced at $312,000, owner will finance. Call Ned at Elite Realty, 555-7970, now.

Forget the Qualifying

Owner will carry loan on charming 4 bedroom, 3-1/2 bath California rambler in superb neighborhood. Enjoy big sunny bedrooms, feast-sized dining room, huge playground & lawn. Priced at $303,000, with below market loan. Call Joe at Elite Realty, 555-7970, today.

You Save Thousands

With owner carrying loan far below market rate, you get low monthly payments while enjoying sumptuous 5 bedroom, 4 bath traditional brick manor. You won't believe that $214,000 gives you diamond-paned windows, manicured lawn, oak floors, huge country kitchen. Call Melinda at Elite Realty, 555-7970, to find out more.

No Points

because owner will carry you on this splendid 4 bedroom, 2-3/4 bath Colorado contemporary, snuggled next to babbling brook. Fieldstone walls, heart of pine cabinets, massive rock fireplaces, giant screened porch. Spacious but warm & cozy. Terrific price of $312,000. To see today, call Tina at Elite Realty, 555-7970.

AD TIP: *Don't be afraid to use questions, expecially in your headlines.*

No Down Payment

Owner will carry loan on this delightful 4 bedroom, 3 bath English Tudor. You not only get a finely crafted home in an executive neighborhood, you get below market financing. For just $303,000, it is a great deal. Call Fredrick at Elite Realty, 555-7970, to see it today.

No Credit Check

because owner will finance you on this wonderful 4 bedroom, 3-3/4 bath California Craftsman in estate neighborhood. Richly restored to its 1924 grandeur, it features the finest luxury touches combined with classic beauty. On sloping lot. Only $325,000. Call Ken at Elite Realty, 555-7970, today.

Special Financing Available

on wonderful 5 bedroom, 4 bath rambler with an exquisite, sun-filled family room. You'll love its bronze-accented country kitchen...gleaming mellow woods...delightful dormer windows. With owner willing to carry below market, it's yours for full price of $312,000. Take advantage today. Call Beverly at Elite Realty, 555-7970.

Low on Cash?

That's no problem with this gorgeous 5 bedroom, 4 bath white brick traditional. Owner will carry you with little or no down. If you like quality touches like whirlpool tubs, brick verandas, graceful weeping willows then call Jimmie at Elite Realty, 555-7970, today. At $315,000, this stunner is sure to move quickly.

Below Market Terms

available on old-world style Victorian, cupcake fantasy of pastels & gingerbread, with 4 bedrooms, 5 baths...lovingly updated. Owner willing to finance at bargain price of $333,000. See it today. Call Fred at Elite Realty, 555-7970.

Terrific Terms

waiting for you on this handsome 4 bedroom, 5 bath Georgian on 1/2 acre lot. Jenn-air range, wool carpets, circular staircase, marble accents. Tasteful home for $312,000. With owner financing below market, can you afford not to see it? Call Lee at Elite Realty, 555-7970, today.

Such a Deal

is waiting for you on this stunning 3 bedroom, 5 bath Williamsburg colonial with owner willing to carry below market. You'll love its high ceilings, open & airy feeling, gleaming gourmet kitchen. Separate office, too. Just $405,000. For a super deal, call Ned at Elite Realty, 555-7970, now.

Low Owner Financing

available on 5 bedroom, 3-3/4 bath brick beauty just across from park. Enjoy convenient downtown living in sumptuous style, with grand living room, floor-to-ceiling French doors, elegant designer kitchen, 2 car garage. Offered at only $298,000. Call Raymond at Elite Realty, 555-7970, today.

Get the Low Down...

on this almost new Yankee Salt Box in elite area. With 4 bedrooms, 5 baths, it's full of old-fashioned charm tastefully combined with modern conveniences. Owner willing to carry on EZ terms at $315,000. Call Ruth Ann at Elite Realty, 555-7970, today.

Low, Low Interest

Owner will finance you at below market rate on this gorgeous New Orleans-style home in a fine neighborhood. With 5 bedrooms, 4 baths, this home offers the finest in luxurious living. Giant 1/2 acre lot filled with trees, flowers, bushes. Yours for just $298,000. Call Joe at Elite Realty, 555-7970, today.

No Loan Fees

Owner will finance terrific 4 bedroom, 2-3/4 bath contemporary. Enjoy dramatic windows overlooking city lights, gleaming oak floors, 2 slate fireplaces, sizzling patio spa. Full price only $265,000. Call Susie at Elite Realty, 555-7970. Better hurry! This one won't last.

EZ Qualifying

Owner financing this dreamy 3 bedroom, 2 bath ranch, nestled in honeysuckle & ivy. You'll adore its homey atmosphere, spacious rooms, 2 huge oak fireplaces. Cradled on 1/2 acre lot for $345,000. Call Jo at Elite Realty, 555-7970, today.

Free & Clear Owner

willing to finance you below market on elegant 3 bedroom, 3 bath perfect family home, with airy & bright den, cheerful eat-in kitchen, giant play area, 3+ car garage. Only $334,000. To see it today, call Rachel at Elite Realty, 555-7970.

Empty Nesters Will Carry

You'll love the below market financing on this stately 4 bedroom, 2-1/2 bath colonial in prestigious neighborhood. Graceful white columns, sweeping emerald lawn, delicate casement windows. A home to cherish for just $303,000. See it today. Call Sue at Elite Realty, 555-7970.

Terrific Financing

available on 4 bedroom, 3 bath seaside stunner. Long & low across the bluffs, this home offers 1950's quality combined with 1990's conveniences. You'll love its free-flowing floor plan, elegant accents, wide windows. With owner carrying below market rate, it's a steal for $315,000. Call Jay at Elite Realty, 555-7970, today.

ASSUMABLE LOAN

Below Market Interest? It's Possible...

when you take over loan on charming 4 bedroom, 3 bath Spanish hacienda, hidden on 1/2 acre lot. You'll adore its terra-cotta tile floors, massive mahogany fireplaces, gleaming paned windows. A real treasure at just $325,000. Call Ty at Elite Realty, 555-7970, for a real deal today.

Possible Below Market Loan

if you're the lucky owner of this sumptuous mountain hideaway, just 25 min. from town. Enjoy clean air, blue skies and the fresh scent of pines all year-round. Luxurious, almost new 5 bedrooms, 4 baths. Unbelievable price of just $315,000. Call Clara at Elite Realty, 555-7970, for details today.

Low Assumable

on gracious 4 bedroom, 5 bath French Normandy on prestigious Buck's Row. With a small down, you can enjoy hand-plastered ceilings, ornate balconies, delightfully large rooms, 3 car garage. Only $425,000. Call Henrietta at Elite Realty, 555-7970, today.

Assume
Low Interest Loan

and enjoy yesterday's interest rate on a very today home—stylish 4 bedroom, 6 bath tri-level built into a hillside. Hundreds of sq. ft. of glass, ceramic tile kitchen, slate-floored den, soaring ceilings. Great area. For $375,000, it's a steal. Call Ken at Elite Realty, 555-7970, now.

You Won't Believe
Your Luck

on this charming 5 bedroom, 4 bath traditional on a heavily wooded acre. In an executive neighborhood, it offers luxurious extras like whirlpool baths, trash compactor, solar hot water, custom workshop/garage. Just $275,000 with an assumable loan. To see today, call Ken at Elite Realty, 555-7970.

Attractive
Assumable

on one of the prettiest houses in the neighborhood. Storybook cottage with rolled roof, brick-walled patio, colorful window boxes, hidden on 1/2 acre. 4 bedrooms, 5 baths make it perfect for a family. Priced at $317,000. How can you beat it? Call Shawntela at Elite Realty, 555-7970, today.

Take Over
Low Payments

on gracious, almost new antebellum-style mansion in executive family neighborhood. With small down enjoy a country-cozy kitchen & family room, entertainment-sized living room, wonderful master suite. Just $315,000. Call Ken at Elite Realty, 555-7970, to see it today.

Forget
the Credit Check

You won't need it when you take over below market loan on this stunning 5 bedroom, 4 bath California contemporary. Set amid tall trees, this cedar-shingled charmer offers walls of windows, gleaming oak floors, top-of-the-line appliances. A must-see at $275,000. Call Jack at Elite Realty, 555-7970, now.

EZ Assumable

on handsome 4 bedroom, 3-1/2 bath Early American home. Radiant with dark woods, plush carpets, wide windows pouring in the sun. In prestigious North Hills, this nearly new showcase is offered at just $275,000. Save thousands! For a terrific deal, call Joe at Elite Realty, 555-7970, right now.

How to Avoid
High Interest

Own the home you've been dreaming about by assuming the low interest loan on this charming New Orleans-style stunner. You'll love its 5 bedrooms (all with balconies), 4 luxurious baths, grand staircase, gourmet kitchen. Not to mention the low monthly payments. Only $315,000. See it today. Call Fred at Elite Realty, 555-7970.

If You've Been Rejected for a Loan...

consider assuming a below market loan on a terrific 5 bedroom, 4 bath secluded contemporary. Enjoy the drama of natural rock, wood & stone. Custom quality, affordably priced at just $265,000. Great neighborhood. Call Ken at Elite Realty, 555-7970, for a look today.

Sweet & Low Assumable

on 4 bedroom, 2-1/2 bath Georgian, built with care just 3 years ago. You'll love its handmade bricks, fan windows, arched doorways. Superb taste throughout. With a small down, assume below market loan. Full price only $315,000. Call Noel at Elite Realty, 555-7970, today.

Assume & Save

when you move into this 4 bedroom, 3-3/4 bath French country charmer on prestigious golf course. European flair in its natural floors, stained glass cabinets, thick beamed ceilings. Wonderful family home. Priced at $245,000. To save, call Ted at Elite Realty, 555-7970, now.

Below Market Interest

Assume low interest loan on delightful 5 bedroom, 2-1/2 bath stone home, resting in sunlit glen just outside town. From its spacious summer porch, enjoy the music of a babbling brook Or warm yourself by the massive rock hearth. Sprawling, comfortable home full of conveniences for just $205,000. Call Ruth at Elite Realty, 555-7970. Hurry.

Save on Interest

when you assume low interest loan on gorgeous 4 bedroom, 3 bath traditional in exclusive area. Mint condition with brick walls, flagstone patio, shining mahogany floors. Yours for only $314,000. Don't pass it up. Call Rosellen at Elite Realty, 555-7970, now.

LOW TAXES

How to Cut Taxes

It's easy when you move into this charming 4 bedroom, 4 bath colonial in fast growing executive neighborhood. Enjoy lowest tax rate in area while living in Early American luxury. Maple cabinets, oak floors, spacious & sunny rooms. Just $245,000. Call Steve at Elite Realty, 555-7970, to save today.

Luxury & Lower Taxes

If you're smart, you'll head over to this elegant Ponderosa-style ranch on 2 acres with low, low taxes. With the money you save, you can entertain friends in its gleaming wood- & window-lined living room. Or on the redwood deck by the free-form pool. A home with many delights for just $310,000. Call Ruth at Elite Realty, 555-7970, for a real deal.

Low Taxes, High Style

Last year's tax bill for this cosmopolitan dream—only $300. 3-story living room with tinted windows, dramatic copper fireplace, 4 bedrooms, 3 full baths, luxurious wraparound deck. Only 10 min. from center city. Priced at $275,000... hurry & call Jo at Elite Realty, 555-7970.

Reduce Your Taxes

by enjoying country-fresh air, blue skies, an acre of woods all your own. Not much of a sacrifice, considering you get a stunning 4 bedroom, 3 bath cedar ranch, with miles of white board fencing. All the luxuries you'd ever want & significant tax savings. Just $302,000. Make the smart move. Call Jim at Elite Realty, 555-7970, to find out how much you could save.

Lowest Tax Rate in County

& some of the prettiest homes—like this traditionally-styled, almost new 3 bedroom charmer. Cherry bannisters, rocking chair front porch, wonderfully warm & cozy eat-in kitchen. Perched on a hill, surrounded by woods, it can be yours for $276,000. Call Vera, today, at Elite Realty, 555-7970, to see this haven.

INVESTMENT VALUE

Lowest Priced Estate in Neighborhood

Surrounded by $500,000 homes, this Oriental palace is a bargain. 5 bedrooms, 4 baths in free-flowing design looking out to garden views. Your oasis of serenity on 1/4 acre. Just $325,000. Snatch it up. Call Alice at Elite Realty, 555-7970.

If You Have Rich Tastes on a Budget

you won't want to miss this Mt. Vernon-inspired colonial, with 4 bedrooms, 5 baths in exclusive neighborhood. Priced far below value at $415,000, it offers handsome detailing, graceful matching fireplaces, airy high ceilings. Rare find. Call Fred at Elite Realty, 555-7970, now.

Enjoy a Mansion for Only $320,000

You'll love living in the Harry Adams home, a marvel of Greek Revival architecture located right downtown. 5 bedrooms, 3 baths, superbly decorated with modern luxuries tastefully concealed. A 1925 stunner that's still captivating, at yesterday's price. Call June at Elite Realty, 555-7970, today.

Live Like a Millionaire for Much Less

You'll feel grand in this Southern-style mansion with its elegant portico, fluted columns, rich atmosphere. 4 spacious bedrooms, 3 full baths. Splendid home with an emerald lawn for only $310,000. If you want a great deal, call Sue at Elite Realty, 555-7970, today.

Want a Prestigious Home for Less Than You Ever Dreamed Possible?

Have the home you deserve—sprawling 4 bedroom, 3 bath Spanish hacienda with its own tower, dramatic leaded glass windows, free-form pool. In a great neighborhood. Bargain-priced at $325,000, it won't last long. Hurry & call Dennis at Elite Realty, 555-7970, now.

Incredible Victorian Value

You'll adore this almost new Victorian stunner, with its whipped cream pastel tints, elegant curlicues, delightful gingerbread. 4 high-ceilinged bedrooms (some with parlor), 2-1/2 antique-looking baths ...character galore for just $201,000. See it to believe it. Call Jim at Elite Realty, 555-7970, today.

Top-of-the-Line Quality —Bargain Basement Price

Suitable for a CEO, this magnificent 4 bedroom, 3 bath contemporary offers the finest in luxurious comfort. Brass highlights, wall of windows, sleek slate fireplaces & floors. You couldn't build it for $301,000. On 1 full acre. Call Fred at Elite Realty, 555-7970, to make a smart move today.

Home of Lasting Value

Tradition-lovers will appreciate the superb styling of this almost new 6 bedroom, 3-3/4 bath Georgian manor. With its winding staircase, solid oak floors, polished cherry cabinets, it's a carpenter's masterpiece. You'll appreciate its warm & open feeling almost as much as its value. At $325,000, this home is far below market. To see it today, call June at Elite Realty, 555-7970.

A Home to Appreciate

You'll fall in love with this gleaming 4 bedroom, 2-1/2 bath Cape Cod, aging ever so gracefully & growing richer with time. This home of quiet quality has heart of pine stained floors, antique newel posts, Chippendale bannisters, many modern conveniences. Sound investment for only $313,000. Call Rich at Elite Realty, 555-7970, today.

If You Appreciate Value...

come see this endearing 5 bedroom, 3-3/4 bath traditional sheltered beneath whispering pines. Enjoy handcrafted elegance, coupled with push-button convenience, in premier neighborhood. Unusual quality, for just $295,000. Call Julianna at Elite Realty, 555-7970, for a look today.

An Investment That Will Pay Off —Immediately

You'll make money the instant you move into this magnificent 4 bedroom, 3 bath California ranch. Worth far more than its $302,000 price, this home offers a gourmet kitchen, Andersen windows, solar hot water, wine cellar, park-view setting. Ideal for family. Call Ed at Elite Realty, 555-7970, today.

For Those Rich in Taste But Short on Cash

one of our city's finest homes...stately colonial mansion on Riverfront Drive. 5 large & luxurious bedrooms, 4 baths, walnut-paneled library, copper kettle kitchen, unique greenhouse dining room. Owner willing to finance at $325,000. Little or nothing down. Call Greg at Elite Realty, 555-7970, today.

Get More for Your $$$

in this long & rambling pueblo with views of the entire valley. Priced to sell immediately, this 4 bedroom, 3 bath stucco is a heritage home featuring hand-carved fireplaces, unique oak doors, old-fashioned French windows. Yesterday's quality at low price of just $225,000. Hurry. Call Fred at Elite Realty, 555-7970, now.

AD TIP: If you are having trouble getting started with an ad, it is always a good idea to try starting from the middle or end and revise it later.

Underpriced at
$324,000

There's no question, this is a quality home. You can tell by its 4 distinctive & stylish bedrooms, 2-1/2 wonderfully large baths, superb "great room." Built to last in 1982, this home is new to the market. Call Rich at Elite Realty, 555-7970, to find out more.

One Thing in Life
That's Certain...

Gray fieldstone construction. 4 bedrooms, 3 distinctively-styled baths. Generous living area & kitchen filled with sunlight, brick, warm woods. Far below replacement cost at $325,000. To see it today, call Hal at Elite Realty, 555-7970.

TRADE

Something to Trade?

Owner willing to barter for down payment on dramatic cedar A-frame, just 20 miles from town. Enjoy the warmth of wood, openness of glass, comfort of 4 generous bedrooms, 3 baths. On 12 acres of woods that belong to you. Full price of $205,000. Call Tim at Elite Realty, 555-7970, if you have something to offer.

Owner Ready
to Swap

high-style city home for open & airy country home comfort. If you'd like a sleek high-tech dream with 4 bedrooms, 3 baths, worth about $215,000, call Ron at Elite Realty, 555-7970, today.

Owner Will
Accept

boat, RV, jewelry, whatever, for down payment on stunning 4 bedroom, 3 bath French Normandy home. Slate blue roof, quaint shutters, terra-cotta tiles, Dutch fireplace, superb gourmet kitchen. Great for entertaining. Appraised at $325,000 ...try any offer. Call Fred at Elite Realty, 555-7970, now.

Let's Talk
Trade

Frustrated farmer wants to move back to city. Will swap delightful 5 bedroom, 4 bath brick traditional on 3 acres for sophisticated downtown home. If $315,000 sounds like a fair exchange, call Tom at Elite Realty, 555-7970, now.

Try a Trade

What will you offer for almost new 4 bedroom, 2-3/4 bath Lindal cedar home, snuggled in 7 acres of woods? Stunning glass & natural woods with your own little lake & boat dock. Just 25 min. from the city. To see it today, call Sue at Elite Realty, 555-7970.

> *AD TIP: Make sure your ads are relevant to the house you are selling. Don't simply reuse the same old ad you used for other listings.*

STYLE

ARCHITECTURE

Architectural Masterpiece

Superb 5 bedroom, 4 bath contemporary with sheets of windows, spiral stairs, lofty ceilings, creative use of beams & railings. A designer wonder on an acre of velvety lawn. Superb opportunity at $375,000. Call Ted at Elite Realty, 555-7970, for a true treasure today.

Frank Lloyd Wright Designed

Unusual opportunity to own a classic American home designed by our finest architect. Generous rows of windows, rosy woods, airy rooms in a delightful natural setting. All this plus 4 distinctive bedrooms, 3 baths, for under $310,000. Call Sue at Elite Realty, 555-7970, now.

Architecturally Striking

Bold 4 bedroom, 3 bath tri-level built into hillside. Huge splashes of color highlight sleek tile interior...with curved glass-block walls, walnut accents, many built-ins. Character home for $315,000. Call June at Elite Realty, 555-7970, to see this unusual property.

Your Own Tara

Thick white columns, graceful curving porch, grand staircase—this 4 bedroom, 3-3/4 bath Southern special will delight any true belle. Elegant taste reflected by rich woods, charming balconies, views of rolling fields. Gracing 2 acres, this storybook home is only $295,000. Call Kenneth at Elite Realty, 555-7970, for a look today.

Southern Mansion

The Old South lives again in this handsome 5 bedroom, 4 bath columned delight. You'll love its stately pillars, delicate shutters, sprawling summer porch. Circled by gentle weeping willows next to bass-stocked pond. Not just a home, a lifestyle. Only $345,000. Call Ed at Elite Realty, 555-7970.

Antebellum-Style Mansion

You'll be waiting for Scarlett O'Hara to come sweeping down its majestic oak staircase. It's only one of the many luxurious features of this 6 bedroom, 4 bath Southern estate. Cradled on 5 acres of wildlife, this newer home offers giant walnut den, eat-in kitchen, huge windows. Yours for only $405,000. Call Ted at Elite Realty, 555-7970, now.

Quaker Charmer

Its simplicity will never go out of style. Delightful 4 bedroom, 5 bath New England home that radiates quiet quality. Mellow oak floors, gentle brick walks, 3 car garage. Surrounded by postcard-perfect English garden. A true haven for only $415,000. Call Suzanne at Elite Realty, 555-7970, today.

Oriental Flair

You'll love its exotic roof, delicate lines, spacious luxury. 5 bedroom, 3-1/2 bath Oriental palace with stunning red decor, bonsai gardens, slatted decks, exquisite gourmet kitchen. Just $325,000. Call Joe at Elite Realty, 555-7970, for a trip to the Far East today.

Queen Anne Manor

Bring your provincial furniture & sterling silver...this home is the lap of luxury. Classic design, with graceful fluted columns, glowing cherry woods, superb craftsmanship. 6 lavish bedrooms, 5 full baths—all in delicate pastels. On 1/2 acre of flowering grounds, this English rose is only $415,000. Call Ken at Elite Realty, 555-7970, for a look at majesty today.

French Provincial Delight

If you like French elegance, you'll love this magnificent 4 bedroom, 4 bath charmer. In a neighborhood of other fine homes, it offers a sun-splashed family room with white brick fireplace, designer kitchen with copper accents, superb schools within walking distance. Only $355,000. Call Suzette at Elite Realty, 555-7970, and say Oui, today.

French Chateau

Inspired by the Loire valley, this gray stone wonder is secluded next to a peaceful brook on its own 1/4 acre. 5 magnificent bedrooms, each with own bath & balcony. Impressive living room dominated by antique hearth. Copper-filled kitchen with sunny breakfast nook. Yours for just $356,000. Call Stephenie at Elite Realty, 555-7970, today.

Magnificent Regency

It's the closest you may ever come to a palace...finely proportioned regency home behind gates in best area. Cobblestone drive, dancing fountains, flower-strewn patio. Plus 5 bedrooms, 4 baths & the most elegant living space you can imagine. Only $400,000. Call Roger at Elite Realty, 555-7970, today.

Grand Victorian

With its creamy pastel exterior, rocking chair porch & lacy gingerbread, this delightful charmer reflects long ago graciousness—yet it's almost new. 4 bedrooms, 4 baths, with airy & bright floor plan concealing a host of contemporary conveniences. Uniquely yours for only $398,000. Call Kenneth at Elite Realty, 555-7970, today.

Swiss Chalet

You'll adore this 5 bedroom, 4 bath shingled stunner, with its gaily painted window boxes, clever wood trim, charming sloping roof. Lovely home with massive den opening to brick patio, giant garage, basketball court, full acre fenced yard. Only $378,000. Get a taste of the Alps. Call Ali at Elite Realty, 555-7970.

Santa Fe Adobe

Artistic retreat offering 4 bedrooms, 5 baths in sun-splashed setting with mountain view. Cool adobe walls, ornate woodwork, smooth colorful tiles, curved fireplace. Ideal Santa Fe home for just $403,000. Call Clarice at Elite Realty, 555-7970, to see its charm today.

Mission-Style Mansion

Elegant & sprawling California mission-style home overlooking rolling fields. Wonderfully thick plaster walls, many windows, luxurious upgrades. 5 very private bedrooms, 3-1/2 baths, a kitchen fit to serve royalty. Proudly offered for the first time at just $398,000. Call Eddie at Elite Realty, 555-7970, for a look.

1928 Spanish Castle

High in the Hollywood hills, you'll find this superb home once owned by a silent film star. With 4 bedrooms, 3-1/2 baths, it offers intriguing surprises like a secret tunnel & concealed doors. Flagstone floors & the sparkling fountain add a classic touch. Just $378,000. Call Ginny at Elite Realty, 555-7970, to own a piece of the past today.

English Estate— One of Humboldt's Finest

2-story Tudor on a walled acre of green in heart of city. Built in 1925 for Redding family, this jewel-like home offers 4 bedrooms, 5 baths, with brick floors, French patios, spa-jetted baths, huge 3 car garage. Proudly offered at $425,000. To see it, call Jim at Elite Realty, 555-7970.

Old-World Spanish

More than 100 years of history created this classic Spanish beauty encircling a fountain-splashed courtyard. Antique tiles, ornate carved woods, elegant leaded glass windows, have been carefully preserved, while modern comforts are hidden inside. On 2 acres of land, this stucco palace offers 5 bedrooms, 6 baths, 4 car garage. Just $450,000. Call Fred at Elite Realty, 555-7970, today.

Italian Villa

Superbly designed, with flowing arched walkways, surprising splashes of tile, high-ceiling splendor—this 6 bedroom, 5 bath villa offers the finest in luxurious family living. Enjoy the glow of copper in the gourmet kitchen...rich gleam of woods in the library...stunning natural beauty of 5 acres of gardens. All for $415,000. Call Jim at Elite Realty, 555-7970, to see it today.

Rustic Ranch

Perfect duplicate of the Ponderosa... sitting high on a mountain, ringed by picture-perfect stockade fence. If you want 5 bedrooms, 5-1/2 baths & the free feeling of the Old West, call Tim at Elite Realty, 555-7970, today. Lasso it for $376,000.

California Contemporary

Enjoy 4,000 sq. ft. of glass, Palos Verde fieldstone & redwood in a stunning view home. 6 bedrooms, 5 baths & 2 acres of wilderness make it terrific for large family or lots of guests. Just $625,000. Call Richard at Elite Realty, 555-7970, for a glimpse of wide-open spaces today.

Victorian Estate

Hard-to-find pastel charmer in mint condition. Located in historic district, this vintage home has been carefully restored to architectural perfection. Offering 6 bedrooms, 4 baths, its classic beauty can be yours for only $386,000. Call Ken at Elite Realty, 555-7970, today.

The Spirit of the Old Southwest

lives again in this sumptuous stucco rambler, with 5 bedrooms, 4 baths. Filled with natural wood windows, terra-cotta floors, rough-hewn beams, this home exudes character & charm. On an acre all your own, it's just $355,000. Call Ted at Elite Realty, 555-7970, & don't forget your southwestern blankets!

Majestic Log Cabin

You'll love the way the setting sun tints the thick logs of this 5,000 sq. ft. cabin. Warmth fills its 5 bedrooms, 4 baths—many with knotty walls, loft areas, huge closets. Wonderful fireplace-warmed kitchen & dramatic family retreat where you'll spend many relaxing hours. With 3 acres, it's yours for $345,000. Call Julie at Elite Realty, 555-7970, today.

ATMOSPHERE

Drama & Sophistication

If you enjoy contemporary drama, take a look at this impressive 5 bedroom, 4 bath masterpiece on an acre of grounds. Light & airy, filled with skylights & glass-block walls, its innovative design offers family privacy yet spacious rooms for entertaining. Just $403,000. Call Jaime at Elite Realty, 555-7970, today.

In a Class by Itself

Stunning half-timbered English Tudor resting in rose garden, its mellow brick walls covered by ivy. 5 bedrooms, 4 baths, leaded glass windows, walnut-paneled den. It radiates a kind of quality available only to the very few. Handsome estate for $415,000. Call Vivian at Elite Realty, 555-7970, for an appointment.

Artfully Elegant

This 4 bedroom, 4-1/2 bath contemporary was designed to turn heads. Filled with hand-painted murals, custom tilework, bold & beautiful accents, it's an artist's delight. Stunningly set on an acre of greenery. For those with eclectic tastes, offered at $375,000. Call Noreen at Elite Realty, 555-7970, to see this unusual home today.

Living—at Its Best

Only rarely does a property as magnificent as this appear on the market. With its winding tree-canopied drive, slate roof, copper gutters, you know no expense has been spared. Majestic 5 bedroom, 6 bath Georgian classic in exclusive setting, with sparkling pool & cabana. Offered at $575,000. To see it today, call Ken at Elite Realty, 555-7970.

A Family Delight

Your entire family will enjoy the splendor & comfort of this wonderful 7 bedroom, 6 bath ranch secluded on 3 acres. With its playground, pool & stable, it's everything a child's heart could desire. You'll love the warmth of its redwood & stone, plus top-of-the-line extras. The peak of comfort & convenience for $425,000. For a look today, call Mary Anne at Elite Realty, 555-7970.

The Ultimate in Luxury

Only the finest fits in this sumptuous 5 bedroom, 6 bath French Regency situated on a choice site in Briarwood Estates. Delightful rock garden surrounds stunning pool & cabana. Proudly offered at $489,000, with some owner financing. If you want the best for those you love, call Tim at Elite Realty, 555-7970, today.

The Art of Luxurious Living

For those who long for luxury...stately 5 bedroom, 6 bath traditional brick with little touches you'll love. Picture-perfect condition, with tennis court, pool, 4 car garage. Priced at $455,000. See it today. Call Joe at Elite Realty, 555-7970.

Details Make the Difference

in this finely styled 5 bedroom Georgian classic resting on the highest point in The Country. Enjoy 3 huge fireplaces, ceramic gourmet kitchen, sparkling pool. For a glimpse of what life can be, at just $503,000, call Regena at Elite Realty, 555-7970, now.

Come Home to a New Beginning

Superb 1957 contemporary crafted for luxury living...with handcrafted ceilings, woodwork, cabinetry. Enjoy 5 huge bedrooms, 4 sumptuously large baths in a home blending pleasure & excitement. Surrounded by a forest, this rambling dream is only $475,000. To make it yours today, call Maryann at Elite Realty, 555-7970.

5,000 Sq. Ft. of Tranquility for $525,000

Stunning 6 bedroom, 5 bath Oriental fantasy, secluded from the street by high walls & bonsai garden. You'll adore its peaked roofs, gentle lines, total harmony, exuberant natural beauty. Call George at Elite Realty, 555-7970, for a piece of paradise today.

World Class Luxury

created for only a few—those who appreciate the beauty of aged woods...the glory of hand-cut crystal...the symmetry of Georgian styling. Majestic 5 bedroom, 6 bath home high on a crest, proudly set in a world apart. Only $575,000. For a special look today, call Malcolm at Elite Realty, 555-7970.

For the Privileged...

A home that harkens backs to a gentler, more gracious era. 5 bedroom, 7 bath, 4,800 sq. ft. Victorian mansion delicately blends yesterday's charm with today's conveniences. Nestled on 3 acres of flowers & shrubs, with a delightful summer gazebo, naturally landscaped pool, splashing fountain. Offered at $475,000. Call Jay at Elite Realty, 555-7970, today.

A Home of Traditions

You'll be proud of this impressive 5 bedroom, 4-1/2 bath colonial resting at the end of a winding poplar-lined drive. Built in 1899, this mansion has been magnificently updated, yet retains its original flavor & charm. Carriage house, outbuildings, antique well-all yours for $565,000. To start a dynasty of your own, call Ken at Elite Realty, 555-7970.

Wall-to-Wall Comfort

For those who love the contemporary look but enjoy feeling pampered...a superbly styled 5 bedroom, 4-3/4 bath Colorado contemporary. All the architectural drama you can imagine, yet warm & intimate feeling. Thoughtful touches like spa-jetted tubs, radiant heat floors, Jenn-air grill. Just $495,000. Call Jill at Elite Realty, 555-7970, for a special treat now.

A Bit of Europe in Buffalo

Imagine a luxurious French mansion in America, with old-world touches like window boxes, statues, marble colonnades. You can find it all in this regal 7 bedroom villa, high in the hills. Designed by a European for his own family, this rare home is priced at $565,000. To see it now, call Alice at Elite Realty, 555-7970.

Are You an Individualist?

If you're looking for a home around $540,000, come see an architectural joy —a home that's fresh, inspiring, almost new yet mellow with woods & views of nature's finest beauties. Secluded in the canyon, this one of a kind delight offers 8 bedrooms, 6 baths, stunning gourmet kitchen. If you enjoy exceptional beauty & style, call Ken at Elite Realty, 555-7970.

Like to Live Like Royalty?

Then do so in this stately & elegant English brick manor—a study of symmetry & style. 4 baronial-sized bedrooms with sitting areas, 5 luxurious baths, walnut-paneled library with massive hearth, 4 car garage. Just $535,000. If you've promised yourself the best, call Tim at Elite Realty, 555-7970, now.

A Home of Distinction

Set on half-moon lot with dancing willows, babbling brook & singing birds, you'll find this superb 5 bedroom, 4 bath American traditional. One of our city's finest homes. Every room shows the hand of a master craftsman. Offered at $615,000. Call Ken at Elite Realty, 555-7970, for a special showing of this one of a kind home today.

Forgotten by Time

Exciting 1920's Greek Revival home that gleams with yesteryear care & pride, yet offers the finest in contemporary comfort. 12 enormous rooms, each superbly styled, on 3 acres of manicured grounds. Offered at $515,000, it's a unique opportunity to live in grandeur. Call Richard at Elite Realty, 555-7970, today.

Pastoral Perfection

Seldom does a home of this quality & refinement reach the market. With its gracefully curved road, secluded park, stunning vistas, this exquisite Southern-style estate offers a lifestyle few ever attain. 7 bedrooms, 9 baths, with a lighted tennis court, free-form pool, cabana, 4 car garage. Just $625,000. If this is for you, call Malcolm, today, at Elite Realty, 555-7970.

AD TIP: Terms like "APR" and "Due on Sale" may make a lot of sense to you, but remember, your readers don't buy homes everyday.

SPECIAL FEATURES

KITCHEN

Professional
Chef's Home

Anyone who cooks will love the kitchen of this charming Normandy estate. Designed by the chef of La Maison, it offers the ultimate in gourmet convenience. You will adore the rest of the house, too, with its superb European style & feel. Very warm, sunny & open. Just $485,000. For a sampling today, call June at Elite Realty, 555-7970.

French Country
Kitchen & Fireplace

Your family will spend hours in this cozy but spacious kitchen/family room, with its crackling fireplace, gleaming copper, mellow wood cabinets & floors. It's the heart of this almost new 17th century—style French farmhouse, featuring 6 bedrooms & 5 baths. Only $475,000. To see today, call Sue at Elite Realty, 555-7970.

Superb
Gourmet Center

If you entertain, consider this elegant 7 bedroom, 5 bath Georgian colonial. Built 4 years ago for the family of a corporate executive, it features a kitchen any true chef would adore. Plus comfort & luxury throughout. Offered at $575,000. If you take your parties seriously, call Fred at Elite Realty, 555-7970, today.

Real Chef's
Kitchen

Imagine all the cooking gadgets you'd ever need, at your fingertips. That's what you get in this handsome 6 bedroom, 6 bath traditional brick with its wonderful designer kitchen. Enjoy the warmth of solarium dining, comfort of your own pool, closeness of your private tennis court. Live in luxury for $505,000. Call Ken at Elite Realty, 555-7970, today.

Old-Fashioned
Farm Kitchen

It's unusual to find such a quality-built home with so much charm. But this 5 bedroom, 7 bath Dutch colonial radiates warmth. Exposed—beam, brick-walled kitchen; massive stone living room fireplace; stained glass window nook. Grace on a scale seldom seen for $525,000. Call Ruth at Elite Realty, 555-7970, now.

FIREPLACE

6 Fireplaces

With the efficient & powerful heating system in this 6 bedroom, 5 bath Georgian beauty, you won't need the fireplaces to keep you warm. But they're perfect to cuddle by. And just another special feature of this stately home with oak floors, chintz drapes & flower boxes. Just $475,000. Call Jack at Elite Realty, 555-7970, today.

Ever Walk
in a Fireplace?

You can, in this almost new English manor with 2 massive stone hearths. A copy of an ancient Yorkshire estate, it's authentic down to the smallest detail. Yet with all the comforts you demand cleverly disguised. Unique home with 5 bedrooms, 7 baths, on 1/2 acre of green for $555,000. Call Barbara at Elite Realty, 555-7970, to see it today.

Big Enough
to Roast an Ox!

Chances are you'll never do that in this gigantic fireplace, but you could. 6 bedroom, 6 bath Tudor-style home with elegant pool, flagstone deck, bubbling fountain, 4-bay carriage house. Yours to command for $465,000. Call Tom at Elite Realty, 555-7970, now.

Fireside
Romance

It'll never disappear from this splendid home—because each of its 5 sumptuous bedrooms glows with the light of its own fireplace. Warmth & charm fill this 14 room white clapboard rambler, with its own apple orchard. A home to love for $525,000. Call Jackson at Elite Realty, 555-7970, today.

Warm Your Hands
& Your Heart

at the 3 antique brick fireplaces in this delightful Cape Cod sitting proudly on its own peninsula. Enjoy the commanding view from its spacious rooms & bay windows. 4 comfortable bedrooms, 7 baths. 15 acres all your own. All for just $512,000. Call Marilyn at Elite Realty, 555-7970, to see this maritime beauty today.

DINING ROOM

24 for Dinner?

It's a piece of cake in this superb brick traditional with its elegant gourmet kitchen & regal dining area. Sculptured ceilings, chandeliers, hand-rubbed cherry china hutch create a wonderfully warm & refined atmosphere. 5 bedrooms, 6 baths on manicured grounds for $534,000. Call Kenneth at Elite Realty, 555-7970, today.

Sun-Splashed Dining

Imagine sun streaming into a flagstone floored solarium overflowing with exotic flowers & a splashing fountain. See it in this stunning 5 bedroom, 4 bath contemporary beauty. A masterpiece of light, air & space, this home is perfect for entertaining or relaxing. If you're looking for something different, under $500,000, call Julie at Elite Realty, 555-7970, now.

A Dining Hall
Fit for a King

Entertainment will be a delight in this regal, mahogany-lined hall that easily holds 18 special guests. You'll love its built-in food warmers, stunning chandeliers, gourmet kitchen. Not to mention the rest of this 5 bedroom, 7 bath manor, a study in superb taste & elegance. Offered at $737,500. To see it today, call Dick at Elite Realty, 555-7970.

Waterford Chandelier

will serve as your stunning centerpiece in the formal dining room of this handsome gray stone mansion. You'll be proud to welcome your friends to this 6 bedroom, 5 bath home, featuring unique architectural accents. On the choicest site in Elmwood, it's just $650,000. To see it today, call William at Elite Realty, 555-7970.

Entertainer's Dream
Dining Room

If you host formal dinners, do it in style —in this gracious antebellum home with imported murals, carved ceilings, graceful chandeliers, warmer buffet & dumbwaiter. Your family will enjoy the 5 luxuriously large bedrooms, 7 spacious baths, 3 acres of countryside for only $535,000. To see, call Vi at Elite Realty, 555-7970.

MASTER BEDROOM SUITE

Your Private Escape

Within this charming 5 bedroom, 4-3/4 bath white clapboard, there's a delightful retreat. Close the master bedroom doors & the floor-to-ceiling French windows, private spa, wonderful dressing areas & your own fireplace await you. Your haven at home for $475,000. Call Ken at Elite Realty, 555-7970, to see it today.

You Deserve It

A sumptuous master bedroom suite that's your own little world. Filled with warmth & luxury, it offers a steaming indoor spa, giant walk-in closets, stunning designer bath, romantic balcony. All in this enticing 5 bedroom, 6 bath Mediterranean villa. Prestige & privacy for $535,000. For a look today, call Ray at Elite Realty, 555-7970.

Hideaway at Home

in a delightful master bedroom suite with French doors opening to your private garden & spa. This elegant home features 5 bedrooms, 4 baths, and 4,100 sq. ft. This French provincial stunner is in a superb secluded neighborhood. Under $500,000. If you want quality & style, call Joe at Elite Realty, 555-7970, today.

Private & Luxurious

You'll spend hours in the fireplace-warmed, wood-filled master bedroom suite set apart from the rest of this rustic stone & glass rambler. You'll love the gentle luxurious charm of its 5 bedrooms & 5 baths, hidden on 5.25 acres of mountainside. Just $486,000. Call Ty at Elite Realty, 555-7970, for a look today.

A World Apart
in the Heart of the City

This sumptuous master bedroom retreat feels far removed. Enjoy your own hot & steamy spa, private fireplace, walk-in dressing areas, giant bath, total seclusion. All within a stunning 3,800 sq. ft. 5 bedroom, 4 bath contemporary. Luscious luxury for $515,000. Call Ruth at Elite Realty, 555-7970, to see it today.

LARGE GARAGE

Car Buff's Delight

Elegant 4 bedroom, 4 bath Georgian with heated 5 car garage & spacious attached workshop. Plenty of room to restore or show off your collection. Excellent taste shows in this 1952 home, with its fine woods, marbles, cobblestone drive. Proudly offered at $554,000. Call Jim at Elite Realty, 555-7970, today.

Give Your Rolls
the Home It Deserves

Park it at this Tom Brownley-designed masterpiece. Unique 6 bedroom, 5 bath traditional, with huge heated workshop/ garage. Classic beauty at its finest, it offers a Tennessee stone fireplace, massive oak beams, superb country styling, 5 wonderful acres. If you're in the market for a $500,000 home, call Ruth at Elite Realty, 555-7970, now.

House & Carriage House

Ancient stone, weathered by time, is carved to perfection in this historic 6 bedroom, 5 bath home & adjoining 4-bay carriage house. At $550,000, it's a marvel of inspired design & thoughtful luxuries. If you want to give your family (& cars) only the finest, see this special property today. Call Jamal at Elite Realty, 555-7970.

RV Garage

isn't all that comes with this millionaire's tribute to his wife. 7,000 sq. ft. in all, this almost new Mediterranean villa offers gourmet kitchen, 4 fireplaces, courtyard swimming pool, marble & oak floors, elevator, 12 bedrooms, 15 baths. On acre overlooking wildlife refuge. $745,000. Call Tim at Elite Realty, 555-7970, now.

More Than
A Garage...

this workshop/4-bay garage is a grease monkey's dream. Well equipped with custom cabinets, hydraulic lift, & tools. With it comes a stunning 5 bedroom, 6 bath contemporary redwood, crafted with tons of stone & glass. Just $550,000. Call Sue at Elite Realty, 555-7970, today.

SPECIAL ROOMS

Unique Music Conservatory

You've seen it in the movies...soaring walls of glass, ferns, circular floor, perfect for a grand piano. It's the centerpiece of this 5 bedroom, 7 bath New Orleans-style home, on a hill overlooking the river. Offered at $650,000, it's a way of life for the chosen few. Call Kim at Elite Realty, 555-7970, if you're among them.

English Library

Life in this splendid English Tudor revolves around a dramatic library filled with gleaming hardwoods, leaded glass, handsome hearth. Bring your leather-bound books, antique furniture, Oriental rugs. This 5 bedroom, 3-3/4 bath manor will show them off to perfection. On 3 rolling acres, its yours for $476,000. Call June at Elite Realty, 555-7970, now.

Separate Artist's/Writer's Studio

Stunning Cotswold charmer on 5 acres of flowers & trees, with delightful office/studio. Walls of glass pour in sunlight, while French doors open to secluded garden. The home itself features 4 sitting/sleeping rooms, 6 full baths, copper & brick gourmet kitchen, breathtaking pool. All for just $525,000. Call Fred at Elite Realty, 555-7970, now.

The Playroom
of Your Children's Dreams

If you want something special for your family, consider this stately 4 bedroom, 3-1/2 bath colonial manor. Exquisitely styled exterior, inside a marvel of artistry & quality. You'll be charmed by the huge play area with its indoor jungle gym, hand-painted murals, built-in slide. A home in a class all its own for $575,000. Call Ken at Elite Realty, 555-7970, for a peek today.

Captain's Lookout & Deck

On a winding street of fine modern homes, this gracious traditional stands out. From its soaring third story juts a sprawling deck, offering a breathtaking ocean view. Quality & elegance fill this almost new home, featuring 5 bedrooms, 5 baths, 3,700 sq. ft. for $450,000. To see for yourself, call Sue at Elite Realty, 555-7970.

ENERGY EFFICIENT

State of the Art
Energy Efficiency

If you want the most out of every dollar, consider this stunning 5 bedroom, 6 bath custom cedar home engineered for maximum energy efficiency & style. All the upgrades you'd expect, plus top-of-the-line solar heating—even the floors stay warm. Offered at $497,000. For a look now, call Steve at Elite Realty, 555-7970.

High Fuel Bills?

Then whittle them down in this elegant Victorian manor, offering nostalgic charm plus the practicality of thermopane windows, 2 zone gas heat, central air, thick insulation. No need to sacrifice warmth or efficiency for style—this home has it all. 4 bedrooms, 7 baths on 2 acres of grounds. Just $435,000. Call Jean at Elite Realty, 555-7970, today.

You'll Stay Warm & Snug

It's hard to find such marvelous energy efficiency in an estate home...but the builder of this 7 bedroom, 7 bath Tudor thought of everything. Massive rock walls, exposed-beam designer kitchen, formal garden & grounds. Luxury & efficiency for $475,000. For a real saver, call Jim at Elite Realty, 555-7970, now.

Peak
Energy Performance

is yours in this sumptuous 5 bedroom, 5 bath contemporary, combining energy efficiency & style. Solar heating keeps the indoor pool, floors & even the garage warm. Hundreds of square yards of thermopane windows look out to a breathtaking view. Offered at $550,000. Call Lee at Elite Realty, 555-7970, today.

If You Worry
About High Fuel Costs...

then see this gorgeous 8 bedroom, 7 bath colonial in a choice setting. Blending the elegance of the old with the efficiency of the new, its mellow woods, stained glass & gentle charm hide a top energy performer. Cradled on 3 acres of park-like grounds, this almost new home is just $476,000. Call Josephine at Elite Realty, 555-7970, today.

ROOM FOR ENTERTAINING

Entertainer's Dream

It's a entertainer's fantasy come true—marvelous 5 bedroom, 3-3/4 bath traditional manor created for elegant entertainment. With its sparkling gourmet kitchen, ornate banquet-sized dining room, softly lit garden with gentle fountains...it's always ready for a party. Offered at $480,000. Call Tom at Elite Realty, 555-7970, for an invitation today.

Entertainer's Ultimate

Wonderful free-flowing contemporary with delightful indoor spa, billiard room, library, dramatic living room. 4 bedrooms, 4 baths, the ultimate entertainment paradise for $650,000. Call Tom at Elite Realty, 555-7970, to see this beauty.

Bring Your Servers

That's all you'll need for a sit-down dinner in this palatial Georgian manor. Gleaming gourmet kitchen, handsome walnut dining room, elegant library, with fireplace for after-dinner drinks. With 6 bedrooms, 4 baths & separate quarters over the garage, overnight guests are no problem. Just $575,000. Call Trudy at Elite Realty, 555-7970, for a look today.

Your Exclusive Showplace

On Holmby Hills Golf Course sits a delightful 5 bedroom, 6 bath colonial brick. Serve cocktails on its sprawling 100' custom brick patio. Relax in the free-form pool or by the family room's toasty fireplace. An elegant home, designed with comfort in mind, for $525,000. To see it, call Vi at Elite Realty, 555-7970.

Entertaining Tonight?

Then why not own a home you'll be proud to show off to your friends? Like this stunning English estate, with its sweeping staircase & leaded stained glass windows. You'll love cooking in the French country kitchen, serving BBQ on the Texas-sized veranda. 6 bedrooms, 4 baths to please everyone's palate. Just $495,000. Call Ruth Ann at Elite Realty, 555-7970, today.

The Joys of Entertaining

belong to you in this 5 bedroom, 4 bath French Regency home. Enjoy gourmet cooking in its elegant, sun-filled kitchen, crowned by a glass-block breakfast nook. Serve meals in a dining room patterned after one of Europe's most prestigious homes. After dinner, relax by the fire in the lion-sized library. Only $525,000. Call Joe at Elite Realty, 555-7970, now.

Be the Ultimate Host

in a home tailored for stylish living & elegant entertaining. 11 room contemporary dream with high-tech designer kitchen, banquet-sized (22' x 28') dining room, soaring & dramatic living room with vaulted ceiling. Surrounded by 2 acres of wildlife. Just $478,000. Call John at Elite Realty, 555-7970, today.

The Last Word in Entertaining

is yours when you live in this magnificent French chateau in the most elite area of Crescent Park. 5 bedrooms, 7 baths. Features a solarium, stables, pool, spa, velvety lawn. The ultimate in luxury for $555,000. Call Fred at Elite Realty, 555-7970, for a vision of beauty today.

Impress Your Friends

with this regal, Mt. Vernon-inspired beauty. Featuring 6 bedrooms, 6 baths, it is a masterpiece of hardwoods, marble, stained glass, luxury. You'll feel like the royalty whenever you descend its grand staircase or tour its acre of grounds. A home your friends will love to visit for $615,000. Call Elizabeth at Elite Realty, 555-7970, today.

High Society Home

You'll know you've arrived when you move into this sumptuous 4 bedroom, 5 bath New York-style brownstone. 3 floors of luxury, crowned by a stunning master bedroom suite overlooking the river. Enjoy the best address in town... for $615,000. Call Kenny at Elite Realty, 555-7970, now.

Love to Throw a Party?

Then do it in this dramatic oceanside home, with 5 bedrooms, 6 baths & a whitewater view that seemingly stretches on forever. Your guests will love relaxing in the pool or spa. You'll love the delightful designer kitchen, with every convenience you'll ever need. Wonderful home in great neighborhood, for $535,000. Call Joe at Elite Realty, 555-7970, today.

The Ultimate Cocktail Party

Whether its a black tie affair or jeans & flannel shirts, this tasteful 4 bedroom, 4 bath colonial will make you shine. Enjoy the spacious brick patio where gentle fountains play. Or the wood-crowned dining room with wide French doors opening to a rose garden. Packed with luxury, this fine home is offered at $496,000. To see it today, call Sue at Elite Realty, 555-7970.

5 or 500 Guest Are No Problem

in this antebellum-style home just 20 min. from the city. You'll have a score of rooms for entertaining friends...or set up tents in the lovely formal gardens. Elegant touches throughout, with 6 bedrooms, library, sewing room, den, 10 baths & all the luxuries you'd ever care for. Offered at $880,000. Call Kim at Elite Realty, 555-7970, for a taste of good old-fashioned Southern hospitality.

Entertain VIPs?

Then do it in a home that's the perfect blend of taste & quality-stunning 5 bedroom, 7 bath Oriental charmer with acre of Japanese gardens. You'll love its classic lines, artistic dashes, soothing natural woods, relaxing spas & pool. A home you'll love living in as well as showing off, for $498,000. Call Steve at Elite Realty, 555-7970, now.

AD TIP: *Price and location are the two most important home buying factors. The newspaper will place your ad by location but you should also include the price.*

ONE-LEVEL

Unique One-Level Design

Life is easy in this 4 bedroom, 4 bath California rambler, a wonderful mix of sun & mellow woods. Nestled on an acre of natural beauty you can enjoy from the sprawling redwood deck or through the many French doors. Easy-reach cabinets, wide halls, spacious baths for $456,000. Call Timothy at Elite Realty, 555-7970, for a look today.

For the Family With Special Needs

Top-quality, easy-care ranch designed with you in mind. Many touches you'll appreciate: wide hallways, 4 roomy baths, low counters plus 6 large bedrooms, mahogany accents, solid oak floors throughout. Steamy spa & pool with wheelchair access. A real find at $445,000. Call Sue at Elite Realty, 555-7970, to see it today.

One-Level Rambler

Sun, warmth, natural woods blend beautifully in this dramatic 5 bedroom, 6 bath contemporary. In a secluded setting just 15 min. from the Medical Center, this home offers an indoor pool, top-of-the-line appliances, exciting brass fireplace. Only $495,000. To see it today, call Jim at Elite Realty, 555-7970.

Sprawling Hacienda

Unique 5 bedroom, 5 bath adobe on one level. Enjoy its fountain-splashed courtyard, ancient tiles, warm & wonderful pool, gleaming hardwood floors, massive wood beams. Designed for easy living, it's offered at $515,000. To see it today, call Lonnie at Elite Realty, 555-7970.

One Story You'll Love

Splendid 6 bedroom, 5 bath French Regency on acre of park-like grounds. Tastefully designed to accommodate everyone's needs, this home offers comfortable one-story living without sacrificing style or quality. Just $511,000. For a happy ending, call Ruth at Elite Realty, 555-7970, today.

PORCHES/PATIOS/SPAS

Juliet's Balcony

A whimsical touch on a delightful home ...4 bedroom, 7 bath French castle with storybook turrets, casement windows, superb patios. You'll love its acre of gardens & trees. Just $495,000. To view today, call Mario at Elite Realty, 555-7970.

Eagle's Nest Spa

From this stunning 4 bedroom, 3-3/4 bath cedar contemporary, you'll find a stairway. It leads up the mountain to a sizzling spa, with a breathtaking valley view. Enjoy long evenings in its bubbles or by the massive orchard stone fireplace in the sprawling family room. A special home for $524,000. Call Mara at Elite Realty, 555-7970, for a bird's-eye view.

Spend Hot Nights on a Cool Summer Porch

& enjoy the fragrant gardenias circling this Victorian fantasy. Enjoy the rich gleam of mahogany, glow of copper-filled kitchen, sparkle of French windows. 5 bedroom masterpiece, lovingly renovated, for $513,000. Call Julie at Elite Realty, 555-7970.

Enjoy Iced Tea & Lemonade

on the long & luscious veranda of this superb California Craftsman with 7 bedrooms & 5 baths. You'll adore its old-fashioned, but updated, country kitchen; gleaming den; elegant dining room. Resting under giant oaks, this home is only $435,000. Call Randy at Elite Realty, 555-7970, today.

The Longest Porch in the World

is what the front porch of this traditional beauty feels like. There's room for outdoor living, dining, playing. You'll love this 5 bedroom, 3-1/2 bath home's gracious charm, as well as its tree-canopied street. Fine home in prestigious neighborhood, for $415,000. Call Ken at Elite Realty, 555-7970, now.

Magnificent Terraces

open to sparkling sea views from this Mediterranean- style villa. Walk through its delightful arches, enjoy its fragrant flowers-as beautiful on the outside as it is on the inside. 5 bedrooms, 5 baths...for $500,000. Call Edward at Elite Realty, 555-7970, today.

Superb Mexican Courtyard

Decked with flowers & filled with fountains, this old-world courtyard creates the focal point for a delightful hacienda. You will adore its colorful tiles, ancient pavers & gracious feel almost as much as you adore the home's quiet quality. 6 bedrooms, 6 baths-all unique for $505,000. Call Sue at Elite Realty, 555-7970, today.

AD TIP: Be specific rather than general.

Luxurious Lanai

stretches entire length of 5 bedroom, 4 bath Florida-style home designed to catch every passing sunbeam. Fill its atrium with flowers...scatter lounge chairs by the patio's delightful pool. If you enjoy fresh air, tropical landscaping & gentle luxury, this home is for you. Just $487,000. Call Joe at Elite Realty, 555-7970, to see it sparkle today.

Gingerbread Front Porch

will captivate you as soon as you see this charming Victorian castle on Turtle Row. 6 bedrooms, 7 baths-with its own miniature tower. Just $512,000. To see it, call Mary at Elite Realty, 555-7970, now.

Old-Fashioned Evenings

can be yours again in this Nantucket-style Salt Box packed with charm. From its rocking chair front porch, watch the ships pass. Curl up with a good book beside the massive hearth. Relax in the spacious master bedroom suite. Only $455,000. Call Sam at Elite Realty, 555-7970, to see this charmer today.

LANDSCAPING

Sculpture Garden All Your Own

You'll love evening strolls in this magnificent garden set with statues. Delightfully landscaped, it's a haven of tranquility & beauty. So is the elegant 12 room brick home Offered at $650,000. Call Marie at Elite Realty, 555-7970, to see it today.

Secluded Meditation Garden

Years of loving care created this oasis of beauty. One of many delights in this 5 bedroom, 6-1/2 bath Georgian manor. Classically styled, with gleaming hardwoods, high ceilings, generous rooms... this home reflects excellence. Just $475,000. Call Elaine at Elite Realty, 555-7970, for a look today.

Enjoy Your Own Bubbling Brook

circling this large & lavish clapboard dream. With its 6 sprawling bedrooms, 5 baths, giant country-fresh kitchen, lion-sized den...it's great for a large family. Acre of lush lawn & 4 car garage. Just $525,000. See your American dream today. Call Sue at Elite Realty, 555-7970.

Lush Formal Gardens

stretch behind this sumptuous 5 bedroom, 6 bath French Regency. You'll love this home's marble floors & hearths, St. Charles kitchen, superbly crafted dining room. Just $565,000. Call Tom at Elite Realty, 555-7970, to see it today.

Your Private Woods

sprawl a full 2 acres behind this elegant redwood & stone contemporary. With 5 bedrooms, 7 baths, you'll never feel crowded-especially with its walls of windows looking out to gorgeous natural views. Just 15 min. from town, this home also offers a pool & 5 car garage. Only $515,000. Call Elizabeth at Elite Realty, 555-7970, today.

Part-Time
Farmer's Dream

Perfect set-up for weekend farmers...a rolling 50 acres, complete with Early American farmhouse. Your family will love its comfort-6 bedrooms, 8 baths, all gleaming with gentle care. Pool, tennis court, 5 car garage, too. Barn & other outbuildings, plus small orchard. All for just $625,000. Call Stephenie at Elite Realty, 555-7970, today.

Lush 2-Story
Atrium

filled with towering plants, dominates this delightful glass & brick contemporary. 5 bedrooms, 4-3/4 baths...all with the open & airy feeling you love. Wonderful eat-in kitchen, dramatic patio, 2 fireplaces in living room. Just $475,000. Call Ken at Elite Realty, 555-7970, now.

24 Acres
& Independence

belong to you in this splendid 6 bedroom, 5 bath English Tudor, reached by a winding drive through rolling hills. A great place to raise a family. Excellent schools nearby. Easy living for $475,000. See it today. Call Vic at Elite Realty, 555-7970.

Fragrant
Citrus Orchard

circles this charming 5 bedroom, 4 bath brick beauty. Enjoy breakfasting on its spacious veranda, evenings on the cool screened porch. A luxury home built for comfort...just $450,000. Call Linda at Elite Realty, 555-7970, to see it today.

> AD TIP: *Try to paint a vivid portrayal of the home you're advertising. This will inspire your prospects to call.*

Rocks, Trees &
Cactus Garden

create stunning setting for this 4 bedroom, 6 bath adobe ranch, built around marvelous inner courtyard. Thick stucco walls keep it cool, while walls of windows & airy design create open feeling. Spectacular sunset views. A home filled with natural beauty for $415,000. Call Roger at Elite Realty, 555-7970, today.

POOL

Olympic-Size Pool

is waiting for you at this grand 5 bedroom, 6 bath ranch, located in choice Sea Hills setting. No problem keeping fit-you'll love this pool's sprawling length & terrific view. 5,000 sq. ft. of luxury for just $457,000. Call Fred at Elite Realty, 555-7970, to check it out today.

Formal Gardens
With Lap Pool

Your friends will think it's part of the lovely garden...it blends so beautifully. They'll never know it's part of your daily routine. Everything about this 7 bedroom, 6 bath Mediterranean-style home radiates refinement. Offered at $555,000. To appreciate it for yourself, call Ruth at Elite Realty, 555-7970, now.

Pool Estate

Life the way you've always imagined it...sparkling blue pool, striped cabanas, sprawling deck dotted with furniture, walls of windows looking over it. Your own pool estate, designed for outdoor fun & indoor comfort. 5 large bedrooms, 4-3/4 baths, every square inch superbly styled. Just $575,000. Call Henry at Elite Realty, 555-7970, for a look today.

Your Own Hot Springs

You'll love the luxurious warmth of this natural hot springs, feeding straight into your wonderful rock pool. Nestled in ferns & towering trees, it's the focal point of a stunning 5 bedroom, 3-1/2 bath contemporary. Generous walls of windows, spacious rooms, airy 2-story atrium...this home is a masterpiece of good taste. Only $615,000. Call Fredrick at Elite Realty, 555-7970, to see it today.

Stunning Naturally Landscaped Pool

Cactus & rocks creep right to the edge of this black-bottom pool, built to capture breathtaking mountain vistas. With the one of a kind pool comes an elegant 6 bedroom, 5 bath Santa Fe charmer...with a sculptured, free-flowing interior you'll adore. Only $575,000. Call Tim at Elite Realty, 555-7970, today.

Pool & Waterfall

You'll love the gentle splash of a waterfall in this rambling 7 bedroom, 5 bath ranch. Set on an acre of natural landscaping, it offers the finest in quality living combined with outdoor beauty. With the pool & Texas-size gas BBQ, it's great for parties. Just $525,000. Call Ken at Elite Realty, 555-7970, to see it today.

AD TIP: How long should an ad be? Long enough to paint a picture of the home and short enough not to skill your pocketbook.

Award-Winning Pool

A masterpiece of flowing sculpture, this pool will delight your eyes, as well as help keep you fit. With it comes a handsome 5 bedroom, 4 bath Georgian manor. You'll love the polished woods gleaming in the library, superb gourmet kitchen, wonderful master bedroom fireplace. 4 fireplaces in all. A true treasure for $545,000. Call Josephine at Elite Realty, 555-7970, today.

Tropical Pool

You'll love this sparkling indoor pool surrounded by fragrant tropical flowers. Great for entertaining or exercising, it's part of a luxurious 5 bedroom, 4 bath traditional brick. Offered at $535,000. Call Fred at Elite Realty, 555-7970, now.

Enjoy Midnight Swims

in the delightful free-form pool of this 5 bedroom, 6 bath California contemporary. Soaring ceilings, huge windows, gleaming tiles, 3 fireplaces make it decorator perfect. It's ready for you at $520,000. Call Jim at Elite Realty, 555-7970, to make an appointment today.

Stay Cool in Your Own Pool

Enjoy your private pool & sizzling Jacuzzi just off the master bedroom of this charming 6 bedroom, 5 bath cedar ranch. You'll love this home's gentle elegance, with sprawling rooms, luxury upgrades, heartwarming decor. All for just $515,000. For a look today, call Suzette at Elite Realty, 555-7970.

CONDITION

WELL CARED FOR

Rare Georgian Showplace

It's hard to find a historical home in such mint condition, but this 4 bedroom, 6 bath manor is special. Gentle loving care throughout. Many original features, plus extras you'll appreciate-like terrific energy efficiency. Just $495,000. To see it today, call Sue at Elite Realty, 555-7970.

The Perfect Estate

Hunting, champagne brunches, chamber music concerts...they'll all fit into this delightful 12 room English manor in impeccable shape. 5 bedrooms, 6 baths on 3 acres of lovely grounds...a showcase for just $875,000. To see for yourself, call Jim at Elite Realty, 555-7970.

Perfection Plus

If you like comfort & charm, you'll love this sparkling 5 bedroom, 7 bath ranch in perfect condition. From the gleaming slate floors to the highly polished hardwoods & shining copper kitchen, it's been well taken care of. Much character for $576,000. Call Ruth at Elite Realty, 555-7970, for a look today.

> AD TIP: *Don't be afraid to use questions, especially in your headlines.*

Decorator-Perfect Estate

All you have to do in this wonderful 7 bedroom, 5-3/4 bath French provincial is bring your furniture. Superb wall & window decorations are already in place. If you like creamy pastels, warm ivories, touches of elegance, this home is for you. Delightful formal gardens, too. All for only $523,000. To see it today, call Kim at Elite Realty, 555-7970.

When Only the Best Will Do

Bring your family to this rugged rock beauty, built into a mountainside. No expense was spared in its construction or upkeep. Featuring 6 bedrooms, den, 7 baths, it's a marvel of open & airy design, coupled with massive handsomeness for only $615,000. For a special showing, call Sue Ellen at Elite Realty, 555-7970, now.

Fussy, Fussy

If you're fussy, head over to this scrumptious 5 bedroom, 5 bath French country home, located in one of the choicest areas of Greenbrier Hills. Immaculate throughout, with latest decorator fabrics & looks. Enjoy your own pool, 5 car garage, tennis court. Just $614,000. Call Kimberly at Elite Realty, 555-7970, to see this beauty today.

Open the Door
to Elegance

Superbly crafted 6 bedroom, 8 bath half-timbered English beauty. Resting on an acre of grounds, this home radiates quiet charm & perfect quality. Top-of-the-line throughout, with tasteful upgrades like spa-jetted tubs & 2-zone gas heat. Just $650,000. Call Malcolm at Elite Realty, 555-7970, now.

You Can See
the Difference

loving care makes in this spotless 5 bedroom, 4 bath French Regency. Built with 1940's quality, this stunning home & grounds reflect only the finest...antique architectural accents, leaded glass, marble floors. All in peak condition at $600,000. To see a real beauty, call Jo Beth at Elite Realty, 555-7970, today.

Beauty
at Its Best

If you enjoy contemporary drama, see this trend-setting 5 bedroom, 4 bath delight. Thoughtfully designed, it offers warm woods, soft carpets, gentle lights ...mastery of space & sun. In perfect shape, this home is offered at only $615,000. Call Thomas at Elite Realty, 555-7970, for a look today.

Cream Puff
Estate

Picture-perfect English manor with 6 bedrooms, 8 baths, cradled on 4 manicured acres behind gates. Red awnings, slate roof, copper gutters...only the best for this home. Inside enjoy the warmth of mahogany, sparkle of Waterford crystal, elegance of teak. Wonderful quality for $650,000. Call Kenneth at Elite Realty, 555-7970, today.

MAINTENANCE-FREE

Carefree Splendor

in this long & rambling redwood, with 5 bedrooms, 5-3/4 baths. Set in spectacular desert scenery, this easy-care home is built so you have time to enjoy its black-bottom pool, tennis court, sprawling deck studded with cactus. A dream come true for $513,000. Call Fred at Elite Realty, 555-7970, today.

The 52 Week
Vacation

is yours in this sumptuous 5 bedroom, 6 bath traditional ranch, located in an exclusive neighborhood. With a billiard room, indoor pool, tennis court, basketball area...your kids will love it. Almost as much as you love its minimum maintenance. Offered at $455,000. To see it today, call Susie at Elite Realty, 555-7970.

Your
Ideal Haven

Oriental country retreat on 3 acres of natural landscaping. Built with the finest teaks, mahoganies, redwoods, this luxurious 4 bedroom, 6 bath home needs little care. All you have to do is enjoy it. Just $515,000. Call Leonard at Elite Realty, 555-7970, for a look.

A Home Where You'll
Have Time to Play

This home demands very little of you, but gives you so much. 5 bedrooms, 6 baths crafted of stone & glass. Little upkeep, so you have time to enjoy its steamy spa, luxurious pool, sweeping vistas. At $455,000, isn't it worth a few minutes to take a look? Call Timothy at Elite Realty, 555-7970, today.

Need More
FREE Time?

Then give it to yourself in this splendid 3 bedroom, 5 bath traditional brick. With its low maintenance, you can enjoy all the things that make you different...while living in comfort & style. Just $424,000. Call Kim at Elite Realty, 555-7970, to see this easy living home today.

Take the Time
to Enjoy Life

in this 4 bedroom, 3 bath Florida rambler ...with skylights that pour in the sun, flagstone patio filled with tropical plants, easy-care natural landscaping. 12 rooms linked by breezeways & patios. Just $395,000. Call Edward at Elite Realty, 555-7970, for a look.

Easy
Estate Living

You'll love the lifestyle of this handsome 4 bedroom, 5 bath English brick manor. Impressive to look at, minimum maintenance makes it a dream to live in. Slate roof and copper plumbing will last forever, all new wiring. At $457,000, it's a golden opportunity. Call Fredrick at Elite Realty, 555-7970, today.

Enjoy Peace of Mind
in Comfort

in this stunning 4 bedroom, 5 bath Colorado contemporary with sweeping mountain views. With its easy-care redwood & stone construction, you'll never have to worry about a paint job. Custom tile roof will last forever & inside everything is the last word in quality. Enjoy carefree living for just $425,000. Call Jackie at Elite Realty, 555-7970, now.

Does Your House
Dominate Your Life?

Then consider this delightful Victorian charmer, blending the best of the old with the comforts of the new. 5 bedrooms, 5 baths, with whimsical gingerbread trim, whipped cream pastels, rocking chair front porch. Recently updated. Only $505,000. Call Vriginia at Elite Realty, 555-7970, to see it today.

Carefree Living

is yours in this sprawling 4 bedroom, 6 bath ranch hidden in the hills just outside town. You'll love its rustic exposed-beam ceilings, stone walls, flagstone floors. Little care required. Even the naturally landscaped yard is low maintenance. A home you'll truly enjoy for $475,000. Call Ken at Elite Realty, 555-7970, now.

QUALITY WORKMANSHIP

The Ultimate in Quality

If you demand the best, consider this 5,000 sq. ft. French Normandy home in our finest neighborhood. Elegant white brick with 4 king-size bedrooms, 6 full baths, luxury touches throughout. Pool & tennis court, too. Proudly offered at $555,000. To see the best today, call Sue at Elite Realty, 555-7970.

Select the Best

by moving into this contemporary English manor featuring only the finest. You can tell by the imported woods, granite counters, marble floors, ultra-plush carpets. 12 room home of grandeur & distinction for only $475,000. Call Tim at Elite Realty, 555-7970, for a look today.

Your Choice?

The best, of course. It's yours in this warm & open 5 bedroom country rambler. Enjoy the mellow look of wood ...open French windows...sunny skylights & flower filled patios. Wonderful family home, on acre of lovely grounds, for $450,000. Call Tom at Elite Realty, 555-7970, to see it today.

Life's Finer Moments

can have no more appropriate setting than this handsome 4 bedroom, 5 bath weathered gray colonial, resting on an acre of towering pines & flowering shrubs. Almost new, this character home offers a fine walnut-paneled den, mahogany library, fireplace-warmed family room. Yours for $495,000. Call Steve at Elite Realty, 555-7970, today.

Premier Home

When only the best will do...lovely traditional brick set on winding drive, with flanking summer porches, 4 fireplaces, expansive veranda. 5 bedrooms, 6 baths, all luxuriously large. Almost new, this gracious home is $455,000. Call Sue at Elite Realty, 555-7970, now.

Surround Yourself With Quality

in this tasteful Cape Cod designed to show off your art & antiques. Gleaming white walls, polished hardwood floors, tons of windows & patios. This 4 bedroom, 5 bath home is packed with old-fashioned character & modern comfort. Real bargain at $375,000. Call James at Elite Realty, 555-7970, today.

Lifestyle of the Rich & Famous

can be yours in this exquisite gray stone beauty nestled beneath ivy & rosebuds on 2 acres. You'll love the inlaid woods, granite counters, top-of-the-line kitchen & 4 baths. Fireplaces warm all 5 bedrooms. Just $450,000. Call Ginger at Elite Realty, 555-7970, now.

First Class Quality

If only the best will satisfy you, try this sumptuous ocean view home on the bluffs. Long & rambling, with 5 bedrooms, 6 baths, this 1950's wood & glass contemporary captures breathtaking natural beauty. Only $395,000. Call Sue at Elite Realty, 555-7970, today.

The Right Track

You're on it in this 4 bedroom, 5 bath Holland Hills stunner. A soaring contemporary built on 3 levels with indoor pool. Enjoy gleaming slate floors, massive bronze fireplaces, lofts & balconies galore. $425,000 will prove you've arrived. Call Joe at Elite Realty, 555-7970, now.

Built to Last

Made to create traditions...handsome 4 bedroom, 6 bath Georgian radiant with quiet quality. Resting on acre of park-like grounds, this home offers a grand staircase, hardwood floors, beveled glass windows, carriage house, garden pool. Just $425,000. Call Roger at Elite Realty, 555-7970, today.

AD TIP: Never write down to your prospects.

If You Want
the Finest...

it's yours in this marvelous 4 bedroom, 4 bath almost new traditional, surrounded by natural beauty. Your family will love its skylight-studded kitchen, long & rambling brick den, huge screened porch, acre of wilderness. Quality & superb comfort for $375,000. Call Jim at Elite Realty, 555-7970, to see it today.

If Your Family
Deserves the Best...

give it to them in this hillside estate just 10 miles from town. Elegant gates welcome you to a 4 bedroom, 5 bath English manor, with pool, championship tennis court, 4 car heated garage with attached workshop. One of the finest things in life for just $435,000. Call Carolina at Elite Realty, 555-7970, now.

In Search
of Excellence

If you want the best then consider this elegant 4 bedroom, 5 bath French Regency offering the ultimate in luxury. In a formal garden setting, it's an architectural masterpiece. Stunning beauty for $555,000. Call Kendall at Elite Realty, 555-7970, today.

High
Standards?

Live up to them in this sparkling 4 bedroom, 6 bath California contemporary, fashioned from Palos Verde fieldstone, glass & redwood. Designed by Thomas Wainwright, this 5,000 sq. ft. marvel offers heated floors, granite counters, marble vanities. On 3 acres for $575,000. Call Carmelita at Elite Realty, 555-7970, today.

Enjoy
Rich Quality

in handsome 5 bedroom, 4 bath colonial estate reached by a winding drive & sheltered under towering oaks. With its paned windows, walnut-paneled den, 5 fireplaces, it offers a lifestyle open to very few. Yours for only $396,000. Call Joe at Elite Realty, 555-7970, now.

AD TIP: Use short sentences. In advertising, anything goes, as long as it communicates. Even a one-word sentence is okay if that word communicates the impact needed.

UNIQUE APPEAL

HISTORY

150 Years in Same Family

Be the first outside owner of this time-mellowed historic colonial, graced with the charm of the past, lovingly updated with today's comforts. Pool, carriage house, 3 car garage. Just $455,000. Call Reed at Elite Realty, 555-7970, today.

1925 Estate

History buffs will love the art deco touches in this run-down 12 room traditional. Built of brick with quality materials, this home needs a little work... but what fun to peel away the present & see the elegant touches underneath. A joy to discover for $325,000. Call Tim at Elite Realty, 555-7970, now.

Authentic Early American Farmhouse

It would take years to gather the materials to duplicate this home-solid maple cabinets, weathered barn siding, thick paned glass. With its sloping ceilings, grand views, ancient garden, this 14 room farmhouse is a true find. Yours for only $315,000. Call Henry at Elite Realty, 555-7970, for a piece of the past today.

Historic Rancho

Its delightful paved courtyard & splashing fountains still echo of fiestas long ago. Feasts were served in the ancient tile-filled dining hall...siestas enjoyed on the spacious colonnaded veranda. Wonderful old-world charm in 4 bedrooms, 6 baths, tastefully updated. Just $425,000. Call Kim at Elite Realty, 555-7970, now.

Old South Plantation

Very few can reach the lifestyle this home reflects-gentle grace, quality woods, elegant marbles. 14 room historical treasure on 3 acres of rolling hills. For $415,000, enjoy yesterday's gracious way of life today. Call Ruth at Elite Realty, 555-7970.

AWARD-WINNING

Blue Ribbon Architecture

Architectural paradise of sloping ceilings, running beams, spiraling staircase, lofty views. You'll love this exciting 5 bedroom, 4 bath contemporary awarded first prize for its innovation & character. Set on acre of hillside, newly listed and offered at $356,000. Call Fred at Elite Realty, 555-7970, today.

Featured in
Architectural Digest

Rarely does a home of this caliber enter the market. Elegant Georgian manor in the best part of town, with 6 bedrooms, 4 full baths. Radiant with gleaming hardwoods, beveled glass, wide archways. Custom pool, spa, 3 car garage. Just $415,000. Call Jonathan at Elite Realty, 555-7970, now.

World Class
Formal Gardens

surround this truly spectacular Italian architectural masterpiece, behind gates on 2 acres. 12 rooms, filled with all the best. An exceptional deal at $455,000. Call Vi at Elite Realty, 555-7970, to see it now.

Interior Design
Showplace

Historic home on park-like grounds in established neighborhood, just re-done by local interior design society. Enjoy the comfort of 5 bedrooms, 6 baths, all in the freshest colors & styles. Grand yet intimate & warm despite its size. Offered at $495,000. Call Barbara at Elite Realty, 555-7970, today.

First Among
Its Peers

Stunning French Normandy, crafted from elegant gray stone & beveled glass. Featuring 5 bedrooms, 5 baths, with a quality that's hard to find in a newer home. Designed for executive living, it is proudly offered at $515,000. Call Timothy at Elite Realty, 555-7970, now.

AD TIP: Most often, it's best to use active verbs and visual nouns.

CELEBRITY OWNED OR VISITED

Cher's Beverly Hills
Estate

New on the market, impressive Greek Revival manor offering 12 bedrooms, 14 baths, free-form pool, cabana, tennis courts, 5 car garage. All the finest at your fingertips for $895,000. Call Fred at Elite Realty, 555-7970, today.

Celebrity
Hideaway

Remarkable log cabin retreat where stars used to relax. Set on acre of grounds just 1 hour from town, this unique home features 4 mammoth bedrooms, 5 baths, natural hot springs, giant rocking chair porch, loads of lush greenery. Rustic delight for $555,000. Call Jim at Elite Realty, 555-7970, to see it today.

Roosevelt Family
Enclave

Unusual family compound with 5 homes, many outbuildings, 3+ acres of grounds gently sloping to lake. Created from limestone & brick, this elegant enclave offers the finest living, plus much seclusion. Offered at $1.2 million. To see it now, call Jill at Elite Realty, 555-7970.

The Home
Georgia O'Keefe Loved

Low & sprawling Santa Fe with sun-splashed rooms & verandas draped with bougainvillea. Cool Southwestern colors throughout 4 bedrooms, 5 baths...with thick hand-hewn posts, adobe fireplaces, curved walls. Delightful, relaxing home with many touches of the artist. Offered at $950,000. Call Victor at Elite Realty, 555-7970, today.

CHAPTER FOUR

FARMS, RANCHES & HORSE PROPERTIES

FARMS & RANCHES

LOCATION/STYLE

Riverfront Wilderness Ranch

Fly into 260 acres of pure paradise in this luxury cattleperson's retreat with complete working facilities. Spacious 12 room log cabin packed with comfort, plus 5 room foreperson's home. Your private domain for $890,000. Call Jason at Blue Star Properties, 555-1100.

1896 Family Homestead

The Allison family carved this 160 acres out of the wilderness long ago, handcrafting the unusual 4 room log cabin still on the property. Today you can enjoy the charm & convenience of a newer 3 bedroom, 2 bath home, yet feel the same sense of pride in the crops this land yields. Home, outbuildings, 90 tillable acres just $187,000. Call Fredrick at Blue Star Properties, 555-1100, today.

Old MacDonald's Farm

Live the way you've always wanted to...giving your family the chance to garden, raise animals, know nature's ways. Come see this delightful 15 acre farm, with old-fashioned windmill & comfortable 4 bedroom home. Just 14 miles from town. Priced to sell at $87,500. Call Frank at Blue Star Properties, 555-1100, today.

Turn of the Century Ranch

Return to old values & real family living in this charming 3 bedroom, 3 bath ranch just 20 min. from town. Built in 1896, it's been carefully updated over the years, reflecting the best of the past, with all the comforts of the present. 10 acres of wilderness, just $105,000. Call Daniel at Blue Star Properties, 555-1100.

Grade "AAA" Dairy Farm

Working farm with 150 acres of loam, 66 in fine pasture & 2 cattle ponds. You will love the up-to-date milking parlor, 3 large barns, 2 silos & much more. Comfortable 3 bedroom, 2 bath brick family home with huge vegetable garden. All for just $315,000. Call Fredrick at Blue Star Properties, 555-1100, today.

Historic Farm

Looking for a home with history? Consider this 1924 homestead nestled on 10 acres. All the modern conveniences mingled with quaint Early American touches you will adore. 3 bedrooms, 2 baths...sparkling bay windows, polished hardwood floors, antique cherry cabinets. A home to cherish for only $102,000. Call Kenneth at Blue Star Properties, 555-1100, now.

> *AD TIP: Humor is fine for coffee breaks, but don't use it in an ad.*

Weekend Farm

Watch your crops grow from the rocking chair front porch of this 1980 manor house with its 12 sprawling rooms of comfort. 145 acres of deep, rich soil plus heavy woods. At night see the deer come to drink at the stream bubbling through your meadow. Fantasy fulfilled for $225,000. Call Jackson at Blue Star Properties, 555-1100, today.

Scenic Cattle Ranch

Real family ranch set in some of the prettiest land you've ever seen. 1200 fenced acres with flowing spring & deep wells, plus quality buildings. Enjoy 2 traditional brick homes, each 4 bedrooms, 2 baths, with breathtaking views. All for only $650,000, with $155,000 down. Call Joey at Blue Star Properties, 555-1100, now.

Fishing Lake With Wharf

plus windmill, fruit trees & terrific views on 10 acre rancho. Traditionally styled 2 bedroom, 2 bath home with freestanding fireplace, satellite dish, solar hot water, office, 3 car garage. Barn/workshop. All for just $79,000, with owner financing. Call Benjamin at Blue Star Properties, 555-1100, today.

Your Own Ponderosa

40 acre very private & beautiful ranch. Whitewater stream packed with trout meanders just yards from delightful 3 bedroom, 2 bath cedar home. New 2 car garage & workshop...just $69,000. Call Tim at Blue Star Properties, 555-1100, and make it yours now.

Storybook Farm

Fully irrigated 5 acre farm with classic 4 bedroom prairie farmhouse. Walls of windows with view stretching to horizon. 2 barns & deep well...$55,000. Call Ken at Blue Star Properties, 555-1100, to see it today.

Get Back to Mother Earth

with 20 acres of deep rich soil all your own. Grow your family's food, while living in the comfort of a sprawling 3 bedroom, 4 bath white frame home. Fenced yard & barn for lots of animals. Just 25 min. from town. Your rural retreat for $88,500. Call Sue at Blue Star Properties, 555-1100, now.

Be Self-Sufficient

on this old-fashioned homestead, with 15 acres of tillable land. You'll love its classic windmill, rocking chair front porch, deep woods. Not to mention the country-cozy 4 bedroom, 3 bath brick home with 2 huge fireplaces & storage galore. Be your own person for only $76,000. Call Kenneth at Blue Star Properties, 555-1100, today.

Farmhouse & Orchard

You'll love the mouthwatering oranges, limes & lemons growing just outside this charming 3 bedroom, 2 bath farm home. Enjoy 2 acres of citrus trees as well as the luxuries of a pool, spa, 3 car garage. Just $99,000. Call Timothy at Blue Star Properties, 555-1100, for a down-to-earth look today.

AD TIP: Don't use too many $5 words.

A Farm for Your Family

Straight out of a picture book, this 15 acre farm is a child's dream come true: sprawling red barn, chicken coops, windmill, old-fashioned homestead. You will enjoy its charm & appreciate all its modern comforts. Back to nature the easy way...for just $105,000. Call Steve at Blue Star Properties, 555-1100, for a taste of the country today.

Old-Fashioned Farm

Return to a simpler way of life with this old-time farmstead. Resting on 10 acres, this delightful, sun-splashed home offers a sweeping staircase, solarium, gingerbread front porch, and a wonderful little stream. At $106,000, far less than a comparable city home. Call Henrietta at Blue Star Properties, 555-1100, to view this charming farm today.

Armchair Farmer

Enjoy the feel of the land without turning a shovel. Sumptuous 200 acre family farm you can supervise from the comfort of your 12 room brick manor. Satellite dish, lake, solar heating, pool...it's a recreational paradise. There is even a 3 bedroom tenant's house. Offered at just $225,000. To see it now, call Lyn at Blue Star Properties, 555-1100.

Like to Get Back to the Basics?

Then discover this country hideaway just 25 min. from the city. With its picturesque 4 bedroom Dutch colonial farmhouse, bright red barn, fenced yard—it's perfect for giving your family the chance to be close to nature. 10 acres of tillable soil you can do with as you please. Great opportunity at $165,000. Call Mike at Blue Star Properties, 555-1100.

Your Own Big Red Barn

is waiting at this 25 acre farm just outside the city limits. Enjoy the fresh scent of a haystack...the good feeling of getting back to nature...the comfort of an old-fashioned 12 room farmhouse with a sunny & cheerful kitchen. Come see what life can be. Just $145,000. Call Joseph at Blue Star Properties, 555-1100, now.

Picturesque Farm

80 acres of views & seclusion, with 30 acres of professionally maintained avocados. Paved road, utilities, oaks, sycamores, seasonal stream, custom 3 bedroom, 2-1/2 bath cedar home. All for only $189,000. Call Samuel at Blue Star Properties, 555-1100, today.

Riverfront Farm

Delightful 4 bedroom, 2-3/4 bath farm home set on 20 acres of rolling hills bordering river. Enjoy your own swimming pond, huge barn, stockade area, miles & miles of woods. All for just $175,000. Call Franklin at Blue Star Properties, 555-1100, for a look today.

Old West Farm

You'll want to saddle right up when you see this 15 acre spread. Pastoral perfection, with a bubbling stream all its own. You'll love its huge barn & old-fashioned style ranch house, featuring 4 bedrooms, 2 baths—all comfortably large but cozy. If you're looking for atmosphere for under $200,000, call Jackson at Blue Star Properties, 555-1100, today.

AD TIP: The words in your ads should match the needs and desires of your readers.

Stake Your Claim Here

on 20 acres of the prettiest apple orchards this side of the Mississippi. All the latest equipment you'll need to turn a profit, plus terrific 3 bedroom, 2 bath white frame beauty. Just $156,000. Call Vivian at Blue Star Properties, 555-1100, and live in the country now.

New England-Style Farm

Imagine a weathered gray colonial on a gentle hill beneath giant pines...with your own maple orchard, pond, red barn. For just $135,000, you can own a 3 bedroom, 2 bath home on 10 acres. Character you won't find in a city home for $145,000. Call Kenneth at Blue Star Properties, 555-1100, for a look today.

Picture-Perfect Farm

You can bring the cows home every night when you live in this charming 3 bedroom, 2 bath brick farmhouse. Enjoy the closeness of nature & the joy of self-sufficiency on this small, but profitable, working farm. 125 acres that belong to you. Only $152,000. Call Vivian at Blue Star Properties, 555-1100.

SIZE

Farmer's Farm—52 acres

Gorgeous scenic beauty. Creek provides irrigation for approx. 40 acres, produces 50 to 60 tons of hay & grazes 50 head. Includes irrigation pump & pipes. Delightful 4 bedroom, 2-story brick ranch, with sun porch, brick & copper kitchen, orchard stone fireplace. Only 15 miles from town. Just $125,000 with $25,000 down, owner financing. Call Tom at Blue Star Properties, 555-1100, today.

Rancher's Pride —60 acres

20 acres of meadows, the rest is grazing & trees. 2 wells, horse barn, hay barn, garage & workshop. Plus stunning 3 bedroom, 2 bath cedar home set on hilltop, with views of rolling fields. Great set-up for $187,000. Call Theodore at Blue Star Properties, 555-1100, to make it yours.

60 Acres of Freedom

Raise your own fruit, nuts, meat, vegetables on this charming 5 acre farm homestead. Clean air, plenty of room to roam ...plus delightful 3 bedroom, 3 bath white frame home, with rosy brick fireplace & 2 car garage/workshop. A home you'll be proud to own for $145,000. Call Marshall at Blue Star Properties, 555-1100, now.

Perfect Start-Up Farm —20 Acres

Comes with barn, tractor, lots of equipment. Enjoy the luxury of a custom 4 bedroom, 2 bath traditional home & pool, with terrific workshop & stunning sunset views. Give yourself a new start for only $165,000. Call Timothy at Blue Star Properties, 555-1100, today.

60 Acre Working Ranch

Fully irrigated. Spacious 8 room rustic ranch house, guest house, pond, large barn, workshop. Spectacular view of 10 mountain peaks. Ski at nearby Mt. Summa. Just $345,000. Call Steve at Blue Star Properties, 555-1100, now.

AD TIP: Use words that appeal to your readers, not to you or your sellers.

PRICE/TERMS

Abandoned Ozark Farm —$49,000

50 acres with pretty but neglected 2-story native rock home. 3 bedrooms, huge family room, stone fireplace, potbellied stove & electric backup heat. Barn, 2 ponds (1 stocked), mature fruit trees, very scenic. With a small down, owner will finance. Call Nicholas at Blue Star Properties, 555-1100, to see this special property today.

6 Acres— $129,000

Woods, meadows, creek & 2,200 sq. ft. rustic redwood home, with 3 cozy bedrooms, 2 baths, sunny loft for guests. Custom kennels, satellite dish & much more. Call Ted at Blue Star Properties, 555-1100. Hurry.

Bargain Farm —$80,000

Peaceful 20 acres in wooded hills. Stylish 2-story, 1,800 sq. ft. contemporary home with 3 bedrooms, 2 baths. Danish fireplace, vast mountain views. Pool with deck. Barn with feeder. Call Suzanne at Blue Star Properties, 555-1100, to see this bargain today.

Forgotten Farm —$39,900

Abandoned yet picturesque. 10 acres of fields with creek, water rights. Forgotten 2 bedroom house. Excellent fishing & hunting. Owner financing with little or nothing down. Call Fern at Blue Star Properties, 555-1100, now.

Neglected Homestead

Rustic cabin on acre next to wildlife refuge. 6 rooms, spacious porches. Huge trees. Ideal for hunters, horseback riders, hikers. Just $19,900. Call Sam at Blue Star Properties, 555-1100, and grab this bargain today.

Create Your Own Homestead

Abandoned 45 acre farm needs hard-working family to rediscover its original charm. Solid 6 room home worthy of loving restoration with weeds to pull & fences to mend. Delightful creek & barn with hand-hewn timbers. Picturesque setting. With very little down, $75,000 full price. Call Jackson at Blue Star Properties, 555-1100, now.

Fixer Farm

Sadly neglected farmhouse needs gentle touch of caring owners to bring it back to life. Charming 7 rooms, full of cozy nooks & crannies, on 15 rich acres of land. Antique stone barn, weed-filled pond, overgrown pasture. Yours for the low price of $55,000. Call Bradley at Blue Star Properties, 555-1100, to see its possibilities today.

Foreclosed Farm —$65,000

Unbelievable bargain for 35 acres of tillable soil, 2 barns, outbuildings, tractors, equipment. Plus delightful 3 bedroom, 2 bath brick farmhouse perched on hill overlooking land that belongs to you. Enjoy country living today. Call Lea at Blue Star Properties, 555-1100.

200 Acre Ranch
—Must Sell Fast

Need quick action on stunning mountain property with its own spring & 3 deep water wells. Plenty of grazing land, big barn, eye-pleasing 3 bedroom, 3 bath cedar custom home. You will adore its sprawling decks, breathtaking views, highway-close conveniences. Priced at just $176,000. Call Leslie at Blue Star Properties, 555-1100.

Desperate Farmer
Needs Help

Owner willing to finance dreamy 4 bedroom, 3 bath Victorian farmhouse on 15 acres of untouched woods & meadows. Perfect for weekend farmer. Priced at just $55,000, with low down & low interest loan. See how good life can be. Call Ty at Blue Star Properties, 555-1100, now.

CONDITION

Young Farmer's
Dream

15 acre Old MacDonald farm in perfect shape, from the cow barns to the sparkling 3 bedroom, 2 bath frame farmhouse. Enjoy old-fashioned living with 10 acres of pasture, huge vegetable garden, even your own bass-stocked pond. Unbelievably priced at $85,000. Hurry & call Ted at Blue Star Properties, 555-1100, before it's gone!

AD TIP: Use headlines that create self-interest and avoid ones that merely provoke curiosity.

Perfect Ranchette
Set-Up

1,800 sq. ft. home on 13 acres with low, low price tag. Just $69,000 gives you 3 bedrooms, 2 baths, dormer windows, big deck, terrific workshop. Near thousands of acres of national forest. Call Deb at Blue Star Properties, 555-1100, today.

If You're an
Armchair Farmer...

come see this spectacular redwood home on 35 rich & beautiful acres. Massive wood beam & glass construction with 4 bedrooms, 3 baths. Oak floors, cedar interior, hot tub room. 3 bedroom foreperson's home, too. Picture-perfect condition. All for just $189,000. Call Tom at Blue Star Properties, 555-1100, now.

A Farm
for the 90's

Unusual high-tech 40 acres, with drip irrigation & latest equipment. Plus stunning architect-designed 3 bedroom, 2 bath contemporary home with sweeping mountain vistas. State of the art living & farming for $198,000. Call Rick at Blue Star Properties, 555-1100, today.

Ranchers:
You Can Take Pride

in this 50 acre poultry & sheep ranch with 30 acres of improved pastures, 3 ponds, creek, 2 outbuildings. Plus spick & span 4 bedroom, 3 bath traditional farmhouse, with, walnut-paneled family room, 2 rock fireplaces. Great atmosphere for only $176,000. Call Matthew at Blue Star Properties, 555-1100, to see for yourself today.

SPECIAL FEATURES

Beef Farm

1,500 acres, big enough for 890 cattle units. Fresh water from natural mountain spring, several ponds, deep wells. Totally fenced, with 2 fine brick homes & 1 brick bunkhouse. A genuine family ranch for $800,000. Call Florence at Blue Star Properties, 555-1100, now.

Alfalfa Ranch

70 irrigated acres & abundant water from both domestic & large agricultural well. Small bungalow with stunning mountain views. Just $235,000. Call Sue at Blue Star Properties, 555-1100.

3-Home Retirement Farm

20 acres in spectacular mountain setting. Main home 3 bedrooms, 2 baths with gingerbread front porch, root cellar, spacious & sunny rooms. Plus newer 2 & 3 bedroom homes, workshop, garden, fruit trees, pond. Just $59,000. Call Jimbo at Blue Star Properties, 555-1100.

Stunning Ocean View

Once a 2 acre rabbit farm, this property sits on a bluff high above the ocean. You'll love the country atmosphere of the 4 bedroom traditional home with wide front porch & wonderful brick fireplace. If you ever want to raise rabbits, there's a specially designed barn as well as other buildings. A real deal for just $135,000. Call Deborah at Blue Star Properties, 555-1100.

Solar & Hydro Power

Unspoiled 10 acre mountain hideaway with 40 ft. solar tower plus waterwheel over large trout creek. During the evening, watch deer cross the meadow to drink in your bubbling brook. Wonderful newer log home with 4 bedrooms, 3 baths. Independence for $65,000. Call Vic at Blue Star Properties, 555-1100.

AD TIP: Make sure your ads are relevant to the house you're selling. Don't simply reuse the same old ads.

HORSE PROPERTY

LOCATION/STYLE

Equestrian
Estate

Settle in at this stunning 4 bedroom, 3 bath Tudor with its own 3-stall barn. You'll love its luxurious feeling, created by gleaming woods, leaded glass, high ceilings. Your horses will love their roomy corrals, next to your own riding ring. Exquisite horse property for just $875,000. Call Jonathen at Blue Star Properties, 555-1100, today.

A Horse?
Of Course!

You'll adore this cozy 2 bedroom country cottage snuggled beneath towering oaks on 2 wooded acres. Enjoy old-fashioned warmth with thoroughly updated kitchen & bath. A charming red barn & plenty of room for riding. All for $135,000. Call Fredrick at Blue Star Properties, 555-1100.

Bring
Your Horse

to this 3 bedroom, 2 bath brick charmer just 10 miles from the city. Warm up next to its massive rosy fireplace... breakfast on the stunning patio entered thru French doors...enjoy the luxury of a master bedroom suite. One acre of delight, plus 2-horse corral & tack room. Yours for $155,000. Call Ruth Ann at Blue Star Properties, 555-1100.

Zoned for
2 Horses

You'll know you're in horse country by the rolling hills, delightful streams, lovely homes. For under $175,000, you can move into this wonderful 3 bedroom, 2 bath contemporary, with its own naturally landscaped acre. Enjoy fresh air, blue sky, open spaces...while giving your horses a home they'll love. Call Suzanne at Blue Star Properties, 555-1100, today.

Horse Lover's
Paradise

Life the way you always dreamed it would be, in this sprawling 4 bedroom, 2 bath newer traditional, with 1/2 acre of fields & meadow for your horses to roam. Spreading oaks, white board fencing, rustic interior create picture-perfect setting. Just $175,000. To see it today, call Josephine at Blue Star Properties, 555-1100.

Horse
Haven

Classic 3 bedroom, 2 bath Victorian beauty nestled on a hill overlooking your 2-stall barn. Watch the horses from your delightful gingerbread back porch. See the sunset from the rocking chair veranda out front. Wonderfully warm home, with skylights to bring in the sun...for only $156,000. Call Clarence at Blue Star Properties, 555-1100, today.

Hey, Cowboy

Bring horses, dogs & kids to this 5 acre spread just 10 min. outside town. Miles of white board fencing, your own pond, rustic 3 bedroom, 2 bath cedar charmer. Pretty as a picture, you can put your brand here for just $175,000. Call Ken at Blue Star Properties, 555-1100, now.

Horse Country

Surrounded by country estates, this old-fashioned 3 bedroom, 2 bath traditional home is a real bargain. Enjoy polished hardwoods, solid cherry cabinets, antique fireplace, together with a 1-stall barn on an acre of natural beauty. Great opportunity at $155,000. Call Jan at Blue Star Properties, 555-1100, to see it today.

Horse Lovers

Give your horses the best in this delightful 3 acre ranch just 20 min. from town. With 2 corrals, 4-stall barn, tack room, fenced & cross-fenced... they'll love it! So will you, because you'll be living in a sprawling 8 room custom redwood home, with lots of glass & stunning mountain views. All for only $187,000. Call Rosalyn at Blue Star Properties, 555-1100, fast.

Great Place for Horses

With 2 acres, fenced pastures, corral, 2-stall barn with tack room. Great place for people, too...with rambling 3 bedroom, 2 bath traditional, featuring exposed-beam family room, 2 fireplaces, cheerful copper kitchen, pool. Only $176,000. Call Gregory at Blue Star Properties, 555-1100, today.

Ideal For Horses

Unspoiled natural beauty surrounds this stunning 1 acre country home. Enjoy your own babbling brook, forest, deer. Plus charming 2 bedroom cottage, with Victorian accents & modern upgrades. Zoned for 2 horses, it's yours for just $145,000. Call Walter at Blue Star Properties, 555-1100, now.

Training Ring

comes with this magnificent 5 bedroom, 4 bath American clapboard classic. Located in a neighborhood of estate homes, you'll love its delightful shutters, sprawling oaks, hand-built brick patio, enticing free-form pool. Terrific 4-stall barn, corral & ring. 2 acres of luxury...for just $225,000. Call Annabelle at Blue Star Properties, 555-1100, and start living a trainer's dream today.

Hang Your Spurs Here

on this pretty little 1 acre spread just 10 min. from town. 2 bedroom country cottage with knotty pine interior, potbelly stove, rocking chair front porch. Plus 3-stall horse barn, corral & miles of riding trails. More than a home, it's a way of life. Just $135,000. Call Jim at Blue Star Properties, 555-1100, now.

Vista's Best Area!

Superb 2 acre horse estate with lighted riding ring, 4-stall barn, tack room, lots more. Elegant 4 bedroom Georgian home offers 2 fireplaces, magnificent view, pool, spa. Fully fenced & landscaped, with own orchard. All for just $225,000. Call Kimberly at Blue Star Properties, 555-1100, today.

Country Manor

Fabulous 4,000 sq. ft. traditional brick on almost 2 acres. Touch of class in its leaded glass entry, sweeping staircase, polished oak floors. 5 bedrooms, 6 baths, all luxuriously large. Pool, too. Huge 5-stall barn with room for arena. Yours for $450,000. Call Ken at Blue Star Properties, 555-1100, now.

Old West Delight

60 acre paradise just 1 hour from city. Rustic redwood ranch house with 3 bedrooms, 2 baths, lots of luxury. Fish & swim in your own trout stream, put your horses in the 3-stall barn. Stockade fencing. Just $335,000. Call Ken at Blue Star Properties, 555-1100, today.

Need a Home for Your Horse?

Then head for the canyon, with its miles of riding trails, acres of land, city-close convenience. This sparkling 3 bedroom, 2 bath contemporary sits next to a gurgling creek, with a sunny redwood deck open to fantastic views. 2-stall barn, fenced corral...all for only $155,000. Call Betty at Blue Star Properties, 555-1100, to see it today.

For Your Horse & You

Country fresh 3 bedroom, 2 bath home nestled in towering pines. Enjoy almost 3,000 sq. ft. of warm & sprawling living area on 2 acres all your own. You'll love the picturesque red barn & tack room. Your horse will love trotting around the countryside. All for only $135,000. Call Mike at Blue Star Properties, 555-1100, to see it today.

Saddle Up!

You'll be ready to ride the moment you see this Old West style ranch. Stockade fencing, rustic log cabin, dark red barn —it's the perfect setting for a part-time cowboy. 3 bedrooms, 2 baths, filled with modern conveniences & the warmth of fine wood. Just $140,000. Call Nicholas at Blue Star Properties, 555-1100, to check it out today.

Ride 'Em, Cowboy!

An honest-to-goodness ranch, with 6-stall barn, tack room, corral, riding ring. Fulfill your dreams on 2 acres of woods, meadows, brooks...in this stunning 3 bedroom, 2 bath California contemporary surrounded by trees. Just $165,000. Call Fred at Blue Star Properties, 555-1100, to see this one now.

Weekender's Horse Ranch

If you love to ride, consider this elegant 4 bedroom, 3 bath French provincial home in an executive neighborhood just outside town. Located on a rolling acre, it features decorator-perfect entertainment areas, free-form pool, cabana, tennis court. Plus 2-stall horse barn & corral. Your private retreat for only $475,000. Call Annabelle at Blue Star Properties, 555-1100, for a look.

Jackson Ranch

Enjoy delightful 4 bedroom, 2 bath custom cedar home on 10 acres in wooded hills, with vast mountain views. Massive rock fireplace, sizzling spa, stockade fencing, pool & deck. For your horses: a barn, feeder & corral. Just $98,000. Call Jim at Blue Star Properties, 555-1100, to see this one of a kind property today.

Bring Your Horse...

to this unique red rock home, with 3 acres of hills & fields for your riding pleasure. You'll love this 3 bedroom, 2 bath stunner's free-flowing design, with brick floors, redwood balconies, tons of glass. Roomy 4-stall barn & riding ring. A genuine delight for $176,000. Call Jean at Blue Star Properties, 555-1100, and bring your horse today.

Old-fashioned Horse Property...

with heated 5-stall barn, generous riding area, feeder...all top-of-the-line. For yourself, a charming 4 bedroom, 3 bath heritage home, lovingly updated for today, with generous sun porch, brick-walled eat-in kitchen, warm & intimate family room. At an old fashioned price of $198,000. Call Gregory at Blue Star Properties, 555-1100, to see it today.

Make Your Horse Happy

at this 1 acre spread just 15 miles outside town. Charming red barn & tack room, natural spring, miles of riding trails. You'll be happy too, in this 4 bedroom, 3 bath traditional brick home, with its warm & wonderful woods, skylights, sunny French windows & doors. A little piece of paradise for $140,000. Call Kenneth at Blue Star Properties, 555-1100, now.

AD TIP: Don't ruin your ad by using too many abbreviations. Studies have shown that too many abbreviations confuse readers.

SIZE

54 Acre Horse Ranch

30 acres of lush, irrigated pasture & easy highway access. 5-bay equipment shed, 12-stall horse barn. Plus sprawling 4 bedroom, 2 bath California ranch home needing tender loving care. Priced at just $135,000, owner will finance. Call Steve at Blue Star Properties, 555-1100, for details on this ranch today.

2 Acres for You & Your Horse

Plenty of room to roam on this city-close spread, fenced & cross-fenced. Features charming 3 bedroom, 3 bath cedar ranch, with artistic touches like stained glass, stenciled floors, custom tilework. 2 corrals, 3-stall horse barn & tack room. Just $144,500. Call Kimberly at Blue Star Properties, 555-1100, now.

6-Stall Barn

comes with stunning brick manor, hidden behind gates in exclusive area. Enjoy the luxury of 6 bedrooms, 5 baths in a home radiant with quiet quality. Perfect for the country squire. Riding ring, too. Your secluded retreat for $550,000. Call Kenny at Blue Star Properties, 555-1100, today.

4 Bedroom Horse Property —15 Miles From City

Bring the farmily, dogs, ponies—there is room for everyone at this sprawling country farmhouse. You'll love its giant apple trees, root cellar, front & back porches. It's life the way it used to be. Huge corral, 3-stall barn, lots of fenced pasture. Only $155,900. Make a real difference in your life. Call Jim at Blue Star Properties, 555-1100, now.

Your First Ranch

3 acres of pure country, with 2 bedroom knotty pine cabin resting in sun-spattered glen. Rustic stockade fencing, 2-stall red horse barn. Surrounded by trees, rocks, babbling brook. Yours for just $99,000. Call Timothy at Blue Star Properties, 555-1100, today.

PRICE/TERMS

Lender Repo Equestrian Center

Highly improved property on 20 acres at city's edge. Brand-new 4 bedroom, 2 bath redwood home with lots of stone & glass. 2 bedroom trainer's home. Extensive stables, paddocks, corrals & 120' indoor freespan arena. Recently appraised at $650,000. Owner will finance or trade. Call Theodore at Blue Star Properties, 555-1100, now.

Horse Property Just Reduced $15,000

You'll get an unbelievable deal on this handsome 5 bedroom, 3 bath country estate located in the foothills just east of town. Enjoy the luxury of your own pool, 3-stall horse barn, lighted riding ring, large corral. Only $225,555—far below appraisal. Call Jonathan at Blue Star Properties, 555-1100, before it's too late. Hurry.

AD TIP: Write more copy than you need then cut out the unnecessary words.

Sacrifice Ranch

Anxious owner needs out of 10 acre ranch with 5-stall horse barn, corral, tack room with shower. Enjoy fresh mountain breezes, clean air, twinkling stars from the redwood decks of this almost new 3 bedroom, 2 bath custom cedar. Charming eat-in pine kitchen, 2 fireplaces, wood-paneled den. Priced to sell at $155,000. Call Marguerite at Blue Star Properties, 555-1100, fast.

Horse Property Low Down/Low Interest

If you've been looking for an affordable horse property, this is your chance. 5 rolling acres, with 2-stall barn & corral, plus delightful 3 bedroom, 2 bath traditional brick beauty loaded with custom upgrades. Owner will finance. $142,000. Call Carolina at Blue Star Properties, 555-1100, today.

EZ to Own Horse Ranch

With little down & low, low owner financing, this stunning ranch in the foothills is remarkably affordable. 4-stall barn, corrals, feeder...plus miles of riding trails behind delightful 4 bedroom, 2 bath Ponderosa-style ranch. You'll love its rocking chair front porch, massive stone fireplace, cozy knotty pine kitchen. $154,500 & it's yours. Call Tom at Blue Star Properties, 555-1100, today.

No Down on Horse Property

If you need a home for your horse, consider this charming 2 bedroom cottage on an acre of wilderness. With its 2-stall barn & corral, it's the perfect starter ranch. Just $98,000. Get back to basics today. Call Nick at Blue Star Properties, 555-1100.

Let's Make a Deal on a Horse Property

Desperate owner needs out of pretty 2 acre spread zoned for 3 horses. With little or nothing down you can have a 3 bedoom, 2 bath white frame cottage with winding staircase, fireplace & solarium kitchen, to call your own. Full price just $86,500. To talk terms today, call Sue at Blue Star Properties, 555-1100.

Bargain Ranch for Armchair Rancher

Priced to sell fast, you'll love this handsome 3 bedroom, 3 bath Cape Cod home sitting on 3 rolling acres. Gorgeous scenery with miles of riding trails, plus a comfortable 2-stall barn & corral. See what $167,400 can give you. Call Joe at Blue Star Properties, 555-1100, now.

Abandoned Home & Horse Barn

Sadly neglected 2 acres needs loving touch. Gently mellowed 3 bedroom farm home, built of solid brick. Lovely antique fireplace & cabinets. Stockade fences need repairing, 2-stall barn is drafty, but for $125,000, you can't beat it. Call Kenny at Blue Star Properties, 555-1100, to see it today.

Low, Low Price on Horse Property

Way below market, this 3 bedroom, 2 bath almost new home is a real bargain. Just $127,000 gives you a full acre of luscious countryside, with barn & tack room. You'll love the home's wide plank floors, hearty fireplace, spacious rooms. Hurry & call Virg at Blue Star Properties, 555-1100, now.

SPECIAL FEATURES

Horse Training Ranch

5 acres with secluded 3 bedroom, 2 bath contemporary home, hidden in forest glen. Horse area offers main building with heated 60' x 115' lighted arena, 9 box stalls, huge tack room, 14-stall barn, 10 outside covered stalls, many extras. All equipment included for $225,000. Call Valentine at Blue Star Properties, 555-1100, today.

View & Horses, Too!

1 acre horse property with stunning 4 bedroom custom white brick. Enjoy mountain view from sweeping veranda or dramatic soaring living room with full French windows. Generous family room with handsome fireplace, cheerful country kitchen. Room for stable, arena, pool. Only $335,000. Call Jimmy at Blue Star Properties, 555-1100, now.

Miles of Riding Trails

run thru the foothills behind this delightful French country home offering 4 large bedrooms, 3 full baths. You'll adore the bleached woods, flower-filled patios, sunny skylights. 2-stall barn & corral for your riding pleasure. All for just $225,000. Call Suzanna at Blue Star Properties, 555-1100, now.

Riding Arena

comes with sprawling 4 bedroom, 2 bath Spanish hacienda located on 2 acres of scenic splendor. Enjoy the comfort of an almost new stucco home with colorful accents & upgrades, plus 3-stall barn, corral & lighted arena. Only $156,000. To see it today, call Tim at Blue Star Properties, 555-1100.

Horse
Walker

is part of this stunning ranch with the feeling of the Old South. You'll love the home's thick white columns & majestic appearance, as well as the 4 giant bedrooms, 3 full baths. Super stables with 7 stalls, riding arena, corrals & walker. For the true horse lover at only $188,000. Call Marshall at Blue Star Properties, 555-1100, today.

CONDITION

Straight From
the Old West

Superb new ranch with all the western charm you'd ever want. Stockade fencing, 4 bedroom log cabin, dusty 4-stall barn set on 5 acres of nature's splendor. Yours for only $175,000. Call Thomas at Blue Star Properties, 555-1100, to see this old western today.

Give Your Horse
the Best...

in this tip-top country charmer set on 3 secluded acres just 15 miles from town. Top-grade equipment, roomy stalls, huge corral. You'll enjoy the 3 bedroom, 3 bath home's mellow feel, with its knotty pine walls, wide windows, stunning views. Just $135,000. Call Fredrick at Blue Star Properties, 555-1100, and start giving the best to your horse (and to yourself) now.

Exquisite
Equestrian Estate

for those who demand only the best. 40 acres with breathtaking mountain views. 4,000 sq. ft. cedar home offers 4 bedrooms, 4 baths, attached greenhouse with sunken hot tub, 3 car garage. For your horses, giant 6-stall barn with tack & feed rooms. Near country club & skiing. Yours for just $315,000. Call Samuel at Blue Star Properties, 555-1100, today.

Easy-Care
Horse Property

Well-kept 3 bedroom frame cottage on 2 acres with 3-stall barn. Built with 1946 quality, this gentle home has been lovingly maintained over the years & thoughtfully updated. Resting under giant oaks & silvery birches, all for $126,000. Call Mary Beth at Blue Star Properties, 555-1100, for a look today.

Immaculate
Horse Property

Spick & span 3-stall barn comes with picture-perfect 3 bedroom, 2 bath Cape Cod. Gleaming fresh paint, shiny hardwood floors, sparkling French windows. All you need is your horse & furniture. Priced at just $128,000. Call Ben at Blue Star Properties, 555-1100, to view this great opportunity today.

AD TIP: Get in plenty of emotional appeal.

CHAPTER FIVE

CONDOMINIUMS & TOWNHOMES

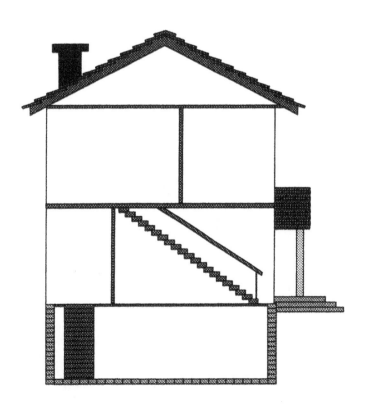

LOCATION

COUNTRY

Heavily Wooded Condo

Nestled in a forest of trees, this dramatic 3 bedroom, 2 bath, 1,300 sq. ft. condo is an exciting blend of sunlight, glass & exposed beams. Overlooking an acre of greenbelt, it offers a fireplace, island kitchen...steps to tennis courts & pool. Just $125,000. Call Julie at All Pro Realty, 555-1100, to see it today.

Enjoy Pastoral Beauty in a Patio Home

You don't have to drive forever to enjoy the country. This carefully planned community with winding sidewalks, towering trees & flowering shrubs, radiates pastoral perfection. Enjoy it through the walls of glass that fill this delightful 2 bedroom, 2 bath patio home. You'll love its ceramic kitchen & steamy hot tub. Vacation at home for only $102,500. Call Ken at All Pro Realty, 555-1100, today.

Feel of the Country, Heart of the City

After a hard day's work enter a worry-free world of fun. Nothing to do in this stunning 2 bedroom, 2 bath modern beauty but take a dip in the pool, get in a few sets of tennis, watch the city lights twinkle from the elegant wrought iron balcony. Fireplace, gourmet kitchen, laundry center. Just $110,000. Call Jim at All Pro Realty, 555-1100.

Cozy Country Condo

A few miles off the highway, you'll find this cheerful condo nestled against the hills. Great country feeling with fireplace, kitchen bay window, warm wood paneling, carport. Your 1 bedroom hideaway just $87,000. Call Linda at All Pro Realty, 555-1100.

Townhome in the Trees

Towering oaks shade the spacious brick patio of this elegant 3 bedroom, 2 bath townhome. You'll love its clean, open feeling. Curl up in front of the rosy-brick fireplace or take a swim in the nearby pool. Comfort & fun for $99,000. Call June at All Pro Realty, 555-1100, to see it today.

WATERFRONT

Waterfront Condo

Watch the ships pull into the harbor from this stunning 2 bedroom, 2 bath contemporary condo lined with glass. You'll adore the bright 14' patio, perfect for parties. Ceramic tile baths, soaring ceilings, gourmet kitchen. Just $145,000. Call Jim at All Pro Realty, 555-1100, today.

Beachfront
Ocean View Condo

Wake up to the waves every morning in this dramatic & open 2 bedroom, 2 bath beachfront beauty. Snuggle up next to its sleek Swedish fireplace. Get a tan on its huge redwood deck. Take leisurely strolls along the sand. Plant shelves, privacy & a whitewater view, only $135,000. Call Virginia at All Pro Realty, 555-1100. Better hurry.

Waterfront Row

A splash of elegance on the prestigious shoreline describes this classic Grecian-style townhome. 3 bedrooms, 3 baths behind gates, with private walled patio, hardwood floors, full-length French windows. Convenient to everything. Only $139,500. Call Linda at All Pro Realty, 555-1100, today.

Riverside Condo

Live in luxury on the 16th floor, with an endless ocean view. Watch the ships sail in as you breakfast on your sunny patio. A tasteful & comfortable home, with white brick fireplace, oak cabinets, 2 huge bedrooms, 2 full baths. Rooftop swimming pool. Only $155,000. Call Geraldine at All Pro Realty, 555-1100.

Lakeside Condo

You'll love to entertain in this handsome 1 bedroom condo with its own dock & water view. Slate fireplace for romantic evenings...top-of-the-line kitchen...spacious loft with skylight. Close to pool, hot tub, tennis courts. Yours for just $89,000. Call Jennifer at All Pro Realty, 555-1100, today.

> *AD TIP: Use the same "tone" throughout your entire ad.*

HILL

Hillside Condo

Breathtaking community perched on hills with stunning city light views. You'll adore this 2 bedroom, 2 bath redwood charmer, filled with unusual accents like crown moulding, trellised private patio, whisper-soft carpets. A luxury home without the work. Only $132,000. Call Lisa at All Pro Realty, 555-1100, today.

Sky-High Condo

Enjoy penthouse living at down-to-earth prices in this sumptuous 3 bedroom, 2 bath suite. Fine wood paneling, gourmet kitchen, slate floors, brick fireplace... plus access to racquetball courts, tennis, pool & spa. High style for low price of $142,500. Call Sue at All Pro Realty, 555-1100, today.

Enjoy New Heights
in Stunning Townhome

You'll love the look of this 3-story colonial charmer with box hedges, brick sidewalks, paned windows. Yet inside there's all the modern warmth & openness you crave. 3 bedrooms, 2 baths stylishly decorated in an award-winning community for $136,000. Call Jan at All Pro Realty, 555-1100, now.

Top of the World
Townhome

Enjoy stunning views from every room of this 3 bedroom, 2 bath lushly land-scaped stucco villa. Secluded on a cul-de-sac, this lovely townhome features an adobe fireplace, tile floors, wide & open living areas flooded with sunshine. Your secret retreat for $147,500. Call June at All Pro Realty, 555-1100.

High on a Hill Condo

Good taste radiates throughout this 2 bedroom charmer perfect for a busy professional. Only 2 miles from downtown, you can enjoy a flower-filled redwood deck, full French windows, plant shelves, stunning ceramic kitchen. Championship pool, spa & playground, just steps away. Close to city park, too. Only $76,000. Call Kenneth at All Pro Realty, 555-1100, now.

DESERT

Desert Dream Condo

Cool pastels fill this 3 bedroom, 2 bath condo. You'll love its tile veranda, just steps from the sapphire pool. Cozy breakfast nook in the skylit kitchen. Elegant master bedroom suite with fireplace. Perfect retreat, close to tennis & golf. Only $142,500. Call Fred at All Pro Realty, 555-1100, today.

Resort Condo

Make every day a vacation in this sun-warmed 2 bedroom, 2 bath delight. Crafted from easy-care redwood & stone with lots of upgrades. You'll have plenty of time to sun, swim, golf. Just $99,000. Call Janice at All Pro Realty, 555-1100, today.

Tan on the 12 Ft. Balcony

of this 2 bedroom, 2 bath desert dream condo just steps from the pool, spa, fine restaurants. If you want an easy-care, stylish home, with soaring ceilings, arched windows & 2 balconies, this is it. Only $87,500. Hurry & call Cary at All Pro Realty, 555-1100, now.

Desert Hideaway

Enjoy easy living in a luxurious planned community, offering golf, tennis, swimming, sunbathing. You'll adore this 3 bedroom, 2 bath townhome... filled with white walls, track lighting, dramatic windows, a flower-splashed patio. Plus very private master bedroom spa. Priced at $105,000. Call Myrna at All Pro Realty, 555-1100, now.

Your Desert Delight

Marvel of adobe, glass & stone blending with the scenic beauty surrounding it. 2 bedrooms, 2 baths & sculptured living space dominated by curved fireplace. One of a kind home, close to pool & tennis, for $125,000. Call Gregory at All Pro Realty, 555-1100, to see it today.

GOLF

On 12th Fairway

You'll love this 2 bedroom, 2 bath upper condo with its sweeping 12' balcony overlooking the fairway. Just steps from the country club, this marvelous home offers a brick fireplace, copper kettle kitchen, greenhouse window. Warmth that is hard to find for $98,000. Call Jim at All Pro Realty, 555-1100, & bring your clubs today.

Golf Course Condo

Life is easy on the greenbelt, especially in this stunning 3 bedroom, 2 bath house of glass. Huge windows bring in soothing tree-filled views...while you enjoy its crackling fireplace, sunning on the giant balcony, relaxing in your spa-jetted tub. Only $102,500. Call Kimberly at All Pro Realty, 555-1100, now.

Your Townhome on the Green

Creamy pastel row house overlooks soothing fairways of Via Mesa Country Club. Enjoy the elegance of 3 bedrooms, 2 baths—all with vaulted ceilings, paned windows, oak trim. Delightful sweeping staircase. Private setting, lush with flowers for $116,000. Call Ken at All Pro Realty, 555-1100, to view this choice townhome now.

Tee-rific Townhouse

You're in the swing of things in this stunning 2 bedroom, 2 bath California contemporary right on a championship golf course. Park your cart out back & keep the clubs in it. This is a gate guarded community with Olympic pool, sizzling spa, tennis courts. You'll love the open feeling of this townhome. All for only $115,000. Call Sue at All Pro Realty, 555-1100, to see it now.

Country Club Condo

More than a home, this 3 bedroom, 2 bath brick beauty is a way of life. A relaxing, easy lifestyle that'll suit you to a tee. Golf, tennis, swimming—all just outside your door. Enjoy the luxury of a gourmet kitchen, oak paneling, white brick fireplace. Just $121,000. Call Steve at All Pro Realty, 555-1100, and start living the good life today.

AD TIP: After someone finishes reading your ad, they should say to themselves, "That sounds like a nice place to live."

RECREATION/LEISURE

Sunrise Racquetball Condo

Exciting 2 bedroom, 2 bath, 1,100 sq. ft. contemporary condo made for carefree living. Enjoy racquetball, tennis, swimming. You'll love the white walls; stylish pastels; track lighting; rock fireplace. Unusually large rooms for $98,000. Call Jim at All Pro Realty, 555-1100, today.

Resort Lifestyle

is yours when you move into this luxurious 3 bedroom, 2 bath condo filled with skylights, balconies, patios. Sail, swim, play tennis. Your choices are endless. 2 car garage & large storage area, too. Only $103,000. Call Steve at All Pro Realty, 555-1100, now.

Carefree Living

comes with this stunning Aspen-like 3 bedroom, 2 bath townhome snuggled in mountains just outside town. Enjoy redwood balconies, soaring ceilings, natural wood trim, rustic rock fireplace in a soothing, tree-filled setting. For your pleasure—tennis, pool, indoor spa & sauna. All only $117,500. Call Jim at All Pro Realty, 555-1100, today.

24-Hour Vacation

Swimming, sailing, tennis, jogging trails suit your lifestyle in this wonderful sunny & bright 1 bedroom condo just 5 min. from downtown. Enjoy fires in its rosy-brick fireplace...city lights from its secluded balcony...sun-splashed breakfasts in its cheery kitchen. No-worry living for $67,000. Call Ted at All Pro Realty, 555-1100.

All Play &
No Work

That's how you'll feel about this spacious 3 bedroom, 2 bath townhome...a marvel of sun, light & space. Exquisite touches like stained glass, brick patio, steaming spa off master bedroom. Easy-care throughout with tennis club around the corner. Only $121,000. Call Susie at All Pro Realty, 555-1100, today & bring your racquet!

Life Can Be a
Year-Round Vacation

when you live in this sumptuous 2 bedroom, 3 bath luxury condo right on Lake Mission Viejo. Park your boat in its dock...get a tan on your 15' balcony... enjoy an ocean view. Luxury upgrades throughout. Just $125,000. To see for yourself, call Roxanne at All Pro Realty, 555-1100, today.

Indulge Your Zest
for Living

in this dramatic 3 bedroom, 2 bath California townhome with vaulted ceilings, greenhouse windows, see-through fireplace. Lushly landscaped grounds, 2 swimming pools, indoor spa, award-winning clubhouse. Just $113,000. Call Sue at All Pro Realty, 555-1100, now.

Recreation &
Relaxation

belong to you in this delightfully open & bright 2 bedroom, 2 bath condo. Skylight in master bedroom, garden tub, family room with wall of windows overlooking a greenbelt view. It's a paradise of birds, flowers & trees. Pool & playground nearby. Only $98,500. Call Jim at All Pro Realty, 555-1100, for a look today.

Enjoy the
Good Life

in picturesque rolling hills with views of scenic open spaces. 2 bedroom, 2 bath upper condo offering gas fireplace, microwave, extra-wide deck, washer/dryer, garage door opener. Close to tennis, pool, spa, clubhouse. Quality living in the country for only $78,000. Call Jim at All Pro Realty, 555-1100, now.

Vacation at Home

Only minutes from beaches, shopping, freeways & business areas, you'll find this delightful 2 bedroom, 2 bath townhome. Set amid waterfalls, palm trees & fountains, it's bright & airy...with tile fireplace, open courtyard, free-flowing floor plan. Tennis, aerobics, swimming. Only $98,000. Call Timothy at All Pro Realty, 555-1100, today.

Make Every Day
a Vacation

in this friendly 2 bedroom, 2 bath Cape Cod condo in a colonial-style village. You'll love its charming gaslight lanterns, brick sidewalks & lush flowers ...almost as much as the maple cabinets, bay windows & stone fireplace. Fitness center, Olympic pool, tennis courts close by. Only $96,000. Call Sue at All Pro Realty, 555-1100, now.

The Good Life

is yours in this soaring 2 bedroom, 2 bath Colorado contemporary condo, with natural wood exposed beams, plank floors, greenhouse windows. Grab your racquet & head for the courts. Enjoy dinner on your balcony overlooking the pool. Close to jogging track. Only $107,500. Call Ann at All Pro Realty, 555-1100, today.

Just for Fun

Carefree 1 bedroom condo in adult community with clubhouse, Olympic pool, sizzling hot tub, BBQ pit. You'll love this home's sun-splashed loft library, full-wall brick fireplace, gleaming ceramic kitchen. Closet space galore, 2 car garage, separate laundry. Only $67,000. If you're ready to make new friends, call Edward at All Pro Realty, 555-1100, now.

For the Fun of Life

Glistening 3 bedroom, 3 bath townhome in trend-setting community close to beach. Soaring windows pour sunlight into 2-story living room circled by a loft. Very private bedrooms, secluded spa, stunning redwood deck with built-in planters. Warm & toasty fireplace. Steps from tennis, racquetball, swimming. All for only $118,000. Call Vera at All Pro Realty, 555-1100, today.

A Lifestyle in Itself

French luxury runs throughout this stunning 3 bedroom, 2 bath townhome in prestigious area. Entered thru a secluded courtyard, this superb home features fireplace-warmed family room/ kitchen, vaulted living room, romantic master bedroom fireplace, walled garden. Exquisite decor. Only $125,000. Call Sue at All Pro Realty, 555-1100, for a private showing today.

> *AD TIP: Don't tamper with a good thing. If an ad gets a good response, run it until the listing is sold or the response slows down.*

CONVENIENCE & NEIGHBORHOOD

Townhome on Bunker Hill

Fabulous 3-story townhome in exclusive area. Enjoy 3 spacious bedrooms, 2 baths, French windows, hardwood floors, sumptuous designer kitchen. Excellent schools in walking distance. Just $145,000. Call Suzie at All Pro Realty, 555-1100, today.

Live in a Williamsburg-Inspired Village

Enjoy the gracious lifestyle of the past surrounded by today's conveniences. Beautiful 2 bedroom, 2 bath townhome on very private cul-de-sac. Brick-walled family room, sprawling yard, rosy warm fireplace. Your colonial treat for $86,000. Call Judy at All Pro Realty, 555-1100, today.

Chic City Condo

You'll love how close this condo is to offices, restaurants & the finest shops. Sophisticated 2 bedroom, 2 bath comfort with slate fireplace, double French doors opening to patio, high-tech gourmet kitchen. Style & grace for $99,000. Call Jimmy at All Pro Realty, 555-1100, to check it out today.

Exclusive Area Only $92,000

If you'd like to live in the best part of town, consider this superb 2 bedroom condo on the 17th floor. Rooftop pool, racquetball court, sun room...all steps away. You'll enjoy this condo's open floor plan with its sweeping wide windows, marble hearth, ceramic kitchen & bath. Call Jasmine at All Pro Realty, 555-1100, for a look today.

Near Parks,
Shops, Schools

Old-world styling radiates throughout this 2 bedroom, 2 bath charmer accented by crown moulding, mahogany trim, solid oak doors. Graceful & airy with 2 balconies & a fireplace, this 1940's delight is just $79,000. Call Ruthie at All Pro Realty, 555-1100, for a peek today.

City Close,
Country Quiet

Superb Victorian-style community nestled downtown. Pastel row houses, window boxes, old-fashioned gas lanterns. This quaint 3 bedroom, 2 bath blue & white townhome offers a walled garden, gingerbread front porch, stunning antique fireplace. Real treasure for only $89,000. Call Jiame at All Pro Realty, 555-1100, now.

New York-Style
Condo

The latest look...sweeping loft condo, with natural exposed beams, huge "great room" with kitchen & fireplace, secluded sleeping area with sprawling closets & baths. High windows stream in sun. Close to everything. Only $92,000. Call Sam at All Pro Realty, 555-1100, today.

Enjoy
Condo Convenience

in this delightful downtown home with 3 bedrooms & 3 baths. Open & airy with skylights, plant shelves, glass doors opening to 2 balconies. Pool, gym & underground parking, too. Just $86,000. Call Josephine at All Pro Realty, 555-1100, now.

Live on Gold Coast Drive
for Only $125,000

At last, the prestigious address you've been waiting for at a price you can afford. Dramatic 1 bedroom condo high above the city. Enjoy sunset views from your private balcony. Fix gourmet meals in your step-saving tile kitchen. Curl up with a good book in front of your stylish see-through fireplace. Call Ken at All Pro Realty, 555-1100, if you're ready to move up today.

Old-Fashioned
Row House

You'll love this gray stone home with its distinctive white shutters & wrought iron gate. Lovingly cared for 2 bedroom, 2 bath charmer with huge fireplace, eat-in kitchen, flower-filled garden. Just $88,000. Call Sue at All Pro Realty, 555-1100, to see it today.

Sick of
Commuting?

Then why do it when you can live in this sophisticated 3 bedroom, 2 bath sky-high condo? Enjoy sparkling city lights through huge walls of glass. Entertain on the stunning brick patio. Relax by the fire in your warm wood-paneled den. Wonderful home, with access to gym & pool for only $123,500. Call Ken at All Pro Realty, 555-1100.

Tired of
Freeways?

Then pick up the key to this chic city condo, with 1,400 sq. ft. of luxurious living. With 2 bedrooms, 2 baths, it's a marvel of glass, soaring beams, gleaming tile floors. Totally contemporary pastel decor & an openness you'll love. At $86,000, isn't it worth a look? Call Fred at All Pro Realty, 555-1100, now.

Your
Downtown Retreat

Hard-to-find 2 bedroom, 2 bath luxury condo gleaming with hardwoods & French windows. Sweeping floor plan, with grand living room, bookcase-lined library, dining area overlooking garden & stained glass kitchen cabinets. All for only $129,500. Call Jim at All Pro Realty, 555-1100, now.

Fun at a
Fashionable Address

You will love this stunning 1 bedroom, 875 sq. ft. condo in an elite neighborhood. White, white walls; track lighting; fireplace; plant shelves & skylights galore. Just steps to pool & fitness center. Only $72,500. Don't miss it. Call Joe at All Pro Realty, 555-1100.

Cosmopolitan
Condo

Sleek black & white dream with 3 bedrooms, 2 baths in guarded building. 14' patio with fountain, hand-painted tile fireplace, solid oak cabinets. A must-see at $82,000. Call Fredrick at All Pro Realty, 555-1100, to see this sophisticated home today.

PRIVACY

Your Private World

Delightful 2 bedroom, 2 bath colonial townhome secluded from neighbors. Trellised patio & spa overlook wooded ravine, charming country kitchen, bay window in living room. Whisper-soft carpets. Just $89,000. Call Sue at All Pro Realty, 555-1100, now.

Honeymoon Hideaway

Romantic 1 bedroom, 750 sq. ft. condo in secluded setting. Enjoy candlelight dinners on walled patio, evenings by the crackling fireplace, whirlpool tub in master bath. For just $72,500. Call Vi at All Pro Realty, 555-1100, today.

The Getaway

Enjoy the lifestyle you deserve in this carefree & stylish 2 bedroom, 2 bath townhome. In an award-winning community offering tennis, pools & lush tropical landscaping, this sunny contemporary feels free & open...with spacious rooms, skylights, sweeping custom staircase. Yours for only $92,500. To see it now, call Vi at All Pro Realty, 555-1100.

Love Nest

Enjoy nature's splendor from the secluded balcony of this 2 bedroom condo. You'll adore its garden bath, skylight in the master bedroom, glowing living room fireplace, warm & cozy den. Your ticket to romance for just $92,000. Call Fred at All Pro Realty, 555-1100, today.

Quiet & Secluded
Condo

In a carefully planned Victorian village, you'll find this charming 1 bedroom pastel paradise. Decorated indoors & out with colors you love, it offers the ultimate in privacy. English garden, greenhouse window, oak floors, antique fireplace. See for yourself how stylish it is. Only $83,000. Call Ruth at All Pro Realty, 555-1100, now.

AD TIP: Make sure your headline calls attention to your ad.

SAFETY & SECURITY

Travel a Lot?

Then consider this delightful 2 bedroom 2 bath townhome in a gate guarded community. Charming rock garden, slate foyer, cathedral ceiling living room with soaring French windows. Upgrades you don't often find in a townhome. Only $78,500. Call Kenneth at All Pro Realty, 555-1100, for worry-free living today.

TV Cameras & Live Guards... PRESTIGE!

You'll love living in this elegant condo complex with its bubbling fountains, curving sidewalks, sculptured landscaping. Only the finest went into this 2 bedroom, 2 bath home, with greenhouse windows, luxury carpets, ceramic kitchen, handsome oak fireplace. If you want the best, for only $88,000, call Tim at All Pro Realty, 555-1100 and make it yours now.

Gate Guarded Community

Nestled in rolling hills, this European-style townhome offers the beauty of hand-painted tiles, a flower-splashed patio, huge brick fireplace. Tennis courts, swimming pools & daycare nearby. Surrounded by other quality homes, this elegant 2 bedroom, 2-1/2 bath retreat is only $94,500. Call Sam at All Pro Realty, 555-1100, to view this beauty today.

> *AD TIP: Read other classified ads—expecially those from top producers.*

VIEW

City Skyline

will add drama to your evenings in this posh 1 bedroom, 18th floor condo. Upgrades like slate fireplace, solid oak cabinets, gleaming ceramic tile floors. Plus delightful balcony with sweeping city view. Only $72,000. Call Jim at All Pro Realty, 555-1100, now.

Forever Views

from this stunning 3 bedroom, 2 bath Colorado-style townhome. You'll adore its rustic redwood & stone construction. Hot tub & pool just around corner. Just $96,500. Call Suzette at All Pro Realty, 555-1100, today.

Overlook Central Park

Walls of windows let you peek over the treetops from this charming 2 bedroom, 2 bath 6th floor condo. Large wrought iron balcony, soaring ceilings, crackling brick fireplace. Just $78,000. Call Vera at All Pro Realty, 555-1100, now.

See the Sailboats

through the walls of glass dramatizing the living & dining areas of this sumptuous 1 bedroom city retreat. Sparkling gourmet kitchen, huge closets, rooftop swimming pool for only $76,500. Call Kim at All Pro Realty, 555-1100, now.

Mt. Baldy View

In this sunny & bright 3 bedroom, 2 bath townhome snuggled in the foothills. Dramatic contemporary design with garden tub, greenhouse window, arched doors... just $88,000. Call Fred at All Pro Realty, 555-1100, today.

SIZE

Perfect Beginning

Charming blue & white 2 bedroom contemporary townhome, has French windows, fireplace-warmed living room, brick patio & BBQ. Convenient to everything. EZ to own at $77,000. Call Jim at All Pro Realty, 555-790, now.

Retire in Style

in this easy-care condo with soaring natural beams, gleaming galley kitchen, guest loft, huge master bedroom suite. Impressive stone fireplace. Hospital, mall, shops close by. Just $65,000. Call Jillian at All Pro Realty, 555-1100, for a look today.

Empty Nesters...

consider this airy & light 2 bedroom California condo with charming redwood patio, inner atrium, cheerful eat-in kitchen. Lots of comfortable living space in carefully planned community with fitness center, pool, shops. Just $75,000. To take a look today, call Sue at All Pro Realty, 555-1100.

AD TIP: Be careful anytime you start talking about loans and finance. Strict guidelines apply.

Why Not Start in Style...

in this sophisticated 1 bedroom city condo on the 14th floor, with stone fireplace, airy loft, stunning skyline view. Hard to find this much class for only $68,000. Call Timothy at All Pro Realty, 555-1100, to see it today.

Ideal First Home

Secluded 2 bedroom patio home, nestled in flowering shrubs. Open & breezy design with walled garden off master bedroom, charming deck off living room, eat-in kitchen with greenhouse window. Many built-ins. Just $75,000. Call Sam at All Pro Realty, 555-1100.

Discover the Joys of Owning a Home

in this stylish 3 bedroom, 2 bath townhouse just 5 min. from center city. Located in a lovely New England-style village, it features weathered gray siding, shingled roof, red shutters. Inside enjoy hardwood floors, bay windows, your own brick fireplace. Just $85,000. Call Ken at All Pro Realty, 555-1100.

A Home of Your Own?

It's possible in this stunning 1 bedroom condo surrounded by skyscrapers. You will love its heart-of-the-city convenience, exposed brick walls, natural beams, gleaming bleached floors. Impeccable shape. Only $72,500. Call Ray at All Pro Realty, 555-1100, now.

Sophisticated Starter

High-tech 1 bedroom condo on 15th floor of terrific building. Enjoy luxury of spiral staircase leading to loft, dramatic Swedish fireplace, stunning balcony with built-in planters. Rooftop pool & gym. Just $81,000. Call Jim at All Pro Realty, 555-1100, to explore the possibilities today.

Perfect for Live-in Relative

Country cottage with '90s style...lovely 2 bedroom, 2 bath traditional townhome, filled with bay windows, oak floors, cute copper kettle kitchen. Mellow woods add warmth, while spacious rooms create airy feeling. Just $73,000. Call Lisa at All Pro Realty, 555-1100, now.

You Can Own a Home

You'll love this stunning 1 bedroom, 750 sq. ft. condo in an elite neighborhood. Take a dip in the luxurious pool. You will adore this home's gleaming designer kitchen, glowing brick fireplace, luxurious whirlpool bath. Best of all, it's only $71,000. Call Fred at All Pro Realty, 555-1100, for a look today.

LARGE SIZE

Tri-Level Townhome

Cleverly designed contemporary dream with 3 bedrooms, 3 baths—all secluded & different. 3 levels ensure privacy, while dramatic "great room" with fireplace promises many happy evenings. Huge patio with pool & gym close by. Comfort & convenience for $145,000. Call Steve at All Pro Realty, 555-1100.

4 Bedroom Townhome

Big families will love the sprawling comfort of this traditional charmer just steps away from an Olympic pool, spa & clubhouse. With almost 2,500 sq. ft., you'll never feel cramped. 3 baths make mornings easy & after school there's a huge yard & playground. Can you believe just $87,000? Hurry & call Vivian at All Pro Realty, 555-1100.

2,500 Sq. Ft. Condo

Hard-to-find giant condo in prestigious area perfect for growing family. 3 bedrooms, 3 baths...within walking distance of superb schools. Enjoy luxury of pool, gym, full security. Plus your own 16' balcony with dramatic mountain view. Low maintenance, high style, just $95,000. Call James at All Pro Realty, 555-1100, now.

Your Penthouse Suite

Sumptuous 4 bedroom, 3 bath penthouse with 360 degree city view. You will love its rooftop terrace, dotted with palm trees & fountains. Dramatic 2-story living room with unusual modern fireplace, gigantic eat-in kitchen, warm & woodsy den. A must-see for $155,000. Call Jim at All Pro Realty, 555-1100, for top of the world view today.

Brady Bunch Condo

Bring the kids to see this airy & bright 3 bedroom, 2 bath condo in great neighborhood. Terrific extras like whisper soft carpets, custom brick fireplace, charming eat-in kitchen. Plus pool, fitness center & 3 playgrounds to keep the kids busy. Can't beat it for $94,000. Call Jack at All Pro Realty, 555-1100, to see it today.

PRICE/TERMS

BARGAIN PRICE

Neglected Townhome

needs gentle care of loving owner. 3 bedrooms, 2 baths in gorgeous park-like setting with view of wooded creek. Begging for fresh paint, new carpets, minor repairs...but offers skylights, loft library, handsome oak fireplace. Ready for action at $83,000. Call Sue at All Pro Realty, 555-1100, for a look today.

Condo Needs TLC

One person's junk is another person's treasure. When you've weeded thru the dirt & grime, you'll find this 1 bedroom classic a dream come true. Clean, straight lines with quality tiles, brass fixtures, rosy red-brick fireplace. Originally sold at $74,500, at $55,000 it's a great opportunity. To take advantage of it today, call Annabelle at All Pro Realty, 555-1100.

Abandoned Brick Row House

It's been years since this once-charming townhome had a good cleaning...but what potential. 3 bedrooms, 2 baths with beveled glass cabinets, oak floors, solid mahogany mantel. True quality beneath the dirt. Only $66,000. Call Fredrick at All Pro Realty, 555-1100, for a great deal today.

Great Condo Bargain

You won't believe the price on this sunny 1 bedroom condo. Just $43,000 gives you spacious master suite, delightful guest loft, gleaming tile kitchen, plus handsome fireplace. View of pool, too. Call Ken at All Pro Realty, 555-1100, today. This won't last.

Price Reduced $10,000

on elegant in-town row home under canopy of trees on quiet street. Wide stone steps lead into spacious & tasteful living room dominated by marble hearth. High ceilings & French windows in all 3 bedrooms. 2 full baths. Need quick sale. Now $85,000. Call Fred at All Pro Realty, 555-1100.

Like New, Priced Less

Dreamy 3 bedroom, 2 bath California condo with 2-story living room, skylights, exposed beams. You'll love its ceramic tile floors, huge kitchen, sunny patio perfect for plants. At $67,000, it's below it's '92 sales price. Call Ken at All Pro Realty, 555-1100, today.

AD TIP: Use "real" language not "real estate" language.

Rock-Bottom Price on Sky-High Condo

If you've been waiting for a great deal, this is it. 2 bedroom, 2 bath condo in super location with gym, tennis court, pool. Enjoy the warmth of your white brick fireplace, the gleam of your gourmet kitchen, the city-lights view from your wrought iron balcony. Terrific quality for only $61,000. Hurry & call Jim at All Pro Realty, 555-1100, today.

French Townhome Just Reduced!

Last of its kind in prestigious planned community. 3 bedrooms, 2 baths with exposed-brick family room, impressive living room, garden view dining & kitchen skylights. 2 fireplaces. Low, low price of just $75,000. Call Mary at All Pro Realty, 555-1100, to see it.

Owner Will Sacrifice Condo

City-lover's delight...1 bedroom with French doors opening to secluded garden balcony. Gracious living room with fireplace flanked by bookcases. Step-saving galley kitchen & walk-in pantry. Sophisticated living for only $63,000. Hurry & call Tim at All Pro Realty, 555-1100, now.

Drastically Reduced Townhome

Desperate owner needs action on charming New England-style townhome just 5 min. from downtown. Delightful country decor throughout 3 bedrooms, 2 baths. Sweeping staircase, bow window overlooking garden, 2 car garage. Only $67,000. Call Vanessa at All Pro Realty, 555-1100, now.

MUST SELL QUICKLY

Got to Go Condo!

Drastic price cut on sunny 2 bedroom, 2 bath condo in great neighborhood. Enjoy sprawling balcony, warm oak fireplace, sumptuous garden tub...just steps from tennis, swimming, FUN. Only $53,000. Call Fred at All Pro Realty, 555-1100, now.

Condo Priced to Sell Fast

Way below market at $52,000, this 1 bedroom charmer is a bargain. Luxurious living room with fireplace, gourmet kitchen, walls of glass opening to balcony with breathtaking view. Better act fast. Call Josephine at All Pro Realty, 555-1100, today.

Can You Move in Tomorrow?

Then you can get a great deal on super 3 bedroom, 2 bath Victorian-style townhome in prestigious area. Cozy up next to its 2 fireplaces...dine on its stunning brick veranda...enjoy the cheerful copper kitchen & 2 car garage. Just $62,000 for the right person. If that's you, call Sue at All Pro Realty, 555-1100.

Condo Close Out

Reduced thousands, this luxurious 2 bedroom, 2 bath contemporary beauty offers custom touches like flagstone fireplace, decorator closets, whirlpool tub, Jenn-air range & over 1,000 sq. ft. of living space. Unbelievable quality for just $73,000. Call Greg at All Pro Realty, 555-1100, to see it today.

If You Need
Fast Escrow...

come see this charming 3 bedroom, 2 bath townhome along the river. Enjoy waterfront delights through your French windows. Relax on your flower filled entry courtyard. Feel the warmth of 2 fireplaces. Priced to sell fast at $76,000. Call Juanita at All Pro Realty, 555-1100, now.

Townhome Owner
in Trouble

Needs quick action on 2 bedroom, 2 bath colonial row house in elite neighborhood. Secluded end home with sprawling garden & view of city lights. Spacious, airy rooms, sprinkled with skylights. Only $61,000. Call Jim at All Pro Realty, 555-1100, today.

Must Close
in 30 Days

Perfect investment or starter home—sweeping 1 bedroom condo in high-rise. 12' balcony for outdoor entertaining, sunken living room with fireplace, sparkling ceramic kitchen with oak cabinets. Only $52,555—if you move fast. Call Ted at All Pro Realty, 555-1100, now. Don't miss out!

Time Running out
for Townhome Owner

Delightful 3 bedroom, 2 bath townhome in private setting near beach. Thick stucco construction with tiled veranda, inner atrium, adobe fireplace. Over 1,500 sq. ft. of living space. Priced to sell fast at $58,000. Hurry & call Alisha at All Pro Realty, 555-1100, for a look today.

Countdown Condo

Perfect place for first time buyer. Needs fast action. 1 bedroom with sunny loft, cheerful galley kitchen, massive orchard stone fireplace. Close to pool, hot tub, tennis courts, jogging trails. Yours for only $51,000. Call Jim at All Pro Realty, 555-1100, to check it out today.

Anxious Owner

wants out of traditional brick townhome on quiet curving street. 3 bedrooms, 2 baths with dormer windows, parquet floors, spacious & bright rooms. Garden & 2 car garage, too. Just $61,000. Hurry & call Fred at All Pro Realty, 555-1100.

FORECLOSURE

Foreclosed Condo

Bank wants quick sale on 1 bedroom luxury condo in skyscraper. Stunning city lights view from 2-story living room, sweeping balcony, huge master suite. Classic white fireplace. Only $51,000. Call Mamata at All Pro Realty, 555-1100, today.

Bank-Owned
Condo

Take advantage of low price on sunny & spacious 2 bedroom, 2 bath California condo in excellent neighborhood. Pool, spa, tennis, underground parking. Plus fireplace, conversation pit & bougainvillea-draped redwood deck. Way below replacement at $55,000. Call Ruth at All Pro Realty, 555-1100, now.

Bankrupt Owner
Will Sacrifice

charming 2 bedroom, 2 bath brick townhome in delightful area, close to excellent schools. Very private cul-de-sac location, enhanced by floor-to-ceiling windows, cozy breakfast nook, bookcase-lined den. Superb value for only $61,000. Call Jamal at All Pro Realty, 555-1100, to see it today.

Lender Orders Sale

of 2 bedroom, 2 bath glass-walled condo in heart of downtown. Steps to offices, shops, museums. You'll love its sleek, sophisticated lines, with upgrades like whirlpool tub, greenhouse window, oak floors. Low, low price of just $52,000. Call James at All Pro Realty, 555-1100. Better hurry.

Condo Close
to Foreclosure

means you get bargain price on dramatic 2 bedroom, 2 bath contemporary filled with sunshine & fresh air. Glorious indoor atrium with towering plants, shiny tile kitchen, exciting exposed-beam ceilings, 2 car garage. Only $53,000. This will go fast. Call Sue at All Pro Realty, 555-1100, today.

OWNER/SPECIAL FINANCING

No Down & Owner Will Carry

Delightful 3 bedroom, 2 bath condo in superb planned community close to shops & freeways. Enjoy mountain views from your spacious balcony. Cuddle up next to your handsome full-wall brick fireplace. With 1,800 sq. ft., plenty of room for a family. Just $76,000 & owner will finance. Call Josephine at All Pro Realty, 555-1100, now.

Sun-Swept
Townhome

A small down payment moves you into this fresh & bright 2 bedroom, 2 bath townhome with terrific river view. You'll love the way the sun sweeps in through the skylights warming the parquet floors. Plants will adore the soaring shelves, greenhouse windows, trellised patio. Packed with upgrades, just $64,000. Call James at All Pro Realty, 555-1100, to see it today.

For Less Than
Rent...

you can own this handsome 2 bedroom, 2 bath condo in an exclusive area. Stylish walnut den warmed by fireplace, with classic arches opening to gracious living room. Health club & pool nearby. With small down & full price of $68,000, owner will finance. How can you pass it up? Call Ty at All Pro Realty, 555-1100, today.

Save $$$$ &
Assume Loan

Dreamy 3 bedroom, 2 bath townhome, nestled on park-like grounds. Enjoy the classic colonial look, with warm woods, paned windows, brick patio & 2 car garage...in a neighborhood you'll love. Only $61,000. Be the first to call Vivian at All Pro Realty, 555-1100.

No Need to Qualify

Owner will carry you on this charming 1 bedroom condo designed for active lifestyles. Low maintenance, with lots of natural sunshine & fresh air. Plus health club, pool, tennis courts & jogging trails. Full price only $62,000. Call Fred at All Pro Realty, 555-1100, and check out this opportunity today.

Nothing Down

& this glamorous 2 bedroom, 2 bath condo can belong to you! Sleek tinted windows, high-tech black & white kitchen, pastel decor, white brick fireplace, soaring ceilings. Full price only $61,000 & owner will carry. Terrific deal. Call Ken at All Pro Realty, 555-1100, today.

Terrific Loan On...

tri-level townhome in friendly family neighborhood. You'll love its 3 king-sized bedrooms, 2 full baths...as well as extra luxuries like 2 balconies, walled patio, fireplace-warmed family room & 2 car garage. Only $85,000 with owner financing. Call Jim at All Pro Realty, 555-1100, now.

Below Market Interest

You'll save thousands with owner financing on this classically styled 2 bedroom, 2 bath condo in prestigious area. Smooth clean lines, with artistic carved nooks, Grecian fireplace, 2 sets of French doors. Superbly decorated. Priced at $78,000, with low down. Call Linda at All Pro Realty, 555-1100, for a look today.

Owner Will Help You

by carrying below market loan on this 3 bedroom, 2 bath brick row home close to everything. With charming bay windows, antique oak mantel & cheerful country kitchen, it's a delightful family home. Only $71,000. For a great deal, call Ann at All Pro Realty, 555-1100.

AD TIP: *Don't be afraid to use questions, especially in your headlines.*

Great Owner Financing

on plush 1 bedroom condo in downtown high-rise. Curved balcony with sweeping city view, sunken living room, charming oak kitchen, underground parking. Top-of-the-line for $43,000. Owner will carry. Call Glendale at All Pro Realty, 555-1100, to see the view today.

Owner Will Carry on Terrific Tri-level

Stunning 3-story townhome, with 3 bedrooms, 2 baths overlooking the park. You'll love its luxurious feel, with gleaming hardwoods, full-length French windows, gentle circular staircase. Delightful walled patio, too. Priced at just $88,000, owner will carry. See it today. Call Kim at All Pro Realty, 555-1100.

No Fuss

If you're always on the run, you'll appreciate this hassle-free 2 bedroom, 2 bath condo with tennis, swimming & sailing at your doorstep. Relax on your sunny balcony. Shop at convenient downstairs boutiques. Spend quiet evenings next to your crackling fireplace. Owner financing means no need to qualify. Just $66,000. Call Jimmy at All Pro Realty, 555-1100, now.

Very Little or No $ Down

on this gorgeous 2 bedroom, 2 bath condo just 10 min. from the city. You'll love its gentle view of rolling hills. Enjoy it from your sprawling balcony or spacious living room. Wood-burning fireplace, microwave, 2 car garage, next door pool...just $55,000. Owner financing makes it easy. Call Jessie at All Pro Realty, 555-1100, to see it today.

Low, Low Down

& you can be the proud owner of this sun-splashed 2 bedroom, 2 bath condo overlooking 12th fairway of championship golf course. You'll adore its easy neutral decor, warmed by mellow woods & rosy brick fireplace. 6 skylights bring in the sun, 1 over the whirlpool tub. Priced at $53,000, owner will carry. Call Jamie at All Pro Realty, 555-1100, to see it today.

Steal of a Deal

Country charm fills this 2 bedroom, 2 bath condo in a tranquil setting. From your 12' balcony, enjoy the music of a waterfall. Warm brick walls, oak floors, spacious & cheerful kitchen, carport. Yours for just $55,000, with owner financing below market. Call Sue at All Pro Realty, 555-1100, now.

INVESTMENT VALUE

Your Hedge Against the Future

Stunning 3 bedroom, 2 bath townhome of unusual quality in sought-after community. Designed for those who appreciate the finer things but don't want the hassle of a house, this luxury home is filled with exotic woods, marble & tile. Very private, yet close to hot tub & pool. Priced at $187,000, far below replacement cost. Call Kenny at All Pro Realty, 555-1100, for a look today.

> *AD TIP: Most often, it is best to use active verbs and visual nouns.*

If You Want to Make Money...

consider this dreamy 2 bedroom, 2 bath condo in rapidly appreciating community. Terrific location on private road. Custom redwood deck, whisper-soft carpets, microwave, ceramic kitchen & bath, 2 car garage. At $81,000, it's way below market. Call Fredrick at All Pro Realty, 555-1100, for a great deal today.

Enjoy Immediate Profit

when you move into this 2 bedroom, 2 bath California-style patio home, located in award-winning community. Open & airy with exposed beams, skylights, classy tile floors, in delightful garden setting. At $66,000, you can't beat it. Call Teddy at All Pro Realty, 555-1100, now.

Value-Packed Condo

Hard-to-find 1 bedroom condo with panoramic view of mountains & city lights. Lovingly cared for by its original owner, this home features many custom upgrades: tile counters, oak cabinets, handcrafted vanity with marble top. Close to health club & pool. Low price of only $55,000. Call Gerry at All Pro Realty, 555-1100, for a look today.

Super Investment

Sought-after 2 bedroom, 2 bath townhome in prestigious gate guarded community. Delightful light pink stucco with red tile roof, heavy oak doors, hand-hewn beams. Genuine hacienda for only $88,000...less than new. Call Jim at All Pro Realty, 555-1100, for a classic home today.

DON'T RENT—BUY!

Why Put $$$ in Your Landlord's Pocket?

when you can enjoy this scrumptious 1 bedroom condo with all the trimmings: health club, Olympic swimming pool, tennis courts, carport. You'll love it's crackling fireplace, sunny kitchen, walls of windows opening to balcony. 2 car garage, too. For only $74,000, it's less than rent. Call Jim at All Pro Realty, 555-1100, to find out more.

If You Can Afford $500/Month Rent...

you can own this charming 2 bedroom, 2 bath Victorian townhome with ginger-bread front porch, antique bronze fire-place, stained glass accents. Priced at just $55,000, with owner financing, you'll save thousands. Call Stephanie at All Pro Realty, 555-1100, to see how easy it is today.

Renters: Get Big Tax Break...

by owning this lush 2 bedroom, 2 bath tropical villa in award-winning com-munity. With its indoor atrium, sliding glass walls, secluded patio, it offers un-usual privacy for a townhome. Low down & full price of $62,000. See it to believe it. Call Tim at All Pro Realty, 555-1100, now.

Renters: Make the Sensible Move

into this delightful 2 bedroom, 2 bath Cape Cod townhome all your own. Enjoy the luxury of a very private garden with hot tub. The warmth of a wood-paneled living room with massive fireplace. The convenience of a 2 car garage with work-shop. Lifestyle that's hard to find in a rental. Just $62,000. Call Kathleen at All Pro Realty, 555-1100.

Finally The Home of Your Dreams

Sophisticated 1 bedroom city condo, with stunning view of twinkling city lights. Room-size bath with garden tub, chande-liered dining, impressive oak fireplace. At $45,000, it's worth a look. Call Leonard at All Pro Realty, 555-1100 & see this unusual offering.

> *AD TIP: As ad expert David Oglivy says, "You can't save souls in an empty church." People must read an ad before they will respond. So make sure your ad counts.*

STYLE

ARCHITECTURE & ATMOSPHERE

Condo That Feels Like a Home

You won't believe you're in a condo when you see this country-fresh 2 bedroom, 2 bath charmer. Cleverly tucked away, secluded from neighbors & noise, there's just an acre of woods to gaze upon. Luxuriously large balcony, giant fireplace, gleaming tile kitchen, carport. Only $65,000 & it can all be yours tomorrow. Call Jim at All Pro Realty, 555-1100, for a look today.

Romantic Villa

You'll fall in love with this softly lit 2 bedroom, 2 bath condo overlooking charming Spanish courtyard with dancing fountains & azure pool. Tiled veranda is perfect for romantic dinners. Bedroom skylights bring in the moon's glow. Lush carpets, oak cabinets. Only $72,000. Call Tim at All Pro Realty, 555-1100, for a little romance today.

Slick & Sophisticated

Contemporary drama fills this 2 bedroom, 2 bath townhome, distinguished by 2-story windows, sunken living room, circular fireplace. Soft fresh colors in impeccable taste, with downtown waiting at your doorstep. Come home to luxury. Only $89,000. Call Beth at All Pro Realty, 555-1100, to see it now.

Designer's Flat

High arched ceilings & abundant windows flood the spacious "great room" of this 1 bedroom condo with light. Island kitchen features all the latest gadgetry. Screened off sleeping area with dressing room & whirlpool bath. For a high tech pleasure, just $87,000. Call Jim at All Pro Realty, 555-1100, fast.

Sophisticated Charm

fills this gleaming 3 bedroom, 2 bath townhome in prestigious neighborhood. Handsome colonial styling with neatly landscaped patchwork garden, solid oak bannisters, sun-splashed breakfast nook. Only $76,000. Call Elizabeth at All Pro Realty, 555-1100, for a look today.

Georgian Townhome

You'll love this elegant address almost as much as you appreciate it's quality. 3 bright bedrooms & 3 baths, with gleaming wood-paneled library, living area opening to garden, shiny copper & brick kitchen. Lots of care for only $81,000. Call Suzie at All Pro Realty, 555-1100, to see it today.

AD TIP: Put the biggest benefit in the headline or beginning of the ad.

European Village Townhome

Move up in the world to this delightful European community tucked away in the foothills. Abundant charm in this 2 bedroom, 2 bath end home with window boxes, skylit kitchen, walled patio & 2 car garage. Mountain views, too. Only $67,000 & it's yours. Call Geraldine at All Pro Realty, 555-1100, now.

Artist's Loft

If you're an individualist, see this magnificent downtown loft. Full wall of windows catches the sunlight, making the brick walls sparkle. Solid oak floors, room-size bath, very secure. Only $91,000. Call Pamela at All Pro Realty, 555-1100, to see something different today.

Architecturally Inspired Condo

Budding architect transformed 2 bedroom, 2 bath contemporary into artistic delight. Jutting balcony, inlaid floors, gleaming granite kitchen-quality galore for $87,000. See for yourself. Call Ken at All Pro Realty, 555-1100, now.

Make New Friends

in this sunny 2 bedroom, 2 bath California dream. Why run off to a crowded health club when 2 pools & spas are right outside your door? Meet your match on the tennis court. Unwind after a hard day's work in the steamy sauna. Enjoy the best in life for only $76,000. Call Judy at All Pro Realty, 555-1100, for a taste of it today.

SPECIAL FEATURES

KITCHEN

Condo With
Country Kitchen

Warm woods fill this charming 2 bedroom, 2 bath condo nestled in a colonial-style village. Delightfully fresh decor, with bay window, redwood deck, oak bannister. Unusual character. All for just $65,000. Call William at All Pro Realty, 555-1100, today.

Professional
Chef's Condo

If you're a serious cook, you'll love this stunning 2 bedroom, 2 bath upper condo with its chef-designed custom kitchen. All the upgrades you can imagine, plus slate fireplace in living room, large balcony, sumptuous master suite & 2 car garage. Only $74,000. Call Sue at All Pro Realty, 555-1100, for a look today.

If You Love
to Cook...

you'll never want to leave this skylight-filled kitchen, trimmed in warm red-woods with hummingbird stained glass window & greenhouse window. It's the heart of this delightful 2 bedroom, 2 bath townhome, accented by French doors, brick patio, oak fireplace. Yours for just $83,000. Call Ken at All Pro Realty, 555-1100, now.

FIREPLACE

Townhome
With 3 Fireplaces

Luxury surrounds you in this impressive 3 bedroom, 3 bath Georgian home, gleaming with solid hardwoods, hand-rubbed bannisters, brass fixtures. Handsome grand staircase with library loft for cozy reading. Huge kitchen with own hearth. Just $98,000. Call Vi at All Pro Realty, 555-1100, today.

Enjoy a
Wood-Burning Fireplace

in this cozy mountain condo, with walls of windows open to towering pines, rugged slopes, gentle deer. You'll love the airiness of this 2 bedroom, 2 bath dream, with natural wood beams, knotty pine kitchen, spacious deck, 2 car garage. Only $65,000. Call Kim at All Pro Realty, 555-1100, for a look at this great bargain today.

Artist-Crafted
Fireplace

is only one of many custom features in this sumptuous 3 bedroom, 2 bath upper condo. You'll adore its textured walls, beveled glass, handsome oak floors. Perfect for entertaining. Just $95,000. Call Joe at All Pro Realty, 555-1100, now.

MASTER BEDROOM SUITE

Sumptuous Suite

is waiting for you in this chic 2 bedroom, 2 bath city condo, just steps from offices & shops. Enjoy bright city lights from the spectacular indoor hot tub of your master bedroom suite. Lush neutral carpeting, elegant brick fireplace, eat-in kitchen. Only $98,000. Call Fred at All Pro Realty, 555-1100, for the suite life today.

Your Townhome Retreat

Enjoy your private hideaway in this 3 bedroom, 2 bath traditional colonial. You will adore the master suite's whisper-soft carpeting, romantic oak fireplace, stunning French doors leading to private garden. Luxurious living for only $96,000. Call Linda at All Pro Realty, 555-1100, for a peek today.

Luxurious Master Suite

is yours when you move into this delightful 2 bedroom, 2-1/2 bath Colorado contemporary townhome in exclusive area. Waterscaped setting, with ponds, footbridges, giant rocks, plus tennis, swimming, sailing. You'll love the rugged feel, with stone fireplace, soaring redwood deck, mellow pine cabinets, 2 car garage. All for just $87,000. Call Fred at All Pro Realty, 555-1100, now.

> *AD TIP: Write as if you are talking to a friend.*

A Condo With Its Own Reward

After you've loaded the dishwasher in your gleaming tile kitchen, put the kids to sleep in the 2 giant bedrooms, checked the crackling fire in your wood-paneled den, you can retreat to comfort in your master suite. Relax in your whirlpool tub ...see the stars from your private balcony...feel the moonlight from the huge skylight over your bed. 2 baths too. Yours for $92,500. Call Jack at All Pro Realty, 555-1100, and get your reward today.

Convenient Yet Private

Classic 2 bedroom, 2 bath city condo with dramatic 15th floor view. Wide & airy living room, 2 sets of French doors, copper kitchen, elegant dining area. Master suite offers luxurious sitting & sleeping area with your own hot tub & private patio. Only $84,000. See for yourself. Call June at All Pro Realty, 555-1100, now.

ENERGY EFFICIENT

Toasty Warm Townhome

Cradled in rolling hills, this aristocratic 3 bedroom, 2 bath brick home will help you save big on utility bills. Stylish & efficient thermopane windows, thick insulation, gas heat throughout free-flowing floor plan. 2 cords of wood for your potbellied stove, too. All for just $97,500. Call Ernestine at All Pro Realty, 555-1100, now.

Cut Your
Utility Bills

by living in this prize-winning energy saver—a sprawling 2 bedroom, 2 bath condo with lots of charm. Doublepane doors open to garden balcony...thick plaster walls hold in heat...delightful wood-burning stove warms family room. Quality & efficiency for only $88,000. Call Tim at All Pro Realty, 555-1100, and start saving today.

Save
Energy $$$$

in this stunning 2 bedroom, 1-1/2 bath redwood & glass thermal-crafted townhome with breathtaking valley view. Triple paned windows, gas heat, solar hot water, 2 heatilator fireplaces, 2 car garage. Stay warm all winter long for just $98,000. Call Dorothy at All Pro Realty, 555-1100, now.

ROOM FOR ENTERTAINING

Entertain Your Friends
in Style

in this airy & open 2 bedroom, 2 bath condo with charming trellised patio, gleaming gourmet kitchen, elegant brick fireplace. Invite your friends for a dip in the pool...play a set of tennis...party in your prize-winning clubhouse. At $87,000, your choices are endless. Call Tina at All Pro Realty, 555-1100, now.

AD TIP: Use testimonials. For example, "Neighbors refer to it as a palace."

Party-Perfect
Condo

You'll feel free & easy in this sprawling 1 bedroom condo with its walls of windows & spacious loft. Set up drinks on your breakfast bar...start a crackling fire in the rock hearth...put lounge chairs on the redwood deck overlooking pool. Yours for $65,000. Call Jim at All Pro Realty, 555-1100, today.

Serve Tea at
Your Townhome

This 3 bedroom, 2 bath traditional charmer is the perfect setting—bay windows, gleaming hardwoods, delightful oak fireplace, walled English garden, 2 car garage. Only $86,000. For a taste of gracious living, call Brian at All Pro Realty, 555-1100, today.

End Your Party
With a Splash

You'll love the huge rooms in this contemporary 2 bedroom, 2 bath condo—perfect for a crowd. Send the overflow out to your 12' balcony...fix snacks in your step-saving ceramic kitchen...end the fun with a swim in your Olympic-size pool. Easy to care for, fun to live in. Just $72,000. Call Samuel at All Pro Realty, 555-1100, now.

Invite
Your Friends

over to this country cozy 2 bedroom, 2 bath townhome nestled in trees & winding sidewalks. You'll love its shiny copper kitchen, polished oak bannister, tasteful terra-cotta tile fireplace. Plus a sweeping rear lawn with a garden that will please everyone's eye. Just $87,000. Call Jim at All Pro Realty, 555-1100, to see it today.

PORCHES/PATIOS/SPAS

Good-bye Tension!

Imagine coming home after a hard day's work & sinking into a sizzling hot tub draped by flowers & hidden by trees. You can in this dramatic 2 bedroom, 1-1/2 bath condo...a marvelous mix of sunshine, classic styling & comfort. Tennis, health center, swimming are all close by for $73,000. Call Ken at All Pro Realty, 555-1100, today.

Italian Tile Spa

is the focal point of this romantic 3 bedroom, 2 bath attached stucco villa located in award-winning community. Set in its own garden, the spa is perfect for private entertaining. Enjoy terra-cotta tile floors, greenhouse windows, 2 car garage. Only $85,000. Call Thomas at All Pro Realty, 555-1100, now.

Invest in Pleasure

in this sleek, sophisticated 1 bedroom city condo with walls of glass open to skyline drama. Enjoy the luxury of a 16' balcony ...an eat-in kitchen splashed by sunshine...the slick look of tile throughout. Huge health club, too. Keep fit for just $65,000. Call Mike at All Pro Realty, 555-1100, today.

For the Fun in Life

Carefree 2 bedroom, 2 bath condo perfect for professional family. Little to do but enjoy your Olympic-size pool, fabulous gym, indoor jogging track. Wood-paneled den, fireplace & breakfast nook add charm. Only $82,500. Call Judy at All Pro Realty, 555-1100, to see it today.

Enjoy Summer Breezes

on the sun-kissed redwood deck of this superb 3 bedroom, 2 bath townhome hugging a hillside. Enjoy warm woods, tons of glass, luxurious upgrades for just $91,000. Call Francesca at All Pro Realty, 555-1100, to see this unusual home today.

> AD TIP: *Don't ruin your ad by using too many abbreviations. Studies have shown that too many abbreviations confuse readers.*

CONDITION

WELL CARED FOR

Champagne Condo

Lots to celebrate in this stunning 2 bedroom, 2 bath modern dream...with its huge 15th floor terrace, spiraling staircase leading to loft, classic gourmet kitchen with dining area. Perfect condition. Only $94,000. Call Sue at All Pro Realty, 555-1100, & break out the bubbly today.

Prim & Proper Townhome

Enjoy gleaming hardwoods, sparkling paned windows, shiny parquet floors in this handsome 3 bedroom, 2 bath colonial home. Built with quality, cared for with pride, it offers 1,800 sq. ft. of gracious living, with a velvety manicured lawn & 2 car garage. Yours for just $82,000. Call Kim at All Pro Realty, 555-1100, to see it today.

Sparkling Fresh Condo

You'll love the fresh look & feel of this 1 bedroom delight with its unique architectural accents, sunken living room, open & airy design. Thoughtful upgrades like ceramic window shelf, gas log fireplace, custom closets. Mint condition...$64,000. Call Kenneth at All Pro Realty, 555-1100, now.

Better Than New Townhome

Cared for by 1 owner for the past 8 years, this Georgian styled home gleams with tender loving pride. 3 bedrooms, 2 baths filled with custom features. Whisper-soft carpets, unusual bow window, hand-built brick patio. Only $74,000. Call Fred at All Pro Realty, 555-1100, for a great deal now.

Cream Puff Condo

Soft peaches & cream decor highlights this sun-sprinkled 2 bedroom, 2 bath high-rise condo located in exclusive area. You'll love its huge terrace, split-level living area, giant master bath. Only the best for $86,000. Call Alisha at All Pro Realty, 555-1100, now.

Pretty as a Picture Townhome

It's unusual to find so much character in a townhome...but this 3 bedroom, 2 bath beauty, in small group of superior homes, has it. Charming gabled roof, window boxes, wonderful airiness inside. Solid quality with microwave, garden tub, 2 car garage. Ready to move at $83,000. To see it today, call Jim at All Pro Realty, 555-1100.

> *AD TIP: Write fast and edit later.*

Designer Condo

Exciting 2 bedroom, 2 bath high-rise condo owned by interior designer. You will adore its fresh, sophisticated look with unique step-down living room, tiled fireplace, high-tech kitchen. Superb condition. $74,500 & you can move in tomorrow. Call Suzanne at All Pro Realty, 555-1100.

Touches of Charm

fill this splendid 2 bedroom, 2 bath townhome located along the waterfront. With its old gas lantern, brick-walled family room, hand-carved cherry stairway, it's a real heart warmer. Immaculate. Just $84,500. Call Frank at All Pro Realty, 555-1100, today.

Tip-Top Townhome

Nothing to do but move into this sunny & bright 2 bedroom, 2 bath California townhome, high on a hill. Clean, sweeping lines, with soaring ceilings, skylights, arched windows. Feels much bigger than 1,800 sq. ft. Only $79,000. Call Ken at All Pro Realty, 555-1100, and make it yours now.

Bring Your Furniture

This charming 3 bedroom, 2 bath traditional townhome is ready & waiting. Almost new, it offers whisper-soft carpeting, cheerful eat-in kitchen, lush walled garden. Day care & playground nearby. Just $78,000. Call Fred at All Pro Realty, 555-1100, fast.

AD TIP: Don't be afraid to use short, choppy sentences.

MAINTENANCE-FREE

No More Yard Work

You'll love the lifestyle of this cheerful 2 bedroom, 2 bath California patio home... open to sea breezes & sunlight. Easy to care for, it leaves time for the things you love: swimming, sailing, sunning on your 15' deck. Only $81,000. Call Jim at All Pro Realty, 555-1100, today.

Home Without Headaches

No need to sacrifice style or quality for efficiency—this 3 bedroom, 2 bath townhome has it all. Gleaming library, French doors opening to patio, stunning designer kitchen & 2 car garage. In a community that's private, well-kept, elegant. Only $99,000. Call Kim at All Pro Realty, 555-1100, now.

Pamper Yourself

in this luxurious 2 bedroom, 2 bath condo with tropical flavor. Lush balcony fragrant with flowers. Sunken living room with walls of windows. Moonlight-filled master bedroom with very private whirlpool bath. Nothing to do but enjoy. Just $89,000. Call Fred at All Pro Realty, 555-1100, today.

Spend Relaxing Weekends

in this rambling 2 bedroom, 2 bath condo with superb recreation right outside your door. How about a few laps in the Olympic-size pool? Or tennis anyone? What about a round of golf? With this easy-care lifestyle you'll never have to spend another weekend doing repairs again. Lovely home, bright & sunny, with open feeling. Only $87,000. Call William at All Pro Realty, 555-1100, to view it today.

If You're a
Busy Person...

consider this classically styled 1 bedroom downtown condo with elegant library & dramatic loft. You'll admire its clean Georgian styling, handsome fireplace, top-of-the-line quality. Only $89,000 & you'll never have to commute again. Call Rick at All Pro Realty, 555-1100, today.

No More
Upkeep

This clean & sparkling 2 bedroom, 2 bath townhome almost cares for itself. You'll love its look: open, bright, with exposed beams & lush landscaping. Delightful inner atrium, too. All for just $78,000. Call Linda at All Pro Realty, 555-1100, to see it today.

Make Your Life
Easier

by moving into this sprawling 3 bedroom, 2 bath condo close to shops, offices, museums. Wonderful city-light view from rambling balcony. Easy-care floors, fresh paint, stunning fireplace. Plus health club & pool. Only $94,500. Call Beth at All Pro Realty, 555-1100, for a simpler life today.

AD TIP: Avoid words that people don't use in everyday conversation.

Give Yourself
the Gift of Time

in this secluded townhome located on cul-de-sac in carefully planned community. No lawn to mow, repairs or trimming... it's all taken care of for you. Just enjoy your luxuriously large living room, sizzling hot tub, 2 gigantic bedrooms, 1-1/2 baths, 2 car garage. Only $87,500. Call Ken at All Pro Realty, 555-1100, today.

The Art of
Carefree Living

is yours in this sumptuous pink & blue condo perched high above the city. Elegantly decorated, its 2 bedrooms, 2 baths offer lavish touches like stained glass, whirlpool tub, cozy window nook. Stunning view. Make it yours for $86,000. Start enjoying life today—call Kim at All Pro Realty, 555-1100.

Maintenance-Free
Townhome

Perfect for the busy family, this stunning 3 bedroom, 2 bath townhome offers the luxury of a private home, combined with the easy life of a planned community. You'll love its elegant double doors, marble hearth, French windows, 2 car garage. You'll appreciate the nearby tennis courts, pool, lots of parking. Only $95,000. Call Suzanne at All Pro Realty, 555-1100, today.

UNIQUE APPEAL

AWARD-WINNING

First Class Condo

Recognized for its outstanding design, this marvelous 1 bedroom condo is a gem to live in. Open, airy, with lots of storage space, its little extras will make your life happy. Unique look, plus lots of places to play, for $76,000. Call James at All Pro Realty, 555-1100, and move up to first class today.

Award-Winning Design

Better-than-new 2 bedroom, 2 bath traditional townhome. Carefully planned to blend homespun charm with contemporary conveniences, it features a wood-burning fireplace, skylights, lots of plant shelves, brick walls. A real prize for only $83,500. Call Rebecca at All Pro Realty, 555-1100, today.

Live in a Prize-Winning Community

You won't believe how easy life is in this stunning 3 bedroom, 2 bath condo. With 2 balconies, skylights, walls of windows capturing the sun, it's truly delightful. Better yet, you'll be living in a community where millions of dollars have been spent to bring you the finest in recreation. Golf, tennis, pools, sailing... it's all waiting for you. Just $94,500. Call Samuel at All Pro Realty, 555-1100, to see it today.

AD TIP: Terms like "APR" and "Due on Sale" may make a lot of sense to you, but remember, your readers don't buy homes everyday.

CHAPTER SIX

MOBILE HOMES

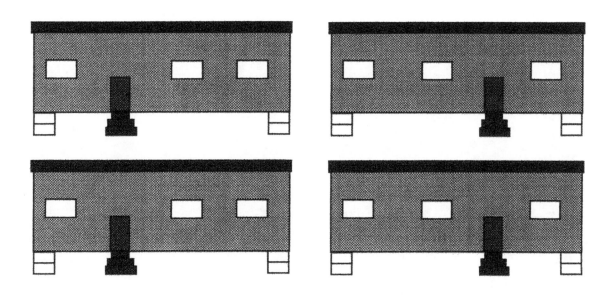

LOCATION/STYLE

"The Orchards"

2 bedroom, 2 bath mobile home in prestigious park. High-tech kitchen, walk-in closets, skylights, air conditioning & lots more. Only $79,500. Call Vivian at All Pro Realty, 555-1100, today.

Coral Ranch
Country Club

Charming 2 bedroom, 2 bath mobile home in resort community. 1,300 sq. ft. of comfort with stunning view of surrounding mountains. Pools, tennis, spacious clubhouse, quiet neighborhood. Home & lot for only $88,500. Call Sam at All Pro Realty, 555-1100, for a look today.

Golfer's
Delight

Live by championship golf course & enjoy ocean breezes. 2 bedroom, 2 bath, 1,600 sq. ft mobile home. Huge screened porch, country kitchen, carport, scads of storage. Just $73,000. Call Suzanna at All Pro Realty, 555-1100, & bring your clubs!

Pearl
Beach

Why rent when you can own your own immaculate 2 bedroom, 2 bath mobile home with breathtaking ocean view? Only $74,500. Call Fredrick at All Pro Realty, 555-1100, now.

Country Club
Exclusive

Doublewide in country club $5,000 below market. 2 bedrooms, 2 baths, family room, all drywall. All for only $35,900. EZ owner financing. Call Kenneth at All Pro Realty, 555-1100, to find out more.

Stunning &
Dramatic

Perfect for entertaining, this 24' x 60' mobile home offers 2 bedrooms, 2 baths in a lovely open floor plan. Wet bar & family room...near beach & shopping. Only $760 a month, including space rent. Call Joe at All Pro Realty, 555-1100, to see this exciting home today.

Quality &
Prestige

Immaculately upgraded to maximum triple with 2 car attached garage, 2 huge bedrooms, 2 baths, cathedral ceilings, drywall throughout, garden tub. You'll adore its delightful "great room" next to custom kitchen. Only $75,000. Shows like conventional home. Call Sue at All Pro Realty, 555-1100, for a look today.

Family Park

Large 3 bedroom, 2 bath mobile home that you can easily convert to 4 bedrooms, in excellent area Exceptionally attractive park. Bring the kids & pets. It's only $49,000. Call Kim at All Pro Realty, 555-1100, today.

Grover Heights

Spacious 1,600 sq. ft., 2 bedroom, 2 bath mobile home with sunken enclosed patio. Delightfully landscaped setting, plus luxury touches like skylights & oak cabinets. Includes all major appliances. Convenient to pool & clubhouse. All for just $45,000. Call Jan at All Pro Realty, 555-1100, now.

5 Star Park

You'll love living in this charming park, with its tall trees & lush bushes. 1988 triplewide, with 2 bedrooms, 2 baths in private setting. Tastefully decorated. Space rent just $300. At $29,000, this won't last! Call Jill at All Pro Realty, 555-1100.

Ocean View Mobile Home
Only $60,000

1,800 sq. ft. of luxury with stunning whitewater view. 2 bedrooms, 2 baths, large kitchen with tiled shelves, family room with wet bar, 2 sheds. Call Sam at All Pro Realty, 555-1100, today.

Everything...

you've ever wanted in a home comes with this delightful 2 bedroom, 2 bath doublewide. Huge family room with wet bar & brick fireplace, built-in appliances, garden tub, compo. roof, total privacy. Only $49,000. Call Fred at All Pro Realty, 555-1100 & make it yours.

Top-Notch

Immaculately upgraded inside & out, this 1992 doublewide offers 2 bedrooms, 2 baths, garden tub, air conditioning, utility room, separate laundry. Huge yard, too. Just $62,775. Call Sam at All Pro Realty, 555-1100, now.

First Class

Gorgeous Villa West doublewide with 1,440 sq. ft. of comfortable living. 2 bedrooms, 2 baths, custom kitchen, like new condition. Bring your kids & pets. Just $51,000. Call Sheila at All Pro Realty, 555-1100, for a great almost new home today.

Live in a Park

5 star park with terrific clubhouse, pool, superb landscaping. You'll love this 3 bedroom, 2 bath triplewide, too. Huge screened porch, towering trees, whisper-soft carpeting, top-of-the-line throughout. Priced to sell fast at only $48,000. Call Ruth at All Pro Realty, 555-1100, today.

> *AD TIP: Watch out for words that have potential double meanings. Back side might easily be taken to mean rear end instead of backyard.*

SIZE

Lots of Home for Your $$$$

Upgraded 24' x 62' with 2 large bedrooms & 2 baths. You will adore its 8' x 18' California room, luxury carpets, family room, extra-large kitchen with pantry, laundry area. On choice corner lot with automatic sprinklers and it's only $49,900. Small pet OK. Call Teddy at All Pro Realty, 555-1100, to see it today.

Triplewide Madison —$41,995

Incredible value in secluded park. 3 large bedrooms, 2 baths, gorgeous round kitchen, decorator carpet & drapes. Outstanding clubhouse & pool, too. No down. VA financing okay. Hurry, this one will not last! Call Clara at All Pro Realty, 555-1100, now. Don't miss out!

1,680 Square Feet

Elegant 2 bedroom, 1-1/2 bath 1986 home with drywall interior, wet bar, skylights, low space rent. Convenient to major malls & freeways. Just $31,000. Call Gerald at All Pro Realty, 555-1100, to see it today.

3 Bedrooms

Skylights, beamed ceilings, waterfront views—you'll love this wonderful extra wide mobile home. Spend evenings on its screened porch, enjoy the privacy of your own yard. 2 baths, too. Space rent $450. Yours for $35,000. Call Caroline at All Pro Realty, 555-1100, for a look at this special home today.

Triplewide Showplace

Delightfully decorated 3 bedroom, 2 bath charmer on choice corner lot. Curl up next to a crackling fire in its huge brick fireplace. Enjoy your plants in the kitchen's greenhouse window. Country fresh, very quiet, only $99,000. Call Thomas at All Pro Realty, 555-1100, to see it today.

> *AD TIP: Long ads are fine, but make sure that they are still tightly written. Remember, in classified ads you're paying by the word. So make each one count.*

PRICE/TERMS

Only $24,000

Charming 1 bedroom mobile home, perfect for the small family. In a security park in picture-perfect Brea Canyon, it offers a delightful screened porch. Call Harold at All Pro Realty, 555-1100, for details on how to see it today.

Luxury at $44,875

24' x 60' Silvercrest with 2 bedrooms, 2 baths. You'll adore its big kitchen with sweeping counters, mirrored closets, mellow earth-tones throughout. Easy-care yet stunning desert landscaping. Call Fred at All Pro Realty, 555-1100, to see this beauty today.

Estate Sale

Spotless 24' wide with 2 bedrooms, 2 baths & yard for pets. Open & airy with beamed family room, chandeliered dining, central air. Low space rent includes all utilities. Vacant & ready for $27,500. Call Edna at All Pro Realty, 555-1100, for a great deal.

Sacrifice Mobile Home

Just on market...1987 24' wide featuring 2 bedrooms, 2 baths, huge elm trees. Eat-in kitchen with dishwasher, central air, compo. roof. Need quick sale. Offered at $29,000. Call Suzanne at All Pro Realty, 555-1100, today. Hurry!

Vacant & Waiting

Immaculate 24' x 60' mobile home with 2 large bedrooms, 2 baths. You'll love its sunken living room overlooking rose garden, formal dining area, warm & intimate family room. 1 year buyer warranty. Only $35,555. Call Jim at All Pro Realty, 555-1100, now.

Picture Yourself in a Beautiful Beachfront Mobile Home for Only $90,000

Custom-built doublewide on the beach with its own boat slip. 2 bedrooms, 2 baths on lushly landscaped lawn in beautiful park, just steps from the sand. Over 2,040 sq. ft. To see it today, call Fred at All Pro Realty, 555-1100.

Own a Cadillac at Ford Prices

Big 1,400 sq. ft. Americana mobile home offers top-quality throughout. Whisper-soft carpet, 2 king-size bedrooms, 2 baths, wet bar, cheerful breakfast nook, large enclosed patio room, elegant fixtures. Located in one of the area's finest parks, with fabulous clubhouse, it's been drastically reduced by desperate owner. Just $37,998. Call Joe at All Pro Realty, 555-1100, now.

Discount Special

Doublewide Lancer with California room, 2 bedrooms, 2 baths. You'll appreciate its custom oak cabinets, water softener, dishwasher, separate laundry. All appliances & great home for only $28,500. Call Susie at All Pro Realty, 555-1100, to see it today.

Low Space Rent

Stunning 24' x 56' home offers 2 bedrooms, 2 baths. Open kitchen off spacious family room & dining area. Custom living room with ceiling fan, built-in desk & breakfast bar. You'll love the detailed brick work on the skirting & patio. With space rent of only $350, isn't it worth a look? Only $33,000. Call Sam at All Pro Realty, 555-1100, to see this bargain today.

Reduced $5,000

Only $15,000 & you own quality 1 bedroom mobile home with garden tub, paneled den, choice corner lot. Pets welcome. Call Richard at All Pro Realty, 555-1100, to see it today.

No Down Repo

Family, adults, pets OK. Take over payments on airy & bright 2 bedroom, 2 bath doublewide on large lot. Call Virginia at All Pro Realty, 555-1100, today.

AD TIP: Try to paint a vivid portrayal of the home you're advertising. This will inspire your prospects to call.

Fixer-Upper

Single wide with 2 bedrooms, 2 baths in 5 star park. All for only $9,995. With very low down & low payments, it's yours. Call Josephine at All Pro Realty, 555-1100, now.

No Qualifying

1994 doublewide in excellent park. 3 bedrooms, 2 baths with charming enclosed patio, sizzling private spa, air conditioning. Family pets OK. Can you believe only $49,900? Call Ted at All Pro Realty, 555-1100. Better act fast.

Trade Your RV For...

this delightful 24' x 60' 2 bedroom, 2 bath mobile home with 8' x 20' sunroom, decorator touches inside & out. Breathtaking mountain views. Easy freeway access. Just $21,000 or ???. Call Ricky at All Pro Realty, 555-1100. Hurry and call today.

Why Rent?

when you can own this sun-splashed 2 bedroom, 2 bath quality mobile home for about the same amount. Nestled in 5 star park, convenient to everything. Call Sam at All Pro Realty, 555-1100, and start owning today.

Owner Will Finance

2 bedroom, 2 bath doublewide with sunny enclosed patio perfect for plants. Corner lot across from state beach. Move in tomorrow. Pets & children welcome. Only $28,500. Call Fredrick at All Pro Realty, 555-1100, today.

Bad Credit
OK

Owner will carry loan on custom 2 bedroom, 2 bath 1,440 sq. ft. Silvercrest. Fully upgraded with dishwasher, Maytag washer & dryer, gorgeous rock fireplace, cathedral windows, wet bar, drywall throughout, vaulted ceilings, spa in master bath. Reduced to $49,999. Call Jo at All Pro Realty, 555-1100.

Assume
Low Interest Loan

on this streamlined like-new doublewide. 2 bedrooms, 2 baths with central air & enclosed Florida room. In prestigious park with clubhouse & pool. Pets welcome. Low down to assume loan at full price of $23,500. Call Jim at All Pro Realty, 555-1100, today.

Low Down
Payment...

moves you into this clean 1 bedroom doublewide...luxury on a budget. All the features you love. Desperate owner will finance at full price of $19,999. Call Sue at All Pro Realty, 555-1100, now.

Below
Market

Spick & span 24' x 60' featuring 2 bedrooms, 2 baths on nicely landscaped over-sized corner lot. Wonderful wood-paneled family room. Pets and children welcome. Just $18,500. Better move fast. Call Elizabeth at All Pro Realty, 555-1100.

AD TIP: *Get in plenty of emotional appeal.*

SPECIAL FEATURES

Bring Your Pets

This super park not only welcomes your pets, it offers one of the lowest space rents in the area—only $330! 2 bedroom, 2 bath beauty is one-owner special with extra storage space, sunny family room, 2 outdoor sheds, quality cabinets. Just $22,000. Call Thomas at All Pro Realty, 555-1100, now.

Own Your Lot

Spacious & bright 2 bedroom, 2 bath doublewide set on "Quake Master" foundation. All the goodies you'd expect, plus small workshop. All for only $87,500. Call Henry at All Pro Realty, 555-1100, to view it today.

Life's a Beach!

when you're living in this skylight-studded 1 bedroom charmer, right on the sand. Put your guests in the bunk room. Entertain in the large living room with glass-walled add-on. $24,500. Call Sue at All Pro Realty, 555-1100, & make the ocean your neighbor now.

Roses Galore

You'll love this peaceful 2 bedroom, 2 bath doublewide circled by a fabulous rose garden. Enjoy their color & fragrance from your sunny Florida room or the sunken living room. Custom cabinets, laundry, all appliances, only $32,000. Call June at All Pro Realty, 555-1100, to smell the roses today.

Fireplace Plus

Sparkling 24' x 60' Silvercrest with 2 bedrooms, 2 baths. Feels like a single family home—brick fireplace, polished cherry cabinets, luxurious garden tub. Just $46,500 & it's yours. Owner financing, too. Call Joseph at All Pro Realty, 555-1100, now.

Security Park

24' wide mobile home featuring 2 king-sized bedrooms, 2 full baths in very private park. Enjoy the breezes on your screened porch or swim in the huge clubhouse pool. Special space rent only $250 per month. Hurry & call Betty at All Pro Realty, 555-1100, for a safe investment today.

CONDITION

Immaculate

2 pets are OK in this near-new 1 bedroom doublewide. All the convenient appliances you love: dishwasher, refrigerator, washer, dryer plus extras like built-in china hutch, walk-in closets, luxury car–pets. Secluded on large private lot, with low space rent. Only $28,500. Call Steve at All Pro Realty, 555-1100, to see it today.

Executive Taste

Doublewide with 2 bedrooms, 1 bath in upscale area with garden tub, mirrored closets, custom kitchen. Enjoy hosting parties. Open living area perfect for entertaining. Yard big enough for spa & BBQ. Low payments, EZ qualifying, full price only $26,500. Call Geraldine at All Pro Realty, 555-1100, today.

Super Sharp

Large 3 bedroom, 2 bath doublewide with vaulted ceilings, giant porch, breezy ceiling fans. Delightful to look at, better to live in. Only $26,500. Convenient to everything. Call Steve at All Pro Realty, 555-1100, now.

Exceptionally Nice

2 bedroom, 2 bath doublewide under shady elm in established park. Family room with fireplace, trellised patio, decorator carpets & drapes. All appliances included. Just $29,950. Call Jim at All Pro Realty, 555-1100, today.

Brand-New Beach Cottage

24' wide 2 bedroom, 1 bath mobile home just 3 min. from the sand. Enjoy its skylights, sunny porch, towering palm tree. 2 bedrooms, 2 baths...1 with luxurious garden tub. Only $39,900 & 6 MONTHS FREE SPACE RENT. Call Samuel at All Pro Realty, 555-1100, for a look today.

AD TIP: *Use words that appeal to your readers, not to you or your sellers.*

CHAPTER SEVEN

VACATION PROPERTIES/ SECOND HOMES

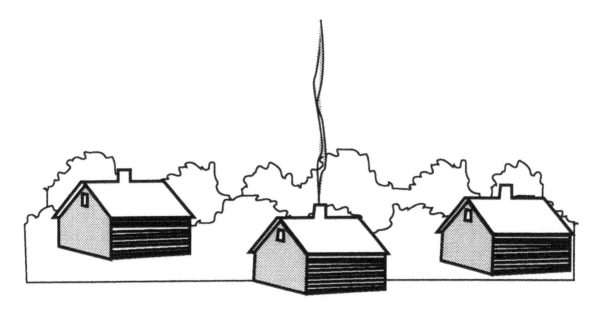

LOCATION

COUNTRY

Weekend
in the Country

in this delightful French-style home. A gem of shining terra-cotta and natural woods tucked away in its own little forest just 2 hours from the city. 3 bedrooms, 2 baths...all peaceful & large with window ledges where song birds perch. One acre of nature's finest. Just $76,000. Call Sue at River Real Estate, 555-1177, today.

Your Own
Wilderness

5 rugged acres of fields, hills & streams with cozy log cabin next to a waterfall. "Great room" with fireplace & kitchen, spacious bedroom, bath & gigantic guest loft make it perfect for weekend "roughing it." Untouched setting... unbelievable price. Just $81,000. Call Kimberly at River Real Estate, 555-1177.

Room to Breathe

in this unusual huge dome home situated on 2 acres in a wildlife sanctuary. Just 2 hours from the city, it's great for weekend "getaways." 3 bedrooms, 2 baths, with dramatic circular fireplace & walls of windows. Enjoy spectacular sunsets, berry-picking, making friends with raccoons & deer...only $76,000. Call Jillian at River Real Estate, 555-1177, and get away today.

Retreat
to the Woods

to this rustic 2 bedroom, 2 bath log cabin, custom-built of hand-hewn beams. With its rocking chair front porch overlooking a rushing trout stream, massive stone fireplace, sprawling country kitchen, it's made for simpler, easier living. 45 min. from town. A bargain at just $66,000. Call Kim at River Real Estate, 555-1177, to see it today.

Hunt & Fish
Heaven

This 5 acre spread has it all...bass-stocked pond, trout stream, wild game, forest. Walk out the door of this sturdy cedar cabin & you're in an outdoors-person's paradise. 2 bedrooms, 2 baths with wood-burning stove & gas heat. An all-year retreat, just $78,000. Call Sam at River Real Estate, 555-1177, to visit heaven today.

WATERFRONT

On Golden Pond

Hard-to-find 1940's lakefront cabin built with quality & care. Massive hand-hewn beams in sprawling living room, wraparound porch with water view, 3 bedrooms, 2 baths, great kitchen. Nestled in 1/4 acre of trees, with own dock. Yours for just $59,500. Call Freddie at River Real Estate, 555-1177, for a look today.

Lakefront
Luxury

If you love comfort, don't miss this stunning 3 bedroom, 2 bath contemporary perched on lakeside bluff. You will adore all its porches & balconies, each with views of waves & sunsets. Spacious glass-lined living room, open to designer kitchen. Black-bottom pool with spa. Make it yours for only $99,000. Call Johnny at River Real Estate, 555-1177, today.

Sunshine &
Sea Breezes

come with this sparkling oceanfront condo, the perfect weekend retreat for busy professionals. Just outside your door, enjoy the luxury of your own private beach, tennis courts, Olympic pool, fitness center. 2 bedrooms, 2 full baths, over 2,000 sq. ft., scads of storage space & balcony brushed by ocean breezes. End your day with a cool drink, watching the sun sink. A real treat for $84,500. Call Paula at River Real Estate, 555-1177, now.

Miles of
White Sand Beach

stretch on either side of this secluded 2 bedroom, 1-1/2 bath Mediterranean-style villa tucked away under waving palms. Very tropical feel, with lush landscaping & many windows. Inside enjoy the tile floors, delightful courtyard, skylights galore. Just $88,000. Call Helen at River Real Estate, 555-1177, to see it today.

AD TIP: Most often, it is best to use active verbs and visual nouns.

Your Summer Place

Wonderful 1950's cottage on the shore. You'll adore its wraparound porch, perfect for wicker & plants. Or try the sparkling sun room completely open to whitewater view. Great kitchen, 3 bedrooms, 2 fully updated baths. A family treasure for just $79,500. Call Ken at River Real Estate, 555-1177, now.

We're at the Lake

That's what you'll tell your friends when you own this stunning cedar delight...3 bedrooms, 2 baths, tailor-made for fun. Every morning, take a spin in the boat, parked at your dock. Sunbathe, water ski, pick berries, watch birds. Each day here is a vacation. End it with a marshmallow roast in your huge rock fireplace. A place for real family togetherness...just $82,000. Call Constantine at River Real Estate, 555-1177, now.

Your Place
at the Shore

You'll love this shoreline cottage's old-fashioned charms almost as much as its modern conveniences. Tastefully updated, it shines with care—from the outdoor refrigerator to the whirlpool tub. Right on the beach, with 3 bedrooms, 2 baths, rooftop patio for sunbathing, outdoor shower. Just $92,000. To see it today, call Kenneth at River Real Estate, 555-1177.

Fisherperson's Paradise

3 bedrooms, 2 baths of custom cedar in a forest glen with running trout stream & game. The whole family will love its waterslide & pool, screened porch, bubbling spa. Sure to be your favorite vacation spot. Just $77,000. Call Betty at River Real Estate, 555-1177, now.

Your Private Beach

comes with this charming 3 bedroom, 2 bath cottage just 2 hours from town. Lovingly cared for over the years, this home sits on a dune, looking out to the water. Enjoy the view from the patio, upstairs balcony, or rooftop sunbathing porch. Only $85,000. Call Joe at River Real Estate, 555-1177, for a look now.

Spectacular Sunsets

will light up your evenings from the balcony of this stunning 12th floor condo. Located right on the beach, this sumptuous home offers an indoor spa, gourmet kitchen, 2 big bedrooms, 2 full baths & over 1,200 sq. ft. of interior living space. Plus tennis, pool, sauna, indoor jogging track. A world of fun for just $65,000. Call Jim at River Real Estate, 555-1177, now.

MOUNTAIN

Weekend Wonderland

It's your refreshing retreat...2 bedroom, 2 bath cedar home high in the mountains with snow in the winter, cool air in the summer, nature's beauty all year-round. Well built for top energy efficiency, it features a sprawling redwood deck, fenced yard, dramatic Swedish fireplace. Only 3 min. to lifts. Just $98,000. Call Linda at River Real Estate, 555-1177, today.

AD TIP: To get a feel for the home, ask the current owners what they like best.

Cozy Ski Cabin

Pretty as a picture, this 2 bedroom, 2 bath log cabin sits in an acre of unspoiled wilderness. Enjoy the rustic life, surrounded by modern comforts. Wood-burning stove, solar heat & hot water, sizzling spa. Minutes to ski runs. Only $52,000. Call Sam at River Real Estate, 555-1177, now.

Bring Your Lift Tickets!

As soon as the snow flies, you'll want to be tucked away in this stunning redwood condo, warming yourself next to a crackling fire. Dramatic mountain vistas through huge window walls, opening to sprawling deck. 2 bedrooms, 2 baths... with fine restaurants, movies, ski runs nearby. Just $75,000. Call Tyrone at River Real Estate, 555-1177, today.

Enjoy Old-Fashioned Christmases

in a real log cabin, high in the mountains, with a fire roaring in the massive rock fireplace, cookies baking in the knotty pine kitchen, snow falling on the acre of land all your own. With 3 bedrooms, 2 baths, & huge 22' x 16' loft, there's plenty of room for friends & family to enjoy the stunning scenery. Your piece of paradise for $105,000. Call Carmelita at River Real Estate, 555-1177, now.

Weekend in the Wilderness

in this rustic 1 bedroom cabin with full bath, nestled on 5 of your own acres. 3 hours from the city, this 1952 redwood charmer offers a wood-burning stove, sun porch, towering pines, peace & quiet. All for only $54,000. Call Kim at River Real Estate, 555-1177, today.

DESERT

Your Desert Oasis

Stunning 2 bedroom, 2 bath contemporary condo overlooking dramatic desert scenery. Enjoy violet, pink & golden sunsets from your huge balcony, or from the deck of the fabulous swimming pool. Golf, shops, museums within walking distance. Only $61,000. Call Stephanie at River Real Estate, 555-1177, for a look.

Tropical Paradise in the Desert

Breathtaking natural beauty indoors & out in this splendid 3 bedroom, 2 bath 1,900 sq. ft. desert palace. Cactus, boulders, trees strewn across 1 acre. Inside your compound, enjoy a lush atrium, lavishly landscaped pool, verandas galore. Cool stucco, with pastel accents. Just $86,000. Call Sam at River Real Estate, 555-1177, now.

Get a Tan

on the 14' balcony of your superbly styled 1 bedroom condo. Airy design with skylights & windows flooding in sunlight. Greenhouse tub, too. Just outside your door, enjoy the pool, golf, fitness club. Only $47,000. Call Josie at River Real Estate, 555-1177, today.

Enjoy Desert Simplicity

in this hard-to-find 2 bedroom, 1-1/2 bath stucco home-delightful 1-level design built around cactus—filled inner courtyard. Of 1950's quality, this home reflects thoughtful touches of the present, like the built-in gas BBQ, secluded spa, breezy ceiling fans. Only $63,000. Call Kim at River Real Estate, 555-1177, for a look today.

Escape to the Desert

to this carefree condo where you have nothing to do but soak up the sun. Golf, tennis, swimming & hiking close by. Stylish pastel decor throughout the 2 bedrooms, 2 baths with plant shelves, gourmet kitchen, huge closets. Just $76,000. Call Sue at River Real Estate, 555-1177, to plan your getaway today.

GOLF

Practice Your Putting

If you love golf, this is it. 2 bedrooms, 2 baths right on championship course. Detached patio home with wide windows, brick courtyard, wonderful feeling of being close to nature. Secluded yet convenient. Just $69,000. Call Vicki at River Real Estate, 555-1177, today.

A Round of Golf a Day

is possible when you live in this sumptuous 3 bedroom, 2 bath condo overlooking the 12th fairway of Via Mesa Country Club. You'll love the convenience & the gracious lifestyle that come with your country club membership. Pool, riding, tennis—take your pick. Every day here is a holiday. Just $108,000. Call Jo at River Real Estate, 555-1177, to see this special home.

Fore!—You

Prestigious golf course home in heart of fast-growing desert community. Almost new, this charming 2 bedroom, 2 bath rambler is hidden by a lushly landscaped lawn. Plantation shutters, whisper soft carpets, cool ceiling fans. You will love its airy & open feeling. Only $79,000. Call Sue at River Real Estate, 555-1177, today.

Golf As a
Way of Life

Enjoy country club living in this elegant 2 bedroom, 2 bath patio home just steps from Singingwood Golf & Country Club. With its low maintenance & easy-care design, you'll have plenty of time for the pool, lounge, tennis courts, restaurant. Lovely peaches & cream decor, with skylights, patio, greenhouse windows. Just $83,000. Call Marcia at River Real Estate, 555-1177, now.

Get Into the
Swing of Things

in this terrific 2 bedroom, 2 bath golf course home right on the 17th green at Lake Shore Golf Course. Airy & open, with lush indoor planters, courtyard fountain & hand-tiled accents. Park your golf cart in the backyard. Only $83,500. To see how good life can be, call Chris at River Real Estate, 555-1177, today.

RECREATION/LEISURE

Four Season
Fun

If you're an active family, come see this impressive 3 bedroom, 2 bath custom cedar on the shore of Lake Shasta. Massive orchard rock fireplace, huge redwood deck, walls of windows with stunning views. In the winter, head for ski slopes just 15 min. away. All-weather fun for only $96,000. Call Ron at River Real Estate, 555-1177, now.

AD TIP: Read your ad aloud and make sure it flows well.

Home Away
From Home

2 hours north of the city, you'll find this charming redwood & stone home tucked away on 10 acres of forest. 3 bedrooms, 2 baths, with a delightful stream gurgling thru its front yard. Enjoy deer, raccoon, squirrels, birds—all in their natural environment. A place to refresh yourself... only $52,000. Call Suzanne at River Real Estate, 555-1177, & start relaxing today.

Resort to This...

Dawn to dark fun in this terrific 2 bedroom, 2 bath beachfront condo. Surf, sail, sunbathe...it's up to you. Your private beach is waiting. Great white-water view from balcony & huge living room. Enjoy the convenience of downstairs restaurant, bar and store, just $57,000. Call Kenneth at River Real Estate, 555-1177, now.

Your Weekend
Hideaway

Exciting 3 bedroom, 2 bath A-frame on 2 acres of trees along unspoiled shoreline. Almost new, this dramatic home features natural woods, exposed beams, massive stone fireplace, huge deck, your own dock. Perfect for relaxing. Just $72,000. Call Walt at River Real Estate, 555-1177, today.

Pack Your Bags
for FUN!

because that's what you get in this delightful 2 bedroom, 2 bath oceanfront cottage in the dunes. Enjoy long walks along the beach...gorgeous sunsets... dips in the surf. It's all yours for only $61,000. Call Sam at River Real Estate, 555-1177, for a look today.

Home for the Holidays

Secluded mountain chalet with dramatic "great room," 2 bedrooms, 2 baths, huge loft for guests. You'll love its warm knotty pine kitchen & island cooking center...almost as much as the hot & bubbly spa off the master bedroom. On an acre of wilderness close to ski slopes, this home is the perfect family retreat. Just $92,000. Call Fredrick at River Real Estate, 555-1177, today.

Make Every Weekend Special

in this unique lakefront home built 3 years ago for a doctor's family. No expense was spared. 3 bedrooms, 3 baths with brick floors, slate fireplace, St. Charles kitchen, 3 car garage. On 2 forested acres with giant stretch of private shoreline. Only $235,500. Call Josephine at River Real Estate, 555-1177, to see it today.

Your Private Playground

Sumptuous 3 bedroom, 2 bath contemporary hidden in the hills, with 3-stall stable. Breathtaking mountain views from living & dining areas. Enjoy the luxury of an indoor Jacuzzi, lava rock fireplace, huge deck. Just $122,000. Call Chris at River Real Estate, 555-1177, for a look today.

Retreat to Your Own Refuge

Old-fashioned 2 bedroom, 2 bath redwood cabin stylishly updated for the '90s. Nestled under towering pines & oaks, this delightful home offers oak floors, stone fireplace, hand-carved china hutch. Plus Jenn-air range, whirlpool tubs, many skylights. Perfection for only $63,500. Call Judy at River Real Estate, 555-1177, today.

Enjoy Your Weekends

in this carefree 2 bedroom, 2 bath town-home located in the heart of a fabulous resort community. Little care required, so you can do all the things you love. Golf, tennis, swim, shop—it's all within easy reach. You'll enjoy this home's free-flowing design with soaring ceilings, & arched windows. Only $81,000. Call Jackson at River Real Estate, 555-1177, today.

CONVENIENCE/NEIGHBORHOOD

Ski Where the Celebrities Do

when you live in this slope-front red-wood condo in prestigious community. 2 bedrooms, 2 baths—large & lush...with thermopane windows, heatilator fireplace, solar hot water. Much character & charm, plus many familiar faces. Just $96,500. Call Sue at River Real Estate, 555-1177, now.

Minutes From Slopes

You'll fall in love with this classic 3 bedroom, 2 bath A-frame tucked away on a hillside just 10 min. from lifts. In summer, enjoy a lake view from your spacious redwood deck. In winter, huddle around the massive rock fireplace. Gourmet kitchen, full-length windows, delightful guest loft. Only $102,500. Call Jimmy at River Real Estate, 555-1177, today.

AD TIP: Show your ads to others—co-workers, family, friends—to make sure your meaning is clear.

Watch World Class Surfing

from sprawling balcony of this classy 2 bedroom, 2 bath condo right on the beach. With sunken living room, skylight in master bedroom, gleaming ceramic kitchen, it's the ultimate in good taste & easy living. Only $81,000. Catch the waves today. Call Kenneth at River Real Estate, 555-1177.

Mingle With the Rich & Famous

in this exquisite 3 bedroom 2 bath home located in a resort where celebrities come to play. Enjoy your own pool, bougain-villea-draped patio, built-in BBQ. This delightful home has white brick walls, curved terrace & lush upgrades. All for just $110,000. For a taste of the good life, call Suzette at River Real Estate, 555-1177, today.

A World of FUN!

lies just outside the door of this sun-splashed 2 bedroom, 2 bath condo, with its own private spa & indoor waterfall. Just steps away you'll find tennis, rac-quetball, golf, swimming, horseback riding. Come home to comfort with a splash. Just $99,500. Call Sam at River Real Estate, 555-1177, and start having fun now.

AD TIP: Tracking the source of your responses will help you plan an effective strategy and save you money.

SIZE

Sprawling Ski Chalet

4,000 sq. ft. of rustic redwood, rock & glass—your 2 bedroom, 2 bath home in the mountains. Enjoy the warmth of the fireplace...warm & mellow country kitchen...lavishly large living area. 2 acres of trees & hills that belong to you. 10 min. to lifts. Only $125,000. Call June at River Real Estate, 555-1177, today.

5,000 Square Feet of Fun!

Your adult playhouse at the beach... with grand living room, huge billiard room, library, screened porch, an acre of sand & trees. There's room for all your grown-up toys & a few friends, too! 4 bedrooms, 3 baths, all for just $110,000. Call Kim at River Real Estate, 555-1177, now.

4 Bedroom Log Cabin

For the family who enjoys crisp, clean air, rugged pines & gentle wildlife—a majestic hand-hewn log cabin built by a rich family as its 2nd home. You'll love the warmth of 3 fireplaces, luxury of 3 full baths (2 with whirlpool tubs), mellowness of solid oak floors. 3 hour drive. Only $156,000. Call Kenneth at River Real Estate, 555-1177, today.

For Big Families

Sprawling 4 bedroom, 3-1/2 bath contemporary on ocean bluffs...just steps from surfing, sunning, swimming. Enjoy relaxing weekends at the beach. You'll love your home's ocean view hot tub, huge windows, gleaming tile. All for just $155,000. Call Fredrick at River Real Estate, 555-1177, now.

Room to Play!

Huge 12 room country home with front & rear porches, fragrant orchard, bubbling stream. Old-fashioned comfort with modern conveniences, just 2 hours from town. Spend weekends getting back to nature...with 10 acres of woods all your own. Room for horse, dogs, pool, lots of kids. Just $76,000. Call Chris at River Real Estate, 555-1177, to see it today.

AD TIP: *Avoid being cute and clever. Credible and convincing will sell more homes.*

PRICE/TERMS

BARGAIN/FORECLOSURE

$50,000
Cabin

Unbelievable value...historic 3 room log home (with utilities) & 10 acres of peaceful woods to roam. Enjoy the rich feel of the past in the massive timbers, huge fireplace, solid cabinets. For a special person. Call Kenneth at River Real Estate, 555-1177, now.

Think You Can't Afford
a 2nd Home?

Then think again—this brand-new lakeside contemporary is a real bargain. Just $55,000 for 3 bedrooms, 2 baths...in long, lean contemporary styling with skylights, porches, sun decks. Right on the beach. Call Benjamin at River Real Estate, 555-1177, today.

Owner
Bailing Out

of delightful 2 bedroom, 2 bath rustic cabin on an acre of woods. Hunt, fish, swim, ski...all just minutes from your door. Inside enjoy the warmth of a stone fireplace, openness of many windows, feel of an old-fashioned front porch. Yours for an unbelievably low $51,000. Call Jack at River Real Estate, 555-1177, today.

2nd Price Cut

Rock-bottom price for wonderful 1 bedroom desert condo just steps from golf, tennis & swimming. Gorgeous pastel decor, garden tub, greenhouse windows, skylights...ridiculously low at $34,500. Better act fast. Call Steven at River Real Estate, 555-1177, now.

Drastically Reduced
Lakefront

Desperate owner needs out of 2nd home ...stunning 3 bedroom, 2 bath Lindal cedar on postcard-perfect shoreline. Watch the geese & ducks from your spacious front deck. At night count the stars thru the huge living room windows. Open & airy with custom upgrades, for only $47,500. See it to believe it. Call Kenneth at River Real Estate, 555-1177, today.

MUST SELL QUICKLY

Owner Wants Out
—Fast

Owner desperate for cash needs family for charming 2 bedroom, 2 bath mountain cabin, just 2 hours from town. Thick log walls, hand-hewn fireplace, knotty pine kitchen...a place you'll treasure for just $29,500. Call Jimmy at River Real Estate, 555-1177, for a real deal today.

Almost in
Foreclosure

If you act fast, you can grab a bargain in this superb 3 bedroom, 2 bath oceanfront condo...close to galleries, shopping, fine restaurants. Whitewater views from huge living area & master suite... slate floors...mirrored walls...top-of-the-line throughout. Below new cost at $76,000. Call Josephine at River Real Estate, 555-1177. Hurry.

Owner Will
Sacrifice

Family-owned 2 bedroom, 1 bath lake-front cottage handed down thru generations. Needs some care but features delightful screened porch, sun room, wonderful view. Only $56,000. Hurry & call Jonathan at River Real Estate, 555-1177.

AD TIP: Write your ads one day then put them down and read them the next.

Needs to
Move Fast

Owner will cut price for quick deal on 2 bedroom, 2 bath mountain cabin, just 20 min. from lifts. Enjoy hand-hewn log construction...artist-crafted fireplace... giant window-filled loft. A home of character for only $41,000. Call Linda at River Real Estate, 555-1177, if you're ready to act.

Condo Owner
Short on Time & Cash

willing to sacrifice his private golf course retreat...spacious & sunny 3 bedroom, 2 bath condo in sought-after location. You will love the smooth contemporary decor, with its airy windows, exposed beams, white walls. Whisper-soft carpets, too. Best of all, watch the sunset from your entertainment-sized balcony. All for only $62,500. For a great deal, call Sue at River Real Estate, 555-1177, now.

OWNER FINANCING/ASSUMABLE

No Down/
Take Over

weekend desert hideaway. 1 bedroom with huge bath, custom decorated in soft pastels with lush plant-filled balcony. Fully furnished, with pool, Jacuzzi, tennis only steps away. Yours for just $42,500. Call Paula at River Real Estate, 555-1177, today.

Assume FHA

on this handsome 2 bedroom, 2 bath mountain retreat just 1 hour outside town. You'll love the clean fresh air... stunning natural beauty...clear skies. Almost new with galley kitchen, huge "great room," gigantic front porch, 2 acres. A must-see at $33,000. Call Jim at River Real Estate, 555-1177, now.

Court Says
Sell

For bargain basement price, you can own this lovely 3 bedroom 2 bath desert retreat located in fast-growing community. Stucco walls, tile floors, veranda, gorgeous cactus. Steps to fine restaurants, art galleries, shopping. Only $29,500. Hurry & call Joe at River Real Estate, 555-1177.

AD TIP: Make sure your headline calls attention to your ad.

Owner
Will Finance

at below market on this superb 2 bedroom, 2 bath lakefront cabin in the mountains. Enjoy your own dock, built-in beds, massive fireplace, large screened porch. Comfort in the woods for just $31,000. Call Ken at River Real Estate, 555-1177, now.

Unbelievable
Terms

Owner will carry loan on this delightful 3 bedroom, 2 bath gabled home with its own swimming pond. Located on 3 acres just 2 hrs. from town, this old-fashioned charmer is a true escape. Just $33,000. Call Linc at River Real Estate, 555-1177, now.

INVESTMENT VALUE/TRADE

Trade Your
Cadillac for...

down payment on fabulous 2 bedroom, 2 bath condo in prestige resort community. Why travel all over the country when sun, golf, swimming & tennis are right outside your door? Enjoy rich woods, marble, skylights...all for only $98,000. Call Ken at River Real Estate, 555-1177, now.

Discover the Secret...

of Apple Valley, high in the mountains. You'll love this stunning 3 bedroom, 2 bath cedar home hugging the ridgeline. Enjoy nature's beauty through Pella windows, redwood decks, your hot & bubbly spa. Garage & workshop, too. Just $102,000. Call Elizabeth Ann at River Real Estate, 555-1177, to find out about it today.

Appreciate Your Advantage

Desperate owner needs quick action on hand-built 2 bedroom, 2 bath mountain cabin. Enjoy a view of forest that belongs to you. 2 acres, bubbling mountain creek, meadow, 100-year-old trees. All utilities in. Just $21,000. Call Suzy at River Real Estate, 555-7870, fast.

A Sound Investment

If you'd like to wake up on weekends to the gentle lapping of waves...the soft cries of sea gulls...the faint kiss of an ocean breeze...come see this rambling 2 bedroom, 2 bath beach cottage. Built with care in 1952, it's been lovingly updated without disturbing any old-fashioned charm. A great investment for only $88,000. Call Ken at River Real Estate, 555-1177, today.

Lowest-Priced Condo in Complex

Turn your playtime into quality time in this stunning 1 bedroom condo, located in an upscale community. Enjoy tennis, swimming, sailing, indoor jogging track ...as well as 1,000 sq. ft. of comfort that feels much larger. Huge windows, lava rock fireplace, designer kitchen. Just $48,000. Call Tina at River Real Estate, 555-1177, now.

STYLE

ARCHITECTURE & ATMOSPHERE

Original Log Cabin

on 3 acres of national forest. Built in 1945 of rough-hewn logs, this sprawling 2 bedroom, 2 bath rustic gleams with rich woods, sparkling windows, mellow cabinets. Needs updating, but at $39,000 ...what a deal! Call Jeanette at River Real Estate, 555-1177, now.

Pioneer Ranch

Carve your own homestead out of 15 acres of wilderness just 2 hours from town. Run-down 3 bedroom, 2 bath ranch house needs work. But with it comes rushing creek, hundreds of trees, sky full of stars at night. Sound worth $29,500 to you? Call Janie at River Real Estate, 555-1177, now.

Lindal Cedar Home

If you want only the best, come see this sumptuous 4 bedroom, 3 bath lakefront home, radiant with natural woods & charm. Huge windows make it feel airy & bright, while you'll love the luxury of its enormous decks. Loft, soaring ceilings, skylights, plus your own dock...for $156,000. Call Jim at River Real Estate, 555-1177, today.

Contemporary Dream

Hard-to-find modern stunner in its own woods. Sheets of glass overlook dramatic lap pool. Extensively landscaped, with waterfalls & garden ponds. 3 bedrooms, 2 baths, with loft balcony above soaring living room. A dream of a price at only $175,000. Call Ned at River Real Estate, 555-1177, now.

Your Connecticut Estate

You'll love this 12 room riverfront estate secluded on 3 acres of greenery. Huge New England clapboard, with shingles, porches, patios, shutters. Inside enjoy lots of sunshine, polished woods, huge rooms. Very tasteful & comfortable. Yours for just $550,000. Call Chris at River Real Estate, 555-1177, today.

> *AD TIP: Don't advertise all of your listings. Put in one or two in each price range and location to attract prospects.*

SPECIAL FEATURES

FIREPLACE

A Fireplace
in Every Room

in this handsome New England Salt Box. Carefully restored to its original 1890 beauty, this gentle charmer features all the modern conveniences. 3 bedrooms with 2 baths & carriage house, too. On an acre of wildflowers 2 hours outside the city for $145,000. Call Jolene at River Real Estate, 555-1177, now.

Unique 1800's Fireplace

dresses up this elegant almost new colonial bordering the river. Superb styling, with high ceilinged rooms, bay windows, shining hardwood floors. 4 bedrooms, 2 baths...all large & sunny. Just $156,000. Call Sara at River Real Estate, 555-1177, today.

ENERGY EFFICIENT

Forget Your Long Underwear

No matter how cold it is outside, you'll stay warm & cozy in this charming 2 bedroom, 2 bath ski chalet. Specially designed to hold in heat, it features triple pane windows, extra thick insulation, highly efficient gas furnace, wood-burning stove. A-frame design on private lot. Just $103,500. Call Jimmy at River Real Estate, 555-1177, now.

Comfort
in the Snow

You won't believe how warm you'll be in this mountainside contemporary. Special care in construction keeps energy costs low. 2 bedrooms, spacious loft & 2 baths. Stunning views. Just $86,000. Call Ken at River Real Estate, 555-1177, to see a real money-saver today.

Save Energy
$$$$

State of the art energy efficiency comes with this futuristic dome home on a lakeshore 3 hours from the city. Specially zoned heat, thermal-crafting & top-of-the-line materials make heating & cooling a breeze. You'll love its sleek look, huge master bedroom, 2 large rooms for the kids & 3 baths. Circular "great room," too. Just $145,000. Call William at River Real Estate, 555-1177, now.

ROOM FOR ENTERTAINING

Enjoy Weekend
Parties

in your picturesque mountain cabin just 2 hours from town. With its huge bedroom, giant loft & spacious living area, you can invite a crowd. Spend afternoons on the ski slopes, evenings in your Jacuzzi for only $76,000. To see it today, call Ken at River Real Estate, 555-1177.

Invite
Your Friends

to this super oceanfront condo just steps from terrific surfing. 2 bedrooms, 2 baths with sunken living room accented by dramatic fireplace, entertainment sized balcony, Olympic pool & spa. For $47,000, you can be the most popular host in town. Call Christine at River Real Estate, 555-1177, now.

Bring Along
a Friend

because they'll all want to visit you in this secluded wilderness retreat just 2 hours from the city. Enjoy a handsome 3 bedroom, 2 bath log cabin along a rushing river. 3 acres of trees & woods that belong to you. Your own sizzling spa & satellite dish. Tons of fun for only $134,500. Call Kim at River Real Estate, 555-1177, for a look today.

Spend Entertaining
Weekends

in your posh 2 bedroom, 2 bath condo in prestigious resort community just 3 hours from town. Far enough away to escape, close enough for convenience, this decorator-perfect condo offers golf, tennis, swimming, sunbathing in an atmosphere of refinement & superb taste. At only $65,000, see for yourself. Call Jillian at River Real Estate, 555-1177, now.

Fun &
Friends

come with this charming 3 bedroom, 2 bath cottage at the lake. You'll love its sun-sprinkled porch, knotty pine paneling, warm country kitchen. Just steps away from 100-year-old oaks & your private dock. Only $66,000. Call Felicia at River Real Estate, 555-1177, today.

SPAS/POOLS

Slip Into Something
More Comfortable

Like the hot & bubbly spa in your private walled garden of this secluded 1 bedroom mountain cabin. High in the hills, it's just minutes from skiing. Yet it feels alone, untouched. Rustic logs, paned windows, oak floors & wood-burning fireplace. Your romantic retreat for just $43,500. Call Christopher at River Real Estate, 555-1177, now.

Take the
Plunge

into the crystal clear pool of this stunning 3 bedroom, 2 bath desert home. Thick stucco construction, cool tile floors & wide windows—perfect for those who enjoy active lifestyles. Golf, tennis, riding...live life to the limit. Just $78,000. Call Anna Marie at River Real Estate, 555-1177, today.

Like to
Skinny Dip?

Then you'll love the very private pool that comes with this 3 bedroom, 2 bath oceanside rambler. No one can look in while you look out to superb water view. Entertainment-sized living room, gourmet kitchen, huge patio. Yours for $199,000. Call Ken at River Real Estate, 555-1177, now.

AD TIP: Long ads are fine, but make sure they are still tightly written. Remember, in classified ads you are paying by the word.

CONDITION

MAINTENANCE-FREE

No-Worry Weekends

are yours in this lakefront condo—a dream of efficiency, space & comfort. 2 bedrooms, 2 baths with a huge patio. With easy-care & luxury features like gas log fireplace, whirlpool tub, walls of windows. Just $76,000. Call Clarence at River Real Estate, 555-1177, today.

The 24-Hour Vacation

Come home from the ski slopes to a roaring fire in your circular hearth. Bunk your guests in the large 20' x 18' loft. You'll love this 2 bedroom, 2 bath easy upkeep cedar home. Just $87,000. Call Vi at River Real Estate, 555-1177, now.

Really Get Away

to this secluded wilderness easy-care ranch with its rustic 3 bedroom, 2 bath home on 30 gorgeous acres. For just $34,500, enjoy your own mountain creek, waterfalls, ancient trees. Call Don at River Real Estate, 555-1177, today.

Don't Lift a Finger

This delightful 2 bedroom, 2 bath golf course condo is spotless. Gleaming ceramic kitchen & baths, slate fireplace, walls of sparkling windows—all you need is your furniture. And your golf clubs. Only $43,000. Call Jim at River Real Estate, 555-1177, now.

Take It Easy

in this superior lakeside home under towering pines. You'll love its country feel. Huge picture window with lake view, warm & toasty fireplace, 3 large bedrooms, 2 baths. Easy care home with an easy price of only $78,000. Call Kenneth at River Real Estate, 555-1177, now.

WELL CARED FOR

World Class Condo

Not a speck of dust in this gleaming 2 bedroom, 2 bath condo at elite tennis club. Plush carpeting and ceramic tile. Balcony overlooks sapphire pool. All for just $48,000. Call Mary Beth at River Real Estate, 555-1177.

Top-of-the-Line Lakefront

Designed to turn heads, this dramatic 2 bedroom, 2 bath contemporary makes the most of its space & view. A tri-level, with balconies, lofts & giant windows, it feels open & airy. Breathtaking lake vistas. All for just $98,000. Call Sue at River Real Estate, 555-1177. Call now.

Shines With TLC

If you're looking for a time-mellowed beach home that gleams with loving care, this is it. 2 bedrooms, 2 baths...all carefully updated. A home for gentle people. Just $66,000. Call Sam at River Real Estate, 555-1177, now.

EQUITY TIME-SHARES

Divorce
Forces Sale

of dramatic contemporary condo. This equity time-share is perched on a mountain overlooking a lake. Close to ski slopes. Sleeps 4. Enjoy one week at peak season for bargain price of just $11,500. Call Tim at River Real Estate, 555-1177, today.

Bask in the Sun
in February

Beachfront 2 bedroom, 2 bath condo in popular Puerta Vallarta. Enjoy one week a year at just $6,500. Call Ken at River Real Estate, 555-1177, to find out about this equity time-share now.

Lawrence Welk
Resort

Gorgeous equity time-share villa at 5-star resort sleeps 6. 2 golf courses nearby, overlooks 14th green. With no down payment, owner will finance at full price of $9,750. Call Marion at River Real Estate, 555-1177, now.

Enjoy
Desert Breezes

One week in Palm Desert from Oct. to January plus bonus time in this equity time-share. 2 bedrooms, 2 baths, full kitchen, 2 large pools, free golf. Sacrifice at $8,800. Call Josie at River Real Estate, 555-1177, today.

Ski
Chalet

Enjoy one week at high season. Attractive A-frame equity time-share with fireplace & hot tub. 3 bedrooms, 2 baths. Only $12,800. Call Kimberly at River Real Estate, 555-1177, now.

> *AD TIP: Put personality into your ads. Then your buyers will know right up front what kind of agent they will be working with.*

CHAPTER EIGHT

INVESTMENT PROPERTIES

LOCATION

5 Acres in
Growth Path

Enjoy living in a comfortable old farm-house—big 4 bedroom, 3 bath rambler with all the latest conveniences—while waiting for your land to appreciate. Flat & studded with towering trees, it offers tremendous potential for subdivision. Your golden opportunity for $189,000. Call Jess at River Real Estate, 555-1177, today.

Duplex on
Golf Course

If you've been waiting for a golf course bargain, consider this delightful custom duplex. Overlooking the 12th fairway at Shamrock Hill, its gentle Cape Cod charm is sure to grab your heart. Thick plaster walls for privacy, totally secluded patios, 2 huge garages. Live in one side while renting the other out. A great deal for only $187,000. Call Joe at River Real Estate, 555-1177, to see it.

Sugar Loaf
Cabin

2 bedroom, 2 bath log home on 3 scenic acres near Goldmine Ski area. Impressive rock fireplace, wide front porch, natural landscaping. Rents for $60/day in winter. Just $52,000. Call Kimmie at River Real Estate, 555-1177, to see it today.

Sought-After
Canyon Cabin

Charming 2 bedroom, 2 bath knotty pine cabin in unspoiled canyon. Towering pines, babbling brook, huge lot. Easy to find tenants, especially with 2 car garage. Only $80,000. Call James at River Real Estate, 555-1177, now.

Ocean View Home
& Guest House

Finally, a way to afford that ocean view home you've been waiting for. This stunning 1950's contemporary with 3 bedrooms, 2 baths is set on 1/2 acre lot, with private guesthouse OK for rental. Let your tenant help pay your mortgage. Just $198,500. Call Lisa at River Real Estate, 555-1177, fast.

CONVENIENCE/NEIGHBORHOOD

2 Fixers
in University Neighborhood

Bring your toolbox & make money on these 2 bedroom, 2 bath older homes, nestled on big lot under giant elms. Great rental history, with low rents. Fix them up & you've got a real money-maker. Charming enough for you to live in, too. Only $74,000. Call Ken at River Real Estate, 555-1177, for a look.

Center City Condo

Perfect rental unit for busy people. 1 bedroom with soaring ceilings, toasty warm fireplace, dramatic city-light view. Easy maintenance, health club, pool. Your opportunity for $65,000. Call Christopher at River Real Estate, 555-1177, today.

Great Rental Neighborhood

Wonderful 3 bedroom, 2 bath family home in established neighborhood near Boeing. Huge brick patio, built-in BBQ, sizzling master spa. Good rental record... positive cash flow. Perfect starter investment for $125,000. Call Karla at River Real Estate, 555-1177, to see it now.

AD TIP: Use the vocabulary of your prospects.

Close to University

Save on dorm fees by investing in this smart townhome within walking distance of Alpha University. With 3 bedrooms, 2 baths, it's tailor-made for roommates. Make money while keeping your student happy. Only $72,000. Call Jacquelyn at River Real Estate, 555-1177, today.

Next to Air Force Base

Perfect for your family or as a rental, this 3 bedroom, 2 bath brick beauty is in a delightful neighborhood. Set far back on 1/2 acre lot, it offers screened porch, giant basement/workshop, convenient 3 car garage. In an area of rapidly appreciating homes. It can be yours for only $81,000. Call Tom at River Real Estate, 555-1177, to take a look.

SIZE

Live in One, Rent the Other

You'll feel good about this charming 3 bedroom, 2 bath vintage Victorian tucked away on a winding street. Gleaming hardwood floors, sunny porches, warm & soothing pastels. Top-of-the-line throughout. You'll also appreciate its delightful 1 bedroom cottage—a great rental that'll help pay your mortgage. Priced at $145,000. See how affordable it is. Call Fredrick at River Real Estate, 555-1177, now.

Two Houses, One Lot

Enjoy the security of steady rental income while living in either of these stunning 2 bedroom, 2 bath Spanish stucco homes. Hidden behind huge gates, both feature polished oak floors, exposed beams, hand-painted tile porches. Sure to please the eye & the pocketbook. All for just $166,000. Call Ken at River Real Estate, 555-1177, today.

Home & Rental

In an established family neighborhood you'll find this vintage Cape Cod, set on a sprawling 1/2 acre. Enjoy the luxury of whisper-soft carpeting, 2 warm brick fireplaces, 3 giant bedrooms, 2 full baths. Over the 3 car garage, there's a charming 1 bedroom rental with huge bay windows. All yours for $154,000. Call Steve at River Real Estate, 555-1177, now.

Cozy Apartment

comes with this handsome 2 bedroom, 2 bath contemporary beauty hidden in the hills just outside town. You'll love its soaring windows, greenhouse tub, sizzling spa—as well as the monthly rent checks from the cozy & cute 2 bedroom apartment over the garage. A smart move for $134,000. Call Julie at River Real Estate, 555-1177, today.

Two on Lot

Elegant 2 & 3 bedroom homes on professionally landscaped 1/4 acre. Share a stunning free-form pool & superb gardens, while you each enjoy the luxury of a Mediterranean-styled villa. Great investment for only $185,000. See for yourself. Call Suzanne at River Real Estate, 555-1177, now.

Home & Duplex

You'll love the luxurious owner's home —3 bedrooms, 2 baths of stately white brick, resting at the end of a circular drive. All the upgrades you can imagine, plus a delightful rear duplex. Both apartments with 2 bedrooms & huge patios. Just $196,000. Call Jim at River Real Estate, 555-1177, today.

AD TIP: Keep track of how your ads are doing by asking prospects where they saw the ad.

Home & Income & 3 Car Garage

Your own piece of paradise—splendid 3 bedroom, 3 bath contemporary with inner atrium, lush landscaping, skylights galore. Very affordable because over your garage, there's a secluded 1 bedroom apartment with a great view. You can't afford to pass this one up at only $189,000. Call Fred at River Real Estate, 555-1177, today.

Live Upstairs, Rent Down

You'll adore this handsome 2 bedroom, 2 bath brownstone in the heart of the city. Glowing mahogany, full French windows, whimsical balconies...it radiates quality & charm. With it comes a superb 2 bedroom, 1-1/2 bath rental featuring exposed brick walls, natural beams, greenhouse windows. Live in style, for less than you ever imagined. Just $192,000. Call Hal at River Real Estate, 555-1177.

Your Private Compound

Hard-to-find estate grounds, with 3 fine homes—perfect for close-knit family. Enjoy the rich look of French provincial styling in each 3 bedroom, 2 bath delight. Pool, 4 car garage, room for tennis courts. Just $275,000. Call James at River Real Estate, 555-1177, to see this one of a kind property today.

Five Cottages & Garden

5 uniquely styled stucco cottages...each with 2 bedrooms, 2 baths. Nestled on an acre of lushly landscaped grounds, with gazebo, brick patios, citrus trees, abundant flowers. Only $325,000. To see how easy it is to own, call William at River Real Estate, 555-1177, now.

Triple Treat

Superb contemporary triplex on waterfront with stunning 3 bedroom, 2 bath owner's unit. Enjoy huge walls of glass overlooking dock, dramatic Swedish fireplace, designer kitchen...while earning extra income on two, 2 bedroom, 2 bath rentals. Only $225,000. Call Kim at River Real Estate, 555-1177, today.

Share a Lot

2 delightful 3 bedroom, 2 bath Spanish villas on 1/2 acre of trees, flowers, shrubs. You'll love the elegant neighborhood, wrought iron gates, picture-perfect look. Room for pool, tennis, RV. Just $186,000. Call Fredrick at River Real Estate, 555-1177, today & bring a friend!

Two Homes on One Acre

Great way to own the home of your dreams...2 homes for the price of 1! Owner's home is Cape Cod clapboard, hidden beneath towering trees. 3 bedrooms, 2 baths, with warm & toasty fireplace, brick patio, 2 car garage. Secluded 1 bedroom rental offers redwood deck & French doors. Offered at only $156,000. Call Mac at River Real Estate, 555-1177, to view it now.

Home & Guesthouse

Superbly decorated 4 bedroom, 2 bath Craftsman with fine wood paneling in the library, fireplace-warmed family room, comfortable & updated country kitchen. Best of all, the 2 bedroom guesthouse makes it very affordable. Just $166,000. To give your family the home of their dreams, call Rick at River Real Estate, 555-1177, today.

Perfect
Bed & Breakfast

Picture this charming 6 bedroom, 4 bath Victorian with high ceilings, French windows, pastel gingerbread trim. See it as a first class inn, filled with antiques. Very spacious, close to everything. Great opportunity for only $153,500. Call Rich at River Real Estate, 555-1177, today.

Ideal As
Country Inn

Rambling 7 bedroom, 4 bath Early American farmhouse cradled on 1/2 acre of trees & flowers. Quiet & secluded, only 20 min. from town. 4 car garage with 2 bedroom apartment. Just $144,000. Call Gregory at River Real Estate, 555-1177, now.

Mansion Approved
for Conversion

Historic family home built by oil baron. Rich details, gleaming hardwoods, circled by trees. Scheduled for conversion into 6 apartments...each uniquely styled & spacious. At $175,000, it's a great opportunity. Call Josie at River Real Estate, 555-1177, fast.

Two
3 Bedroom Homes

with 2 baths each, on rambling 2 acre lot high in the mountains. California styling with huge windows, charming redwood decks, tile floors. In great family neighborhood with excellent schools. Only $186,000 for both. Call Kenny at River Real Estate, 555-1177, now.

4 Bedroom Home
With Rental

Plenty of room for big family in this sprawling ranch on a cul-de-sac in upscale neighborhood. Enjoy country-fresh kitchen, party-size family room, 3 full baths. Plus money-making 2 bedroom, 1 bath guesthouse hidden by trees. Only $156,000. Give your family a treat. Call Suzanne at River Real Estate, 555-1177, today.

AD TIP: Use headlines that create self-interest and avoid ones that merely provoke curiosity.

PRICE/TERMS

FIXER-UPPER

2 Unit Fixer

FHA repo...1 bedroom front, 2 bedroom, 2 bath rear home. 2 car garage. Possible 7x gross after repairs. Asking $90,000. Call Sam at River Real Estate, 555-1177, now.

Fix It Up

Vintage Victorian with 5 bedrooms, 4 baths. Ideal for large family or subdivide into apartments. Marvelous hardwood floors, wood windows, rocking chair front porch. Only $124,500. Call Ken at River Real Estate, 555-1177, for a super bargain today.

Rental Fixer

Solid 3 bedroom, 2 bath brick desperately needing paint & repairs. But you are starting with 1/2 acre of land, oak floors, copper plumbing. Great rental area. Just $66,000. Call Jim at River Real Estate, 555-1177, to see it today.

Hire a Handyperson

& turn this charming 2 bedroom, 2 bath stucco cottage into a real money-maker! On huge terraced lot in elite area, it offers handsome oak fireplace, wrought iron fencing, many windows. Perfect rental. Just $65,000. Call Thomas at River Real Estate, 555-1177, now.

Neglected Home With Rental

Built with 1940's quality, this 3 bedroom, 2 bath traditional is sadly in need of care. Peeling wallpaper, leaky sinks, cracked windows. Lots to do, but great potential. Especially with its tucked away 1 bedroom rental unit. Only $122,000. Call Joe at River Real Estate, 555-1177, to take a look.

BARGAIN

Priced to Sell

Need quick action on 2 bedroom, 2 bath starter home in good rental neighborhood. Delightful white frame with screened porch, huge kitchen & wood-accented living room. Only $54,000. Call Christy at River Real Estate, 555-1177, today.

Owner Leaving State...

needs out of prestigious golf course condo overlooking 8th fairway of Via Mesa Country Club. Second home or rental. 2 bedrooms, 2 baths with Olympic pool, indoor jogging track, sauna. A steal for only $172,000. Call Jimmy at River Real Estate, 555-1177, now.

AD TIP: *Use the vocabulary of your prospects.*

2-Family Home
for the Price of One

If you & a friend are looking for homes, consider this 1/2 acre with 2 & 3 bedroom redwood & stone cottages. Enjoy custom quality & comfort at below tract-home prices. Just $104,000 for both. Call Ken at River Real Estate, 555-1177, for a look today.

Investor
Liquidating

so this 3 bedroom, 2 bath beachfront home is a bargain, especially with its charming 2 bedroom rental. Comfortable Cape Cod styling in both...with fireplaces, country kitchens, great location. Only $165,000. Hurry & call Richard at River Real Estate, 555-1177, now.

$10,000
Below Appraisal

for this impressive contemporary duplex located downtown. 2 bedrooms, 2 baths each, with fireplace, redwood decks, designer kitchens. Very private. Offered at $154,000. Call Kim at River Real Estate, 555-1177, for a real bargain today.

MUST SELL QUICKLY

Behind Payments
Must Sell Now

Desperate owner needs out of charming 2 bedroom, 2 bath traditional beauty with two 1 bedroom guest houses. Hardwood floors, towering trees, close to schools & shopping...great opportunity for only $145,000. Call Noel at River Real Estate, 555-1177, fast.

Distress Sale!

Escrow fell thru...need fast action on 2 bedroom, 2 bath oceanfront condo with own boat slip. Whitewater view, huge balcony, cozy fireplace...high rent potential. Grab it for $98,000. Call Kenneth at River Real Estate, 555-1177, today.

Must Close
by Year's End

Investor must sell 2 bedroom, 2 bath mountain cabin just 5 min. from town. Solid redwood, with spacious sun porch, updated bath, terrific view. Live in or rent out. Either way, it's a money-maker. Only $77,000. Call Jim at River Real Estate, 555-1177, now.

Need Quick
Takeover

on vintage Victorian with charming owner's unit & 2 downstairs rentals. Enjoy high ceilings, gleaming hardwoods, 3 sunny & cheerful bedrooms, 2 baths plus steady income. And at $133,000, it's a real deal. Call Sally at River Real Estate, 555-1177, today.

Price Slashed
to Move Fast

Owner needs out of 2 bedroom, 2 bath ski cabin near White Horse slopes. Hand-hewn logs, massive rock fireplace, huge loft, warm knotty pine kitchen. Can you believe only $42,000? Be the first to call Dick at River Real Estate, 555-1177.

AD TIP: Get inspiration from others— including the current homeowner.

FORECLOSURE

Government Owned
Repo

Just a small down payment gives you a delightful 2 bedroom, 2 bath starter home perfect for small family or rental. Great tree-shaded neighborhood with good schools & many parks. Full price only $43,000. Call Jim at River Real Estate, 555-1177, to find out more.

Foreclosed
4-Unit Fixer

Great deal on terrific home close to beach. Huge owner's unit with 4 bedrooms, 2 baths, rooftop sun porch. Three 1 bedroom rentals in back. Needs work, but livable. Only $122,000. Call Samuel at River Real Estate, 555-1177. This one will go fast.

Home & Guesthouse
Near Foreclosure

Comfortable 3 bedroom, 2 bath white traditional on choice corner lot with delightful 1 bedroom guesthouse. Worth thousands more than $122,000. Call Fred at River Real Estate, 555-1177, to see it today.

Bank
Wants Out

Snappy 1 bedroom city condo great as rental or for the busy professional. Loft den overlooks huge living room dominated by impressive circular fireplace. Step-saving ceramic kitchen, whirlpool bath...only $53,500. Call Linda at River Real Estate, 555-1177, now.

Forced to
Foreclose

on charming 3 bedroom, 3 bath Cape Cod in family neighborhood with cozy studio guesthouse. Only $94,500 & it's yours. Call Fredrick at River Real Estate, 555-1177, today.

OWNER/SPECIAL FINANCING

Investors:
No $$$ Down

on this sparkling 1 bedroom condo close to beach. Features include a 16' balcony, wood-burning fireplace, microwave, washer and dryer. Just $43,500. Call Sue at River Real Estate, 555-1177, today.

Low Down,
Positive Cash Flow

You'll love this delightful 3-unit building. Each unit has 2 bedrooms, 2 baths, rosy brick fireplace, old-fashioned charm. Located in quiet neighborhood, close to university, hospital, parks. Full price only $110,000. Call Ron at River Real Estate, 555-1177, and start making money now.

Duplex—
Low Down

will make you owner of this spick & span 3 bedroom, 2 bath California Craftsman with tidy duplex tucked in behind. Enjoy lavishly large living room with mahogany mantel, window-lined dining, elegant country kitchen. All this plus rental income for just $145,000. Hurry & call Sal at River Real Estate, 555-1177, today.

Bayfront Duplex at
Below Market Financing

Enjoy low interest owner financing on this classy duplex facing the bay. 3 bedrooms, 2 baths each, with marble fireplace, 2 full baths, gourmet kitchen. Stunning views from front porches. Priced at only $186,500. Call Elizabeth at River Real Estate, 555-1177, fast.

Owner Will
Carry Note

on this charming courtyard of storybook cottages with winding sidewalks, rolled roofs, fragrant flowers. Six homes, 2 bedrooms, 2 baths each, with patios. Only $199,500. Call Kenneth at River Real Estate, 555-1177, today.

LOW TAXES

Cut
Your Taxes

Enjoy tax benefits as well as steady income from this money-making duplex in popular neighborhood. 3 bedrooms, 2 baths each, with private redwood decks, towering trees, separate garages. Your own gold mine for just $144,500. Call Elizabeth at River Real Estate, 555-1177, today.

Make More
$$$

by reducing your taxes when you own this income-producing home & guesthouse. Located in a prestigious area, this 4 bedroom, 3 bath colonial offers a library, wood-paneled family room, majestic living room. Knotty pine guesthouse features 2 bedrooms, brick patio. Rent one or both...offered at $176,000. Call Sue at River Real Estate, 555-1177, now.

Need a Tax Break?

Consider this deluxe duplex hidden in the hills. Custom-built. Features a handsome 2 bedroom, 2 bath upper unit with mellow pine kitchen, leafy view living room, gorgeous cactus garden. Downstairs is a charming single—all knotty pine with custom cabinets. Make it yours for just $145,000. Call June at River Real Estate, 555-1177, today.

INVESTMENT VALUE

Two for the
Price of One

Save big when you live in this impressive white columned colonial located in prestigious neighborhood. 4 bedrooms, 3 baths with grand staircase, oak floors, wonderful screened porch. With it comes airy & bright 2 bedroom guesthouse perfect for rental. Just $176,000. Call Kimberly at River Real Estate, 555-1177, now.

A
Buy-to-Rent

First time investors—see this delightful 3 bedroom, 2 bath stucco in established family neighborhood. Easy-care construction with gorgeous naturally landscaped yard. Packed with quality, it commands high rent. Just $134,500. Call Jan at River Real Estate, 555-1177, today.

Investor's
Delight

Spick & span 2 bedroom, 2 bath condo at elite tennis resort. Enjoy it yourself or rent it out. Fireplace, greenhouse windows, huge balcony. 1 hour from city. Just $33,000. Call Jimmy at River Real Estate, 555-1177, now.

Investor's Dream

You'll build up equity fast in this breezy 3-unit townhome...a marvelous blend of contemporary styling & old-fashioned charm. Almost new, it features two 2 bedroom, 2 bath units & 1 single on almost an acre. Tall trees, wrought iron gates, French windows...just $178,000. Call Ann at River Real Estate, 555-1177, for a look.

Second Chance!

Great-looking condo right on sand just fell out of escrow. Need fast action. 1 bedroom with 14' balcony overlooking water, slate fireplace, gleaming ceramic kitchen. Just $77,000. Hurry & call Dick at River Real Estate, 555-1177, to see it today.

4 Bedroom —$154,500

You'll love how low your monthly payments will be in this sprawling 4 bedroom, 3 bath California Craftsman. Imagine 2,500 sq. ft. with sunny country kitchen, yard for football, rosy red brick fireplace...for less than rent. You can do it because this charmer comes with two 2 bedroom, 2 bath rental units. Call Maryann at River Real Estate, 555-1177, now.

EZ Income

is yours with this neat & tidy duplex under tall trees in a quiet neighborhood. Spanish styling with 2 bedrooms, 2 baths each, brick patios, arched windows. Just $122,500. Call Annalisa at River Real Estate, 555-1177, today.

Beginning Investors

Get started with this little or nothing-down condo, close to freeways, schools, shops. 1 bedroom with sunny loft overlooking pool. Great bachelor pad. Just $42,000. Owner will finance below market. Call Phillip at River Real Estate, 555-1177, today.

Let Your Tenants Pay Your Mortgage

when you live in this stunning 4 bedroom, 2 bath traditional brick in prestigious area. You'll love its arched windows, hand-built patio, skylight-filled kitchen...almost as much as you'll love the monthly checks from your 2 rental units. All for $145,000. Call Joe at River Real Estate, 555-1177, fast.

First Time Investors

Perfect starter home...2 bedroom, 2 bath Spanish villa in good area, with massive oak beams, carved wood fireplace, stunning terra-cotta tile floors. Easy to care for, great rental. Just $66,000. Call Fred at River Real Estate, 555-1177, today.

Build for Your Future

by investing in this sought-after neighborhood. New-on-market, classic 2 bedroom, 2 bath log cabin on 1/2 acre lot. Surrounded by ancient trees next to babbling brook, it offers a rocking chair front porch, stained glass windows, charming wood-burning stove. Great rental. Just $77,000. Call Kathleen at River Real Estate, 555-1177, for a look at this investment today.

Pocket High Rents

from this flashy 2 bedroom, 2 bath duplex on riverfront. Prestigious address, plus bleached floors, sky-high windows, solid oak cabinets. For quality tenants. Only $176,000. Call Gerald at River Real Estate, 555-1177, now.

Small Investment, Big Rewards

Terrific new resort condo in exclusive area. Tennis, golf, swimming are just steps outside the door of this 2 bedroom, 2 bath stunner. Skylights, exposed beams, whirlpool tub...make it your vacation paradise or enjoy rental income. At $65,000, this won't last. Call Frederico at River Real Estate, 555-1177, today.

Want Financial Security?

Then invest in this handsome triplex with ideal 3 bedroom, 2 bath owner's unit. You'll love its clean, smooth lines, accented by gleaming hardwoods & big windows. Tenants will enjoy the quality of their 2 bedroom, 2 bath homes. Unusual opportunity for only $195,000. Call Sam at River Real Estate, 555-1177, now.

Enjoy Steady Income

from this one of a kind Spanish courtyard in sought-after area. Five 2 bedroom, 2 bath stucco homes, plus three 1 bedroom units. Nestled in lush landscaping with fountain, trellised patios, towering palms. Just $375,000. See for yourself. Call Kenneth at River Real Estate, 555-1177, today.

An Investment That Will Pay Off Every Month

when you own this superbly styled traditional duplex on quiet family street. 3 bedrooms, 2 baths each, with hardwood floors, private patios, separate garages. Live in one, rent the other. A fantastic investment for only $164,000. Call Kim at River Real Estate, 555-1177, now.

Get Out of the Stock Market

& enjoy rich rewards every month from this money-making triplex in great area. 2 bedrooms, 2 baths each, both with exposed brick walls, lofty ceilings, gleaming gourmet kitchens. Great for the serious investor. Only $189,000. Call Margaret at River Real Estate, 555-1177, to check it out today.

Live in a $200,000 Home for Much Less

You'll be surprised at how low the monthly payments are when you live in this friendly 4 bedroom, 2 bath Cape Cod. Spacious & luxurious, it features 2 fireplaces, sparkling country kitchen, bay windows & a delightful 2 bedroom, 2 bath guesthouse. Rent can cut your payments almost in half. Call Ken at River Real Estate, 555-1177, today.

Smashing Value

Delightful triplex walking distance to beach. Huge 3 bedroom, 2 bath owner's unit has rosy red fireplace, whisper-soft carpeting, & balconies brushed by ocean breeze. Great investment or living. Just $205,000. Call Jim at River Real Estate, 555-1177, now.

Investors:
Turn-Key Rental

Immaculate 4 bedroom, 3 bath home with pool, in excellent family neighborhood. Near shopping, freeways, super schools. Positive cash flow possible. Offered at only $154,900. Call Kimberly at River Real Estate, 555-1177, for details.

Be the Landlord

& love it in this charming 3 bedroom, 2 bath white traditional surrounded by citrus trees & fragrant flowers. You'll adore its hardwood floors, leaded glass windows, elegant brass accents. Luxury plus income from two 1 bedroom rentals. Only $187,000. Call Annette at River Real Estate, 555-1177, for a look at this charmer today.

Plan Now for
Your Retirement

by investing in this terrific duplex high on a hill just outside the city. Walls of windows, redwood decks, plenty of parking ...these two 2 bedroom, 2 bath units are sure to rent fast. Almost new, too. Only $145,000. Call Kim at River Real Estate, 555-1177, today.

Get Rich Gradually

with monthly income from this delightful country cottage. 2 bedrooms, 2 baths nestled next to running creek, with 1/2 acre of land. Tenants will love its massive brick fireplace, secluded atmosphere, updated kitchen. A great investment for only $76,000. Call Sue at River Real Estate, 555-1177, now.

Put Your Money
to Work for You

in this stunning 2 bedroom, 2 bath condo on Melrose Street. Close to restaurants, shops, offices. Busy renters will love its free-flowing design, with spiral staircase, high-tech kitchen, dramatic fireplace. Bargain at $84,500. Call Constantine at River Real Estate, 555-1177, today.

Looking for a
Sound Investment?

Then head out to this 4 bedroom, 2 bath country charmer right on the city's growth path. For only $65,000, you get a sun-filled eat-in kitchen, elegant oak staircase, crown moulding throughout. Plus full acre of flat land. If you can spot potential, call Fred at River Real Estate, 555-11770, now.

Great for
Investors

2 room, 1 bath cottage suitable for rental on 4.3 acres of land. Half hour drive from city. Close to new developments. Only $54,500. Call George at River Real Estate, 555-1177, today.

AD TIP: *Feel free to mention brand names in your ads. Capitalize on all the advertising major compaines to do promote thier products.*

STYLE

ARCHITECTURE & ATMOSPHERE

Spanish-Style Duplex

Enjoy the fresh look of whitewashed stucco accented by red tiles & blue shutters in this charming duplex. 2 bedrooms, 2 baths each, with hardwood floors, wood-burning fireplace, updated baths. Rent one or both. Your choice for just $123,500. Call Jim at River Real Estate, 555-1177, now.

Your Bread & Butter

Classic 3 bedroom, 2 bath traditional brick with shady elms & giant oaks. Cute & cozy 1 bedroom guest cottage. 1/2 acre, with pool. Just $146,000. Call Vi at River Real Estate, 555-1177.

Charming Craftsman & Cottage

Sprawling 3 bedroom, 2 bath California Craftsman with rock fireplace, beamed dining area & sweeping staircase. On heavily landscaped 1/2 acre lot with 1 bedroom, 1 bath guesthouse. Totally private. Just $187,000. Call Joey at River Real Estate, 555-1177, for a look.

Hideaway Home & Rental

You'll never be alone in this rustic 3 bedroom, 2 bath redwood, a marvel of natural wood, stone & glass. Secluded on a private road, it comes with charming 2 bedroom, 1 bath guesthouse. Both for just $134,500. Call Melissa at River Real Estate, 555-1177.

Spanish Courtyard

Be a grandee in this stunning stucco palace with three 1 bedroom apartments & lavish 2 bedroom, 2 bath owner's unit. On an acre of gardens, it's yours for only $405,000. Call Tim at River Real Estate, 555-1177, now.

Cape Cod Beauty

You don't have to be a thrifty New Englander to appreciate the value of this comfortable 2 bedroom, 2 bath Cape Cod duplex. Cheerful gray siding with white shutters & brick sidewalks. Enjoy hardwood floors, spacious rooms, private decks. $156,000 for both. Call Vince at River Real Estate, 555-1177, fast.

Live in the Penthouse

of this stunning contemporary with six 2 bedroom, 2 bath units under your lavish suite. You'll adore the city-light view, plus the 3 bedrooms, 2 baths. Not to mention the monthly rent checks. Just $395,000 & it's yours. Call Jason at River Real Estate, 555-1177, today.

Small Town Charm

If you're looking for a vintage 3 bedroom, 2 bath home with quality upgrades, consider this sparkling white traditional. Nestled under tall trees by a gentle creek, it radiates quiet character. Includes stunning 1 bedroom apartment. Just $165,000. Call Beth at River Real Estate, 555-1177, now.

CONDITION

Picture-Perfect & Steady Income

Live in the prettiest home on the block & enjoy extra income. You can do both in this 3 bedroom, 2 bath brick colonial circled by huge flower gardens. Your tenant will adore the spacious 2 bedroom, 2 bath guesthouse with its own fireplace & screened porch. All for just $154,000. Call Jimmy at River Real Estate, 555-1177, today.

Quality Duplex

Hard-to-find custom duplex in quiet neighborhood. 3 bedrooms, 2 baths each, with gleaming oak cabinets, whisper-soft carpets, professionally landscaped yard. Lots of care. Yours for only $143,000. Call Julie at River Real Estate, 555-1177, to see it today.

Pride of Ownership Home & Rental

Gentle 1945 charmer glows with tender loving care. Delicately upgraded, keeping original woods & windows. 3 bedrooms, 2 baths, plus sunny & bright 1 bedroom rental. Just $124,000. Call Sam at River Real Estate, 555-1177, to see it today.

Duplex You'll Be Proud to Share

Unusually spacious 2 bedroom, 2 bath duplex in family neighborhood close to downtown. Built of cedar with lots of glass, it offers exciting design & efficient comforts. Almost new for just $135,000. Call Tim at River Real Estate, 555-1177, for a look today.

Custom-Built, Maintenance-Free 3 Units

You'll love the look of this soaring redwood contemporary styled like a single family home. Two 2 bedroom, 2 bath units, 1 single...all free & open with skylights, decks, multi-level design. One year new. Only $162,000. Call Kimberly at River Real Estate, 555-1177, now.

Historic Home

Restored & converted to 6 handsome rental units, this 1898 charmer was the talk of the town. Impressive Victorian with formal garden, wrought iron fence, 5 car garage. Character & income, just $199,500. Call Fred at River Real Estate, 555-1177, today.

Condo in Award-Winning Community

Enjoy a luscious 2 bedroom, 2 bath upper condo in prestigious resort community. Wood-burning fireplace, huge balcony, walls of windows with mountain view. Live in it yourself or rent it out. Either is easy. Just $44,000. Call Fred at River Real Estate, 555-1177 and make it yours today.

First Time Offered

Almost new redwood & cedar condo close to ski slopes. 2 bedrooms, 2 baths & huge loft for guests. You'll adore the massive stone fireplace, impressive decks, delightful hot tub. Great rental. Just $35,000. Call Jennifer at River Real Estate, 555-1177, today.

Be the First

to see this 2 bedroom, 2 bath mountain cabin perfect for rentals. Just 15 min. from the city, it's nestled in its own little forest. Knotty pine interior, skylights, potbellied stove. Only $38,500. Call Chris at River Real Estate, 555-1177, fast.

AD TIP: As ad expert David Ogilvy says, "You can't save souls in an empty church." People must read an ad before they will respond. So make sure your ad counts.

CONCLUSION

Advertising, whatever its form, rests on solid principles. Things like fashioning copy to play up the reader's potential personal gain. But no matter how closely we rely on these principles—no matter how faithful we are to their spirit—the magical ingredient in any ad is you. You, the writer, select the words, rhythm and style that can make a home come alive. We trust this book has helped. What happens next is up to you.

SELLING WORDS

LOW-PRICED HOMES

LOCATION

award-winning
community
breathtaking view
established
neighborhood
friendly family
neighborhood
intimate
isolated
jog to beach
magnificent view
majestic view
private
rising home values
stable neighborhood
steps to surf & sun
traditional neighborhood

EXTERIOR

artfully landscaped
artist's studio
brick
bungalow
cabin
clapboard
colonial flavor
colonial shutters
cottage
cream puff
doll house
enormous trees
fantastic trees
fixer
garden delight
gazebo
gigantic trees
glass

EXTERIOR, continued

heavily wooded
homestead
ivy-covered brick
lodge
majestic trees
mighty trees
monumental trees
old apple tree
overwhelming trees
phenomenal trees
picket fence
picturebook
prodigious trees
redwood
renovate
restore
rocking chair front porch
rough-hewn cedar
screened porch
shake roof
sleeping porch
spreading trees
summer porch
towering trees
vast trees

INTERIOR

bay window
breakfast nook
cedar closets
custom-comfort
exposed-beam ceiling
family atmosphere
farm-style kitchen
free-flowing
French windows

INTERIOR, continued

galley kitchen
generously sized
grand staircase
greenhouse windows
hard-to-find
light & airy
maple floors
mellow wood
natural woods
nooks & crannies
open style
pantry
party-perfect
planter shelves
polished hardwood
room to play
rosy brick fireplace
skylights
soft pine

ADJECTIVES/ PHRASES

affordable
artfully landscaped
bargain
beauty
big
charming
cheerful
chic
classic
colonial flavor
custom
custom-comfort
distinctive
efficient

ADJECTIVES/ PHRASES,
continued

endearing
estate
free-flowing
fun
gracefully
handcrafted
hard-to-find
huge
lovingly restored
natural rustic charm
nostalgia
old-fashioned
old-time
perfect starter home
picturebook
probate
quaint
rambling
real family living
romantic
storybook
thoughtfully updated
time-mellowed
turn-of-the-century
under market
unusual
use your imagination
vacant
vintage
well-kept
yesteryear charm

MID-RANGE HOMES

LOCATION

at end of a country road
carefully planned
close to
country
elite
executive family neighborhood
fashionable
greenbelt
hillside
ocean view
peaceful neighborhood
prestigious
sunset view
waterfront

EXTERIOR

brick patio
brownstone
bubbling creek
colonial
courtyard
delightful stream
emerald lawn
fruit trees
house of glass
pool
rock garden
rolling lawn
stockade fencing
sweeping lawn
trellised patio
trim white fence
velvety lawn

INTERIOR

ceramic kitchen
chair rail mouldings
chef-designed kitchen
cherry bannisters
crown moulding
designer kitchen
energy efficient
French country
garden tub
garden view dining
gourmet kitchen
ideal for entertaining
mint
spa-jetted tub
whirlpool tub

ADJECTIVES/ PHRASES

adobe
art deco
authentic
contemporary
custom-built
delightful
dramatic
Early American
elegant
European flair
favorite
flair
fresh
gracious
handcrafted
heritage
independence
New England
Old-world

ADJECTIVES/ PHRASES, continued

original
perfect
quality
quiet quality
relaxing
soothing
sophisticated
splendid
sprawling
stunning
thoughtfully
tradition
unspoiled

PRESTIGE HOMES

LOCATION

choice setting
choicest site in _____
estate neighborhood
hilltop
in the woods
oasis
prestigious address

EXTERIOR

circular drive
columned porch
copper plumbing
double chimney
estate
flowering shrubs
forest
formal garden setting
giant oaks
half-timbered
hung with ivy
ivy-covered chimney
manor
mansion
masterpiece
Mediterranean
pool & cabana
redwood balconies
shangri-la
showplace
slate roof
stately trees
tennis
towering oaks
tree-canopied drive
trees
Tudor
weathered stone
white board fencing

INTERIOR

antique newel posts
Berber carpets
bleached floors
bubbly spa
butler's pantry
Chippendale bannisters
double fireplace
Dutch tile fireplace
exposed brick
hand-troweled
home gym
honey birch cabinets
hot & sizzling spa
imported wall coverings
inlaid hardwoods
Jenn-air range
king-sized
lava rock fireplace
leaded glass windows
lush atrium
luxurious master suite
mahogany paneling
marble hearth
Maytag appliances
Mexican tile
richly restored
sculptured living space
see-thru fireplace
slate entry
slate fireplace
solid marble basins
St. Charles kitchen
stained glass
vaulted ceilings
walls of glass
walnut paneled library
warmth of fine wood

ADJECTIVES/ PHRASES

artfully elegant
artistic
best
blue chip
champagne
cherished
details
discriminating
dramatic
European
finest
first class
gem
gentleman's
Georgian
handcrafted
heritage
historic
innovative
intimate
jewel-like
lasting
luxurious
magnificent
majestic
perfect
premier
privileged
rare
rich blend
richer with time
solid
sprinkled
traditional
treasure
ultimate
unique
warm
world class

FARMS, RANCHES & HORSE PROPERTIES

3-stall barn
air strip
automated
carve
cattle ponds
close to freeway
corral riding arena
create
crystal creek
deep water well
domain
drip irrigation
Dutch barn
family farm
feeder
fenced & cross-fenced
flowing spring
forgotten
fresh air
grazing
hand-hewn
historic
homestead
horse walker
hunting estate
hydro power
independent
lighted arena
loam
meadows
mighty pretty spread
mountain brook
mouthwatering
native rock
natural spring
nature
neglected
Old MacDonald
old West
old-fashioned

orchard
paddocks
pasture
paved road
pioneer
plank floors
Ponderosa
pride
put your brand
red barn
rich soil
riding trails
rolling hills
root cellar
satellite dish
scenic
self-sufficient
silos
solar power
swimming pond
tack room
tillable soil
vegetable garden
white board fencing
windmill
working
zoned for...

CONDOMINIUMS & TOWNHOMES

balcony
bubbling Jacuzzi
carefree
championship golf course
colonial
cosmopolitan
curved balcony
designer
dramatic
dreamy loft
easy-care
entertain
entertainment-sized
extra-wide deck
fitness center
free-flowing
fun
gate guarded security
gourmet kitchen
greenbelt
guest loft
health club
high-tech kitchen
indoor jogging track
indulge
island kitchen
just outside your door
last of its kind
lifestyle
lighted tennis courts
low maintenance
maintenance-free
microwave
Olympic size pool
open & airy
over the treetops
pamper yourself
patio home
planned community
playground
private
recreation
redwood deck

resort
rooftop pool
sauna
secluded
skylights
skyline
skyscraper
sleek
slick
soaring
sophisticated
sparkling
splash!
steps to...
stunning
sun-filled loft
to play
traditional
tucked away
underground parking
vacation
village
walls of glass
waterfalls
well cared for
wood-burning fireplace
worry free
zest

MOBILE HOMES

5 Star park
air conditioning
all appliances
beamed ceilings
breezy ceiling fans
brick work on skirting
California room
clubhouse
corner lot
custom closets
drywall throughout
enclosed Florida room
enclosed patio
enclosed porch
extra storage
family park
garden tub
huge swimming pool
low space rent
lushly landscaped
maximum triple
pets welcome
"Quake Master" Foundation
screened porch
skylights
upgraded
very private
walk-in closets
walk-in closets
washer/dryer
wet bar
workshop

VACATION PROPERTIES/ SECOND HOMES

at the shore
BBQ
country-fresh kitchen
country
hideaway
holidays
lakefront
loft
luxurious
ocean view
paradise
playground
refuge
resort
rustic
sanctuary
simple
Swedish fireplace
weekend
wilderness

INVESTMENT PROPERTIES

architect-designed
bed & breakfast
build up equity fast
carriage house
ceiling fans
country inn
custom duplex
custom triplex
deluxe duplex
easy to rent
easy-care
fat rent checks
Grannie apartment
great rental neighborhood
great rental
growth path
guesthouse
income-producing
low monthly payments
Mom & Pop apartment
money-making
monthly income
path of progress
penthouse
perfect for rentals
positive cash flow
potential
private patios
professionally
landscaped
rent 1 or both
rental-ready
separate garages
steady income
studio
styled like single family home
thick plaster walls
turn-key rental
two for price of one

Fair Housing Administration

Real Estate Advertising Regulations

Part 109—Fair Housing Advertising

Sec.
109.5 Policy.
109.10 Purpose.
109.15 Definitions.
109.16 Scope
109.20 Use of words, phrases, symbols, and visual aids.
109.25 Selective use of advertising media or content.
109.30 Fair housing policy and practices.

APPENDIX I TO PART 109—FAIR HOUSING ADVERTISING

AUTHORITY: Title VIII, Civil Rights Act of 1968, 42 U.S.C. 3600-3620; section 7(d). Department of HUD Act, 42 U.S.C. 3535(d).

SOURCE: 54FR 3306, Jan. 23, 1969, unless otherwise noted.

Part 109.5   Policy.

It is policy of the United States to provide, within constitutional limitations, for hair housing throughout the United States. The provisions of the Fair Housing Act (42 U.S. C. 3600, *et seq.*) make it unlawful to discriminate in the sale, rental, and financing of housing, and in the provision of brokerage and appraisal services, because of race, color, religion, sex, handicap, familial status, or national origin. Section 804 (c) of the Fair Housing Act, 42 U.S. C. 3604 (c), as amended, makes it unlawful to make, print, or publish, or cause to be made, printed or published, any notice, statement, or advertisement, with respect to the sale or rental of a dwelling, that indicates any preference, limitation, or discrimination because of race, color, religion, sex, handicap, familial status, or national origin, or an intention to make any such preference, limitation, or discrimination. However, the prohibitions of the act regarding familial status do not apply with respect to *housing for older persons,* as defined in section 807(b) of the act.

Part 109.10   Purpose.

The purpose of this part is to assist all advertising media, advertising agencies and all other persons who use advertising to make, print, or publish, or cause to be made, printed, published, advertisements with respect to the sale, rental, or financing of dwellings which are in compliance the requirements of the Fair Housing Act. These regulations also describe the matters this Department will review in evaluating compliance with investigations of complaints alleging discriminatory housing practices involving advertising.

109.15   Definitions.

As used in this part:
    (a)   *Assistant Secretary* means the Assistant Secretary for Fair Housing and Equal Opportunity.
    (b)   *General Counsel* means the General Counsel of the Department of Housing and Urban Development.
    (c)   *Dwelling* means any building structure, or portion thereof which is occupied as, or designed or intended for occupancy as, a residence by one or more families, and any vacant land which is offered for sale or lease for construction or location thereon of any such building, structure, or portion thereof.
    (d)   *Family* includes a single individual.

(e)   *Person* includes one or more individuals, corporations, partnerships, associations, labor organizations, legal representatives, mutual companies, joint-stock companies, trusts, unincorporated organizations, trustees, trustees in cases under title 11 U.S.C., receivers, and fiduciaries.

(f)   *To rent* includes to lease, to sublease, to let and otherwise to grant for a consideration the right to occupy premises not owned by the occupant.

(g)   *Discriminatory housing practice* means an act that is unlawful under section 804, 805, 806, or 818 of the Fair Housing Act.

(h)   *Handicap* means, with respect to a person—

(1)   A physical or mental impairment which substantially limits one or more of such person's major life activities.

(2)   A record of having such an impairment, or

(3)   Being regarded as having such an impairment.

This term does not include current, illegal use of or addiction to a controlled substance (as defined in section 102 of the Controlled Substances Act (2) U.S.C. 802). For purposes of this part, an individual shall not be considered to have a handicap solely because that individual is a transvestite.

(i)   *Familial status* means one or more individuals (who have not attained the age of 18 years) being domiciled with—

(1)   A parent or another person having legal custody of such individual or individuals; or

(2)   The designee of such parent or other person having such custody with the written permission of such parent or other person. The protections afforded against discrimination on the basis of familial status shall apply to any person who is pregnant or is in the process of securing legal custody of any individual who has not attained the age of 18 years.

Part 109.16   Scope.

(a) *General.* This part describes the matters the Department will review in evaluating compliance with the Fair Housing Act in connection with investigations of complaints alleging discriminatory housing practices involving advertising. Use of these criteria will be considered by the General Counsel in making determinations as to whether there is reasonable cause, and by the Assistant Secretary in making determinations that there is no reasonable cause, to believe that a discriminatory housing practice has occurred or is about to occur.

(1) *Advertising media.* This part provides criteria for use by advertising media in determining whether to accept and publish advertising regarding sales or rental transactions. Use of these criteria will be considered by the General Counsel in making determinations as to whether there is reasonable cause, and by the Assistant Secretary in making determinations that there is no reasonable cause, to believe that a discriminatory housing practice has occurred or is about to occur.

(2) *Persons placing advertisements.* A failure by persons placing advertisements to use the criteria contained in this part, when found in connection with the investigation of a complaint alleging the making or use of discriminatory advertisements, will be considered by the General Counsel in making a determination of reasonable cause, and by the Assistant Secretary in making determinations that there is no reasonable cause to believe that a discriminatory housing practice has occurred or is about to occur.

(b) *Affirmative advertising efforts.* Nothing in this part shall be construed to restrict advertising efforts designed to attract persons to dwellings who not ordinarily be expected to apply, when such efforts are pursuant to an affirmative marketing program or undertaken to remedy the effects of prior discrimination in connection with the advertising or marketing of dwellings.

[54 FR 3308, Jan. 23, 1989, as amended at 55 FR 53294, Dec. 28, 1990]

Part 109.20   Use of words, phrases, symbols, and visual aids.

The following words, phrases, symbols, and forms typify those most often used in residential real estate advertising to convey either overt or tacit discriminatory preferences or limitations. In considering a complaint under the Fair Housing Act, the Department will normally consider the use of these and comparable words, phrases, symbols, and forms to indicate a possible violation of the act and to establish a need for further proceedings on the complaint, if it is apparent from the context of the usage that discrimination within the meaning of the act is likely to result.

(a) *Words descriptive of dwelling, landlord, and tenants.* White private home, Colored home, Jewish home, Hispanic residence, adult building.

(b) *Words indicative of race, color, religion, sex, handicap, familial status, or national origin*—(1) *Race*—Negro, Black, Caucasian, Oriental, American Indian.

(2) *Color*—White, Black, Colored.

(3) *Religion*—Protestant, Christian, Catholic, Jew.

(4) *National Origin*—Mexican American, Puerto Rican, Philippine, Polish, Hungarian, Irish, Italian, Chicano, African, Hispanic, Chinese, Indian, Latino.

(5) *Sex*—the exclusive use of words in advertisements, including those involving the rental of separate units in a single or multi-family dwelling, stating or tending to imply that the housing being advertised is available to persons of only one sex and not the other, except where the sharing of living areas is involved. Nothing in this part restricts advertisements of dwellings used exclusively for dormitory facilities by educational institutions.

(6) *Handicap*—crippled, blind, deaf, mentally ill, retarded, impaired, handicapped, physically fit. Nothing in this part restricts the inclusion of information about the availability of accessible housing in advertising of dwellings.

(7) *Familial status*—adults, children, singles, mature persons. Nothing in this part restricts advertisements of dwellings which are intended and operated for occupancy by older persons and which constitute *housing for older persons* as defined in part 100 of this title.

(8) *Catch words*—Words and phrases used in a discriminatory context should be avoided, e.g., *restricted, exclusive, private, integrated, traditional, board approval or membership approval.*

(c) *Symbols or logotypes.* Symbols or logotypes which imply or suggest race, color, religion, sex, handicap, familial status, or national origin.

(d) *Colloquialisms.* Words or phrases used regionally or locally which imply or suggest race, color, religion, sex, handicap, familial status, or national origin.

(e) *Directions to real estate for sale or rent (use of maps or written instructions).* Directions can imply a discriminatory preference, limitation, or exclusion. For example, references to real estate location made in terms of racial or national origin significant landmarks, such as an existing black development (signal to blacks) or an existing development known for its exclusion of minorities (signal to whites). Specific directions which make reference to a racial or national origin significant area may indicate a preference. References to a synagogue, congregation or parish may also indicate a religious preference.

(f) *Area (location) description.* Names of facilities which cater to a particular racial, national origin or religious group, such as country club or private school designations, or names of facilities which are used exclusively by one sex may indicate a preference.

Part 109.25   Selective use of advertising media or content.

The selective use of advertising media or content when particular combinations thereof are used exclusively with respect to various housing developments or sites can lead to discriminatory results and may indicate a violation of the Fair housing Act. For example, the use of English language media alone or the exclusive use of media catering to the majority population in an area, when, in such area, there are also available non-English language or other minority media, may have discriminatory impact. Similarly, the selective use of human models in advertisements may have discriminatory impact. The following are examples of the selective use of advertisements which may be discriminatory:

(a) *Selective geographic advertisements.* Such selective use may involve the strategic placement of billboards; brochure advertisements distributed within a limited geographic area by hand or in the mail; advertising in particular geographic coverage editions of major metropolitan newspapers or in newspapers of limited circulation which are mainly advertising vehicles for reaching a particular segment of the community; or displays or announcements available only in selected sales offices.

(b) *Selective use of equal opportunity slogan or logo.* When placing advertisements, such selective use may involve placing the equal housing opportunity slogan or logo in advertising reaching some geographic areas, but not others, or with respect to some properties but not others.

(c) *Selective use of human models when conducting an advertising campaign.* Selective advertising may involve an advertising campaign using human models primarily in media that cater to one racial or national origin segment of the population without a complementary advertising campaign that is directed at other groups. Another example may involve use of racially mixed models by a developer to advertise one development and not others. Similar care must be exercised in advertising in publications or other media directed at one particular sex, or at persons without children. Such selective advertising may involve the use of human models of members of one sex, or of adults only, in displays, photographs or drawings to indicate preferences for one sex or the other, or for adults to the exclusion of children.

Part 109.30   Fair housing policy and practices.

In the investigation of complaints, the Assistant Secretary will consider the implementation of fair housing policies and practices provided in this section as evidence of compliance with the prohibitions against discrimination in advertising under the Fair Housing Act.

(a) *Use of Equal Housing Opportunity logotype, statement, or slogan.* All advertising of residential real estate for sale, rent, or financing should contain an equal housing opportunity logotype, statement, or slogan as a means of educating the homeseeking public that the property is available to all persons regardless of race, color, religion, sex, handicap, familial status, or national origin. The choice of logotype, statement or slogan will depend on the type of media used (visual or auditory) and, in space advertising, on the size of the advertisement. Table I (see appendix I) indicates suggested use of the logotype. Table II (see appendix I) contains copies of the suggested Equal Housing Opportunity logotype, statement and slogan.

(b) *Use of human models.* Human models in photographs, drawings, or other graphic techniques may not be used to indicate exclusiveness because of race, color religion, sex, handicap, familial status, or national origin. If models are used in display advertising campaigns, the models should be clearly definable as reasonably representing majority and minority groups in the metropolitan area, both sexes, and, when appropriate, families with children. Models, if used, should portray persons in an equal social setting and indicate to the general public that the housing is open to all without regard to race, color religion, sex, handicap, familial status, or national origin, and is not for the exclusive use of one such group.

(c) *Coverage of local laws.* Where the Equal Housing Opportunity statement is used, the advertisement may also include a statement regarding the coverage of any local fair housing or human rights ordinance prohibiting discrimination in the sale, rental or financing of dwellings.

(d) Notification of fair housing policy—(1) Employees. All publishers of advertisements, advertising agencies, and firms engaged in the sale, rental or financing of real estate should provide a printed copy of the nondiscrimination policy to each employee and officer.

(2) Clients. All publishers or advertisements and advertising agencies should post a copy of their nondiscrmination policy in a conspicuous locations wherever persons place advertising and should have copies available for all firms and persons using their advertising services.

(3) Publishers' notice. All publishers should publish at the beginning of the real estate advertising section a notice such as that appearing in Table III (see appendix I). The notice may include a statement regarding the coverage of any local fair housing or human rights ordinance prohibiting discrimination in the sale, rental or financing of dwellings.

APPENDIX I TO PART 109—FAIR HOUSING ADVERTISING

The following three tables may serve as a guide for the use of the Equal Housing Opportunity logotype, statement, slogan, and publisher's notice for advertising:

Table I

A simple formula can guide the real estate advertiser in using the Equal Housing Opportunity logotype, statement, or slogan.

In all space advertising (advertising in regular printed media such as newspapers or magazines) the following standards should be used:

Size of advertisement	Size of logotype in inches
1/2 page or larger	2X2
1/8 page to 1/2 page	1X1
4 column inches to 1/8 page	½X½
Less than 4 column inches	*

*Do not use.

In any other advertisements, if other logotypes are used in the advertisement, then the Equal Housing Opportunity logo should be of a size at least equal to the largest of the other logotypes; if no other logotypes are used, then the type should be bold display face which is clearly visible. Alternatively, who no other logotypes are used, 3 to 5 percent of an advertisement may be devoted to a statement of the equal housing opportunity policy.

In space advertising which is less than 4 column inches (one column 4 inches long or two columns 2 inches long) of a page in size, the Equal Housing Opportunity slogan should be used. Such advertisements may be grouped with other advertisements under a caption which states that the housing is available to all without regard to race, color, religion, sex, handicap, familial status, or national origin.

Table II

Illustrations of Logotype, Statement, and Slogan. Equal Housing Opportunity Logotype:

EQUAL HOUSING OPPORTUNITY

Equal Housing Opportunity Statement: We are pledged to the letter and spirit of U.S. policy for the achievement of equal housing opportunity throughout the Nation. We encourage and support an affirmative advertising and marketing program in which there are no barriers to obtaining housing because of race, color, religion, sex, handicap, familial status, or national origin.

Equal Housing Opportunity Slogan:
"Equal Housing Opportunity."

Table III

Illustration of Media Notice—Publisher's notice: All real estate advertised herein is subject to the Federal Fair Housing Act, which makes it illegal to advertise "any preference, limitation, or discrimination because of race, color, religion, sex, handicap, familial status, or national origin, or intention to make any such preference, limitation, or discrimination."

We will not knowingly accept any advertising for real estate which is in violation of the law. All persons are hereby informed that all dwellings advertised are available on an equal opportunity basis.

INDEX